"*The Therapist's Notebook for Teletherapy with Children and Adolescents* [illegible] telehealth for children and adolescents. Parts 1 and 2 provide valuable [illegible] and materials. Parts 4 through 12 provide readers with interventions that can be easily implemented through telehealth. These interventions address a wide variety of topics such as mindfulness, emotions, anxiety, trauma, and attachment. For therapists working with children via telehealth, this book is a valuable asset to have within reach of your computer."

Robert Jason Grant, EdD, LPC, RPT-S, *AutPlay® Therapy, author of* The AutPlay Therapy Handbook *and* Play Interventions for Neurodivergent Children and Adolescents

"When I first started doing teletherapy with kids, I thought, 'How am I supposed to keep their attention through a screen?' This book is the answer I wish I had. It's packed with 50 creative interventions that take teletherapy from 'just talking' to fully engaging. I love how it covers everything – even using green screens to make therapy feel magical. The chapters on culture and gender especially spoke to me because they bring inclusivity and representation front and center. This toolkit can help you make teletherapy effective, fun, and transformative. If you work with young clients online, you need this on your shelf."

Carmen Jimenez-Pride, LCSW, RPT-S, ICST-P, RST-C/T, *host of the Diversity in Play Therapy Summit*

"This book makes the monotony of teletherapy feel full of possibility. It's thoughtfully packed with creative, developmentally-attuned interventions designed to spark connection and play, even through a screen. The authors offer ideas that are as practical as they are imaginative. A definite go-to guide for bringing joy, movement, and intention back into the virtual therapy space."

Jamie Watson, LMFT, RPT-S, *instructor of clinical mental health counseling, University of Western States, and owner of Jamie Watson Consulting, Inc.*

"This impressive resource provides a comprehensive overview of everything you need to know about teletherapy with youth. Whether you're new to teletherapy, brushing up on knowledge, or supervising clinicians, this book provides a wealth of ideas for strengthening your work in an online environment. With innovative strategies for engaging youth with varied clinical needs, this practical guide is filled with useful information and inspiration."

Morgan Cooley, PhD, LCSW, *associate professor of social work, Florida Atlantic University*

THE THERAPIST'S NOTEBOOK FOR TELETHERAPY WITH CHILDREN AND ADOLESCENTS

This practical text provides mental health professionals with the tools to deliver effective and engaging teletherapy with children, adolescents, and families.

The Therapist's Notebook for Teletherapy with Children and Adolescents: Creative Interventions for Effective Online Therapy provides systemic teletherapy activities and interventions for a variety of topics and presenting problems for working with children, adolescents, and families. Fifty chapters are arranged into 12 parts: setup and preparation, materials, self of the therapist, assessment and goals, interventions for use with multiple presenting problems, working with emotions, strengthening attachment, anxiety and trauma, neurodivergence, gender, culture, and green screens. Over 70 leading experts provide step-by-step guidelines on setup, instructions, processing, and suggestions for follow-up for assessments and interventions that are grounded within foundational therapy theories/models and evidence-based practice. This comprehensive guide explores both new intervention strategies and ways to adapt in-person therapy assessments and interventions for telehealth.

This book provides creative inspiration and practical advice for novice and experienced family therapists, clinical social workers, counselors, play therapists, psychologists, psychiatrists, and practitioners in related fields.

Rebecca A. Cobb, PhD, LMFT, is a clinical professor for Seattle University's Master of Arts in Couples and Family Therapy program. She also has her own Seattle-based private practice where she provides supervision as an American Association for Marriage and Family Therapy (AAMFT)-approved supervisor and supervision mentoring to AAMFT-approved supervisor candidates. She is the editor of *The Therapist's Notebook for Systemic Teletherapy*, has authored numerous journal articles and book chapters, is a former president of the Washington Association for Marriage and Family Therapy (WAMFT), and has won awards from AAMFT, WAMFT, and the National Council on Family Relations. When she isn't working, she enjoys hot yoga, hosting dinner parties, razor clamming, and spending time with her partner and the small humans who have almost succeeded in making her a morning person.

THE THERAPIST'S NOTEBOOK FOR TELETHERAPY WITH CHILDREN AND ADOLESCENTS

Creative Interventions for Effective Online Therapy

Edited by Rebecca A. Cobb

Routledge
Taylor & Francis Group
NEW YORK AND LONDON

Designed cover image: © Christine Walsh Borst

First published 2026
by Routledge
605 Third Avenue, New York, NY 10158

and by Routledge
4 Park Square, Milton Park, Abingdon, Oxon, OX14 4RN

Routledge is an imprint of the Taylor & Francis Group, an informa business

ISBN: 978-1-032-36241-0 (hbk)
ISBN: 978-1-032-36240-3 (pbk)
ISBN: 978-1-003-33091-2 (ebk)

DOI: 10.4324/9781003330912

Typeset in Stone Serif
by codeMantra

Access the Support Material: www.routledge.com/9781032362403

For Charlie, who brings so much joy to those around her by enthusiastically dancing to her own tune.

And for Laney. "Nana's a good girl."

CONTENTS

CONTRIBUTORS

Cover Contributor

Christine Walsh Borst, PhD, LMFT, is an artist, therapist, and creative entrepreneur. She left her role as an assistant professor in family therapy to pursue a creative career, which includes but is not limited to writing and illustrating children's books and tearing up old magazines to make pretty pictures. Her published books include *What Is Coronavirus?*, *For the Love of Organs: A Quasi-Educational Collection of Poems*, *Us: An Introduction to Pronouns*, and *Drawing the Sun*, a book about the journey to the authentic self. Additionally, she runs a private coaching practice, where she supports clients in connecting with their wild selves. When she isn't having fun at work, she is hanging out in Colorado with her husband (the other Dr. Borst), her three wonderful children, and their two dogs and kitten. You can find her on Instagram at @thechristineborst or www.christineborst.com.

Chapter Contributors

Rachel A. Altvater, PsyD, RPT-S, is an award-winning, pioneering expert, leader, researcher, international trainer, author, and supervisor. She is the owner of *Creative Psychological Health Services*, past president of the Maryland/DC Association for Play Therapy, clinical advisor for PlaySpace, and clinical consultant for Hopscotch. Dr. Altvater authored the book *Perspective: Contemplating the Complexities of Our Realities*, published her research on technology use in play therapy, and is a contributing author in numerous scholarly texts on implementing digital technologies in play therapy practice.

Sophia Ansari, LCPC, LPCC, RPT, is an international speaker, author, educator, and owner of the Let's Play Therapy Institute. She delivers engaging workshops worldwide, teaching mental health professionals, caregivers, and educators about the transformative power of play. Sophia earned a Bachelor of Science in Biology from Wright State University and a Master of Arts in Mental Health Counseling from the University of Cincinnati.

Jessica Bahr, MA, LMFTA, is a couples and family therapist who works primarily with individuals and children, especially those with ADHD and/or those who are LGBTQ+. She is the owner of a private practice, Jessica Bahr Counseling, and sees clients exclusively via telehealth.

Lauren Baxley, PhD, LMFT, is a licensed marriage and family therapist and AAMFT-approved supervisor and mentor in Florida. She has experience working with youth and families as a crisis response therapist, school-based therapist, and private practice provider. She served as a family therapist within the Veterans Affairs (VA) system for seven years helping to establish family therapy services. She enjoys mentoring, supervising, and teaching graduate students part-time as faculty in the Marriage and Family Therapy program at the University of South Florida.

Kristen E. Benson, PhD, LMFT, is an AAMFT-approved supervisor, an associate professor, and director of the Marriage and Family Therapy doctoral program at Virginia Tech. Her research, clinical work, and teaching centers on social justice and liberatory practices, with a focus on providing ethical and inclusive therapy to LGBTQ+ people and relationships.

Kristina Betz, LMFT, is a certified autism-informed professional, certified mental health and nutrition clinical specialist, and holds advanced Gottman training. She provides therapy to individuals, couples, and families at Integrated Therapy Services in University Place, Washington. She is passionate about helping individuals and couples live meaningful, authentic lives, drawing on a combined approach of narrative, person-centered, and Bowenian family therapy. Integrating somatic techniques and modern biological research, Kristina emphasizes the mind-body connection while addressing trauma, communication, connection, and life transitions. She fosters an empathetic, collaborative space where clients can reclaim trust, intimacy, and desire and cultivate deeper, more fulfilling relationships.

Nefeteria L. Bolin, MA, LMFTA, is a staff therapist who works with individuals, couples, and families at MEND Seattle. Her work is the collective efforts of CBT, EFT, and narrative therapy, with a focus on empathetic teaching/coaching and practices originated from humanistic therapeutic approaches.

Deborah J. Buttitta, PsyD, LMFT, is an assistant professor and AAMFT-approved supervisor in the Marriage and Family Therapy program at California State University, Northridge. Her collective work centers on addressing diversity issues in clinical practice and creating educational opportunities that foster personal and professional growth. She utilizes postmodern and strength-based approaches in her private practice in Los Angeles, California.

Chelsea L. Cheney, MA, LMFT, is a PhD candidate in the Couple and Family Therapy program at the University of Iowa. She is also an AAMFT-approved supervisor candidate and works at a private practice providing individual, couple, and family therapy, primarily through telehealth.

Katelyn O. Coburn, PhD, LIMHP, CMFT, LCFMT, is an assistant professor at the University of Nebraska-Lincoln, AAMFT-approved supervisor, and therapist who specializes in LGBTQ+ inclusive therapy and relational, societal, and religious trauma. Their clinical and research work focuses on intervening in the societal and relational factors that negatively impact the mental health and well-being of nonbinary people and LGBTQ+ communities to reduce health disparities. They primarily use internal family systems therapy and anti-oppressive, nervous system, and trauma-informed frameworks in their work.

Megan Conrad, MA, LMHC, is a clinical supervisor and mental health therapist who specializes in working with children and individuals, particularly those who are neurodivergent. Megan is the owner of a private practice, High Hopes Therapy Services.

Danerys Crown, MS, LMFT, is a co-creator and director of the Marriage and Family Therapy training internship program at the Tampa VA. She is an AAMFT-approved supervisor and mentor who specializes in working with individuals, couples, and families in the veteran population.

Adam D. Davis, MA Ed, is the co-founder of Game to Grow, a non-profit organization dedicated to the use of games for therapeutic, educational, and community growth. He has been a professional therapeutic game master since 2011. In addition, Adam developed the CoRe Gaming program at the Atlantic Street Center utilizing video games to teach dialectical behavioral therapy skills, served as an educator at Seattle's Woodland Park Zoo, and taught fourth-grade literacy for Seattle Public Schools. Adam is a contributing author to *Therapeutically Applied Role-Playing Games*; *Integrating Geek Culture into Therapeutic Practice; Game Play* (3rd ed.); and *The Walking Dead Psychology*.

Barry L. Duncan, PsyD, is a therapist, trainer, and researcher with over 17,000 hours of clinical experience. He is the developer of the Partners for Change Outcome Management System (PCOMS) and leader of the team responsible for PCOMS scientific credibility and evidence-based status. Better Outcomes Now, the web application of PCOMS, brings his clinical experience and investigative spirit to life. Barry has over 150 publications, including 18 books, addressing measurement-based care, common factors, and the importance of client privilege in all aspects of therapy.

Christie Eppler, PhD, LMFT, is a professor for Seattle University's Master of Arts in Couples and Family Therapy program. She is an AAMFT-approved supervisor who has a private practice in Seattle, Washington. She is the editor of *Cultivating Systemic Resilience in Therapy: Applications and Interventions for Families, Relationships, and Individuals*. The focus of her clinical practice and research is systemic resilience and narrative therapy.

Jacqueline Florian, PhD, LMFT, is an assistant professor at Alliant International University. Her clinical work and research focus on supporting and advocating for immigrant communities and mixed-status families.

Karen Fried, PsyD, LMFT, is a family and educational therapist and consultant in Los Angeles, California. Karen uses the Oaklander Model of child therapy in her private practice and is the president of the Violet Solomon Oaklander Foundation. She trains child and adolescent therapists and educators in the United States and internationally.

Gabrielle C. Gebel, PhD, LMFT, is a faculty member and AAMFT-approved supervisor in the Marriage and Family Therapy program at the University of Rochester School of Medicine and Dentistry. She has a clinical caseload at the university's internal clinic, Strong Family Therapy Services, and owns a private practice. She has interests in medical family therapy, reproductive justice, couples therapy, and providing trauma-informed and LGBTQ+ affirming care.

Eliana Gil, PhD, LMFT, RPT-S, ATR, is a founding partner of the Gil Institute for Trauma Recovery and Education and a senior consultant for Starbright Training Institute for Child and Family Play Therapy. She is a former president of the Association for Play Therapy and the author of *The Healing Power of Play*, *Play in Family Therapy*, *Helping Abused and Traumatized Children*, *Posttraumatic Play in Children*, and many other publications.

Teddy Goyer, MS, LMFT, is a queer, neurodivergent, and disabled therapist practicing in Los Angeles, California. They specialize in providing queer-, trans-, and neurodiversity-affirming therapy. Their approach integrates talk therapy with support, tools, and accommodations, assisting clients in navigating neurodivergence and other marginalized identities in a world not often designed to meet their needs.

Cary McAdams Hamilton, LMHC-S, CMHS, RPT-S, CDWF, is a clinician, educator, and mother of two. She serves as Director of Play Therapy at Antioch University Seattle, owns Olympia Therapy, and has led the Washington Association for Play Therapy as president twice. An international presenter and author, Cary specializes in play therapy, neurodiversity, and sensory sensitivities. With over 20 years of experience working with and parenting neurodivergent children, she shares parenting insights through her platform, Playful Wisdom. She believes play is the universal language of children, reflecting their resilience, curiosity, and capacity to grow into extraordinary, successful adults.

Martha Hernández, PhD, is the Director of Spanish Training and Associate Director of Family Support Services. She is a bilingual psychologist, supervisor, and professor. Her areas of focus include working with couples and families, families with children with a chronic illness, grief, and loss, and immigrant mental health, with a specialization on the Latine community. She focuses on social justice and the impact of social drivers on mental health. Additionally, she teaches courses and trains students to provide services in Spanish.

Katherine M. Hertlein, PhD, LMFT, is a professor and Associate Dean of Faculty Affairs and Professional Development at the Boonshoft School of Medicine at Wright State University. She has published over 100 articles and book chapters and 12 books. Dr. Hertlein was awarded a Fulbright Core Scholar Award and, in this role, served as a guest lecturer and researcher at the University of Salzburg in Salzburg, Austria. Dr. Hertlein's work has been featured in various media outlets, including *Men's Health*, *The APA Monitor*, *The Atlantic*, and *The Huffington Post*. She lectures nationally and internationally on technology, couples, and intimacy.

Fiona Hill, LPC-S, RPT, is the owner of Lighthouse Play and Consulting where she provides child and family therapy and supervision. She specializes in childhood trauma, attachment disruption, and varying developmental needs within the family system. She has a sub-specialty of incorporating digital tools into therapeutic practice.

Jennifer L. Hodgson, PhD, LMFT, served as an AAMFT-approved supervisor, professor, co-creator, and former director of the Medical Family Therapy doctoral program at East Carolina University. She is a principal consultant with Health Management Associates and an elected member of her county's board of education.

Hailee Hughston, MA, LMFTA, is a graduate of Seattle University's Master of Arts in Couples and Family Therapy program where she interned at Twin Lakes Counseling in Federal Way, Washington. She has experience working with neurodivergent youth and specializes in treating anxiety and depression.

Kevin B. Hull, PhD, LMHC, RPT, CGP, is an associate faculty member with Liberty University and owner of Hull and Associates, P.A., a private practice in Lakeland, Florida. Dr. Hull is a registered play therapist, certified group psychotherapist, and specializes in using electronic devices in play therapy and in working with children, adolescents, and families on the autism spectrum. He has published numerous books, chapters, and articles related to neurodiversity.

Krupali S. Joshi, MA, LMFTA, is a relational psychotherapist at Insight Mental Health Group in Washington, where she works virtually and in person with individuals, couples, and families, drawing on postmodern and strengths-based frameworks to foster change and resilience. Krupali earned a Master of Arts in Applied Psychology from the University of Mumbai and a Master of Arts in Couples and Family Therapy from Seattle University.

Jacob Kajiwara, MS, LMFT, is a licensed therapist in California whose work centers on supporting Asian Americans. He addresses themes of identity, attachment, and relationships, helping clients navigate intergenerational/intercultural conflict and foster meaningful connections. His approach is grounded in person-centered care, creating a safe space for healing and self-discovery.

Lorin C. Kelly, PhD, LIMHP, LCMFT, CMFT, is the owner of Kelly and Associates Therapeutic Services in Lincoln, Nebraska. She is an AAMFT-approved supervisor, eye movement desensitization and reprocessing (EMDR)-certified therapist, and EMDR consultant in training who primarily works with Black, Indigenous, and People of Color (BIPOC), queer, and trans communities. She strives to sit with her clients and assist them in realizing and processing their trauma through anti-racist, systemic, and inclusive ways.

Adrian Knauss, PhD, LMFT, BCB, is a medical family therapist who serves as faculty at the Methodist Family Medicine Residency program of Oak Ridge, where she is involved in integrated behavioral healthcare, curriculum development, wellness initiatives, and patient and family advocacy within systems of care. Her research interests include psychophysiology and biofeedback, integrated behavioral healthcare, and residency education.

Richard Lamb, PhD, LCMHC, is the Director of the Neurocognition Science Laboratory at the University of Georgia. His research focuses on the use of psychophysiomeasurement and technology tools such as virtual and synthetic environments to provide access to mental health treatments for rural, veteran, and underserved populations, assessment of mental status, and understanding of socioemotional health for all. Using advanced technologies such as machine learning and artificial intelligence, he seeks to shape the biopsychosocial aspects of mental health to promote learning and well-being across the lifespan. He has taught courses in counseling research, technology integration, education, neuroimaging, psychophysiomeasurement, psychometrics, and clinical reasoning.

Ariel Landrum, LMFT, ATR, is a narrative therapist certified in Geek Therapy® and co-host of *Happiest Pod on Earth*, a podcast exploring Disney mediums as tools for therapy and education. Ariel helps clients reframe stories around trauma, belonging, and identity, working with survivors of childhood sexual abuse, the Asian American and Native Hawaiian/Pacific Islander and LGBTQIA+ communities, and military families. She has specialized in telehealth since 2016 and authored *Waves of Grief: A Guided Grief Journal*. Based in Los Angeles, Ariel supports the Filipino American community through mental health initiatives and enjoys gaming, food adventures, and travel.

Tiffany Alexis Leal, MA, LMFTA, owns and operates a Seattle-based private practice, Bloom Therapy PNW. Tiffany completed a certificate program in play therapy and specializes in working with children, adolescents, and families. She has written book chapters, presented on telehealth interventions, and was awarded the 2024 Washington Association for Marriage and Family Therapy Professional Poster Award for her presentation on "The Creative Use of Poetry Interventions in Teletherapy."

Chrystal McDowell, PhD, LMFT, is the Director of Group Mental Health programs at Florida State University, where she leads the development and implementation of therapy services, emphasizing emotional regulation and group interventions. Her research examines evidence-based practices for neurodiverse populations and the barriers that prevent families of children with autism spectrum disorder from accessing appropriate healthcare.

Kathryn McNiel, LMFT, is a private practice owner and is licensed in Wisconsin and Washington. She has advanced training in EMDR and specializes in trauma, anxiety, and relationship issues.

Lindsay V. Miller, MACFT, LMFTA, is a graduate of Seattle University's Master of Arts in Couples and Family Therapy program and practices in the greater Seattle area.

Shyrea Minton, EdD, LPCC, is a professor and department chair of educational psychology and counseling at California State University, Northridge. Her research explores ways to leverage community strengths and social and cultural capital as protective factors for minoritized clinicians-in-training and P-12 student populations. She has a small telehealth private practice, in which she uses strengths-based approaches and mindfulness practice.

Sarah Moran, LMFT, RPT-S, is a clinician and supervisor in Olympia, Washington. She specializes in play therapy, AutPlay® therapy, and supporting children and their families through change (including adoption, divorce, grief/loss, chronic illness, and medical trauma). Sarah is the past president of the Washington Association for Play Therapy and currently serves on the AutPlay Advisory Board. She has published numerous chapters contributing to the field of play therapy and neurodiversity.

Amy A. Morgan, PhD, LMFT, is an assistant professor in the Department of Family Science at the University of Maryland's School of Public Health. She is also a core faculty member in the Couple and Family Therapy Master's Program. Her research focuses on the health and resilience of families affected by incarceration, exploring their experiences during incarceration and the re-entry process. She also examines family relationships more broadly, with expertise in separation and reunification, parenthood, intimate relationships, and relational therapy. Dr. Morgan is also an AAMFT-approved clinical supervisor and maintains a private practice in the D.C. Metro area.

Amy R. Nelson, LCSW, RPT-S, is a play therapist, SEL coach, keynote speaker, and founder of *Emotional Milestones*, an organization that aims to improve children's social and emotional well-being. She is passionate about motivating and inspiring early childhood educators to develop knowledge and strategies to better support neurodiversity and inclusion in the classroom. She is also the author of the award-winning children's book *Every Bunny Can Learn: A Tail of Inclusion.*

Emerald Niakan, MA, is a graduate of Seattle University's Master of Arts in Couples and Family Therapy program and where she interned at Connection Therapy Center in Seattle, Washington. Emerald approaches her clinical work as a living poem, both mystical and deeply rooted in physical life. She sees the ecological intersections between self and world as invitations to restore humility and create an inner spaciousness that beckons the inherent reciprocal connection of heart, body, mind, and Earth.

Carmen V. Nieto, MS, MFT-I, is a bilingual marriage and family therapy intern working toward licensure in Nevada. She is interested in the early social, cultural, and family influences that impact cognition and development and hopes to work toward the expansion of accessibility for mental health resources within Hispanic and Latinx populations.

Aaron Norton, PhD, LMFT, is an associate professor of marriage and family therapy at Texas Woman's University. His research focuses on the role of technology in couples and families and the practice of relational teletherapy.

Maxine Notice, PhD, LMFT, LMHC, NCC, is an associate professor at Abilene Christian University (Dallas), AAMFT-approved supervisor, avid researcher, and private practice owner. Dr. Maxine values the education of trainees to promote the growth of skills and clinician preparedness. She spends much of her time working with and advocating for couples and families who are underserved and underrepresented.

Jason Perry, PhD, LCMHC, is an assistant teaching professor in the Counselor Education program in the Department of Interdisciplinary Professions at East Carolina University. He was the 2013 recipient of the Association for Humanistic Counseling's distinguished Emerging Leader Award and is an active member of the North Carolina Counseling Association. Postmodern and constructivist career strategies for community ex-offenders are at the center of his current research interests. Dr. Perry embraces the values of the humanistic psychology of Alfred Adler and Carl Rogers, which emphasize person-centeredness, the importance of the therapeutic alliance, and unconditional positive regard.

Jaclyn Cravens Pickens, PhD, LMFT, is an associate professor at Texas Tech University. Her research focuses on the intersection of technology and romantic relationships (internet infidelity) as well as within the mental health profession (relational teletherapy education and training).

Jacob B. Priest, PhD, LMFT, is an associate professor and director of the Couple and Family Therapy program at the University of Iowa. He is also a clinical associate professor in the LGBTQ and Weight Management Clinics in the Department of Internal Medicine at the University of Iowa Carver College of Medicine.

Lisa René Reynolds, PhD, LMFT, is the assistant director of online faculty at The Family Institute at Northwestern University's Master of Science in Couples and Family Therapy program. She is an AAMFT-approved supervisor and has private practices in New York and Connecticut. She is also the author of *Creative Play in Family Therapy: Effective Strategies and Interventions for Child-Centered Treatment* and *Parenting through Divorce: Helping Your Kids Thrive During and After the Split.*

Kimberly Riley, DSW, LMFT, is an assistant clinical professor at Seattle University in the Couples and Family Therapy program, where she enjoys teaching students clinical care skills and how to treat children and adolescents. She is also in private practice and contracts as the local Head Start program's Mental Health Consultant. In both university and private practice settings, Dr. Riley enjoys being an AAMFT-approved supervisor and supporting therapists entering the field of Marriage and Family Therapy. She is licensed in Washington State, California, and Oregon.

Karrison A. Rimon, MS, MFT-I, is a marriage and family therapy intern working toward licensure in Nevada. Karrison is interested in serving children and adolescents with the goal of creating and supporting safe spaces for diverse clientele. Karrison works toward improving upon mental health resources for youth both virtually and in person in an effort to eradicate the stigma surrounded by mental health.

Bianca Rodriguez, MA, LMHC, CMHS, works at Seattle Children's Hospital as a bilingual case manager serving Spanish-speaking families and supporting research projects as a clinical research coordinator.

Kayla Sellers, MA, tLMFT, is a couple and family therapy doctoral student at the University of Iowa. She also works for an Iowa City-based private practice, where she provides couple and family therapy services and supervision as an AAMFT supervisor candidate.

Megan Simmons, MS, LMFT, is an AAMFT-approved supervisor at a community survivor services agency and has served as an adjunct instructor for Seattle University's Couples and Family Therapy program and Seattle Pacific University's Marriage and Family Therapy program. Her work focuses on the impact of relational and interpersonal violence on families. She is dedicated to training new therapists in trauma-informed care to equip emerging therapists with the tools needed to address complex trauma within family systems.

Tiffany Smith, PhD, LMFT-S, LPC-S, NCC, is the Clinical Director at Flower Mound Counseling in the Dallas/Fort Worth Metroplex. Her work focuses on innovative approaches to family therapy in virtual settings and she has authored several publications on play therapy via telemental health.

Paul R. Springer, PhD, LMFT, is a professor in the Marriage and Family Therapy program at Virginia Tech. As an AAMFT-approved supervisor, he has worked with students on how to deliver telemental health services to rural underserved communities since 2008.

Dana J. Stone, PhD, LMFT, is a professor and program coordinator for the Marriage and Family Therapy program at California State University, Northridge. She is an AAMFT-approved supervisor and supervisor mentor and has a telehealth private practice. Her work focuses on students and early-career MFTs with marginalized identities bringing their whole selves into their clinical work.

Eric L. Ström, JD, PhD, LMHC, is a licensed attorney and licensed mental health counselor in Seattle, Washington. Eric has taught as an adjunct instructor at a range of clinical graduate programs. His clinical experience has been focused on working with combat veterans, and he currently provides clinical counseling, clinical supervision, and legal/ethical consultation through his private practice.

Dania Tawfiq, PhD, is an assistant teaching professor at Florida State University, specializing in human development and family science. In addition, Dr. Tawfiq is a private practitioner, where she integrates her academic insights with practical applications to support individuals, couples, and families. Her work emphasizes the importance of fostering healthy relationships and promoting emotional well-being.

Simran K. Uppal, MA, LMFTA, specializes in supporting teens, adults, and families, with a strong focus on BIPOC communities. Her expertise spans anxiety, depression, obsessive compulsive disorder eating disorders, and women's issues. Simran was honored with the Student Poster Award from the Family Therapy section of the National Council on Family Relations for her work on *Creative Teletherapy Interventions that Honor Indian Culture*, reflecting her commitment to culturally responsive care and innovative therapeutic approaches.

Kimberly N. Usbeck, MS, MFT-I, is a marriage and family therapy intern working toward licensure in Nevada. Kimberly's work focuses on supporting children and adolescents, creating safe and welcoming spaces for young clients to explore their emotions and navigate challenges. She is committed to promoting mental health awareness and fostering understanding, working to ensure that families feel empowered to seek the support they need.

Darlene M. Vander Schuur, MACFT, LMFT, is a Seattle University graduate and Ballmer scholar. She owns her own private practice, which specializes in folx with trauma and neurodiversity. Her published works center around telehealth considerations.

Amanda Veldorale-Griffin, PhD, LMFT-S, is a professor of marriage and family sciences at National University. She also has a private practice in which she specializes in working with transgender individuals and their families.

Ying-Shui Wang, MA, is a graduate of Seattle University's Master of Arts in Couples and Family Therapy program, where she interned at Stories of Hope in Monroe, Washington. She is passionate about working with children and their families and supporting healthy parent-child interactions.

Katharine P. Wenocur, DSW, LCSW, RPT-S, is the coordinator of the Child Trauma and Play Therapy concentration at Thomas Jefferson University. Dr. Wenocur provides play therapy to children and young families impacted by trauma, loss, and other life challenges and supervises clinicians seeking play therapy training and credentials.

Michael R. Whitehead, PhD, LMFT, RPT-S, is the creator of Integrative Systemic Play Therapy and author of *Treating Children with Disruptive Behavior Disorders: An Integrative Play and Systems Theory Approach to Oppositional, Aggressive, and Antisocial Behavior.* He specializes in family-based solutions at Aspen Grove Family Therapy in Twin Falls, Idaho. A seasoned educator and presenter, he teaches and supervises future therapists while presenting nationally on parenting, behavior management, and play therapy. Dr. Whitehead has co-authored works on disruptive behavior treatment and held leadership roles in professional organizations.

Anna Wilson, LMFTA, specializes in helping children and teens manage anxiety, depression, and neurodivergence. She is passionate about empowering young people and their families to build resilience and emotional well-being. Anna meets clients where they are in their journey, providing personalized, compassionate care to families across the greater Pacific Northwest.

Julianna Wisneski, MS, LMFT, PLMFT, has a clinical focus in trauma, attachment, and parenting and serves clients in both private practice and community mental health. At Embark Counseling Services, Julianna provides mental health therapy to couples, families, and children/teens. She also supports parents, families, and children/teens in their journey toward healing at a Missouri domestic violence shelter. Julianna has completed a 150-hour play therapy certification course and is working toward becoming a Registered Play Therapist.

Taylor Young, PhD, LMFT, is a clinical assistant professor of behavioral health at the Greater Lawrence Family Health Center Family Medicine Residency program in Lawrence, Massachusetts, where he focuses on integrating behavioral health into medical care and educating family medicine residents. He has a background in behavioral health integration, providing support to patients, their families, and medical providers. His research focuses on spirituality within healthcare, integrated behavioral health, and LGBTQIA+ health.

Kalen D. Zeiger, PhD, LMFT, CCTP, CFTP, is core faculty in the Couple and Family Therapy program at Antioch University. They also serve as the Director of Clinical Development and Outreach at Radiant Counseling and Wellness Center in the Denver Metro Area of Colorado. Kalen focuses on clinical work and research with LGBTQ+ populations, trauma and resilience, identity development, and inclusive healthcare.

FOREWORD

As we know, when the world shut down in early 2020, so did much of what we assumed was foundational to doing therapy, especially with children and teens. The familiar rhythms of the playroom or office gave way to webcams and unfamiliar interfaces. Many clinicians found themselves trying to recreate their work in a format that felt, at first, disconnected from so much of what we thought we knew about the therapeutic process.

And yet, something remarkable emerged: creativity. Clinicians didn't just adapt – they reimagined. They asked new questions. They honored the needs of their clients in new ways. And in doing so, they opened up possibilities that had long been underutilized or overlooked. That spirit runs throughout this book.

This isn't simply a collection of translated in-person activities. It's a reflection of what can happen when we center connection, flexibility, and clinical integrity across platforms. It brings us back to the heart of the work: *what* we're doing, *why* we're doing it, and *how* we can do it in ways that are responsive and relevant.

Each one is a reminder that teletherapy is not a fallback or lesser alternative. It is a necessary, valid, and often essential mode of care. During the height of the pandemic, telehealth use expanded rapidly, with nearly one in four U.S. adults accessing care virtually (U.S. Department of Health and Human Services, 2023). Research has since confirmed what many clinicians already knew: virtual care is not only effective, but it can also help reduce access barriers that have long limited mental health treatment for underserved and marginalized populations (Dorsey & Topol, 2021). It provides clients with multiple ways to access treatment and to engage with interventions in ways that reflect their needs, strengths, and realities, which is central to ethical and effective practice. Teletherapy offers a different space with different tools, and it expands what's possible.

In *The Therapist's Notebook for Teletherapy with Children and Adolescents: Creative Interventions for Effective Online Therapy*, you'll find interventions using everything from puppets to digital collages, green screens to tabletop role-playing games. There are chapters that walk you through how to set up a session, explain teletherapy to caregivers, and use physical or digital materials to bridge the distance between clinician and client. There are also interventions tailored for specific needs: supporting emotional regulation, strengthening attachment, honoring cultural identity, and working with neurodivergent youth, to name just a few.

What I especially appreciate about this collection is that it doesn't assume one-size-fits-all. Included are more than 70 contributors who bring diverse clinical voices, populations, and approaches for your consideration. Importantly, embedded throughout is the recognition that we, as therapists, matter too. There's a full section on the self of the therapist, including reflections on energy management and practicing as a therapist with attention-deficit hyperactivity disorder. That kind of attention to the clinician's experience is not only refreshing, but also necessary.

The interventions span a range of styles and approaches. Some are structured and directive, while others are more exploratory and open-ended. Many reflect familiar foundations, while others push into areas not often addressed in traditional therapy texts, such as gender expression through avatars or the use of anime in sessions with neurodiverse teens. There are ideas in here that were new even to me, and I've been immersed in this space for a long time. That's one of the things I love most about this field. Good clinical work means we never stop learning. When we stay attuned to our clients – their needs, their comfort, their goals, their interests, and their culture – we're called to keep listening, adapting, and growing. That alone is reason enough to keep this book within reach.

More than the techniques themselves, what stands out is the commitment woven throughout these chapters, a commitment to meaningful, connected work. Therapy in a virtual space remains rich and relational when we bring our full selves to the process. Curiosity, intention, and a little playfulness go a long way in helping us meet clients exactly where they are.

This book is full of ideas you can use right away. It also offers reminders: stay flexible, present, and curious. Keep learning – from your clients, from trusted colleagues, from supervision, and from the moments that surprise you. Let the client's needs, interests, and worldview guide your work.

I hope you find inspiration here. I certainly did.

Jessica Stone, PhD, RPT-S, ACC
Virtual Sandtray, LLC

References

Dorsey, E. R., & Topol, E. J. (2021). Telehealth transformation: COVID-19 and the rise of virtual care. *Journal of the American Medical Informatics Association, 28*(3), 393–398. https://doi.org/10.1093/jamia/ocaa301

U.S. Department of Health and Human Services, Office of the Assistant Secretary for Planning and Evaluation. (2023, January). *Who used telehealth services during the COVID-19 pandemic?* https://aspe.hhs.gov/sites/default/files/documents/7d6b4989431f4c70144f209622975116/household-pulse-survey-telehealth-covid-ib.pdf

PREFACE

At the start of the pandemic, when navigating my own challenges with the transition to online therapy, I was inspired to create a practical resource that would compile creative ideas that could be used in working with children, adolescents, adults, intimate relationships, and families via teletherapy platforms. With the encouragement of my mentor, Dr. Lorna Hecker, who created *The Therapist's Notebook* series over 25 years ago (e.g., Hecker & Deacon, 1998; Hecker & Sori, 2007; Sori & Hecker, 2003, 2008), I reached out to clinicians from all over to write chapters on creative teletherapy interventions that they had been using in their practice. My plan was to publish one book, *The Therapist's Notebook for Systemic Teletherapy: Creative Interventions for Effective Online Therapy* (2024), but I had no idea what an overwhelming response my call for proposals would elicit. This first book had room for 40 chapters. I received inspiring, high-quality ideas for more than twice that. In realizing that there was enough material to publish a second book, I set aside chapters focused on working with children and adolescents. That's how *The Therapist's Notebook for Teletherapy with Children and Adolescents: Creative Interventions for Effective Online Therapy* came about.

There are 50 chapters in this book, written by over 70 talented clinicians/authors, each of whom has contributed their own unique and creative ideas to this text. Their work in this book is divided into 12 sections: *Setup and Preparation, Materials, Self of the Therapist, Assessment and Goals, Interventions for Use with Multiple Presenting Problems, Working with Emotions, Strengthening Attachment, Anxiety and Trauma, Neurodivergence, Gender, Culture,* and *Green Screens.*

Part 1: Setup and Preparation addresses practical considerations that therapists can use to create a successful online therapy practice when working with children and adolescents. Chapter 1 addresses legal and ethical considerations of teletherapy with children and adolescents, focusing on how to determine whether it is appropriate to practice online therapy. Chapter 2 addresses ways in which to successfully engage children, adolescents, and families in teletherapy, including how to set up an effective structure for sessions. Chapter 3 provides instructions for ways in which to explain teletherapy to guardians of children and adolescent clients and answer questions commonly asked about the teletherapy experience. Chapter 4 provides practical advice on setting up confidential spaces from which to conduct teletherapy with children and adolescents. Chapter 5 focuses on ways in which to provide trauma-informed care and consider client safety.

Part 2: Materials reviews both physical and digital materials that may be used in teletherapy with children, adolescents, and families. This section includes an overview of materials that may be used (Chapter 6), instructions on ways in which to acquire and/or create cost-effective hand puppets for use in teletherapy intervention (Chapter 7), a description of therapeutic care packages that can be sent to clients in preparation of interventions that require the use of physical materials (Chapter 8), information on how to use virtual playrooms in teletherapy (Chapter 9), and instructions on how to create digital tools consent forms (Chapter 10).

Part 3: Self of the Therapist addresses unique personal considerations for therapists who practice with children and adolescents online. Topics in this section include consideration of the influence of therapists' attitudes about technology and teletherapy (Chapter 11), ways in which to keep up energy while conducting online therapy with children and adolescents (Chapter 12), and suggestions specific to therapists with attention-deficit hyperactivity disorder (Chapter 13).

Parts 4–11 focus on approaches for working with specific topics/populations. The organization of these chapters is inspired by that of the original *Therapist's Notebook* series. Most chapters provide an objective, a rationale for use that is grounded in research/evidence-based practice, steps necessary for setup, instructions for conducting the intervention, guidance on how to process the intervention with client systems, an example vignette (in which client names and identifying features from any actual cases have been altered), suggestions for follow-up, and possible contraindications. Each chapter also lists materials required for both therapists and clients. This text assumes that both clients and therapists have access to a computer or another device that has a working camera and audio, has a screen large enough to adequately see the video of another person/people, and can be used to connect to working Wi-Fi and/or the Internet. It also assumes that therapists use a teletherapy platform that is consistent with required Health Insurance Portability and Accountability Act laws and regulations. Though most chapters are grounded in a particular systemic therapy theory or model, they can be adapted and used from your own approach.

Part 4: Assessment and Goals provides step-by-step instructions on how to assess and/or identify goals of therapy through the use of the virtual crystal ball activity (Chapter 14), family photograph genogram (Chapter 15), digital photo tree of life (Chapter 16), digital collage (Chapter 17), mixed-media aquarium (Chapter 18), online child outcome rating scale (Chapter 19), and online child session rating scale (Chapter 20).

Part 5: Interventions for Use with Multiple Presenting Problems presents instructions on how to conduct interventions that can be applied for use with many different presenting problems and client populations, including the use of bibliotherapy (Chapter 21), a virtual dollhouse (Chapter 22), puppet reflecting teams (Chapter 23), and scavenger hunts (Chapter 24). Chapter 25 presents ways in which to break up teletherapy sessions with different short activities designed to increase child and adolescent engagement.

Part 6: Working with Emotions addresses creative ways in which to engage children, adolescents, and families with emotions and mindfulness via teletherapy. Chapter 26 provides instructions for creating customizable feelings charts using photos that clients take depicting varied emotions. Chapter 27 describes the use of a mindful drawing application that is available for free on the internet that facilitates the mindful expression and processing of feelings. Chapter 28 provides step-by-step instructions on setting up a school-based mindfulness program via teletherapy.

Part 7: Strengthening Attachment presents instructions on the use of interventions designed to strengthen the connection between members of the client system, including virtual conjoint family drawings (Chapter 29), virtual therapeutic gaming (Chapter 30), the family gift intervention for families living apart (Chapter 31), and online child-parent relationship therapy (Chapter 32).

Part 8: Anxiety and Trauma includes chapters aimed at addressing anxiety and trauma. Chapter 33 provides instructions on the use of a virtual teddy bear that can be used to address medical anxiety and trauma. Chapter 34 describes ways in which to use extended reality-based exposure therapy to address post-traumatic stress disorder, phobias, and anxiety for children and adolescents. Chapter 35 addresses ways in which to use visual cues to enhance the comfort and safety of child and adolescent clients during teletherapy appointments.

Part 9: Neurodivergence includes descriptions of interventions that are particularly fitting with neurodiverse clients, though the tools and interventions within this section may be used with diverse populations and presenting problems. Chapter 36 describes the use of virtual sensory play therapy, Chapter

37 describes the use of anime with neurodiverse teens, and Chapter 38 explains how to implement therapeutically applied tabletop role-playing games in online therapy.

Part 10: Gender provides instructions on the use of interventions aimed at addressing gender in teletherapy intervention with children, adolescents, and families. Chapters 39 and 40 introduce the gender-celebratory safe relationships genogram for use with transgender and nonbinary adolescents and their parents. Chapter 41 describes the use of an intervention in which queer and gender diverse youth are invited to dress up a virtual doll or avatar to process gender expression in a playful way. Chapter 42 provides guidance on ways in which to therapeutically support trans and gender diverse children and adolescents by giving them control over their physical and vocal visibility during teletherapy sessions.

Part 11: Culture includes descriptions of interventions designed to facilitate conversations regarding culture. Chapter 43 describes the use of digital cultural play genograms. Chapter 44 describes the use of a fill-in-the-blank poem that can be used to support clients in identifying who they are, connect with where they're from, and share this story with others. Chapter 45 explains how to have families create a puppet play telenovela. Chapter 46 describes the use of an ancient Indian board game to address various therapeutic goals, cultural identity exploration, and the navigation of everyday challenges. Though Chapters 45 and 46 are aimed for use with clients who identify with particular cultures, they may be adapted for use with diverse populations.

Part 12: Green Screens explains how to set up a green screen for therapeutic engagement of child and adolescent clients (Chapter 47). Examples are provided for several playful interventions that can be conducted through a green screen, including appearing and disappearing objects (Chapter 48), a floating objects illusion (Chapter 49), and an invisibility cloak illusion (Chapter 50) designed to facilitate therapeutic discussions in an imaginative way.

With a little creativity, teletherapy allows for the application of engaging interventions for use with children, adolescents, and their families. My hope is that this book provides you with continued inspiration of creative interventions for your practice in the same way that chapter authors have inspired me.

References

Cobb, R. A. (Ed.). (2024). *The therapist's notebook for systemic teletherapy: Creative interventions for effective online therapy.* Routledge.

Hecker, L. L., & Deacon, S. A. (Eds.). (1998). *The therapist's notebook: Homework, handouts, and activities for use in psychotherapy.* Routledge.

Hecker, L. L., & Sori, C. F. (Eds.). (2007). *The therapist's notebook volume 2: More homework, handouts, and activities for use in psychotherapy.* Routledge.

Sori, C. F., & Hecker, L. L. (Eds.). (2003). *The therapist's notebook for children and adolescents: Homework, handouts, and activities for use in psychotherapy.* Routledge.

Sori, C. F., & Hecker, L. L. (Eds.). (2008). *The therapist's notebook volume 3: More homework, handouts, and activities for use in psychotherapy.* Routledge.

ACKNOWLEDGMENTS

This book was only possible because of the talent, time, and effort of the skilled clinicians who contributed their innovative ideas to this text. It was truly a pleasure working with each of you. Thank you for all that you did and for everything that you taught me throughout the process.

Thank you to Dr. Lorna Hecker, editor of *The* [original] *Therapist's Notebook*, who provided inspiration, encouragement, and guidance in submitting the proposal for this book.

I also want to thank Heather Evans at Routledge, who had the idea of expanding my initial book proposal into two, which led to this text, and to Julia Giordano at Routledge, who stepped in for Heather and supported me in the editing process.

Thank you to Seattle University's College of Arts and Sciences for supporting this project through the Dean's Research Fellowship and Student Assistantship Award. In addition, the Roundglass India Center's Raman Family Faculty Grant generously supported the development of *Moksha Patam: Integration of an Ancient Indian Board Game into Culturally Relevant Teletherapy* (Chapter 45). These awards made it possible to have two fabulous research assistants work with me on this book. Not only did they contribute keen editorial assistance, but they were also each honored with awards at professional conferences for their presentations on chapters that they contributed to this book. Tiffany Alexis Leal won the Washington Association for Marriage and Family Therapy's (WAMFT) 2024 Professional Poster Award for her presentation on *The Creative Use of Poetry Interventions in Teletherapy: "Where I'm From"* and Simran Uppal won the National Council on Family Relations (NCFR) Family Therapy Section's 2024 Best Student Poster Award for her presentation on *Creative Teletherapy Interventions That Honor Indian Culture.* I'm proud of you and am so grateful to have had the opportunity to work with each of you. Thank you also to WAMFT and NCFR for supporting Tiffany and Simmi in their work and for acknowledging the caliber of their contributions to the literature on culturally responsive creative teletherapy interventions.

Christine, Jacob, Amanda, and Lauren, thanks for letting me talk you into another collaboration. I always love a good excuse to work with old friends!

Finally, to Adam, Addison, and Charlie, thank you for helping me to remain playful and for bringing so much joy to my life. I love you.

Part 1

Setup and Preparation

CHAPTER 1

CAN WE MEET REMOTELY?

LEGAL AND ETHICAL CONSIDERATIONS FOR TELETHERAPY WITH CHILDREN AND ADOLESCENTS[1]

Eric L. Ström

Teletherapy is defined as any use of technology as a medium for delivering clinical services to a client who is in a physical location separate from the clinician. Under this definition, teletherapy refers to services delivered via synchronous audio/video telehealth platforms, phone, email, text, and other virtual environments. Thus, the defining features of teletherapy are the use of technology and physical separation of the clients' and clinician's locations.

When determining how best to apply legal and ethical standards in the context of technology, start by analogizing the situation to the "physical" world. Generally, ethical and legal standards of clinical work in the physical world apply to clinical work in the virtual world. However, teletherapy presents several unique issues to consider regarding ethical and legal aspects of practice. Among the most important of these is determining when it is appropriate to conduct teletherapy with a client or client system.

When considering whether it is appropriate to conduct teletherapy, ask yourself the following questions:

1. Who is the client?
2. Is it legal for me to conduct teletherapy given my physical location and the physical location of my clients?
3. Have I received the proper training to conduct teletherapy?
4. Is teletherapy sufficiently effective for this client in this situation?
5. Are there other contextual factors that might make in-person therapy a better option?
6. If in-person therapy is a better option or if I'm not legally allowed to provide teletherapy given jurisdictional limitations, do clients have accessibility to alternate services?

The following outlines the necessary considerations when assessing who the client is, working within jurisdictional limitations, teletherapy training, the effectiveness of teletherapy services, contraindications of teletherapy given presenting problem(s), and accessibility of alternate services for children, adolescents, and family systems.

DOI: 10.4324/9781003330912-2

Identifying the Client

Just as when delivering clinical services in person, the first fundamental step of providing therapy with children, adolescents, and family systems is to explicitly identify who the client is. In systemic teletherapy, there are three primary options when it comes to identifying the client.

First, the relationship can jointly be the identified client. In this case, there would be one single treatment record and each member of the relationship would have a right to access the record, but authorization would need to be obtained from each member before any information could be released to a third party.

Second, there could be two (or more) separate individual clients. In this case, the clinician would have separate and distinct treatment records in each client's name. Session notes from joint sessions would be documented in each treatment record. In this case, each client would have a right to access their individual record, and each would need to provide authorization before any information about them could be released to a third party.

Third, it is also possible to have just one individual client. In this case, one member of the relationship would be identified as the client and the other member(s) would attend teletherapy sessions as non-client collateral contacts. In this scenario, there would be one treatment record in the client's name, and only the identified client would have a right to access the treatment record or to authorize disclosure of information.

Identifying the client is vitally important when conducting teletherapy because this determination defines who is owed duty of care, who has legal decision-making authority, and which jurisdiction(s) determine the laws and regulations that apply to services. Until a client has reached the legal age of decision-making autonomy, state law will define who is able to exercise the minor client's legal rights on their behalf, including consent to treatment, the right of confidentiality, and who has the legal right to access the treatment record.

Age of Decision-Making Autonomy

The age at which a minor may independently consent to behavioral health treatment varies considerably from state to state. For example, the age of independent autonomy is 12 in California (Mental Health Services for Minors, 2011), 13 in Washington State (Outpatient Treatment of Adolescent, 2019), 16 in New Jersey (Consent by Minor to Treatment, 2015), and 18 in Nebraska (Infants and Juveniles, 2019). The details and nuances of these legal standards of autonomy are different in every state. Therapists who work with minors must have specific understanding of precisely how these rules apply in their state(s) of practice.

Once a minor has reached the age of independent autonomy and decision-making authority in accordance with the law in their jurisdiction, they may consent to treatment without the consent of an adult, exercise the rights of confidentiality, and authorize (or decline to authorize) the disclosure of information about their therapy. However, if they have not yet reached the age of decision-making authority in the jurisdictions in which both the client and therapist are physically located, an adult with legal decision-making authority may have the legal right to consent to treatment, access the record, and authorize disclosure on the client's behalf.

Legal Decision-Making Authority

If a child or adolescent is not of age to independently consent to behavioral health treatment in the jurisdictions in which both the minor and the therapist are physically located, the therapist must consider who has legal decision-making authority over them. In general terms, state law typically creates three types of legal decision-making authority. These are shared, joint, and sole decision-making authority.

Shared decision-making authority is typically the default for biological parents. Shared decision-making authority can also be granted by a court to a child's guardian or to adoptive parents. With shared decision-making, each parent can independently consent to services or terminate services. Each parent can independently access their child's treatment record, and each parent can independently consent to having the treatment record released to a third party. This default decision-making authority can be altered by court order or by agreement between the parents. The two most common alternatives when this default is modified are joint decision-making authority or sole decision-making authority.

With *joint decision-making authority*, the consent of both parents is required to initiate clinical services. Because joint consent is needed, each parent can independently terminate services by withdrawing their consent. Each parent can also independently access the child's treatment record. However, the consent of both parents is required before the treatment record can be released to a third party.

Lastly, with *sole decision-making authority*, only one identified parent can consent to and terminate services. That parent is also the only one who can access the treatment record and consent to having the treatment record released to a third party.

When a parent is exercising decision-making authority on behalf of their minor child, at a minimum, it is best practice to expressly ask the presenting parent whether or not they have legal decision-making authority for the child and to obtain a copy of any applicable custody orders, parenting plans, or other relevant legal documentation. Since laws that define how decision-making authority is identified and applied vary by jurisdiction, it is always important to obtain legal guidance on how parental decision-making applies in the locations in which you and your clients are physically located.

Jurisdictional Limitations

When providing teletherapy, health care is legally considered to occur in both the clients' and the clinician's physical locations simultaneously. Therefore, the laws and regulations of the jurisdiction the clinician is physically located in and of the jurisdiction(s) the clients are physically located in during teletherapy both apply (American Association for Marriage and Family Therapy, 2015; American Counseling Association, 2014; American Mental Health Counselors Association, 2020). Accordingly, to determine what legal standards apply, consider (1) the clinician's physical location, (2) the physical location of client(s), and (3) the clinician's location of licensure.

The Clinician's Physical Location

Generally, clinicians must be licensed in and follow all applicable laws and regulations regarding teletherapy practice in the location in which they are physically located while teletherapy services are taking place. This means that if a clinician is physically located outside of the jurisdiction of their license, they might be restricted from providing teletherapy from that location. This is true even if clients are in the location of the clinician's licensure and even if the clinician is just temporarily in that location.

The Client's Physical Location

Likewise, clinicians must follow all applicable laws and regulations regarding teletherapy practice in the locations in which their clients are physically located while teletherapy services are taking place. This usually includes a requirement for the clinician to be licensed by the state(s) their clients are located in. Many states have clear statutory requirements for licensure when providing teletherapy to clients located in those states. Other states express this requirement as policy rather than statutory law (e.g., New York State Office of the Professions, 2021). In many cases, this means that if a client is outside of the location in which the therapist is licensed, they must have permission from that other state before they can provide teletherapy services to a client located in that state. This is true even if the client is just temporarily in that location.

These jurisdictional issues are compounded when a clinician engages in teletherapy with children, adolescents, and family systems. When a minor child is the identified client and the child's parents are in different locations, the clinician needs to comply with the applicable laws and regulations of each state and/or country that has jurisdiction over the clinical relationship. Likewise, when a family or relationship is the identified client and members are in different locations, the clinician needs to comply with applicable laws and regulations for all jurisdictions members of the family or relationship are located in.

Consider a therapist doing family therapy with a family made up of a mother, father, and 13-year-old son. The father, son, and therapist are all physically located in Washington State and the mother lives in New Jersey. In this situation, the therapist would need to comply with licensure rules in both states at once. Dependent on the rules of each state, this may require the therapist to be licensed in two different states to provide therapy to this family. If the clinician were physically present in another state (e.g., Florida), this could mean that the therapist needs to be licensed in three different jurisdictions all at once.

Some states, however, have provisions that allow for temporary practice. This means that under certain circumstances, those states will allow a clinician to provide teletherapy, under a license from the clinician's state, to a client located within that other state. These temporary practice rules range anywhere from 15 to 90 days (Exceptions to Licensure: Jurisdiction, 2015; Regulation of Professions and Occupations – Exemptions, 2013). Similarly, some states allow temporary practice only for specific purposes, such as the recent relocation of a client (Exemptions from Licensure, 2021) or in case of an emergency (Exemptions, 2018). Defining what situations may constitute a valid "emergency" is up to the discretion of the applicable regulatory board(s).

Therefore, if the mother in the aforementioned example was only temporarily located in one of the states in which there are temporary practice rules, the therapist may only be required to be licensed in the state in which they and the other family members are located, though they would still need to comply with licensure rules for both states while practicing with this family. However, let's say that the son, rather than the family, has been identified as the client. The individual client and the therapist could invite the mother and father to participate in one or more sessions for support. In that case, the healthcare is being delivered only in locations of the therapist and the son and the jurisdictions that each of the parents is located in would generally not have a legal basis to regulate the therapy.

Additionally, differing ages of consent for treatment can make the determination of whether you can legally conduct therapy with minors increasingly complex when teletherapy involves more than one state. Consider the aforementioned family made up of a mother, father, and 13-year-old son. Let's say that the son and father, who are located in Washington, want the son to be in therapy. The mother, however, who lives in New Jersey, does not want the son to be in treatment. In this situation, both Washington law and New Jersey law apply to the clinical service. Under Washington law, the son is an independent and autonomous decision-maker. Under New Jersey law, a 13-year-old does not have independent decision-making authority. If the mother, who has joint decision-making authority with the father, were to not want their son to be in therapy and the son wanted to attend therapy, inconsistency between these state laws would create a true ethical and legal dilemma because there would be no course of action that would simultaneously abide by the legal rules in both jurisdictions, even if the therapist were licensed in both states. When laws applicable to your licenses and/or the clients with whom you are working are inconsistent, consult with an attorney.

Just as when delivering clinical services in person, the client must be explicitly identified prior to providing systemic therapy and all participants must have a shared understanding of that identification. Identification of the client defines who has entered into a clinical relationship with the clinician and therefore the location(s) in which therapy is taking place. Issues of legal jurisdiction and licensure requirements then flow directly from the physical location of the identified client(s).

The Clinician's Location of Licensure

Within the United States, healthcare largely continues to be regulated on a state-by-state basis. When providing teletherapy across state lines, the rules and regulations (including licensure requirements) require a state-by-state analysis due to the variation between states. For example, some states have temporary practice provisions, some allow for temporary licensure, and some simply require full licensure. With a *temporary practice provision*, a state may allow an out-of-state clinician to provide services to a client located in that state for a limited amount of time or for a limited number of sessions. *Temporary licensure*, on the other hand, is when a state grants a license to an out-of-state therapist for a limited time, context, or purpose (e.g., natural disaster or crisis response work).

There are a few narrow federal legal provisions allowing clinicians to provide teletherapy across state lines while being exempted from state regulation in some very limited contexts. One such example applies to clinicians providing healthcare services as employees of the United States Department of Veterans Affairs (Health Care Providers Practicing via Telehealth, 2018). Most (if not all) states have implemented exceptions to state licensure requirements for employees of the federal government when providing healthcare services as part of their federal employment. This has particular relevance for children whose parents frequently relocate from one state to another because of federal employment or military orders. In such cases, it might make the most sense for the family to seek services from a federally employed therapist who is likely to be able to provide continuity of care to the child regardless of the state the parents relocate to.

However, there are no general national policies or rules that allow the delivery of teletherapy across state lines. Some multi-state agreements, or "compacts," have been created to facilitate state-to-state credential portability for clinicians with equivalent licenses in different states. These compacts apply only to clinicians who hold specific types of licenses and only in states that have joined the compacts. The types of licenses covered and the number of member states increase year by year.

Many teletherapy clinicians choose to become licensed in more than one jurisdiction to allow them the flexibility of travel. For example, a clinician who spends summers in Minnesota and winters in Texas may choose to seek licensure in both states to continue their clinical work throughout the year. This also allows them access to a wider array of clientele (i.e., clients who are physically located in both Minnesota and Texas). Other clinicians may maintain licensure in several jurisdictions simultaneously simply to allow access to a larger pool of clients with whom they can work. This can be particularly important for clients who travel often between different jurisdictions. For example, a child who lives primarily in Kansas but travels often to Illinois to stay with their grandparents may avoid large gaps in treatment by having a therapist who is licensed in both Kansas and Illinois.

In the case of international teletherapy, laws and regulations of the jurisdiction the clinician is physically located in and the jurisdictions clients are physically located in during teletherapy both apply just as they do with teletherapy that crosses state lines. While many other nations regulate the practice of psychology, very few countries specifically regulate the practice of counseling or marriage and family therapy. However, it is possible that another country might limit or restrict the services a clinician licensed elsewhere can provide either when they themselves are physically located in that country or when a client is physically present in that country.

The bottom line is, if the clinician and client(s) are physically located in different jurisdictions during a teletherapy session, the clinician has an obligation to ensure the clinical work is in compliance with the laws, rules, and policies of all jurisdictions involved. The best way to maintain practice within appropriate legal and ethical boundaries is to:

1. Include a statement in the informed consent indicating what jurisdiction(s) you are licensed in, and therefore what physical location(s) clients must be in to provide services.
2. Identify who the client is.
3. Identify the location(s) of the identified client(s) during each teletherapy session.
4. In advance of conducting teletherapy, verify authorization to provide clinical services in each client location.
5. When in doubt about another jurisdiction's licensure requirements or temporary practice provisions, contact that jurisdiction's licensing board for more specific guidance about licensure and any applicable exceptions.

Given these jurisdictional complexities when providing services via teletherapy, it is vital to have a plan in place to support effective continuity of care and/or transfer of care in response to jurisdictional restrictions. An example of this could be if the client or the clinician needs to temporarily travel outside of the state of the clinician's licensure. In this case, the clinician should consider requesting temporary practice permission from the state in which they are traveling, temporarily pause clinical services, or terminate care and refer the client to a different provider.

Teletherapy Training

Just as the specific requirements for licensure vary from jurisdiction to jurisdiction, so do the requirements for specific training and continuing education in teletherapy. Some jurisdictions have requirements regarding specific teletherapy training that must be completed before a clinician may deliver teletherapy services. Some jurisdictions have a teletherapy continuing education requirement. Some jurisdictions have both requirements.

Even in jurisdictions in which specific training in teletherapy is not required, the ethical standard of care still requires that clinicians develop competency for safe and effective delivery when providing clinical services via teletherapy (American Association for Marriage and Family Therapy, 2015; American Counseling Association, 2014; American Mental Health Counselors Association, 2020). Clinicians should therefore:

1. Be aware of and follow any relevant jurisdictional regulations regarding training and continuing education in teletherapy.
2. Seek training opportunities to develop and enhance practice specifically as it relates to teletherapy and alternative modes of virtual interaction. This may be particularly relevant to work with children and adolescents who may need a variety of creative online therapy interventions to maintain engagement.

Effectiveness of Teletherapy

In addition to applicable laws and regulations, services should be provided via teletherapy only when such services are effective and appropriate for individual clients (American Association for Marriage and

Family Therapy, 2015; American Counseling Association, 2014; American Mental Health Counselors Association, 2020). Research indicates that teletherapy is just as effective as in-person services for many clinical conditions including adjustment disorder, anger management, anxiety, depression, eating disorders, post-traumatic stress, and substance use (Braeuer et al., 2022; Lazur et al., 2020; Slone et al., 2012; Turgoose et al., 2018; Varker et al., 2019). In fact, teletherapy may be even more effective than in-person therapy for some clinical presentations such as depression (Luo et al., 2020). Teletherapy may be especially effective in the formation of the therapeutic alliance between clients and clinicians, especially when working with children and adolescents (Braeuer et al., 2022; Slone et al., 2012; Stiles-Shields et al., 2014). While these studies demonstrate the potential effectiveness of teletherapy as a modality, it is still important to assess the applicability and effectiveness of this modality on a client-by-client basis.

Contraindications of Teletherapy

There may be instances in which teletherapy is contraindicated or in-person services may be more effective than teletherapy. Teletherapy may not be appropriate for clients with severe mental illness or when there is a safety risk for the client or others. For example, unless clients are currently involved in other in-person treatments, carefully consider referring them to in-person service providers if any of the following are of concern within the client system:

- There is a serious mental health diagnosis
- There are indicators of severe dysregulation or profound dissociation
- There is a history of self-harm
- The client demonstrates indicators of uncontrolled substance abuse or dependence
- There are indicators that domestic violence may be taking place in the child's household or among the child's family members (Myers et al., 2017)
- There is concern that the child may be experiencing abuse or neglect
- There are indicators that the confidentiality of teletherapy is compromised and the client's safety may be at risk as a result. This may be of particular concern for adolescents who have reached the age of legal decision-making authority but may not be able to ensure their own online security and privacy when using computing devices that are shared with, or accessed by, parents or other family members. In this case, others may be obtaining information about the adolescent's therapy even though they may not have any legal authority to access the adolescent's treatment record or participate in the adolescent's therapy.

Accessibility of Alternate Services

As more clinicians transfer their practice to telehealth, fewer in-person services may be available. Finding specialists for particular presenting problems may be extra challenging, especially for those in rural communities. Additionally, busy families may struggle to coordinate their schedules to make time for therapy services, especially if service providers have limited appointment options available. Often, online therapy is the most effective way that families may be able to come together to access services at the same time, especially if one or more person is physically in another location. If in-person services necessary to meet the client's needs are not available due to geographic availability of services, client mobility, cost of travel, limitations of client schedules, or cost of in-person services available, it may be in the client's best interest to participate in teletherapy services, at least until other services become available. This may help to avoid situations in which clients have no services at all.

Questions to Consider

As it relates to determining whether teletherapy is appropriate, consider the following:

- Who is the identified client?
    - Is the child/adolescent old enough to have legal decision-making autonomy under applicable law? If not, who has legal decision-making authority for the child?
    - Is more than one person present in treatment? If so, are these family members participating in the role of a client in the family system, or are they participating in a support role to the child/adolescent?
    - Do all participants understand the nature of their role as a client or as a non-client?
- Where is/are the client(s) physically located?
- Am I legally allowed to practice with the client(s) given their physical location(s)?
- Are there provisions allowing temporary practice in the location(s) in which the client(s) is/are located?
- Is teletherapy appropriate for the client given their age, cognitive and emotional development, presenting problem, and other unique factors? Why or why not?
- If in-person services would be better suited for the client, is there an accessible option for this available to them?
- What are the positive and negative implications if services are temporarily paused or terminated?
- If services must legally be paused or terminated, how might I address the client's need for continuity of care?

Note

1 Adapted from Ström, E. L. (2024). Can we meet remotely? Legal and ethical considerations for systemic teletherapy. In R. A. Cobb (Ed.) *The therapist's notebook for systemic teletherapy: Creative interventions for effective online therapy* (pp. 3–10). Routledge. https://doi.org/10.4324/9781003289920-2

References

American Association for Marriage and Family Therapy. (2015). *2015 AAMFT code of ethics*. https://www.aamft.org/Legal_Ethics/Code_of_Ethics.aspx

American Counseling Association. (2014). *2014 ACA code of ethics*. https://www.counseling.org/docs/default-source/default-document-library/ethics/2014-aca-code-of-ethics.pdf

American Mental Health Counselors Association. (2020). *2020 AMHCA code of ethics*. https://www.amhca.org/HigherLogic/System/DownloadDocumentFile.ashx?DocumentFileKey=24a27502-196e-b763-ff57-490a12f7edb1

Braeuer, K., Noble, N., & Yi, S. (2022). The efficacy of an online anger management program for justice-involved youth. *The Journal of Addictions & Offender Counseling, 43*(1), 26–37. https://doi.org/10.1002/jaoc.12101

Consent by Minor to Treatment, New Jersey Revised Statutes, § 9:17A-4 (2015).

Exemptions, Code of the Dist. of Columbia, §3-1205.02 (2018).

Exemptions from Licensure, Utah Code, 58-60-107 (2021).

Exceptions to Licensure: Jurisdiction, Ariz. Rev. Stat., 32-3271. (2015).

Health Care Providers Practicing via Telehealth, 38 C.F.R. § 17.417 (2018).

Infants and Juveniles, Neb. Rev. Stat., 43-2101 (2019).

Lazur, B., Sobolik, L., & King, V. (2020). *Telebehavioral health: An effective alternative to in-person care*. Milbank Memorial Fund.

Luo, C., Sanger, N., Singhal, N., Pattrick, K., Shams, I., Shahid, H., Hoang, P., Schmidt, J., Lee, J., Haber, S., Puckering, M., Buchanan, N., Lee, P., Ng, K., Sun, S., Kheyson, S., Chung, D. C., Sanger, S., Thabane, L., & Samaan, Z. (2020). A comparison of electronically-delivered and face to face cognitive behavioural therapies in depressive disorders: A systematic review and meta-analysis. *eClinicalMedicine, 24,* Article 100442. https://doi.org/10.1016/j.eclinm.2020.100442

Mental Health Services for Minors, California Health & Safety Code § 124260 (2011).

Myers, K., Nelson, E. L., Rabinowitz, T., Hilty, D., Baker, D., Barnwell, S. S., Boyce, G., Bufka, L. F., Cain, S., Chui, L., Comer, J. S., Cradock, C., Goldstein, F., Johnston, B., Krupinski, E., Lo, K., Luxton, D. D., McSwain, S. D., McWilliams, J., North, S., & Bernard, J. (2017). American telemedicine association practice guidelines for telemental health with children and adolescents. *Telemedicine Journal and e-Health: The Official Journal of the American Telemedicine Association, 23*(10), 779–804. https://doi.org/10.1089/tmj.2017.0177

New York State Office of the Professions. (2021). *Guideline 9: Engaging in telepractice*. https://www.op.nysed.gov/professions/marriage-and-family-therapists/professional-practice/engaging-telepractice

Outpatient Treatment of Adolescent, Revised Code of Washington, § 71.34.530 (2019).

Regulation of Professions and Occupations – Exemptions, Fl. Stat., 32 § 491.014. (2013).

Slone, N. C., Reese, R. J., & McClellan, M. J. (2012). Telepsychology outcome research with children and adolescents: A review of the literature. *Psychological Services, 9*(3), 272–292. https://doi.org/10.1037/a0027607

Stiles-Shields, C., Kwasny, M. J., Cai, X., & Mohr, D. C. (2014). Therapeutic alliance in face-to-face and telephone-administered cognitive behavioral therapy. *Journal of Consulting and Clinical Psychology, 82*(2), 349–354. https://doi.org/10.1037/a0035554

Turgoose, D., Ashwick, R., & Murphy D. (2018). Systematic review of lessons learned from delivering tele-therapy to veterans with post-traumatic stress disorder. *Journal of Telemedicine and Telecare, 24*(9), 575–585. https://doi.org/10.1177/1357633X17730443

Varker, T., Brand, R. M., Ward, J., Terhaag, S., & Phelps, A. (2019). Efficacy of synchronous telepsychology interventions for people with anxiety, depression, posttraumatic stress disorder, and adjustment disorder: A rapid evidence assessment. *Psychological Services, 16*(4), 621–635. https://doi.org/10.1037/ser0000239

CHAPTER 2

ENGAGING CHILDREN AND ADOLESCENTS IN TELETHERAPY

Karrison A. Rimon, Carmen V. Nieto, Kimberly N. Usbeck, and Katherine M. Hertlein

Families have turned to teletherapy due to its invaluable benefits. For example, telebehavioral health gives families broader access to providers, greater flexibility with scheduling, and the convenience of receiving care at home (Dombo et al., 2014; Weinsberg & Rolnick, 2020). Due to its advantages, teletherapy can be a desirable solution for many families; however, it also has challenges that place psychotherapists in a predicament as to how to approach treatment with children and adolescents. The following addresses ways in which to determine roles, set a structure, create rituals, stay active, and pay attention to the little things to successfully engage children, adolescents, and their families in teletherapy.

Determining Roles

At the onset of therapy, explicitly identify who the client is to help determine each person's roles for teletherapy. Consider the legal age of decision-making autonomy in the jurisdiction(s) in which you are licensed and the client is located to determine whether legal guardians need to be involved in treatment. If clients are old enough to have decision-making authority and can consent to treatment on their own, discuss whether they would like to involve any family members in treatment, and if so, what that might look like. If clients are not old enough to consent to treatment, consider who has legal decision-making authority over the client in identifying any adults that legally must be involved in any decision-making regarding treatment. See Chapter 1 for additional legal and ethical considerations. Also consider the client's preferences for treatment, whether they prefer individual therapy, family therapy, or a combination of the two, and your perceptions of the efficacy of each form of treatment given the client's unique needs and presenting problem(s).

Whether children and adolescents are seen individually or as part of a larger client system, caregiver involvement plays a crucial role when conducting therapy. Prior to the onset of therapy, have an explicit conversation with legal guardians about teletherapy and its treatment format (see Chapter 3 on explaining teletherapy to guardians) and involve other members of the client system as you would in in-person sessions. When children and adolescents are seen individually, inform caregivers that they should be physically present within the location from which they attend teletherapy, though not necessarily in the same room unless they are doing family therapy.

DOI: 10.4324/9781003330912-3

Unless youth are of legal age to consent to therapy and legal guardians are unaware that the client is attending therapy, or the youth prefers that you not involve others in the therapeutic process, make plans to check in with at least one guardian at the start and/or end of each session. For example, you may meet with parents at the beginning of each session to inquire about the onset of new symptoms or any changes to previous symptoms. You may choose to end sessions with caregiver involvement as well. For example, at the end of sessions, you may review treatment objectives and discuss with caregivers ways in which they can support progress toward identified goals outside of session.

Younger children and adolescents who are not technologically savvy may need additional support from caregivers to navigate technology, especially when assessments or interventions require the use of apps, websites, or other devices with which they are unfamiliar. Some may benefit from having caregivers open websites or apps for them. Others may need more support throughout the session, depending on their own developmental needs and the needs of the assessment or intervention. Work with caregivers at the start of each session to ensure that technology can be successfully navigated and make plans accordingly and to mitigate any disturbances to the flow of the session.

Everyone must know their roles in the teletherapy process (Hertlein et al., 2021). Help families collaborate to determine the following:

- Who will be responsible for telling everyone it's time to attend therapy?
- Who will bring any necessary materials to the session?
- Who will sign into the teletherapy session?
- Who will align the camera to ensure that everyone can be seen by the therapist?
- Who will be responsible for tech support if something goes wrong with the device, software, or internet during the session? How will that person be accessed if they are not in session at the time that help is needed?
- Who will schedule the next session and ensure that the time works for everyone's schedule?
- Who will set any necessary materials aside to save for the following session?
- Who will make sure that homework assignments are completed between sessions?

Each of these topics may require a negotiation process that can be part of the therapeutic agenda.

Setting the Structure

When caregivers are in a support role and children and adolescents attend therapy by themselves, help caregivers establish a consistent space from which children and adolescents can attend teletherapy (Maheu et al., 2018). Teletherapy can occur in any room where a child can be safely left alone and has privacy. Depending on the type of therapy offered, there may be more appropriate places to hold sessions than others. For example, many young people prefer to have therapy in their bedrooms. This may be a place where they feel comfortable having confidential conversations online. This arrangement might also provide a stimulating environment full of objects that capture their attention and may prevent them from fully being attentive in teletherapy. To the extent to which you are able, work with children, adolescents, and guardians to establish an emotionally and physically safe place from which to attend sessions that minimizes distractions. In addition, consider the needs of specific interventions or approaches to therapy and the qualities of the client's physical space that are necessary to successfully implement those interventions or approaches.

An ideal space from which children and adolescents can attend teletherapy is safe, private, equipped with objects required for therapy intervention, and free of unnecessary distractions.

- ***Safe:*** Work with caregivers to ensure that the space from which children and adolescents attend teletherapy sessions is devoid of potentially dangerous objects. Consider the client's developmental age in assessing safety of their physical space. This is particularly important for young children and adolescents who may have a history of self-harm. See Chapter 5 for more ideas on identifying safe spaces for teletherapy.
- ***Private:*** An ideal room for teletherapy has doors that may be closed to ensure the privacy of their sessions. Consider the age of the client and if they are old enough to be alone with doors closed. Ask caregivers if others will need to access anything in the room during the session and avoid spaces that others may need access to during the session if possible. Support clients in acquiring and/or setting up a noise machine if necessary. If a noise machine is not available, apps and websites may be accessed from a cell phone and used for this purpose. See Chapter 4 for more information on confidentiality in teletherapy with children and adolescents.
- ***Equipped with objects required for therapy intervention:*** For assessments and interventions that require particular materials, work with caregivers to organize necessary materials in the therapy space prior to the start of session. For example, a designated play space with appropriate toys may be set up in a child's bedroom for use in teletherapy sessions. Likewise, caregivers may help to set up a space on the kitchen table for an activity that may require a large, flat surface and crafting materials.
- ***Free of unnecessary distractions:*** While some distractions may be inevitable (e.g., toys for use in therapy intervention), other distractions may be avoided by asking caregivers to remove these from the physical and/or virtual environment. For example, you may ask that clients leave cell phones out of the room from which teletherapy is attended if they're not necessary for a specific intervention. Likewise, if children and adolescents have a habit of accessing websites and apps that are not necessary for intervention, you may ask that caregivers change parental settings on the device from which teletherapy is accessed the inhibit their use.

Many clients may not have access to an ideal space. When one is not available, help clients and caregivers prioritize qualities such as safety and privacy when determining the best space from which to attend sessions. Work collaboratively with children, adolescents, and their caregivers to determine what would enhance the therapeutic space.

It may be of benefit for children and adolescents to use a different space for their individual portion of the session and have them join caregivers in a different physical space during portions of the session in which caregivers are involved. Using a laptop computer may ease this transition. For example, a parent may join their child in the first portion of a session from the living room. When the time comes for the child to meet individually with the therapist, the parent may move the laptop computer to the child's bedroom and set it up in a way that allows the therapist to see the designated play space that they have set up for teletherapy before leaving the room.

Develop a plan for how caregivers will know when it's time to join teletherapy sessions. For example, the therapist may text a caregiver, the child/adolescent may make a specific sound (e.g., horn, bell, song, funny voice/noise), or the child/adolescent may go get their caregiver(s). If the plan is to retrieve their caregiver, discuss with adults where they will be located to make the transition as quick as possible.

Develop a backup plan with caregivers in case something happens that requires that they return before the originally planned time. For example, if there is a safety concern, the child/adolescent needs help navigating technology, or they walk away from the screen and don't return, having a backup plan in place will allow you to get help from an adult who is present within the client's physical location should the need arise.

Creating Rituals

Children and adolescents benefit from having a consistent routine. In therapy, consistency of routine supports therapeutic engagement by helping clients know what to expect next. Teletherapy, however, lacks the natural transition rituals that are inherent to in-person therapy, such as traveling to the therapy office, sitting in the waiting room, and walking to the therapy room with the therapist. Support engagement of child and adolescent clients by creating rituals that they can engage in each time that they attend a teletherapy session (Smith et al., 2023).

The following are examples of possible rituals that you, clients, and caregivers may build into the regular routine of teletherapy:

- Get a snack and drink before each session
- Play a song at the start of each session
- Select a fun virtual background
- Change the written name that appears on the teletherapy platform to something silly
- Take a restroom break
- Take a dance party break
- Clean up materials at the end of each session

Any ritual will promote a level of expectation and predictability into sessions, thus allowing children and adolescents to relax and more fully engage in the therapy process.

Staying Active

Successful teletherapy with children and adolescents requires active engagement throughout the entirety of each session. To maintain client engagement, prepare materials in advance, alternate activities, maintain the illusion of eye contact, and be authentic.

Prepare materials. Children in in-person therapeutic environments often step into some version of a play therapy room filled with engaging toys and games. In virtual environments, have clients and/or caregivers come to session with physical materials for use in therapy assessment and intervention or be prepared with virtual tools. This means logging into any necessary websites, programs, or applications in advance and having all relevant links ready to ensure seamless transitions between activities, avoid unnecessary lag time, and ultimately avoid the loss of client interest. See Chapter 6 for more information on materials for therapy at a distance.

Alternate activities. Include a variety of different activities that clients can engage in, even within the same session. Strategies may include alternating between virtual interventions (e.g., use of websites, apps, gaming devices, virtual reality), movement activities (e.g., scavenger hunt; see Chapter

24), sensory play (see Chapter 36), and mindfulness-based activities (see Chapter 28). See Chapter 25 for additional ideas on breaking up teletherapy sessions.

Maintain the illusion of eye contact. Direct eye contact is not possible in virtual settings. However, "high eye contact" is associated with higher ratings of perceived empathy in teletherapy sessions (Grondin et al., 2022). Attempt to create an illusion of eye contact by looking near your camera. You must, however, also keep visual contact with the client's image on your computer, requiring that you inadvertently take your eyes off of the camera. This may make it look to clients as though you aren't looking at them (Hertlein et al., 2021). To maintain the illusion of eye contact while still allowing for a continued visual of the client on your screen, center the client's video under your camera, while keeping your eyes centered near the camera (Reynolds et al., 2024). The angle at which you look at the screen versus the camera should be no more than seven degrees (Tam et al., 2007). In some cases, this means altering your video equipment (e.g., moving your camera) and/or software (e.g., changing settings in the camera app to make one's face larger in the frame) so you look as if you are looking into the camera.

Be authentic. Your own level of authenticity can go a long way in increasing client engagement. Tap into your own history and identify what created engagement and meaning for you as a child and adolescent. Consider ways in which you might intentionally maintain focus and keep up your own energy during sessions (see Chapters 12 and 13). Additionally, consider your use of technology and how your own likes, dislikes, and experience with it may influence your use of these resources in therapy with children and adolescents (see Chapter 11). Make adjustments as needed.

Paying Attention to Little Things

Finally, pay attention to the little things. Engage with the client's environment by asking questions or making conversation about things that you notice or see. For example, the following make great conversation starters:

- Toys that you might see in the space where the client is physically located
- Art on the client's wall
- Graphics on the client's clothing
- Family pets that may be present during the session

Carefully observe client actions and reactions (e.g., smiles, frowns, when it appears that they might be looking at something else in the room or on their screen). Make the covert over by asking about these things and discussing them (Reynolds et al., 2024; Springer et al., 2024).

References

Dombo, E. A., Kays, L., & Weller, K. (2014). Clinical social work practice and technology: Personal, practical, regulatory, and ethical considerations for the twenty-first century. *Social Work in Health Care, 53*(9), 900–919. https://doi.org/10.1080/00981389.2014.948585

Grondin, F. G., Lomanowska, A. M., Poiré, V., & Jackson, P. L. (2022). Clients in simulated teletherapy via videoconference compensate for altered eye contact when evaluating therapist empathy. *Journal of Clinical Medicine, 11*(12), Article 3461. https://doi.org/10.3390/jcm11123461

Hertlein, K. M., Drude, K. P., Hilty, D. M., & Maheu, M. M. (2021). Toward proficiency in telebehavioral health: applying interprofessional competencies in couple and family therapy. *Journal of Marital and Family Therapy, 47*(2), 359–374. https://doi.org/10.1111/jmft.12496

Maheu, M., Drude, M., Hertlein, K., Lipschutz, P., Wall, K., & Hilty, D. (2018). An interprofessional framework for telebehavioral health competencies. *Journal of Technology in Behavioral Science, 3*(2), 108–140. https://doi.org/10.1007/s40596-018-0988-1

Reynolds, L. R., Springer, P. R., Taylor, N. C., Bischoff, R. J., & Cobb, R. A. (2024). Building therapeutic relationships via teletherapy. In R. A. Cobb (Ed.) *The therapist's notebook for systemic teletherapy: Creative interventions for effective online therapy* (pp. 21–28). Routledge. https://doi.org/10.4324/9781003289920-5

Smith, T., Norton, A. M., & Marroquin, L. (2023). Virtual family play therapy: A clinician's guide to using directed family play therapy in telemental health. *Contemporary Family Therapy, 45*(1), 106–116. https://doi.org/10.1007/s10591-021-09612-7

Springer, P. R., Taylor, N. C., & Bischoff, R. J. (2024). Overcoming lack of visual and auditory cues in online sessions. In R. A. Cobb (Ed.) *The therapist's notebook for systemic teletherapy: Creative interventions for effective online therapy* (pp. 11–17). Routledge. https://doi.org/10.4324/9781003289920-6

Tam, T., Cafazzo, J. A., Seto, E., Salenieks, M. E., & Rossos, P. G. (2007). Perception of eye contact in video teleconsultation. *Journal of Telemedicine and Telecare, 13*(1), 35–39. https://doi.org/10.1258/135763307779701239

Weinsberg, H., & Rolnick, A. (2020). *Theory and practice of online therapy*. Routledge.

CHAPTER 3

EXPLAINING TELETHERAPY TO GUARDIANS

Katharine P. Wenocur

It is critical to collaborate with guardians of children and adolescents seeking treatment at the onset of therapy and throughout (Goodyear-Brown, 2020). Although the convenience of teletherapy makes it a compelling option for care, guardians may experience worry as a result of both the reason for seeking therapy and uncertainty regarding the nature of therapy itself. Explaining the mechanics of therapy and youth-specific modalities can increase comfort with and buy-in to therapy. This ultimately increases session attendance and effectiveness of intervention (Wark, 2015). Similar care should be taken to orient guardians to the nature of teletherapy. Teletherapy can raise additional questions, particularly related to the logistics of accessing videoconferencing technology and about assisting their child in participating in teletherapy in a meaningful way. Families may benefit from discussions about both the therapeutic and technological aspects of teletherapy. These conversations set clear expectations for teletherapy at the onset of services, ensure a smooth transition to starting therapy, and open lines of communication between the therapist and guardian should challenges related to the format arise.

Prior to beginning teletherapy, schedule a videocall with guardians of child and adolescent clients via the telehealth platform that you plan to use for sessions. Set aside 15–30 minutes to (1) inquire about their experience with therapy and technology, (2) discuss the treatment format, (3) explain the benefits of teletherapy, and (4) answer any questions that the family might have.

Inquiring about Experience with Therapy and Technology

Adult, adolescent, and child clients may have a wide range of knowledge and comfort with both therapy and technology. Explain that teletherapy is a unique approach to therapy in which the therapist and clients utilize a variety of physical and digital tools throughout sessions. Inquire about their experience with therapy. If they have prior experience with therapy, ask about what's worked for them and what they might want that's different from their previous experience. Then inquire about their experience with computers and any other digital tools that you may use in teletherapy assessment and intervention. Client responses will guide you in determining what might need to be explained about teletherapy and in identifying the level of support that may be required in navigating technology throughout treatment.

Discussing the Treatment Format

Explain your own approach to teletherapy and the tools that you use in treatment. This discussion should likely include an introduction to the teletherapy platform, digital tools used in teletherapy

DOI: 10.4324/9781003330912-4

assessment and intervention, the use of objects within the client's physical location, and expectations regarding participation on the part of guardians and/or other family members.

- ***Teletherapy platform:*** Provide a "tour" of the teletherapy platform that you use. Explain the basic functions such as clicking on the videoconferencing link, using the chat feature, and adjusting the platform's video or audio settings. It may also be helpful to share that the platform is Health Insurance Portability and Accountability Act (HIPAA) consistent, and what this means in terms of ensuring confidentiality. Also, explain the limitations to confidentiality as it relates to the possibility of conversations being overheard by others present within the client's physical location and discuss safeguards for addressing this concern (see Chapters 2 and 4).
- ***Other digital tools:*** Outline the digital tools that you use in your teletherapy practice. For example, you might say that a wide array of digital materials may be used to support the therapeutic process. These may include:
  - Computer programs (e.g., PowerPoint)
  - Digital white boards
  - Digital cameras and/or photographs
  - Websites with content for therapeutic assessment/intervention (e.g., virtual sand tray, virtual dollhouse)
  - Music
  - Videos
  - Videogames
  - Virtual reality hardware/software
  - Virtual backgrounds
  - Green screens

  Provide a few specific examples to illustrate the use of the aforementioned digital tools and explain the ways in which you use these tools for therapy assessment and/or intervention. For example, you might access a virtual dollhouse (see Chapter 22) and explain the therapeutic benefit of this tool to illustrate the use of a website used for therapeutic intervention.

  Inquire about any hardware that the clients have available to them that they might be able to use in sessions (e.g., gaming devices, virtual reality hardware) and what software they have available on those devices.

  If you use a digital tools consent form (see Chapter 10), explain that you will provide this prior to the first session to detail the use of digital tools and allow guardians to provide consent to the use of digital tools prior to their use.
- ***Use of objects within the client's physical location:*** Explain that sometimes you have clients use physical objects that are available to them for assessment and intervention. Provide examples of materials that you typically use and explain the ways in which you use these tools for therapy assessment and/or intervention. For example, you might explain how you incorporate sensory play through the use of physical objects and explain the therapeutic benefit of this approach (see Chapter 36).

Inquire about the availability of tools necessary for any specific interventions that you commonly use. If you plan to send clients a "therapeutic care package" with necessary physical tools at the onset of therapy (see Chapter 8), discuss this as well.

- ***Guardian participation:*** When working with children and adolescents who are not old enough to consent to treatment on their own, explain that successful teletherapy is dependent on caregiver involvement, just as it is with in-person treatment. Set clear expectations regarding their expected participation in each session and their required roles for any additional support that may be needed (e.g., joining at the start and/or end of each session, being on call for help with technology or any safety concerns; see Chapter 2).

Explaining the Benefits of Teletherapy

Provide guardians with justification for the use of teletherapy beyond simple convenience. Share research on the efficacy of teletherapy and the ways in which teletherapy may help to increase attendance and engagement. The following information may be provided to support with this endeavor.

- ***Effectiveness:*** In a meta-analysis of 20 studies, no significant differences were found in outcome measures between synchronous teletherapy and in-person therapy (Lin et al., 2022). This means that, if properly trained in teletherapy, clinicians can successfully implement in teletherapy most modalities that they are trained to practice in in-person sessions. Reassure caregivers that their child will receive high-quality therapy online.
- ***Attendance:*** Teletherapy providers typically have increased attendance rates for sessions involving children and adolescents (Nicholas et al., 2021). When families encounter challenges that might otherwise require them to cancel in-person therapy appointments (e.g., car needing repair, sick parent, snowstorm), teletherapy often allows for therapy to continue without interruption.
- ***Engagement:*** Minors generally report high satisfaction with teletherapy (Nicholas et al., 2021). Children and adolescents can be successfully engaged in teletherapy by determining and clarifying the roles of each person in the therapeutic process, setting a clear structure, creating rituals, and staying active by preparing materials in advance and alternating therapeutic activities (see Chapter 2). The tools of teletherapy, including internet-based games and videoconferencing, may already be familiar to children and adolescents. Therefore, they may feel that teletherapy contains familiar elements of their daily lives and may be more willing to engage with therapy when delivered via this medium.

Answering Questions

While a comprehensive, pre-treatment conversation can prepare families for the clinical and logistical details of participating in teletherapy, expect to engage in ongoing conversations regarding teletherapy and ask caregivers if they have any questions about the process.

It can be helpful to anticipate common questions that caregivers may ask and be prepared to answer them. For example:

- ***Is teletherapy confidential?*** Telehealth platforms that have signed a HIPAA business associate agreement (BAA) commit to the highest level of security to prevent unauthorized sharing of data (U.S. Department of Health and Human Services: Office for Civil Rights, 2023). Finding out whether your platform has signed a BAA and explaining this level of protection to caregivers can mitigate concerns about confidentiality. It can also be helpful for caregivers to know that clinicians commit to the same level of confidentiality in data management during teletherapy sessions as they would during face-to-face sessions.

- ***What should I do while my child is in teletherapy?*** Explain to caregivers that they should allow their child to access the teletherapy session from a private location, but remain nearby and available for a conjoint or caregiver-only component of the session, as needed. Caregivers might find it helpful to consider a task that can occupy the time of the session, but from which they can be easily called away (e.g., watch a television show or fold laundry).
- ***How do I know that my child isn't just playing games?*** Similar to communication with caregivers regarding in-person sessions, it is beneficial to discuss the child's treatment plan and some examples of the modalities – including online games – that you might use during the course of treatment. Caregivers can benefit from knowing the therapeutic purpose behind games and activities that may also be played for recreational purposes.
- ***How will I know if my child is benefitting from teletherapy?*** Ask caregivers about any changes they see in their child and discuss observations of how their child is doing in sessions. Clear, consistent communication with the clinician helps caregivers to best understand their child's progress.

Answer any questions that caregivers might have and proactively address any concerns. Periodically assess the family's satisfaction and comfort with the format of therapy and provide ongoing information about updates to the teletherapy platform, digital and physical tools used in assessment and intervention, and state and federal regulations regarding the use of telehealth. Clear, open lines of communication with guardians can set children and adolescents up for a successful teletherapy experience.

References

Goodyear-Brown, P. (2020). *Parents as partners in child therapy.* Guilford Press.

Lin, T., Heckman, T. G., & Anderson, T. (2022). The efficacy of synchronous teletherapy versus in-person therapy: A meta-analysis of randomized clinical trials. *Clinical Psychology: Science and Practice, 29*(2), 167–178. https://doi.org/10.1037/cps0000056

Nicholas, J., Bell, I. H., Thompson, A., Valentine, L., Simsar, P., Sheppard, H., & Adams, S. (2021). Implementation lessons from the transition to telehealth during COVID-19: A survey of clinicians and young people from youth mental health services. *Psychiatry Research, 299*, Article 113848. https://doi.org/10.1016/j.psychres.2021.113848

U.S. Department of Health and Human Services: Office for Civil Rights (2023, October 18). *FAQs on telehealth and HIPAA during the COVID-19 nationwide public health emergency.* https://www.hhs.gov/sites/default/files/telehealth-faqs-508.pdf

Wark, L. (2015). Explaining the use of play to parents. In C. F. Sori, L. Hecker, & M. E. Bachenberg (Eds.), *The therapist's notebook for children and adolescents: Homework, handouts, and activities for use in psychotherapy* (pp. 3–8). Routledge.

CHAPTER 4

CONFIDENTIALITY IN TELETHERAPY WITH CHILDREN AND ADOLESCENTS[1]

Eric L. Ström and Rebecca A. Cobb

Just as with in-person services, confidentiality is a critical aspect of providing safe and effective teletherapy services to children and adolescents. While all the rules and standards of confidentiality that apply to conventional practice settings apply to teletherapy service (American Association for Marriage and Family Therapy, 2015; American Counseling Association, 2014; American Mental Health Counselors Association, 2020), there are additional considerations regarding confidentiality specific to teletherapy practice, especially when working with children and adolescents. In addition to state laws, regulations, and requirements regarding confidentiality in teletherapy, consider the teletherapy platform, use of external websites and applications, privacy on devices used by clients, the therapist's physical environment, and the client's physical environment.

HIPAA-Consistent Platform

All teletherapy services must be provided via a platform that is consistent with federal Health Insurance Portability and Accountability Act (HIPAA) standards. Some video conferencing services have HIPAA-consistent and non-HIPAA-consistent versions of the platform. The version of the platform that you use for teletherapy services must be consistent with HIPAA standards and must issue a HIPAA business associate agreement to the therapist.

Use of External Websites and Applications

Some creative therapeutic interventions may require access to websites and applications that may not be HIPAA consistent (e.g., see Chapter 22 on the virtual dollhouse and Chapter 30 on virtual therapeutic gaming). When this occurs, explain to clients the difference between the HIPAA-consistent therapy platform and the use of any other websites or applications that may be accessed during therapy. If non-HIPAA-consistent chat functions are available through the website or application being used, instruct clients to dialogue with you in a way that is HIPAA compliant, such as through your teletherapy platform. Explicitly discuss strategies for maintaining confidentiality and any identified risks to confidentiality. Consider creating a digital tools consent form to inform clients and caregivers about the steps they can take to support the safe and effective use of technology in teletherapy and to provide

DOI: 10.4324/9781003330912-5

any appropriate acknowledgement and acceptance of risk to privacy that allows clients to consent to the use of digital tools in therapy (see Chapter 10).

Privacy on Client Devices

Additionally, therapists should have sufficient technical understanding to help clients assess whether their device and online environment are sufficiently secure and private. When working with adolescents who are old enough to consent to therapy on their own and who do not want their caregivers to know that they are in therapy, you may discuss the possibility of others accessing data stored on the device that they use to attend teletherapy if others have access to that device. Likewise, if you know that a client is joining teletherapy from a school-provided device, discuss how data relating to teletherapy that is stored on the client's school computer might be vulnerable to being accessed by the client's teachers or school administrators.

Therapist's Physical Environment

Confidentiality requirements regarding the therapist's physical environment are similar to that of in-person services. However, clinicians working from home offices should take additional measures to support confidentiality if other people are physically present in their environment. The following steps may be taken to help safeguard your physical environment from possible breaches to confidentiality:

- Lock office door(s) while in session.
- Sound-proof the room used to deliver teletherapy.
- Use a headset so only your side of the conversation may be overheard from your physical location.
- Use noise machines to prevent your side of the conversation from being overheard.

You may consider scanning the room with your camera to provide clients with a visual of your physical location to ease any concerns that they may have regarding confidentiality. If you have a pet that attends session with you, you might intentionally scan your camera to your pet, introduce the pet, and ask if it is okay if they attend session with you or if they would prefer that they not listen in. This can help to set younger clients at ease and demonstrate the importance that you place on maintaining confidentiality within your environment. If special circumstances necessitate supervisors or other healthcare providers being present in your physical location, disclose this information to clients prior to the start of teletherapy sessions.

Client Physical Environments

Unique to teletherapy is that the client's physical environment is generally outside of the therapist's control. This means that therapists must work with clients and their caregivers to set up confidential spaces for teletherapy and assist them in assessing who might be able to see or overhear teletherapy sessions from their physical location.

The following suggestions may assist clients in setting up their physical environment in a way that supports confidentiality:

- Discuss with caregivers the need for privacy during portions of therapy sessions in which children and adolescents are alone with the therapist.
- Help clients and their caregivers identify a space to engage in teletherapy where privacy may be maximized.
- Instruct clients to close and, as appropriate, lock the door(s) to the room(s) where they will be during session.
- Support caregivers in helping anyone who is not attending therapy avoid the space in which teletherapy will be taking place while sessions are occurring. This may be particularly important when there are other children and adolescents within the household.
- Encourage clients attending session individually to use a headset so only their side of the conversation may be overheard in their physical location. A limitation of this is that clients may not be able to hear if another person were to enter the room while wearing a headset or noise-cancelling earphones. If others entering the space in which clients attend teletherapy is a concern, use best judgment in determining the course of action that is least likely to compromise confidentiality.
- You may practice talking with children and adolescents in the designated therapy space while a caregiver leaves the room, shuts the door, and moves to different spaces of the home to see if your discussion can be heard from different locations within the home. This may help to prevent others from inadvertently overhearing content from sessions. Help clients and caregivers consider vents or other ways in which noise may travel in the client's physical location, even to spaces that may be farther away.
- Work with children, adolescents, and their caregivers to determine whether a noise machine may be necessary to prevent others in the client's physical location from overhearing their side of the conversation. If a noise machine is not available, an application can be downloaded on the client's phone or tablet that can be used to make white or brown noise. This device can then be placed on the inside of their door at the start of session.
- When noise traveling throughout the client's physical location is inevitable, work with caregivers to develop a plan for remaining in locations from which conversations may not be easily overheard while still providing age-appropriate supervision for client safety.

To assess confidentiality in the client's physical location, ask the following:

- Where are you joining therapy from today?
- Is there anyone else there with you?
- Where [is/are] your [mom/dad/brother(s)/sister(s)/etc.]?
- Do you think anyone else might be able to overhear our conversation?

If you are concerned about someone being able to overhear the conversation and clients are old enough to read and type, you can type these questions into the chat function of your teletherapy platform and have clients do the same with their responses.

Many children and adolescents may not have a private space available from which they can attend teletherapy. For example, many children share rooms with siblings, do not have locks on their doors, or may have other children run into the room in the middle of the session. If others are present in the client's physical location during a session, consider asking an adult to help secure the space for confidentiality. If the presence of others appears unavoidable, consider what topics and activities might allow therapy to continue in an appropriate way given the circumstances. For example, when others who are not a part of therapeutic services join the client's physical location midway through session, you might shift the conversation from a more emotionally charged topic to do an activity that is less likely to lead to the client divulging more sensitive information that they may not want others to hear or that may not be of therapeutic benefit for others to hear until further processing has occurred. In addition, use caution in initiating discussion of topics addressed in previous sessions to avoid sharing confidential information with others who are physically present in the client's location. For clients who are old enough to read and type, you might consider alternative or adjunct forms of communication that may add an additional level of confidentiality, such as typing more sensitive information into the teletherapy platform chat function rather than discussing the information out loud. Otherwise, when teletherapy may be contraindicated given the presence of others, work with clients to assess whether the session should continue or whether it would be best to resume your work when confidentiality is more likely to be maintained.

Note

1 Adapted from Ström, E. L., & Cobb, R. A. (2024). Confidentiality in systemic teletherapy. In R. A. Cobb (Ed.) *The therapist's notebook for systemic teletherapy: Creative interventions for effective online therapy* (pp. 18–20). Routledge. https://doi.org/10.4324/9781003289920-4

References

American Association for Marriage and Family Therapy. (2015). *2015 AAMFT code of ethics*. https://www.aamft.org/Legal_Ethics/Code_of_Ethics.aspx

American Counseling Association. (2014). *2014 ACA code of ethics*. https://www.counseling.org/docs/default-source/default-document-library/ethics/2014-aca-code-of-ethics.pdf

American Mental Health Counselors Association. (2020). *2020 AMHCA code of ethics*. https://www.amhca.org/HigherLogic/System/DownloadDocumentFile.ashx?DocumentFileKey=24a27502-196e-b763-ff57-490a12f7edb1

CHAPTER 5

TRAUMA-INFORMED CARE AND SAFETY CONSIDERATIONS FOR TELETHERAPY WITH CHILDREN AND ADOLESCENTS

Darlene M. Vander Schuur, Lindsay V. Miller, Nefeteria L. Bolin, and Megan Simmons

It is important to deliver all mental health services with sensitivity to the potential of trauma and consideration of client safety (Gerber et al., 2020). This is true for both in-person and teletherapy services. The following provides unique considerations for teletherapy to support trauma-informed care and client safety. It is not an exhaustive summary. Rather, it highlights components of trauma-informed care and safety considerations that are unique to teletherapy services with children and adolescents, including the setup of sessions, the client's environment, the therapist's environment, the virtual environment, and assessing for and addressing trauma responses.

Establishing Setup of Sessions

Trauma and maltreatment can greatly affect the participation of children and adolescents in therapy. For example, children with trauma histories may have shorter attention spans, which may impact their ability to engage in treatment for longer periods of time. When engaging in teletherapy specifically, long periods of time spent on the computer or other devices may be particularly triggering for clients who have experienced trauma or vicarious trauma through the use of technology (e.g., cyberbullying, being recorded unknowingly, technology-facilitated intimate partner violence; Pickens & Norton, 2024). Some clients may benefit from shorter and/or more frequent sessions to amplify engagement. Transversely, time spent in each therapy session can be split so that half of the time can be spent with children or adolescents and the other half can be spent with caregivers (Burgoyne & Cohn, 2020).

Set expectations for caregiver involvement either prior to the start of therapy or in the first session. Include psychoeducation on the rationale for caregiver involvement and discuss what structure will work best (e.g., inviting caregivers to the beginning and/or end of sessions). In the development of the session structure, consider any emotional support from caregivers or family members that may be helpful. Involve others as needed to enhance the efficacy of treatment.

DOI: 10.4324/9781003330912-6

The Client's Environment

In teletherapy, the client's physical environment is generally outside of the therapist's control. Yet, the client's physical environment greatly impacts the process of teletherapy. For example, a sibling or parent unexpectedly entering the room in which teletherapy is taking place can be incredibly disruptive to the therapeutic process. Simply the possibility of interruption (e.g., knowing that a family member might overhear a conversation or walk into the room during the session) may inhibit children and adolescents from talking about certain things (Springer et al., 2024).

Beyond the general need for confidentiality, children and adolescents who have experienced trauma and abuse may have additional concerns that need to be addressed. Clients who have experienced abuse may not feel safe to disclose maltreatment if the person who perpetrated the abuse is present in the household. In this case, the fear of retaliation for disclosure may prevent them from sharing this information altogether or until they have more privacy. For those who are gender nonconforming and/or belong to the LGBTQIA+ community, using preferred names and pronouns and discussing this part of their identity may feel uncomfortable or unsafe. Likewise, some children and adolescents may not be comfortable with certain members of the household knowing that they have experienced certain traumas and may not want to discuss their experience knowing that others may be able to overhear the conversation.

Though therapists can't control the client's environment, they may work with clients and their caregivers to create safe spaces for teletherapy (see Chapter 4). The following provides guidance on how to help clients identify spaces for teletherapy and engage in continued safety assessment throughout teletherapy.

Identifying Safe Spaces for Teletherapy

Discuss with clients and caregivers how to prepare a therapeutic space for teletherapy (Romney & Garcia, 2021; Stewart et al., 2017). Discuss the importance of privacy and of attending therapy from a space that is both physically and emotionally safe. For many children and adolescents, home may be a place where trauma has occurred or may otherwise not feel like a safe space. Discuss with clients their comfort with attending teletherapy from their current physical location and work with them to make any adjustments that might be necessary. For example, you might work with clients to schedule appointments for days or times when fewer people are home (Burgoyne & Cohn, 2020). Alternatively, many schools offer private rooms through their counseling offices and are willing to allow teletherapy sessions to occur within school hours. After-school programs or libraries may also be amenable to quiet private rooms. Clients often think of brilliant strategies for creating safe and private spaces for therapy when given the opportunity. Empower clients to help identify solutions that feel right for them.

Assessing Safety

Take note of where clients are physically located during teletherapy sessions to ensure physical safety, especially in the event of an emergency. At the start of each session, assess the physical location of clients. This is especially important if it appears that they are in a location that looks unfamiliar or if they have a virtual background that inhibits you from seeing their physical surroundings. If they are located somewhere other than their home or another location for which you have a physical address, acquire the physical address of their location. This is vitally important to support clients in any crisis situation in which outside help, such as caregivers, a crisis team, medical assistance, or law enforcement, should be called upon.

Regularly assess for the presence of others in the client's physical location, especially if there is reason to believe that abuse may be occurring or if there are any other safety concerns. You may ask who else is in the room with them, or you may ask where other members of the household are located (Stewart et al., 2017). If others are present or you have reason to believe that others may be able to overhear your conversation, avoid talking about anything that could put clients at risk of harm. If someone doesn't appear to be physically present in the room with the client but may be able to overhear the conversation, and if children and adolescents are able to read and type, you may use the chat function on the teletherapy platform to assess safety and communicate if needed.

Safety Planning

As with in-person therapy, assess regularly for any relevant safety concerns and conduct a safety plan as needed. At the onset of therapy, identify and discuss resources that are available to clients. Since resources vary by location and clients typically benefit from services that are within close physical proximity, familiarize yourself with resources available within each client's physical location (Springer et al., 2024). Keep documentation of these resources readily available so you can quickly access them in the event of an emergency.

Have children and adolescent clients identify an adult who will be physically nearby each session that you can call if you become concerned about their safety. For children, this may be the person who initiated therapy for them. For adolescents who are of age to consent to therapy, this may be someone else that the adolescent has identified as a preferred point of contact. Obtain a release of information, if appropriate, and discuss instances in which you might contact this person. Obtain their phone number and keep this readily available each session so you can quickly call them if needed. For example, if a young child begins climbing on unstable furniture in session and can't be redirected, or a teenager exhibits signs of suicidal ideation mid-session, having accessible emergency contact information will allow for the fastest possible safety intervention.

When confidentiality is a concern, work with children and adolescents to create a code word or phrase that they can use to inform you of instances in which they do not feel safe because of others in their environment or if their conversation is no longer private. Ideally, this word or phrase should be a common saying that would not arouse suspicion when spoken or could be easily typed into the telehealth platform's chat feature (Briere et al., 2020). Alternatively, you can work with clients to develop another way of signaling safety concerns using virtual backgrounds or other tools available through the teletherapy platform (see Chapter 35).

For children and adolescents who are in crisis or have a history of self-harm, collaborate with clients and caregivers on safety planning. Identify current triggers and work with children, adolescents, and families to identify when triggers are likely to occur. Inquire about objects present within the client's physical location that may be used for self-harm. Work with clients and caregivers on setting up a safe environment both during and between sessions.

Also work with children, adolescents, and caregivers to identify what to do if they are in immediate danger and need to leave their physical location during or outside of sessions (Briere et al., 2020). For example, you might work with clients to identify trusted people and have the client inform them that they may be called on for safety, have a packed bag, develop an escape route, and have relevant contact information programmed into their phone or written on a piece of paper that they can easily access when needed (e.g., therapist, crisis line, 9-1-1, nearby shelters). Finally, when there is imminent risk to client safety, abide by legal guidelines and send appropriate people to conduct a well check or call emergency services as needed.

The Therapist's Environment

Be aware of how your own environment may also impact a client's experience in teletherapy. In addition to ensuring privacy of your space (see Chapter 4), organize your work environment to create a professional and calming space that resembles that of an in-person therapy office (Springer et al., 2020). Refrain from having beds in the background, especially when working with clients who have experienced sexual abuse (Burgoyne & Cohn, 2020). Consider the physical or virtual background that clients see surrounding your image and the message(s) that may be portrayed through this space. If you are providing telehealth from an in-person office, consider showing clients the entirety of your office and inviting them to share their space as well. This may help to set clients at ease knowing that no one else is present in your physical location. You may also choose to display certain overt or subtle messaging to create a felt sense of safety (Veldorale-Griffin, 2024). For example, you may display your name and pronouns on your screen to show support as an LGBTQIA+ ally, which may help some children and adolescents feel more comfortable in sharing their own pronouns and discussing their identity.

The Virtual Environment

Logistically speaking, clients often battle with connectivity issues due to unstable internet (Eppler, 2021) and poorly functioning or outdated tech. Young children may push buttons, abruptly ending sessions, mute themselves, or inadvertently shift their screens, placing the child out of view of the camera (Eppler et al., 2022). Continued visual and auditory contact with clients in teletherapy, however, is important for assessing safety and providing trauma-informed care. The following addresses these concerns by providing instructions on working with clients and their caregivers to set up teletherapy equipment to maximize visual contact and identify support people if technological failure occurs.

Setting Up Equipment

Prior to the first session, provide caregivers with resources and instructions on how to join the virtual session. During the first session, confirm with the caregiver that a computer, tablet, or phone with a reliable internet connection will be available for each teletherapy session. Ideally, clients should have access to a computer for session attendance. This allows better visibility of the client's body, which is especially important for younger children, who may be more likely to move around while using a tablet or phone, making it more difficult to maintain visual contact.

Work with caregivers to set up devices in a way that maximizes your view of clients and ensures working audio. This may mean guiding them on how to position their camera, adjust lighting, or move seats at the start of each session. If a larger device is unavailable, placing phones and tablets on stands may help to increase visibility and stability. Technologically savvy children and adolescents may be able to do this without the support of caregivers and may eventually learn to check equipment on their own without prompting.

Discuss the importance of visual and audio contact throughout the entirety of each session. Explain that this allows you to make sure that they are safe and doing okay, especially when discussing difficult topics (Springer et al., 2024).

Identifying Tech Support

Identify a person who will support with any technological difficulties that may occur during the session. When working with adolescents, this may be the client themselves. For younger children and adolescents who may need more help, work with caregivers to identify someone within the client's physical location who will be available to help with tech support if necessary during sessions. Ask that caregivers provide you with contact information for that person so you can reach out to them directly by phone if needed.

Identifying Alternative Plans

Establish a contingency plan for tech failure (e.g., frozen screens, loss of audio, loss of internet service; Galindo, 2020). Plans can include using the chat box function within the telehealth platform if audio or video is lost, connecting from a different device, moving to a phone call for the remainder of the session, or rescheduling.

Addressing Confidentiality

If abuse has occurred through technology (e.g., cyberbullying, sexual abuse), remind clients of steps taken to ensure confidentiality, remind them that sessions are not recorded, and possibly even move away from the screen enough so clients can see your entire clothed body to help reduce stress. In addition, explain that your meetings will all occur over a Health Insurance Portability and Accountability Act (HIPAA)-consistent therapy platform. Describe the ways in which HIPAA compliance helps to protect client confidentiality and safeguard against anyone else being able to see, overhear, or otherwise be a part of your conversations. When you utilize websites and other digital tools that may not be HIPAA compliant, explain potential risks to confidentiality. For example, describe ways in which IP addresses may be recorded on websites and explain that others who have access to their computer could see which websites they have visited during teletherapy sessions.

Trauma Responses

Throughout each teletherapy session, observe and assess clients for trauma responses and address them proactively as needed. When equipment is set up properly, you should be able to see and listen for signs of hypo- and hyperarousal, indicators that a client may be experiencing a trauma response. Even when conducting creative therapeutic assessments and interventions that require visual contact with something other than clients themselves, try to maintain simultaneous visual contact with the client's face and as much of their body as possible. Having a second computer screen may allow for greater visual contact with both the client and other websites, applications, or computer programs. When this is not possible, pay special attention to auditory cues that may indicate hypo- or hyperarousal.

Assessing Hypo- and Hyperarousal

The virtual environment plays an important part in the therapeutic process, especially as it relates to processing trauma and identifying important cues indicating the client's ability to engage in treatment (Glass & Bickler, 2021). Maximum therapeutic benefit happens when clients stay within their window of tolerance (Rothschild, 2000; Siegel, 2020). The best indicators as to whether clients are within their window of tolerance are often nonverbal cues. Therefore, you must be aware of changes in skin coloration, gaze, body motion, and body posture to identify when clients experience hyperarousal (e.g., emotional dysregulation) or hypoarousal (e.g., dissociation). Unfortunately, teletherapy may provide a limited view of clients, making it more difficult to assess for these important cues that indicate when critical next steps are necessary.

Addressing Hypo- and Hyperarousal

In preparation for more difficult activities and topics of conversation, and before any trauma processing, provide psychoeducation. To establish a common language and understanding, provide clients and caregivers with a description of typical hyper- and hypoarousal responses. This can help all parties identify when dysregulation may occur. Teach techniques that children, adolescents, and their caregivers can use to stay within their window of tolerance. Mindfulness exercises, breathing and grounding exercises, and relaxation techniques are all great methods of helping clients access their parasympathetic nervous system, ground in the "here and now," slow down emotion responses, and maintain attention (Racine et al., 2020). As with any therapy intervention, apply a trauma-informed approach in the application of these exercises. For example, don't require that clients close their eyes during mindfulness activities. Rather, you may provide this as an option if it feels comfortable for them.

During any virtual trauma work, pay close attention to any visual and auditory cues that may be noted. Frequent eye movement, sensorimotor agitation, reddening of the skin, and elevated tone of voice could indicate hyperarousal. Conversely, staring into space, physical rigidity, and paling of the skin might be signs of hypoarousal (Rothschild, 2000). Verbalizing these noticed changes to clients can aid in shifting clients back into their window of tolerance, especially when followed up with a centering or grounding technique. For adolescent clients, you can also ask that they describe their experiences using the common language of hypo/hyperarousal presented in the initial psychoeducation phase.

If attempts to move clients back into their window of tolerance are unsuccessful or if they abruptly disconnect from teletherapy while in a heightened state, while experiencing dissociation, or while other concerns regarding the safety of self or others are present (e.g., suicidal ideation), call the identified emergency contact, ask them to physically join the child or adolescent in the room in which they are currently located, and guide them in providing any necessary support (Springer et al., 2024).

To maintain engagement and avoid dysregulation, it can be helpful to bring a sense of playfulness to sessions, rather than simply focusing on topics of trauma. Offer an array of creative interactive therapy opportunities. For clients who struggle with making decisions, you might avoid offering too many options at once. Rather, offer two activities and ask which of the two they prefer. Some children and adolescents, however, thrive in the consistency of a routine in which they engage with the same activities each session. Attend to the unique needs of each client in finding this balance. Finally, assess the effectiveness of teletherapy and refer to in-person providers within proximity of the client's physical location if needed (Springer et al., 2024).

References

Briere, J., Lanktree, C., & Escott, A. (2020). *Trauma teletherapy for youth in the era of the COVID-19 pandemic: Adapting evidence-based treatment approaches*. Adolescent Trauma Training Center, University of Southern California.

Burgoyne, N., & Cohn, A. S. (2020). Lessons from the transition to relational teletherapy during COVID-19. *Family Process, 59*(3), 974–988. https://doi.org/10.1111/famp.12589

Eppler, C. (2021). Systemic teletherapists' meaningful experiences during the first months of the coronavirus pandemic. *Journal of Marital and Family Therapy, 47*(2), 244–258. https://doi.org/10.1111/jmft.12515

Eppler, C., Vander Schuur, D. M., & Correa, N. (2022). COVID-19 and clinical training: Diverse interns' perspectives and collaborative recommendations. *Journal of Feminist Family Therapy, 34*(3–4), 370–389. https://doi.org/10.1080/08952833.2022.2141956

Gerber, M. R., Elisseou, S., Sager, Z. S., & Keith, J. A. (2020). Trauma-informed telehealth in the COVID-19 era and beyond. *Federal Practitioner, 37*(7), 302–308.

Glass, V. Q., & Bickler, A. (2021). Cultivating the therapeutic alliance in a telemental health setting. *Contemporary Family Therapy: An International Journal, 43*(2), 189–198. https://doi.org/10.1007/s10591-021-09570-0

Pickens, J. C., & Norton, A. (2024). Assessing appropriateness of teletherapy for intimate partner violence. In R. A. Cobb (Ed.) *The therapist's notebook for systemic teletherapy: Creative interventions for effective online therapy* (pp. 180–185). Routledge. https://doi.org/10.4324/9781003289920-34

Racine, N., Hartwick, C., Collin-Vézina, D., & Madigan, S. (2020). Telemental health for child trauma treatment during and post-COVID-19: Limitations and considerations. *Child Abuse & Neglect, 110*, Article 104698. https://doi.org/10.1016/j.chiabu.2020.104698

Romney, J., & Garcia, M. (2021). TF-CBT Informed teletherapy for children with autism and their families. *Journal of Child & Adolescent Trauma, 14*(3), 415–424. https://doi.org/10.1007/s40653-021-00354-0

Rothschild, B. (2000). *The body remembers: The psychophysiology of trauma and trauma treatment.* Norton.

Siegel, D. J. (2020). *The developing mind: How relationships and the brain interact to shape who we are* (3rd ed.). Guilford Press.

Springer, P., Bischoff, R. J., Taylor, N. C., Kohel, K. & Farero, A. (2020). Collaborative care at a distance: Student therapists' experiences of learning and delivering relationally focused telemental health. *Journal of Marital and Family Therapy, 46*(2), 201–217. https://doi.org/10.1111/jmft.12431

Springer, P. R., Taylor, N. C., & Bischoff, R. J. (2024). Overcoming lack of visual and auditory cues in online sessions. In R. A. Cobb (Ed.) *The therapist's notebook for systemic teletherapy: Creative interventions for effective online therapy* (pp. 25–28). Routledge. https://doi.org/10.4324/9781003289920-6

Stewart, R., Orengo-Aguayo, R., Cohen, J., Mannarino, A., & De Arellano, M. (2017). A pilot study of trauma-focused cognitive–behavioral therapy delivered via telehealth technology. *Child Maltreatment, 22*(4), 324–333. https://doi.org/10.1177/1077559517725403

Veldorale-Griffin, A. (2024). Using background images to signal messages via teletherapy. In R. A. Cobb (Ed.) *The therapist's notebook for systemic teletherapy: Creative interventions for effective online therapy* (pp. 29–31). Routledge. https://doi.org/10.4324/9781003289920-7

Part 2
Materials

CHAPTER 6

MATERIALS FOR THERAPY AT A DISTANCE

Rebecca A. Cobb

In-person therapy with children and adolescents typically relies on the use of a wide range of toys and/or art supplies to support the therapeutic process (e.g., Ray et al., 2013; Sinason, 1988). Though online therapists are inhibited from physically sharing objects that are present within their office, teletherapy doesn't need to be devoid of playful materials. Teletherapy with children and adolescents may include materials that are (1) acquired from objects present within the clients' physical location, (2) physically located in the therapist's office, and (3) digital in form. The following provides ideas of each of these forms of materials for use in teletherapy assessment and intervention.

Materials in the Client's Physical Location

Assess physical materials that are available to clients through discussion with caregivers in initial sessions. Depending on the activities that you hope to do in session, this may include art supplies, toys, hand puppets, video games, and virtual reality hardware and software. Though you can request that caregivers acquire specific materials for therapeutic intervention, many clients may not be able to afford additional materials for therapy. Be creative in using the resources that are already present within the client's physical environment!

For example, when practicing online child-parent relationship therapy (see Chapter 32), you may request that clients bring toys that they already have and enjoy playing with to the space in which teletherapy will take place. Alternatively, if the clients have a portable device that they can use to attend teletherapy, you may request that they attend session from any confidential space that might be designated for play and already has toys available in it. Likewise, you may conduct a scavenger hunt in which clients move throughout their physical location to seek specific objects and bring them back to the device from which they are attending therapy (see Chapters 24 and 36).

If clients do not have specific materials that are necessary for intended therapeutic assessment and intervention, consider sending a therapeutic care package (see Chapter 8).

Materials in the Therapist's Office

Though you don't need to have materials available in your physical location to conduct creative teletherapy interventions with children and adolescents, specific objects may enhance the therapeutic process. These materials will be dependent on your own preferences and intended therapeutic interventions.

For example, you may choose to share physical objects that you think clients will enjoy as a sort of "show and share" to enhance therapeutic rapport. This works particularly well if you've heard a client

DOI: 10.4324/9781003330912-8

discuss their fondness of a certain thing and you have something related to their interest that you feel comfortable showing them. If you have a well-behaved pet that is typically present with you during sessions, you might also introduce your pet and share a little bit about them. This can be particularly engaging for children who may be shy about the therapeutic process. Other materials may be intervention specific, such as use of books for bibliotherapy (see Chapter 21) and puppets for puppet reflecting teams (see Chapters 7 and 23).

Digital Materials

A wide array of digital materials may also be used to support the therapeutic process. These may include:

- Computer programs (see Chapters 14, 17, 18, 33, 39, 40, 43, and 46)
- Digital whiteboards (see Chapter 29)
- Digital cameras and/or photographs (see Chapters 15, 16, and 26)
- Websites with content for therapeutic assessment/intervention (see Chapters 19, 20, 22, 27, 38, 41, and 44)
- Music (see Chapter 25)
- Videos (see Chapters 21 and 37)
- Videogames (see Chapter 30)
- Virtual reality hardware/software (see Chapters 9 and 34)
- Virtual backgrounds (see Chapter 35)
- Green screens (see Chapters 47–50)

Other chapters within this book provide examples of the use of the aforementioned digital materials. Be creative in your own identification of additional age-appropriate digital tools. When using digital materials with children and adolescents, consider the use of a digital tools consent form to inform clients and legal guardians about the benefits and risks of digital tools in therapy prior to their use (see Chapter 10).

References

Ray, D. C., Lee, K. R., Meany-Walen, K. K., Carlson, S. E., Carnes-Holt, K. L., & Ware, J. N. (2013). Use of toys in child-centered play therapy. *International Journal of Play Therapy, 22*(1), 43–57. https://doi.org/10.1037/a0031430

Sinason, V. (1988). Dolls and bears: From symbolic equation to symbol: The significance of different play material for sexually abused children and others. *British Journal of Psychotherapy, 4*(4), 349–363. https://doi.org/10.1111/j.1752-0118.1988.tb01038.x

CHAPTER 7

HOMEMADE PUPPETS

Rebecca A. Cobb

Online virtual puppets are available for use in online therapeutic assessment and intervention (Fried, 2024). However, having physical puppets available for use in teletherapy intervention can be useful for many activities, especially since the act of physically moving puppets while voicing them can be powerful for children and adolescents in projecting emotions and acting out behaviors (Carter & Mason, 1998). This can be especially helpful for children who tend to be quieter or more resistant in therapy (Gil, 2014). In this book alone, there are two different interventions that rely on the use of physical puppets. Chapter 45, *Puppet Play Telenovela,* requires that clients have puppets available to participate in the intervention. Chapter 23, *Puppet Reflecting Teams for Telehealth Family Therapy,* requires that therapists have puppets available to conduct the intervention. Optionally, clients may also use puppets for this intervention. In addition, puppets are a great resource to have "on hand" (pun intended) for open-ended play in teletherapy with children and adolescents. Hand puppets, however, can be expensive, especially when building a collection with a variety of options.

The following describes several cost-effective ways in which clients and therapists may create or acquire puppets for use in these activities, including (1) sock puppets, (2) paper bag puppets, (3) stuffed animal puppets, and (4) finger puppets. Advantages and disadvantages of each puppet type are also discussed.

Sock Puppets

Sock puppets may be created using old socks and any other crafting materials that may be available. Ideal socks for this activity may be ones that no longer fit, need mending, or have lost their other half. Assess the age of clients when listing potential materials that may be used for this activity (e.g., needle, scissors) and ask adults to support children in creating their puppets as needed. Avoid asking young children for these materials so they don't inadvertently bring clothing items that their caregivers would rather not use. Minimally, sock puppets may be created with socks and markers, though having more materials available is ideal.

Materials

- Socks
- Markers

DOI: 10.4324/9781003330912-9

- Glue
- Scissors
- Yarn
- Thread and needle
- Fabric
- Buttons

Advantages

Sock puppets are durable and may be the most cost-effective way of acquiring a small number of hand puppets for both clients and therapists. Their mouths can easily be moved and it can be a fun activity to make them. It's also a great way to make use of old socks that may not otherwise serve a purpose anymore!

Disadvantages

Clients and therapists may not have many socks available for the creation of sock puppets. They also require time to make.

Paper Bag Puppets

Paper bag puppets may be created using small paper bags and other available crafting materials (see Figure 7.1). Ideal bags for this activity are just a little larger than a hand and are free of writing or other images. Brown paper bags commonly used for sack lunches are perfect for the creation of paper bag puppets and are often readily available. Assess the age of clients when listing potential materials that may be used for this activity (e.g., scissors) and ask adults to support children in creating their puppets as needed. Minimally, paper bag puppets may be created with paper bags and writing utensils, though having more materials available is ideal.

Materials

- Small paper bags
- Markers, crayons, colored pencils, and/or pens
- Glue
- Scissors
- Construction paper
- Googly eyes
- Yarn
- Pom poms

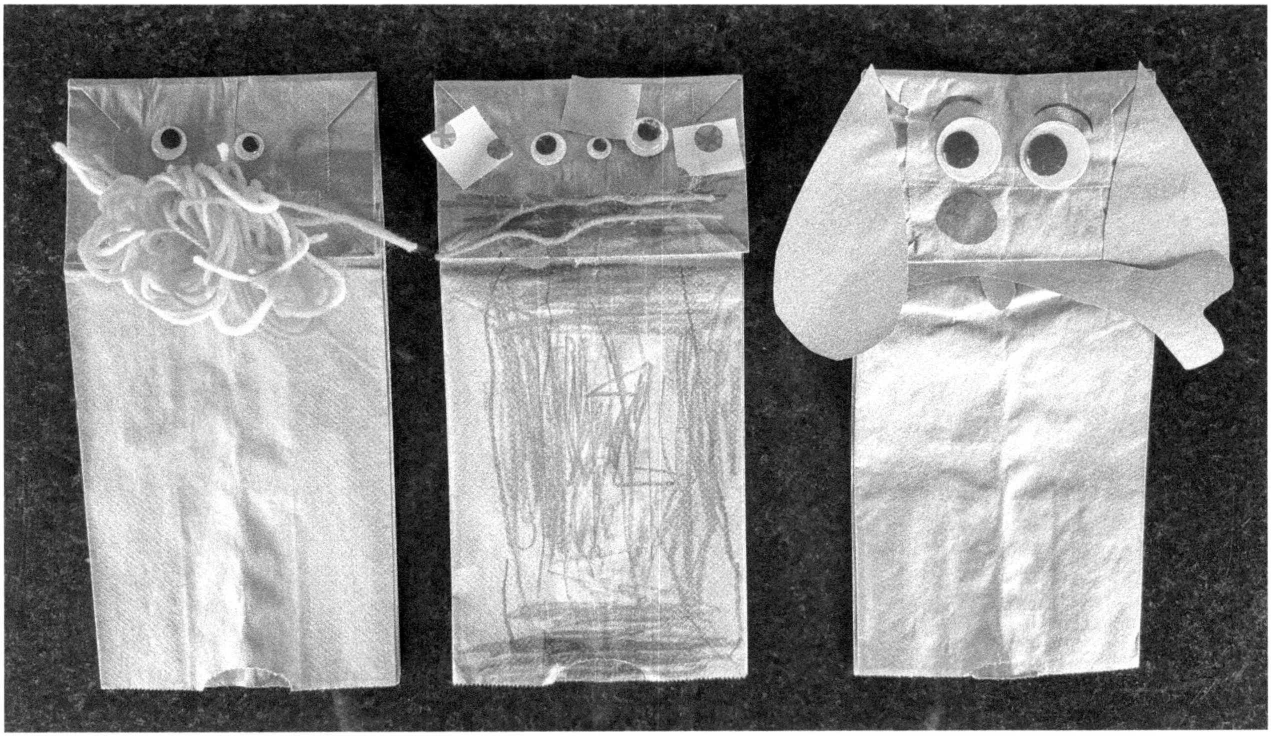

Figure 7.1 Paper bag puppets. Credit: Charlie, Addison, and Mama.

Advantages

Paper bag puppets may be the most cost-effective method of acquiring a wide array of hand puppets for both clients and therapists. Their mouths can easily be moved and it can be a fun activity to make them.

If clients don't have access to required materials, or if buying materials appears to be too financially burdensome, you may easily send clients materials to create paper bag puppets (see Chapter 8).

Disadvantages

Paper bag puppets may become wrinkled or torn easily, especially if the puppets are engaged in more aggressive behavior. They also require time to make.

Stuffed Animal Puppets

Old stuffed animals may be purchased at a low cost from resale shops and converted into hand puppets with the following steps (Foraker-Koons & Sori, 2016):

1. Select and acquire a stuffed animal.
2. Cut it open – preferably at the seam or a place where your hand would ideally be placed for manipulating the puppet.

3. Remove some of the stuffing, leaving some inside the head and limbs.
4. *Optional:* Sew a glove into the puppet to provide a more finished look and prevent the remaining stuffing from falling out.

Materials

- Stuffed animals
- Scissors
- Glove
- Needle
- Thread

Advantages

Stuffed animal puppets are cost effective and durable. They are also typically able to move their arms.

Disadvantages

Though more cost effective than buying hand puppets, stuffed animal puppets require financial resources to purchase the materials required to make them and transportation to a location where used stuffed animals can be purchased. Creating them also requires time. In addition, most stuffed animal puppets cannot be manipulated to move their mouths.

Finger Puppets

To collect a wide variety of finger puppets, it can be helpful to purchase them from someone who makes them by hand, so you can submit special requests. Etsy, an online store where shop owners sell handmade items, is a great option for this. Many shops may not advertise special requests; however, you may message them in advance of purchase to ask if they are able and willing to make small alterations in the puppets that they create (see Figure 7.2). For example, consider asking if available finger puppets can be made with diverse skin tones and facial expressions depicting a variety of different emotions. Many shop owners will happily oblige this request, especially if they are aware of the intended therapeutic purpose of the puppets.

Advantages

Finger puppets are durable and will last a long time. They are also small, portable, and do not require time to make if purchased from someone else.

Disadvantages

Finger puppets cost more money than paper bag puppets, sock puppets, and stuffed animal puppets. They are also limited in the ability to move parts (e.g., arms, mouth).

Figure 7.2 Finger puppets custom made by cherylasmith.etsy.com at the start of the COVID-19 pandemic. Credit: Rebecca A. Cobb.

Consider the advantages and disadvantages of each method of acquiring puppets before obtaining your own. If time allows, discuss available options with clients and caregivers and work with them to acquire materials in ways that are most fitting given their unique needs and desires.

References

Carter, R., & Mason, P. (1998). The selection and use of puppets in counseling. *Professional School Counseling, 1*(5), 50–53.

Foraker-Koons, K., & Sori, C. F. (2016). A guide to making puppets without breaking the bank. In C. F. Sori, L. L. Hecker, & M. E. Bachenberg (Eds.), *The therapist's notebook for children and adolescents* (2nd ed., pp. 327–329). Routledge.

Fried, K. (2024). Virtual puppet play therapy. In R. A. Cobb (Ed.) *The therapist's notebook for systemic teletherapy: Creative interventions for effective online therapy* (pp. 70–78). Routledge. https://doi.org/10.4324/9781003289920-17

Gil, E. (2014). *Play in family therapy* (2nd ed.). Guilford Press.

CHAPTER 8

THERAPEUTIC CARE PACKAGES

Rebecca A. Cobb

Some therapeutic activities may rely on the use of physical materials that clients do not have access to or that may be difficult for clients to acquire. If you plan to conduct assessments or interventions that require specific materials, consider mailing a "therapeutic care package" to clients at the onset of therapy (see Figure 8.1). This may be particularly helpful for clients who are not able to afford additional materials. For example, many clients may not have a working printer available in their home. Yet, you may easily include several printed worksheets in a therapeutic care package for ease of use in future sessions. Even if clients have the financial resources to purchase required materials, therapeutic care packages may serve as an engaging way to welcome new clients to your teletherapy practice.

Figure 8.1 Therapeutic care package.

DOI: 10.4324/9781003330912-10

Preparing Materials

When preparing therapeutic care packages, include materials that clients may use for several different therapeutic interventions. For example, you might include:

- Printed worksheets
- Coloring pages
- Construction paper
- Small paper bags
- Googly eyes
- Yarn
- Pom-poms
- Pipe cleaners
- A glue stick
- Crayons
- Play-dough
- Fidget toys
- Latex balloons

Consider diversity, equity, and inclusion, and incorporate materials that allow your clients to see themselves in what you send (Chang et al., 2005). For example, you might include Crayola's Colors of the World Crayons to ensure that clients have coloring materials that match their skin tone and that of other members of their system.

Also consider specific interventions that you might want to conduct in future sessions or materials that you might want to make available for more client-led activities that clients may not have available to them. For example, the above-listed materials would prepare clients to participate in the mixed-media aquarium (see Chapter 18), puppet play (see Chapters 7, 23, and 45), and sensory play activities (see Chapter 36), among many others.

For a more cost-effective and time-efficient process, prepare therapeutic care packages in bulk. Then, add materials as needed to fit the needs of each client.

Discussing with Clients

After having an initial intake session with caregivers and scheduling a follow-up session, ask caregivers for permission to mail a package to them with materials for subsequent sessions. Request that once it arrives, caregivers keep the package in a safe place without opening it prior to the next session, though you might encourage them to show children/adolescents that a package has arrived for them and that they'll be able to open it during their therapy session. This can be an exciting way to engage children and adolescents at the very start of therapy, similar to the excitement that many children experience when they enter a play therapy room full of new toys for the first time!

Then, ask caregivers to make the package available at the start of the next session and invite child and adolescent clients to open the package. Some children may need help opening the package or may need oversight from an adult to ensure that they don't use all the materials at once. Provide guidance as needed.

Finally, request that clients and/or caregivers put these materials in a special space and wait until the next therapy session to use them again, unless you've given them a homework assignment that requires their use. When working with younger children, ask caregivers for help to ensure that the materials are available for the next session(s) and be prepared with alternative interventions if materials have been used or are not available.

Reference

Chang, C. Y., Ritter, K. B., & Hays, D. G. (2005). Multicultural trends and toys in play therapy. *International Journal of Play Therapy, 14*(2), 69–85. https://doi.org/10.1037/h0088903

CHAPTER 9

VIRTUAL PLAYROOMS

Richard Lamb and Jason Perry

Materials for Therapists: Timing device. A second computer monitor and augmented reality (AR) headset to join clients directly in the AR environment are optional. If using a headset, you will also need a minimum of 4 square feet in a seated position or 6.5 square feet for room-scale settings to move around.

Materials for Clients: AR hardware and a minimum of 4 square feet in a seated position or 6.5 square feet for room-scale settings to move around.

Objective

Play therapy typically requires the use of a play therapy room equipped with a wide variety of physical materials. AR offers a unique opportunity to provide children and adolescents with virtual playrooms with which they can interact. The objective of this chapter is to provide an overview of the use of AR-based playrooms in teletherapy intervention.

Rationale for Use

Play therapy is a form of psychotherapy in which play is used to help children express and communicate complex feelings and thoughts (Cochran et al., 2023). Between 77% and 84% of children who take part in play therapy illustrate significant positive changes in behavior and emotional expression (Ashby et al., 2020). Most play therapy, however, requires the use of a play therapy playroom that requires significant space and a significant number of play items to ensure continuous engagement over time (Lamb et al., 2018; Lamb & Etopio, 2021). This is particularly challenging for therapists who work virtually and cannot provide clients access to required resources. Advancements in AR, however, offer a unique opportunity to provide clients with virtual playrooms for use in teletherapy.

AR is defined as technologies which combine in a significant way the real world overlaid with a digital construct (Lamb et al., 2024). What sets AR apart from other multimedia systems or interactive digital displays is the opportunity to integrate real-world items. AR playrooms allow clients to see and interact with their current physical environment through a virtual overlay of the AR environment, which may then have additional virtual objects placed within it. To accomplish this, AR-based playrooms use head and body sensors for tracking movement, realistic computer graphics, high-definition visual displays, and other sensory input tools to create presence for clients in controlled digital environments.

DOI: 10.4324/9781003330912-11

Figure 9.1 Child playing with a puppy in a simulated AR environment. Credit: University of Georgia Neurocognition Science Laboratory.

An advantage of AR-based playrooms is the ability to quickly and easily add items to the virtual environment to make the playroom more client-centered, meet specific client needs, and support client engagement, exploration, and experimentation (Stutey et al., 2019). For example, if a client would like to have a specific toy or item, the therapist can add it via downloadable content. Figure 9.1 illustrates an example of an AR-based environment with a child playing with a puppy.

Play therapy interventions using AR-based playrooms serve as an effective method for addressing emotional, behavioral, and cognitive concerns for clients between the ages of 3 and 12 by allowing for natural expression through play without the need for traditional play therapy room materials. When compared to existing treatments, studies suggest that AR-based play is as effective as real-life play and potentially more engaging for children (Zuo et al., 2022), especially if alternative materials are not available for use in teletherapy intervention.

Setup

Prior to introducing the idea of AR playrooms with clients, familiarize yourself with AR equipment and technology. Practice using AR on your own so you are well versed in both technical procedures and the virtual experience itself. The following describes the steps necessary for setup in an initial therapy session and between sessions.

First, involve children and adolescents, along with caregivers, in the following conversations regarding the use of AR-based playrooms in teletherapy.

1. ***Explain the use of AR playrooms in therapy and how they differ from in-person playrooms.*** Describe the perceived benefits of AR playrooms in helping clients progress toward the goals of therapy. Focus on the ability to introduce items that you may not otherwise be able to provide access to while doing teletherapy and the potential for clients to test and experiment in the environment without fear of damaging items.

2. ***Assess the availability of AR equipment, physical space, and caregiver involvement.*** A minimum of 4 square feet in a seated position or 6.5 square feet for room-scale settings is required for clients to physically move around while they are immersed within the virtual environment. In your assessment, ensure that the space available will allow you to maintain visual contact with clients during the activity through the teletherapy platform and that the client's physical environment is safe (e.g., no nearby stairs or breakable objects). Explain that a caregiver must be available during therapy sessions to provide support with AR equipment as needed. If AR equipment, required space, or caregiver involvement are not available, consider other options for therapeutic intervention.

3. ***Discuss the length of treatment and time typically spent in the AR environment.*** Plan for a total of 10–20 weeks with AR playroom sessions lasting between 20 and 45 minutes per session. Plan at least one session to teach clients how to use the AR equipment and at least three to four sessions to specifically work with clients to integrate and transfer strategies into the real world.

4. ***Explain potential harm which can occur with the use of the AR environment, identify ways in which to mitigate these barriers, and discuss what clients and caregivers should do if they occur.*** AR-based playrooms generate digital data related to each client's psychological and physiological state. Discuss potential limitations to client confidentiality. In addition, explain that simulation sickness is a potential barrier to treatment. Discuss how clients can exit the AR environment any time that this occurs by simply removing the AR headset.

   To prevent simulation sickness, use a timing device to limit the client's headset usage to the recommended 10–30-minute timespan. Some clients may need tolerance training prior to intervention to mitigate simulation sickness. Begin with shorter immersive experiences until clients have demonstrated the ability to withstand longer periods of involvement. Should simulation sickness occur, you can (a) suggest they get fresh air or have a fan blow cool air on them; (b) ask the client to redirect their gaze to a distant object or the horizon; or (c) have the client lie on their back. Continue to monitor them until the symptoms resolve. If the symptoms do not resolve within 10–20 minutes, refer them to their primary care provider and reassess the use of AR for this client.

5. ***Discuss how the AR system works.*** If clients have access to their own AR equipment and are familiar with their system, this may require little explaining. If caregivers are familiar with the system and child or adolescent clients are not, support caregivers in providing a tutorial. Then, explain how the AR system will be used in subsequent sessions to support play therapy intervention.

6. ***Acclimate to the AR Environment.*** Allow children and adolescents the opportunity to try using AR equipment. This may be done in the initial session in which AR is discussed or in a subsequent session. Caregivers may also support this endeavor outside of sessions.

   Following practice, inquire about the client's experience and assess for any possible simulation sickness that may have occurred. Provide tolerance training as needed by having clients practice being in the virtual environment for shorter periods of time and then increasing time spent in the virtual environment until they can withstand longer periods of time without simulation sickness.

7. ***Assess the client's interest in participating.*** Initial screening of the client should capture baseline information related to the child's likes and dislikes, behavioral or emotional concerns, and the child's experiences interacting with digital environments. Avoid forcing clients to participate in AR-based playrooms and identify alternative interventions as needed.

Then, if clients appear interested in participating, complete the following steps between sessions.

8. ***Select a virtual environment.*** Virtual playroom environments can be obtained online through the headset store or downloaded from the development company. Align AR-based items in the playroom with the client's preferences. Consider caregiver and client assessment, as well as your own.

9. ***Provide the virtual environment to caregivers.*** Virtual environments can be made available through download via a computer file transfer from the therapist's website. Provide any additional instructions that may be necessary to help caregivers upload the environment to their AR hardware.

Instructions

In the next session, conduct the following steps.

1. ***Check with caregivers to ensure that the virtual environment has been uploaded to the AR hardware.*** If it hasn't been uploaded, ask that caregivers do this in session. Provide support as needed. Test the broadcasting feature of the AR headset to an external monitor so you can observe what the client is seeing.

2. ***Review AR controls.*** Ask for support from caregivers as needed. Explain that you will observe their actions throughout the experience and can also provide guidance.

3. ***Describe what the AR environment will be like.*** Discuss how long you intend for the experience to last, what they are going to see, hear, and potentially "feel" within the environment.

4. ***Obtain assent from the client and consent from the client's caregiver(s) to begin the experience.*** When working with younger children, caregivers may place the headset on the client's head when they are ready. Have caregivers support in adjusting the headset as needed so clients are comfortable.

5. ***Allow time for virtual play.*** Establish a permissive environment within the AR playroom and allow clients to lead the experience by asking them to interact with the virtual environment and items within it as they please. Also, allow clients the opportunity to solve any "problems" that may arise within the AR environment without intervening unless your help is requested. Provide coaching and support as needed if clients get confused about the items in the environment.

   Throughout the activity, observe client interactions with their virtual environment. Reflect on their emotions, thoughts, and experience in the virtual playroom as they interact with it. Also, look for signs of simulation sickness or distress and request support from caregivers as needed.

6. ***Prepare to exit the environment.*** Provide a 30-second to 1-minute warning to inform clients that their time in the headset is coming to an end.

7. ***Exit the environment.*** At the appointed time, ask clients to press the escape button or remove the headset.

8. ***Monitor for signs of discomfort or simulation sickness.*** Observe clients for ten minutes with the aid of caregivers to ensure that they are not experiencing any negative effects associated with the environment (Lamb et al., 2021). If simulation sickness does occur, provide guidance to caregivers on steps to take to mitigate the effects. If clients are feeling well, you can begin the processing portion of the intervention during this time.

Processing

Processing may occur both during play and upon its conclusion. Processing should focus on helping clients reflect on their emotions, thoughts, and experience in the virtual playroom. This may occur through simple reflection statements or summaries of observations regarding the client's play. Depending on your theoretical approach, you may further process by making connections between the client's experience within the virtual playroom and real-life scenarios.

Vignette

Luis (9) was a male child of Honduran descent enrolled in a local elementary school in the southeastern United States. Luis and his parents moved from Honduras approximately a year prior to meeting with the therapist, leaving behind significant violence, fallout from a natural disaster, and severe poverty. In the initial teletherapy session, Luis's parents explained that the trip from Honduras to the United States took approximately seven months. During that time, Luis was unable to attend school and had gaps in his education. While he seemed to enjoy his current class and teacher, Luis had not been completing schoolwork and showed signs of increased anxiety over the last four months. When talking with his teacher, he expressed some concern about what he would do over the summer after school ended.

Luis's mother expressed concerns about his trouble sleeping and the change in his mood. She noted that the travel to the United States was difficult for the family. There was significant uncertainty related to meeting their basic needs and concerns about the family's safety as they traveled. She noticed that Luis had trouble maintaining his friendships in and out of school. Since moving in with extended family, Luis was more likely to interact with his cousins than other children outside of the household, though he spent more time alone in his room than he had prior to their move. When he did play with his cousins, he typically enjoyed playing with his cousin's video games and virtual reality set.

This information identified Luis as a potential candidate for AR-based play therapy to help him express, resolve, and restructure his behaviors and emotions as he interacted with others in school and at home. The therapist asked the family if they might be able to use Luis's cousin's virtual reality equipment during the next session. Luis's mom confirmed between sessions that it would be available for their use.

During the second session, the therapist used a psychoeducational approach to explain to Luis and his mother how the AR system worked and what he would see in the AR playroom. In addition, the therapist explained what play therapy was and focused on reassuring Luis that he was able to make his own decisions and interact with the environment in the ways that he wanted. The therapist laid out a 15-session plan in which Luis would be placed in various digital environments of his choice and with items he wanted to interact with. The therapist offered a list of potential items that could be placed in the virtual environment through a menu of items within the environment. Luis selected a balloon-filled environment in which he could pop, throw, and interact with the balloons (see Figure 9.2). Luis also selected an environment in which he could build large-scale sand structures in three dimensions and "enter" the items as he built them (see Figure 9.3). Lastly, Luis selected an AR environment in which he could interact with an artificially intelligent puppy avatar with which he could play games, talk, and do other tasks such as access specific psychoeducational materials (see Figure 9.4).

Figure 9.2 AR-based balloon game. Credit: University of Georgia Neurocognition Science Laboratory.

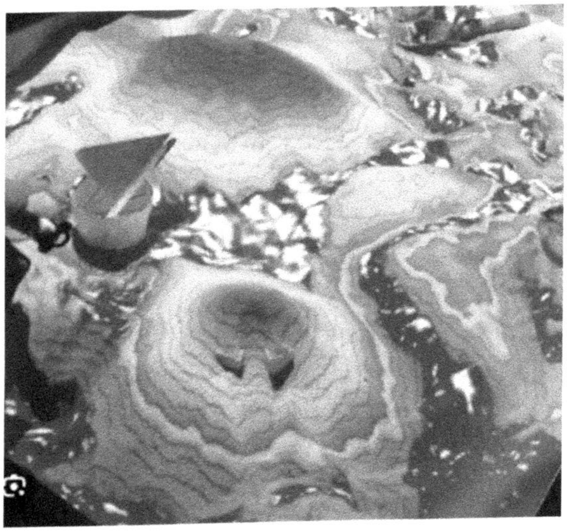

Figure 9.3 AR-based interactive sand table. Credit: University of Georgia Neurocognition Science Laboratory.

Within the AR environment, Luis could move around the playroom and interact with items. Ambient noise included music and other sounds which were controlled by Luis, giving him a sense of control over his environment. Of all the environments Luis selected, he most seemed to enjoy the sand table and his interactions with the avatar puppy.

During initial sessions, Luis easily spent 30 minutes in the environment and often did not want to exit it. During this time, the therapist saw what Luis saw on a separate computer monitor through a broadcast feature associated with the AR headset. As Luis interreacted with the environment, the therapist provided brief reflections on his actions without offering judgment. For example, when Luis played with the balloons, they said, "I see you popped the red one." As Luis grew more comfortable with the AR environment, the therapist began to provide encouragement, promoted more reflection on his feelings, and worked with Luis on strategies to help him negotiate his environment. For example, "If you're feeling nervous, what's one thing you can do to help you feel better?"

About 30 seconds to a minute before the specified end time, the therapist would warn Luis that his time in the playroom was about to end. Only once during one of the early sessions did Luis experience

Figure 9.4 AR interactive puppy. Credit: University of Georgia Neurocognition Science Laboratory.

discomfort in the form of a headache when he was in the headset. This was remedied by allowing Luis to remove the headset and sit for a few minutes. After resting, the remaining portion of the session consisted of processing the experiences with a focus on identifying specific physical, cognitive, and emotional responses to the virtual environment.

Over time, Luis gained increased comfort with verbally expressing his feelings and his worries about the future of his family and their transition to the United States, both with the therapist and with his parents. Even though the future wasn't clear, Luis and his parents were able to engage in continued conversations about the safety and future of their family, and the concerns that had initially brought Luis to therapy began to dissipate.

Suggestions for Follow-Up

After sessions involving AR therapy, maintain consistent follow-up to ensure clients are integrating their experiences effectively. Encourage clients to reflect on their AR experiences by keeping a journal and noting any emotions, thoughts, or behaviors that arise. Schedule regular check-ins to discuss progress, address any challenges, and adjust therapeutic strategies as needed. Provide clients with additional resources, such as relaxation techniques or mindfulness exercises, to help them manage any residual stress or anxiety they may have from the AR experience. Reinforce the importance of practicing coping strategies learned during AR sessions. Additionally, consider incorporating feedback from clients about their AR experiences to continually refine and enhance the therapeutic process. This feedback can help identify what aspects of AR therapy are most beneficial and which areas may need adjusting.

Contraindications

AR hardware costs can limit accessibility for clients. Additionally, physiological conditions (e.g., epilepsy, seizures) may be triggered by the AR environment. Respiratory or cardiovascular concerns could also lead to negative outcomes due to physiological stress. Psychological factors, such as emotional instability, may impact AR-based play therapy. In addition, children who are unable to successfully work the controls may not fully engage with the environment and may be further destabilized because of frustration with environmental interactions. Thoroughly assess to determine whether AR-based play therapy is appropriate for use with each client prior to implementing it and provide alternative interventions as needed.

References

Ashby, J. S., Tobin, G. K., & Jin, M. K. (2020). Adlerian play therapy and adventure therapy: Complementary interventions for comprehensive theory. *The Journal of Individual Psychology, 76*(2), 187–200. https://doi.org/10.1353/jip.2020.0000

Cochran, N. H., Nordling, W. J., & Cochran, J. L. (2023). *Child-centered play therapy: A practical guide to therapeutic relationships with children*. Routledge. https://doi.org/10.4324/9781003260431

Lamb, R., & Etopio, E. (2021). Therapeutic extended reality. In H. G. Kaduson & C. E. Schaefer (Eds.), *Play therapy with children: Modalities for change* (pp. 241–257). American Psychological Association. https://doi.org/10.1037/0000217-016

Lamb, R., Etopio, E., & Lamb, R. E. (2018). Using virtual reality in play therapy. *Play Therapy*, 13(1), 22–25. https://doi.org/10.1037/0000217-016

Lamb, R., Firestone, J., Kavner, A., Almusharraf, N., Choi, I., Owens, T., & Rodrigues, H. (2024). Machine learning prediction of mental health strategy selection in school aged children using neurocognitive data. *Computers in Human Behavior, 156*, Article 108197. https://doi.org/10.1016/j.chb.2024.108197

Lamb, R., Hand, B., & Kavner, A. (2021). Computational modeling of the effects of the science writing heuristic on student critical thinking in science using machine learning. *Journal of Science Education and Technology, 30*(2), 283–297. https://doi.org/10.1007/s10956-020-09871-3

Stutey, D. M., Klein, D. E., Wubbolding, R. E., & Dunnigan, N. (2019). Therapists' perceptions of the reality play therapy model. *International Journal of Play Therapy, 28*(2), 69–78. https://doi.org/10.1037/pla0000092

Zuo, T., Jiang, J., van der Spek, E., Birk, M., & Hu, J. (2022). Situating learning in AR fantasy, design considerations for AR game-based learning for children. *Electronics, 11*(15), Article 2331. https://doi.org/10.3390/electronics11152331

CHAPTER 10

DIGITAL TOOLS CONSENT FORMS

Rachel A. Altvater and Ariel Landrum

Digital tools consent forms inform clients about the use of digital tools in therapy assessment and intervention and should be used whenever technology is integrated into child and adolescent therapy treatment. The use of digital tools consent forms ensures that clients are fully informed about the use of technology in their sessions (Ceranoglu, 2010). It promotes transparency between therapists and clients, ensuring that the methods of assessment and intervention are aligned with the values and preferences of all parties involved (Trachsel & Holtforth, 2019). For example, digital tools consent forms may outline the use of external websites, gaming platforms, virtual reality, therapeutic apps, online assessments, and other digital tools.

Digital tools consent forms also provide the opportunity to communicate how digital tools will be used in treatment and inform clients about the benefits and risks of digital tools in therapy (Horne-Moyer et al., 2014). While digital tools can enhance therapeutic outcomes, they also pose risks to client confidentiality. For example, many websites and apps that may be accessed through teletherapy intervention are not Health Insurance Portability and Accountability Act (HIPAA) compliant and may collect protected health information (PHI) such as the client's internet protocol (IP) address. Just like a home address, an IP address can tell a lot about a person's location and, potentially, their personal habits. IP addresses are considered PHI and are therefore protected under HIPAA. Digital tools consent forms allow clients to acknowledge and accept any potential risks to privacy that may come from using digital tools in therapy and consent to their use. Therapists may also use digital tools consent forms to communicate any security measures taken on the part of the therapist while using digital tools, such as avoiding the use of chat functions via websites that are not HIPAA compliant and communicating via the telehealth platform instead.

The following template illustrates how you might structure a digital tools consent form when incorporating digital tools into therapy. Adapt it to fit your practice's specific needs and your client's unique circumstances. Consider applicable legal, ethical, and professional guidelines relevant to your license, jurisdiction, and clinical setting and obtain a legal review of your digital tools consent form prior to use.

This example does not cover other digital products used in therapy settings, such as electronic health records, telehealth platforms, or communication tools like phone and fax systems. Understanding this distinction will help you tailor your consent process more accurately to the specific technologies employed in your therapeutic practice. You may wish to combine all digital products into one consent form, especially if your practice regularly integrates digital tools in treatment. Alternatively, if you use digital tools irregularly in your practice, you may create a supplemental consent form for those specific cases.

DOI: 10.4324/9781003330912-12

Consent for Use of Digital Tools in Treatment

In therapeutic play, children often tell their caregivers they are "just playing." However, during digital play sessions, beneficial therapeutic work occurs. Play is a child's natural mode of communication, and technology is a modern communication facilitator. Using technology in therapy allows further insight and connection into a child's world, enabling clinicians to further understand and assist children in navigating their struggles. The use of technology in therapy is not for leisurely purposes. Rather, digital tools for teletherapy are carefully selected for assessment and intervention that is likely to yield therapeutic benefit.

Digital Tool Selection

Various styles and types of digital tools will be considered for use in your child's treatment. For example, digital tools used in therapy may include, but are not limited to, smart device applications such as "apps," social media, gaming, and YouTube. Each tool serves a specific therapeutic purpose and is chosen for its potential to facilitate effective therapeutic interventions and support your child's treatment goals.

To address the diverse needs of children and adolescents, our digital tool selection is tailored to match different developmental stages. For younger children, digital tools might focus on games that require simple, interactive tasks that enhance verbal communication and emotional recognition. Teenagers might engage with games with more complex digital scenarios that challenge problem-solving skills and promote mature discussions.

Your child's therapist will consider your child's clinical needs, the needs identified in your child's treatment plan, their personal interests, and what interventions can be facilitated with each digital tool. This tailored approach ensures that each child receives the most appropriate and effective therapeutic interventions.

The following are examples of specific digital tools that may be used during therapy sessions:

- ______________________________
- ______________________________
- ______________________________
- ______________________________
- ______________________________
- ______________________________

Policies and Procedures

Gaming can be a very personal experience. Depending on the style and type of gaming, it can often require your child's openness, making them more emotionally vulnerable. Additionally, specific themes and gameplay styles may be triggering, particularly if they have a trauma history. Your child must be aware of this and be open to communicating their needs and expectations with their therapist. Even if not emotionally or mentally triggering, games can be challenging to master, such as learning controls or understanding the rules.

As we incorporate digital tools into our therapy sessions, it is important to establish clear guidelines to ensure a safe and effective environment for all involved. There are certain expectations around gaming, including online prosocial engagement and behavior. Your child's therapist will review these expectations with you before engaging in the gameplay. Throughout gameplay, your child's therapist will also remind your child of them. Below, you will find detailed examples of our policies and procedures that govern the use of these tools. These guidelines are designed to protect privacy, enhance security, and promote an understanding of how these digital interactions are managed:

- There may be instances where an app is to be downloaded on a smart device. Caregiver permission will be obtained before any downloads. It is the caregiver's discretion to review the terms and conditions associated with downloads on any device.
- Comprehensive support will be provided, including training on using digital tools effectively. Technical assistance is available through [contact information], supplied in session by the clinician, or tutorial information provided before the session to ensure you and/or your child can utilize these tools confidently and securely.
- Before entering into a digital space, ensure you're in a private, safe, and secure location. You may use additional measures to ensure confidentiality in the space that you're in, such as wearing headphones and playing white or brown noise.
- Before engaging with digital tools in therapy, shut off any notifications that may pop up on your device and remove digital assistant devices (e.g., Alexa, Google) from your space.
- Before gameplay, switch your game into "hidden mode," so other players you may be friends with do not see you're in the game.
- Your child and therapist may need to "friend" each other to be in the same game or on a private server. If that is the case, after gameplay, the therapist will "unfriend" your child as part of maintaining privacy and confidentiality.
- There is a possibility your child's friends will notice they have a new friend on their list during the limited-time gameplay.
- Your child will not be allowed to invite others into a game. Only the therapist will be allowed to add individuals to the game and only do so if these individuals are part of treatment (such as group therapy, family therapy, couple's therapy, or in situations where collateral with the proper release of information has been set up).
- Neither your child nor their therapist will record any other part of sessions, and no session content is to be shared publicly without proper consent and documentation to do so.
- If a digital tool has a chat component, the therapist will not communicate via the tool's platform and they will instruct the child to only use the chat component via the teletherapy platform.
- The therapist will not disclose personal identification information using digital tools (e.g., addresses, names, dates of birth, or that we are in an online therapy session).
- If digital spaces require a login feature, your child and their therapist will use non-primary email addresses, create usernames that are not identifying, and create avatar names that are non-identifying.
- The therapist will not disclose usernames, login information, or account information to others. Only approved individuals, such as guardians, will have access to this information.

- In case of a technology failure, alternative methods for continuing the session will be immediately implemented to ensure continuity of care.
- Use of digital tools is a part of therapeutic work and not included as a reward system in session.
- The clinician will actively monitor digital engagement, assess for safety and responsible use, and reinforce appropriate limits when necessary. If the clinician is concerned about the safe use of technology, the clinician will notify you and assist you in setting appropriate screen boundaries and limits.
- You will be notified of any significant changes to this consent form.
- Should we discontinue any digital tool currently in use, you and your child will be informed in advance, and we will discuss alternative solutions tailored to therapeutic needs.
- Clients can request access to their digital records by contacting their therapist directly. All requests will be addressed within a legally compliant timeframe.
- Your feedback is invaluable. Please share your experiences or concerns regarding the digital tools used in your therapy through [feedback mechanism] or directly with your child's therapist.

Confidentiality and the Use of Digital Tools

Your child's therapist strives to protect private health information, which includes demographic, background, and session information. Though the platform used to conduct teletherapy is HIPAA consistent, sometimes technology-based interventions deemed useful and therapeutic by your therapist may not comply with HIPAA standards. In providing consent to use these technologies, you agree to allow your child to access non-HIPAA-compliant digital tools for the purpose of teletherapy assessment and intervention. Some examples of what information these platforms may have access to include:

- Your IP address
- Suggestions on content based on having received "cookies"
- Knowledge of types of games or websites used and time spent on them
- Shared records of chat conversations, images, or screenshots
- Attempts to contact your child's therapist on unsecured platforms and any response, or lack thereof, to them

Though you opt in to use these digital platforms, your child's therapist will still prioritize maintaining confidentiality. This includes using private servicers whenever possible, not sharing logging information, and continued communication through HIPAA-consistent software.

Accessibility and Accommodations

We are committed to ensuring our digital tools are accessible to children with diverse abilities. Accommodations, such as customizable user interfaces and content adjustments, will be available to meet your child's specific needs.

Feedback and Evaluation Process

To continually enhance the efficacy of our digital tools, we will periodically seek feedback from you and your child. This process will help us assess the suitability and impact of the tools used and make necessary adjustments to our practices. Your insights are invaluable in shaping a responsive and effective therapeutic environment.

I have read the above and release my child's therapist of liability for using technology that does not comply with HIPAA standards for treatment.

You may revoke your consent any time. Should you choose to withdraw consent, please notify us in writing. We will discuss the implications of ongoing therapy and explore alternative methods of supporting your child's therapeutic journey.

______________________	______________________	______________
Client Printed Name	Client Signature	Date
______________________	______________________	______________
Legal Guardian Printed Name	Legal Guardian Signature	Date
______________________	______________________	______________
Therapist Printed Name	Therapist Signature	Date

Processing with Clients

To establish a clear understanding and agreement on using digital tools in therapy, discuss digital tools consent forms and their contents with clients before asking them to sign them (Horne-Moyer et al., 2014). The following provides guidelines on leading these discussions.

- ***Clearly explain each section.*** Go through the consent form section by section with clients and their caregivers. Ensure that they understand each part's meaning and how it relates to their therapy. This helps in building an informed consensus and mitigates any misunderstandings.
- ***Demystify digital lingo.*** As you explain the consent form, define any technical terms or jargon such as 'IP address.'
- ***Discuss the importance of privacy and security.*** In advance, consider how comfortable you feel explaining the intricacies of data protection taken on your end of the process. If you don't feel confident in your ability, consult with experts to learn how your client's data will be protected, what happens during a data breach, and the measures that should be taken to ensure client privacy.
- ***Personalize the experience.*** Tailor your discussion to your client's needs and circumstances. This personalized approach makes the information more relevant and easier to understand.

- ***Encourage questions.*** Invite clients and their caregivers to ask questions. Provide answers and clarification as needed. This is crucial to ensure that they fully understand their consent.
- ***Confirm understanding and consent.*** Ask clients if they understand all parts of the consent form and agree to use digital tools as described. This confirmation should be obtained without pressure, ensuring consent is given freely and informedly. Also, explain that they can withdraw consent at any time.

Maintaining Regular Updates

Consent forms should be adaptable and viewed as dynamic entities. Regular updates to your digital tools consent form are essential to ensure that your therapeutic practices remain at the forefront of technological and ethical standards. Just as software updates can introduce new features or change existing ones, new digital tools or updates to existing tools might necessitate updates to your consent forms. This ensures that they accurately reflect the technologies you're using in practice.

This ongoing review process is also an opportunity to enhance therapeutic efficacy and client safety. By staying informed about the latest developments in digital tools and adjusting the consent form accordingly, you ensure that you are using the most effective, secure, and ethical approaches available. Regular updates are not just about compliance; they are about enhancing therapeutic effectiveness. Key areas to focus on during updates include client feedback, technological advancements, legal and regulatory changes, and professional guidelines and best practices.

- ***Client feedback:*** Client and caregiver feedback can provide valuable insights into the effectiveness of digital tools used in therapy. Incorporating this feedback into practice protocols and digital tools consent forms can significantly improve client outcomes and satisfaction with services provided.
- ***Technological advancements:*** As new tools and technologies emerge, their potential for therapeutic application should be evaluated and, if appropriate, integrated into practice. This requires updating the digital tools consent form to include these new tools, ensuring clients are informed and consent to their use. Particularly after significant software updates, it's crucial to review how these changes impact your therapy tools and revisit the consent forms to reflect any new data handling or privacy implications.
- ***Legal and regulatory changes:*** Legal standards governing the use of digital tools in therapy vary by jurisdiction and can evolve rapidly. Regular reviews of local and national regulations are necessary to ensure compliance and protect both clients and therapists.
- ***Professional guidelines and best practices:*** As professional bodies update guidelines and best practices, reflect these changes in your digital tools consent form as needed. This alignment ensures that your practice is compliant and represents the highest professional standards.

Obtain a legal review of your digital tools consent form and any updates that you make to it prior to use. Regularly consult with legal professionals, identify a means of receiving regular updates from your licensing board(s) on evolving laws and regulations, and stay engaged with other professional bodies to ensure compliance with laws and regulations relevant to your digital tools consent form. Staying informed is not just about compliance; it's also about safeguarding your practice and clients.

Diversity, Equity, Inclusion, and Belonging

As you embark on creating or updating your digital tools consent form, it's crucial to embrace the principles of diversity, equity, inclusion, and belonging. These interconnected concepts are foundational in ensuring a therapeutic environment that is responsive to and respects the varied identities and needs of all clients (Alegria et al., 2010). Diversity involves acknowledging and valuing the rich dimensions of differences within your client base, from cultural backgrounds to personal identities. Equity seeks to provide fair treatment, access, and opportunity by actively addressing and overcoming barriers that might hinder full participation. Inclusion ensures that clients feel supported and valued, contributing to a therapeutic setting where everyone can participate fully. Beyond inclusion, belonging aims to foster a deeper sense of intimate connection and community, making clients feel not just included but integral to and actively involved in the therapeutic process. With these guiding principles in mind, consider the following approaches as they relate to the use of digital tools in therapy.

- ***Diversity:*** Ensure that the digital tools that you use in therapy allow clients to "see themselves" in the materials. For example, offer games in which clients may choose or create avatars with a wide array of skin tones and hair colors/styles. Also consider languages offered, closed captioning capabilities, culturally specific imagery, and alignment with cultural norms and values.
- ***Equity:*** Not all clients may have equal access to technological tools due to socioeconomic or other factors. Likewise, some clients may not be able to use digital tools during certain days and/or times for religious reasons, though some clients may allow exceptions to using a computer for the use of accessing therapy. Consider alternative options for intervention when needed.
- ***Inclusion:*** To ensure that an inclusive therapeutic environment is fostered, consider any biases that may be perpetrated by digital tools, particularly those that involve artificial intelligence or data algorithms. Review these tools regularly to ensure that they do not perpetuate existing biases or create new ones. Be open to adjusting the tools that you use in your practice as needed.
- ***Belonging:*** Encourage clients to provide feedback on digital tools and interactions, affirming that their insights are crucial to the therapy process. Strategies such as regular follow-ups to solicit their views and adapting digital content based on input can reinforce their impact on the therapeutic journey. Additionally, guide clients in extending the skills and connections fostered through digital tools to build supportive networks outside the therapy setting, enhancing their sense of community and belonging both during and beyond therapy sessions.

References

Alegria, M., Atkins, M., Farmer, E., Slaton, E., & Stelk, W. (2010). One size does not fit all: Taking diversity, culture and context seriously. *Administration and Policy in Mental Health, 37*(1–2), 48–60. https://doi.org/10.1007/s10488-010-0283-2

Ceranoglu, T. A. (2010). Video games in psychotherapy. *Review of General Psychology, 14*(2), 141–146. https://doi.org/10.1037/a0019439

Horne-Moyer, H. L., Moyer, B. H., Messer, D. C., & Messer, E. S. (2014). The use of electronic games in therapy: A review with clinical implications. *Current Psychiatry Reports, 16*(12), Article 520. https://doi.org/10.1007/s11920-014-0520-6

Trachsel, M., & grosse Holtforth, M. (2019). How to strengthen patients' meaning response by an ethical informed consent in psychotherapy. *Frontiers in Psychology, 10,* Article 1747. https://doi.org/10.3389/fpsyg.2019.01747

Part 3

Self of the Therapist

CHAPTER 11

THERAPIST'S ATTITUDES ABOUT TECHNOLOGY AND TELETHERAPY[1]

Rebecca A. Cobb, Chrystal McDowell, and Dania Tawfiq

Therapists' attitudes about technology may influence their creative use of technological resources, assessments, and interventions. For example, when perceived difficulties in online therapy increase, therapeutic presence decreases (Rathenau et al., 2022), thereby allowing one's relationship with technology to negatively impact the therapeutic relationship. Likewise, a therapist's own enjoyment of particular digital tools, or lack thereof, may influence the tools that they make available in teletherapy services, whether or not these tools may be of benefit to clients.

The following questions are designed to encourage therapists to evaluate their attitudes about technology and its use in therapy. This assessment may be used as an initial check-in and revisited over time to reflect on self-of-the-therapist dynamics that may impact one's use of digital tools in therapy assessment and intervention.

1. What is your relationship with technology?
2. What/who has most influenced your attitudes about/relationship with technology?
3. What do you enjoy about working through this medium?
4. What do you not enjoy about working through this medium?
5. What are your first memories of using a computer, the Internet, or other forms of technology? What feelings are associated with these memories?
6. Over the course of your lifespan, what have been your favorite activities on the computer?
7. What have been your favorite video games?
8. Have you enjoyed interactive activities or more solitary activities?
9. Who have you included in your technologically based activities?
10. Rank the following technology-based activities in order of your preference:
    - Talking with friends/family via videochat
    - Messaging friends/family
    - Watching shows/movies
    - Reading ebooks or listening to audiobooks

DOI: 10.4324/9781003330912-14

- Playing multiplayer video games
- Playing solitary video games
- Engaging in social media
- Researching
- Shopping online
- Listening to music
- Other: ___________________

11. How have your likes and dislikes related to computers, the Internet, and other digital tools changed at different developmental levels?
12. What feelings, memories, or insights have you gained about your relationship with technology by reflecting on these questions?
13. How might your own experience and relationship with technology influence the ways in which you conduct teletherapy?
14. How may a negative or positive bias toward technology impact your relationship with clients?
15. Have you received any telehealth training?
16. How might your experiences with telehealth training and education influence your perceptions about the modality?
17. How might you access further education and/or training to change your relationship with technology in ways that may be of benefit to your therapeutic practice?

After evaluating your experience and attitudes about technology, consider any changes that you might make regarding the use of digital tools in your practice. If you feel uncertain or lack confidence in your use of technology, consider additional training to increase confidence in providing teletherapy services (e.g., Glass & Bickler, 2021; Hertlein et al., 2014; Pickens et al., 2020) and practice engaging in unexplored technology-based activities to discover, or rediscover, fun new ways to engage clients via telehealth!

Note

1 Adapted and expanded from Sori, C. F. (2016). Therapist's attitudes about play. In C. F. Sori, L. L. Hecker, & M. E. Bachenberg (Eds.), *The therapist's notebook for children and adolescents: Homework, handouts, and activities for use in psychotherapy* (2nd ed., pp. xxii–xxiii). Routledge.

References

Glass, V. Q., & Bickler, A. (2021). Cultivating the therapeutic alliance in a telemental health setting. *Contemporary Family Therapy, 43*(2), 189–198. https://doi.org/10.1007/s10591-021-09570-0

Hertlein, K. M., Blumer, M. L. C., & Smith, J. M. (2014). Marriage and family therapists' use and comfort with online communication with clients. *Contemporary Family Therapy, 36*(1), 58–69. https://doi.org/10.1007/s10591-013-9284-0

Pickens, J. C., Morris, N., & Johnson, D. J. (2020). The digital divide: Couple and family therapy programs' integration of teletherapy training and education. *Journal of Marital and Family Therapy, 46*(2), 186–200. https://doi.org/10.1111/jmft.12417

Rathenau, S., Sousa, D., Vaz, A., & Geller, S. (2022). The effect of attitudes toward online therapy and the difficulties perceived in online therapeutic presence. *Journal of Psychotherapy Integration, 32*(1), 19–33. https://dx. doi.org/10.1037/int0000266

CHAPTER 12

KEEPING UP ENERGY

Maxine Notice and Julianna Wisneski

Maintaining an adequate amount of energy is imperative in conducting sustainable therapy with children and adolescents. Energy is essentially the maintenance of our driving force to think consciously, remain engaged, and establish and maintain a secure therapeutic connection with young clients.

Imagine yourself in a low energy session, tired or restless in your seat, sounding monotone, and talking at your screen instead of with your client. This may be an accurate picture of how we experience ourselves on some occasions. Now imagine an alternative scenario where you're excited, curious, and creatively draw young clients into the therapeutic process. These contrasting visions create a vivid picture of our need for healthy amounts of therapeutic energy. When therapists are energetic in their work, therapy is typically more engaging for clients who may otherwise struggle with their own engagement in the process.

When practicing via teletherapy, both therapists and clients run the risk of lessened energy during sessions. Prolonged sitting in front of a computer may result in strain on the body. Increased screen time places pressure on the eyes. Even the effort required to hear properly through an online platform may require additional energy (Enns, 2021). When the energy in teletherapy sessions is low, children and adolescents may redirect their energy toward alternative sources, often easily accessible at their fingertips or elsewhere in their physical location. While technology bridges the gap between physically distant locations, it is our own internal meter of energy that drives all connecting features of the therapeutic relationship.

Working with children and adolescents via teletherapy creates a unique opportunity for therapists to calibrate their energy levels within the therapeutic space. Young clients may require a range of energy from their therapists. It is vital that therapists use their skills to assess each client's needs and to devise appropriate plans for keeping them engaged. The following offers suggestions for therapists to maintain high levels of energy to bolster engagement of children, adolescents, and their families throughout teletherapy sessions. Suggestions are organized by things that you can do related to teletherapy setup, in sessions, between sessions, and outside of sessions.

Setup

Creating the proper therapeutic space is a key feature of clinical success and the maintenance of effective energy through teletherapy sessions. To set up a work environment that is conducive of energy, consider the following.

- ***Create a comfortable environment from which to work.*** Be creative and customize your workspace to best fit your needs and preferences. For example, consider adjusting your chair,

DOI: 10.4324/9781003330912-15

desk, and computer setup to be more ergonomic and less wearing on your body. When working from a home office, establish a space that is separate from areas of the home commonly associated with rest and relaxation, such as the bedroom and living room.

- ***Let the light be your guide.*** Consider the lighting in the room in which you conduct sessions. If you find that your energy is lower when the lighting is dimmer, bring more light into the room by opening curtains or blinds, turning on overhead lights, or bringing in additional light sources (e.g., lamps). Explore the use of warm and cool lighting in your therapeutic space and their influence on your energy level.
- ***Add items to your workspace that bring joy and energy.*** Surround yourself with colors, images, and objects that are lifegiving to you. Consider the use of fragrances, decor, plants, inspirational quotes, and pictures. This is where creative expression comes into play! Surrounding yourself with items that are uplifting, motivating, and/or remind you of your "why" can be just the energy booster needed to get through those last few sessions of the day.
- ***Set up and use reliable technology sources.*** To avoid stress and the energy exertion required to manage technological difficulties (McLean et al., 2021), preparation is key. Focus on what is within your control to help prevent last-minute stressors. For example, make charging any necessary devices part of your end-of-day routine to avoid the depletion of energy caused by rushing around to find a charger between sessions. Likewise, turn on your computer and log into any necessary programs in advance of meetings to prevent unexpected computer updates from interfering with the start times of your sessions.
- ***Collaborate with caregivers.*** Address privacy with both caregivers and children. Draw attention to how a child's engagement or energy can be impacted by disruptions in privacy as you work to maintain energy throughout the session. Also, ask that caregivers provide any necessary tools for therapeutic activities (e.g., art supplies, devices, specific toys) in advance of sessions to avoid any unnecessary pauses in the momentum of therapy.
- ***Decrease screen fatigue.*** Staring at a screen all day conducting teletherapy can leave your eyes feeling strained and fatigued (Enns, 2021). Use blue light glasses or screen protectors to avoid ocular stress that can contribute to depleted energy levels during session.

In Sessions

In session is the key time at which your energy level will be felt and experienced by clients. To keep your energy up during this critical time, consider the following.

- ***Read the (virtual) room.*** Make a regular practice of assessing client energy and engagement. If clients appear tired or distracted, you may need to turn up your own energy to help them re-engage. There may be times, however, when you want to curb the expression of your energy to help clients re-center. For example, if a client is in an anxious state or experiencing a manic episode, you may want to calm yourself first to support clients in doing the same. Attend to the needs of each client by assessing prior to adjusting your own presence.
- ***Monitor your voice and other forms of nonverbal communication.*** Your voice is a powerful tool, as energy can be translated through the cadence of your voice. Be mindful of the volume, tone, and pace of your speech. Modeling higher energy levels can subtly encourage

clients to rise to match yours. The use of hand gestures and facial expression can help with this as well. For example, when conducting a teletherapy session in which a child tells you that they did something that they're proud of, consider clasping your hands in front of you so that they're visible on the screen and smiling just a bit bigger than you would if you were in an in-person session.

- ***Get up and move around.*** Movement can help both clients and therapists in keeping energy high during sessions (see Chapter 25). Start a virtual session by facilitating a game of "Simon Says" or "Freeze Dance" to help younger clients exert excess energy and help set them up for success as they embark on a period of prolonged sitting while in session. Incorporate chair yoga or stretching breaks to add movement into sessions and help manage energy levels. Though it may seem as if teletherapy renders you unable to use your body as a tool in therapeutic interventions via online platforms (Heiden-Rootes et al., 2021), chapters throughout this text challenge this assumption and provide creative ideas for how to do so.
- ***Use your imagination.*** With the exponential growth of technology, there are always new technological advancements available to use in sessions with clients. Incorporate new technology, apps, and platforms to invigorate and engage young clients (Borenstein, 2022). Consider applying creative interventions suggested throughout this book to engage in new and energetic ways.

Between Sessions

Effectively using your time between teletherapy sessions can help to avoid screen fatigue, muscle tension, and ocular strain, allowing you the ability to focus on refreshing and re-energizing yourself throughout the workday. Consider implementing the following suggestions between sessions.

- ***Avoid back-to-back sessions.*** Allow appropriate amounts of time to transition between sessions to create a healthy and sustainable teletherapy practice.
- ***Take restorative breaks.*** During breaks, step away from screens, take a minute for mindfulness, and socialize with others (Heiden-Rootes et al., 2021).
- ***Move your body.*** Do simple stretches and exercises such as yoga poses, or alternate seating positions to reduce muscle and ligament tension while encouraging correct posture (Enns, 2021).
- ***Nourish your body.*** Consider making homeostatic changes for upkeeping your energy. Avoid relying on caffeine and other temporary first-order change items. Consider making second-order changes to your practice, such as hydrating with water for sustainable results. Time between sessions is a great opportunity to replenish your energy with high-quality, energy-rich foods to give you the boost you've been looking for.
- ***Move beyond your immediate environment.*** Make a conscious effort to take a break, look outside, and peer into the distance. A change in scenery has the potential to help reset between sessions.
- ***When ready, prepare for re-engagement.*** Get back into the therapeutic mindset by taking a glance at your notes from the previous session or creating a session agenda. Developing a routine to re-engage can support in mentally preparing to hold space for and engage clients throughout sessions.

Outside of Sessions

Time outside of work has a great impact on your time and energy in session and is a great place to implement meaningful changes. As you read the following, consider what things you're doing well and what changes you might make.

- ***Maintain a manageable caseload.*** Your telehealth caseload may look different than an in-person therapy caseload, and this number may vary for each clinician. Explore what supports your energy and thus the quality of services you're able to provide.
- ***Establish a distinct end to the workday.*** When working from home, this could look like closing the door to your office outside of work hours or creating an end-of-workday ritual (Koons-Beauchamp, 2024). Be mindful of how you mark the close of your workday to support you in being fully present and recharging when you're not working.
- ***Limit screen time outside of business hours.*** Excessive time in front of screens can play a toll both physically and mentally on your energy. Avoid excess technology use before and after work to provide a much-needed break for your eyes and your mind.
- ***Connect with others who energize you.*** You might consider creating your own ecomap (Hartman, 1978) and making note of which people and/or organizations are lifegiving to you. Then, assess the ways in which you spend your time and consider ways in which you might be able to spend more time with those who provide what you most need.
- ***Get a different perspective.*** Seeking insight from other professionals is a great way to keep energy up around treatment planning and case conceptualization. Collaborate with other professionals or consider doing co-therapy (McLean et al., 2021). Also, consider joining or starting a professional consultation group.
- ***Seek clinical supervision.*** Use this to circumvent isolation and conceptualize creative interventions (Heiden-Rootes et al., 2021). Through routine or periodic supervision, access a supportive environment to discuss self-of-the-therapist issues related to the complexities of teletherapy work.
- ***Engage in personal therapy.*** If you find that burnout, depression, compassion fatigue, or other personal factors are contributing to low energy in session, consider engaging in personal therapy.

Continue to reassess your own needs and the needs of your clients. By continuously incorporating small changes that create renewable energy, you have the potential to boost energy on both sides of the computer screen, therefore prioritizing your own well-being and more effectively engaging children, adolescents, and their families in teletherapy.

References

Borenstein, L. (2022). Imagination and play in teletherapy with children. *American Journal of Play, 14*(1), 13–32.

Enns, V. (2021, April 19). Building counselors' resilience to zoom fatigue. *Psychology Today*. https://www.psychologytoday.com/us/blog/resilience-and-connection/202104/building-counselors-resilience-to-zoom-fatigue

Hartman, A. (1978). Diagrammatic assessment of family relationships. *Social Casework, 59*(8), 465–476. https://doi.org/10.1177/104438947805900803

Heiden-Rootes, K., Ferber, M., Meyer, D., Zubatsky, M., & Wittenborn, A. (2021). Relational teletherapy experiences of couple and family therapy trainees: "Reading the room," exhaustion, and the comforts of home. *Journal of Marital and Family Therapy, 47*(2), 342–358. https://doi.org/10.1111/jmft.12486

Koons-Beauchamp, D. (2024). The "commute home": End-of-day letting-go rituals for online therapists. In R. A. Cobb (Ed.) *The therapist's notebook for systemic teletherapy: Creative interventions for effective online therapy* (pp. 38–40). Routledge. https://doi.org/10.4324/9781003289920-10

McLean, S. A., Booth, A. T., Schnabel, A., Wright, B. J., Painter, F. L., & McIntosh, J. E. (2021). Exploring the efficacy of telehealth for family therapy through systematic, meta-analytic, and qualitative evidence. *Clinical Child and Family Psychology Review, 24,* 244–266. https://doi.org/10.1007/s10567-020-00340-2

CHAPTER 13

STAYING IN YOUR SEAT

A GUIDE FOR TELETHERAPISTS WITH ADHD

Jessica Bahr

Many therapists with attention-deficit hyperactivity disorder (ADHD) are skilled at pretending to be a neurotypical therapist, but this approach may lack authenticity and contribute to a feeling of disconnect with one's true self. Allowing yourself to be your full self in therapy is beneficial for both you and your clients. This is especially true when working with children and adolescents, who excel at detecting inauthenticity and may be exploring ways in which to be their own authentic selves. This becomes especially important when working with children and adolescents who have ADHD themselves, as it can be therapeutically relevant and meaningful for their therapist to model living a neurodivergent life free of shame. By leaning into ADHD, you can embrace your strengths and discover how to work *with* your perceived shortcomings rather than against them. The following offers suggestions on ways in which therapists with ADHD can provide the best therapy possible while honoring how their neurodivergent brains work.

Being a Therapist with ADHD

People with ADHD need both structure and novelty to thrive, but one often comes at the expense of the other. For example, a 9-to-5 job provides structure, but not a lot of novelty; a freelance job provides lots of room for novelty, but not a lot of structure. Being a therapist is a great job for people with ADHD because it incorporates this balance of both structure and novelty. Your days are scheduled the same way in that you have a number of hour-long sessions (i.e., structure), but each hour you meet with different people and discuss different issues (i.e., novelty). Additionally, being a therapist allows for built-in breaks, which are crucial for people with ADHD due to the increased likelihood of spending hours at a time invested in something that may lead to overstimulation and burnout.

Therapists with ADHD also inherently have strengths that facilitate the therapeutic process. They often have incredible relational skills that help in deeply attuning to clients (Honos-Webb, 2008). They also feel things very strongly, which can be beneficial when mirroring emotions back to clients, since their deep feelings may point out things that others may not realize. Their brains also work very quickly, which helps to connect points in clients' lives and stories that others might miss. These relational abilities are useful when working with children and adolescents because they support in translating client symptoms and feelings into language that helps clients understand and accept themselves.

DOI: 10.4324/9781003330912-16

Teletherapy can be especially well-suited for therapists with ADHD. Conducting virtual sessions allows for less pressure to be seen as "normal," which can be distracting. It also allows for more control over sensory input (e.g., brightness and noise levels, both in physical space and on screen), and therefore lowers the risk of overstimulation. The following offers suggestions for teletherapists with ADHD to employ while working with children and adolescents. These suggestions revolve around paying attention, staring at a screen, sitting still, completing progress notes on time, and self-care.

Paying Attention

A common misconception about people with ADHD is that they have a hard time paying attention to things. While this is partially true, it is more complicated. People with ADHD more so have difficulty with prioritizing tasks and information. This can also become an issue in the therapy room, where the therapist listens to someone talk and can get lost when needing to prioritize and process information. In addressing this concern, you have several options.

- ***Admit to clients when you get distracted and miss something that they said.*** You might say something like, "I'm so sorry. Would you mind repeating the last thing you said?" Clients are usually receptive to this and appreciate you asking for clarification, as opposed to you pretending to understand. By modeling these behaviors yourself, children and adolescents can learn to feel more empowered to ask clarifying questions themselves, which promotes agency and self-acceptance.
- ***Incorporate your tangential thought into your reflection*** (Honos-Webb, 2008). For example, if a teenager says something happened to them this week that sounds similar to a plot line on a show they like and you get distracted by this thought, you might incorporate your distraction into the conversation and say, "What do you think this character would do in your situation?" Often, tangential thoughts will resonate with clients and may be of therapeutic benefit to discuss if addressed in a way that is client centered and goal focused. When doing this, employ the same rules that you would normally apply to self-disclosure. For example, are you bringing this up because you think it may resonate with your client(s)? Or do you just want to talk about a TV show? Self-disclosure can be useful when intentional and employed for the benefit of clients.
- ***Save the thought for later in session.*** Tangential thoughts can be important and worth returning to. However, they are usually less time sensitive than attending to what your client is currently discussing. If your tangential thought is related to your client and would be of benefit to discuss later that session, you might write a quick note for yourself using a few key words to remind you to return to the thought at a more appropriate time.
- ***Save the thought for after session.*** Thoughts that aren't client-related or that don't need to be addressed in session can be saved for later by writing them down and then returning to them at a more appropriate time. To avoid getting further distracted by writing down your thought in its entirety and focusing on the details, simply write key words. For example, if a client mentions they have family in Georgia, and you think "What's the capital of Georgia? Is it Atlanta? What about Georgia the country?" you can make a simple note to yourself such as "caps of GA?" and then turn your attention back to your client.

Staring at a Screen

Other helpful tips for staying engaged while doing teletherapy and staring at a screen for an extended period of time include the following.

- ***Set up your workspace for success.*** Cater your surroundings to be comfortable, free of distraction, and professional enough to remind your brain that you are doing something important.
- ***Minimize the number of windows and tabs open on your computer.*** This minimizes tangential thoughts pertaining to other open tabs. Alternatively, if you need to have multiple tabs open on your computer, have two separate windows open – one with the multiple tabs and one with only your telehealth video software. Then, minimize the window with multiple tabs so it's out of sight unless you need to actively use it for teletherapy assessment or intervention.
- ***Cover or uncover the clock on your computer.*** Make this decision based on which option is least distracting for you. Some ADHD therapists will fixate on the minutes passing by. Others will constantly wonder what time it is.
- ***Make your face preview hidden or visible.*** Some therapists get distracted by looking at their preview too much. Others get distracted from wondering what they look like, so being able to see the preview is calming and therefore less distracting. Make this decision based on which option is least distracting for you.
- ***Limit other distractions.*** Keep your phone out of sight and on silent if possible. If your phone allows it, consider turning on the "Do Not Disturb" mode to allow certain notifications to come through if needed. This can be useful if you have children or dependents and are their point of contact for emergency situations. It can be distracting to wonder if anything important is happening while your notifications are off, so ensuring you'll know if something important happens can be helpful.

Sitting Still

People with ADHD often have trouble sitting still or abstaining from fidgeting because movement helps them process information. Likewise, children move around more when their working memories are being challenged and their brains are more alert (Farrar, 2011). Since fidgeting is a crucial component in working memory and working memory is an important part of being a therapist, allow yourself to fidget in ways that aren't overly distracting to your clients. Some ways to fidget without distracting children and adolescents too much from a session include the following.

- ***Sit different ways in your chair.*** Swiveling, crossing your legs, or sitting in various forms of criss-cross or having your legs under you can be more comfortable and reduce leg bouncing. Leg bouncing is acceptable, but can be distracting, and perhaps indicative of anxiety or restlessness. You may also consider a standing desk, yoga ball, treadmill, stationary bike, or something to put your feet on.
- ***Play with quiet fidget toys.*** Fidget spinners, fidget rings, Rubik's cubes, hair clips, and string are all great options. Some fidget toys are noisy and distract from the session. Before playing

with fidget toys in session, play with them outside of session and assess the amount of noise that they make. Avoid using any fidget toys that clients might be able to hear. Many children and adolescents also benefit from playing with fidget toys during sessions. Consider showing clients the fidget toys that you use and discuss with caregivers the possibility of acquiring similar toys for use in teletherapy and other settings in which clients may benefit from using them.

- ***Doodle or color.*** Consider whether you are able to simultaneously maintain the illusion of eye contact with clients. If doodling or coloring keeps your eyes away from the camera, employ other options. Doodling and coloring, however, are usually great options during phone calls.
- ***Incorporate movement into your sessions.*** The beauty of working with children and adolescents via teletherapy is that they often need to move around during sessions as well, and movement can be incorporated into therapy very naturally. When you encourage clients to move around, take the opportunity to move around too! See Chapter 25 for ways in which to incorporate movement into sessions.

Additionally, wear comfortable clothing to avoid unnecessary fidgeting and distraction caused by discomfort. Avoid clothes with itchy tags or fabrics and clothes with loud buckles or zippers. Clothes specifically for work purposes can help put you in the right mindset to do therapy, helping with focus. Some therapists also find that wearing shoes indoors can help them get into a productive mindset.

Completing Progress Notes on Time

Meeting deadlines and completing tasks that require sustained effort can be challenging for people with ADHD (Wender & Tomb, 2017). Progress notes need to be done by a certain time and require sustained effort. The following are some structures that can be helpful in completing notes on time.

- ***Use multi-colored pens for subjective objective assessment plan (SOAP) notes.*** When taking notes in session, use one color for S and O, another for A, and another for P. This saves mental energy later when trying to determine which notes go into the progress note. Thinking critically about the "color" of client statements can help you to stay engaged in session and pay attention. Having colorful pens at arm's reach also allows you to write and draw things for assessment and intervention with child and adolescent clients in a fun and engaging way!
- ***Have ambient background noise.*** Consider whether music with lyrics is distracting for you. If it is, either play music without lyrics or try listening to music in a language that you don't know so you don't get distracted by the words.
- ***Challenge yourself to complete notes quickly.*** This can help to avoid hyper-fixating on them. For example, set a timer for five minutes for each note. The alarm going off gives you a sign to wrap up.
- ***Incorporate notes into your work routine in a way that works for your unique needs.*** People with ADHD benefit from structure and having a structured time to do notes makes them feel more concrete and harder to put off. You could complete notes during your breaks between clients or set aside time after you've finished seeing clients for the day. Taking screen breaks and moving your body between sessions may be important, however, so consider what works best for you. If you work in a group practice or agency setting, you might also consider setting aside

a time to work on progress notes at the same time as others with whom you work to help you stay engaged and motivated.

Self-Care

Care for yourself is of the utmost importance. Set up structures that make self-care fun and doable. The following provides things to consider.

- ***Take frequent breaks.*** Disengage from the screen during these breaks. It can be tempting to begin another task, but this may not be a good idea during ten-minute breaks since transitioning back to teletherapy can be difficult.
- ***Move around in between sessions.*** Some therapists find that the more they find ways to move around between sessions, the less impulse they have to move around in sessions.
- ***Take your medication if that works for you.*** Consider getting a pill tray, since it's easy to forget if you already took your meds, and easy to forget about meds altogether.
- ***Drink enough water.*** This can be especially important if you're taking stimulant medication.
- ***Get enough sleep.*** Sleep is important to overall functioning, and ADHD symptoms can increase when you are tired (Nadeau et al., 2011).
- ***Maintain other passions.*** It's easy to get hyper-focused on work and burn yourself out. Try to have other things in your life that you're excited about to balance out work.
- ***Work out regularly.*** This can help to physically release the emotions you held earlier that day. Alternatively, you might do a vigorous workout in the morning before seeing clients. There is some evidence that this might increase attention span (Wender & Tomb, 2017).
- ***Be honest with yourself.*** It's okay to have things you don't automatically excel at, and accepting these things about yourself is the first step to improving them. Maintain kindness and compassion toward yourself throughout this process.
- ***Allow yourself to gracefully switch to new routines.*** As routines lose their novelty, they might become boring and uninteresting. It is more important to stay organized and on top of things than it is to stick to any one particular method. For example, if using an online calendar starts to become difficult, see if using a physical planner feels better. Either way, you're still keeping track of your appointments, and you can always switch back to old methods later if new methods get boring.

Contraindications

The goal of the aforementioned strategies is not intended to "overcome" any barriers or to mask better. Rather, the goal is to better connect with child and adolescent clients by showing up authentically and ready to focus on their needs. The suggestions offered here may not work for everyone. Try the ones that you think might be most fitting for you, assess their impact on your clinical work and personal wellbeing, and make adjustments as needed.

References

Farrar, A. (2011). *ADHD*. Twenty-First Century Books.

Honos-Webb, L. (2008). *The gift of adult add: How to transform your challenges & build on your strengths*. New Harbinger Publications.

Nadeau, K. G., Littman, E. B., & Quinn, P. O. (2011). *Understanding girls with attention deficit hyperactivity disorder*. Advantage Books.

Wender, P. H., & Tomb, D. A. (2017). *ADHD: A guide to understanding symptoms, causes, diagnosis, treatment, and changes over time in children, adolescents, and adults*. Oxford University Press.

Part 4

Assessment and Goals

CHAPTER 14

VIRTUAL CRYSTAL BALL

Lauren Baxley and Danerys Crown

Materials for Therapists: PowerPoint or another computer program that can be used to compile images, digital image of a crystal ball, and clip art or other digital images. An initial set of images, including an image of a crystal ball, is included as supplemental materials to this book.

Materials for Clients: None. A printed copy of a crystal ball or inflated balloon, crayons, colored pencils, and/or markers are optional.

Objective

The crystal ball technique first discussed by Erickson (1954) and later modified by de Shazer (1985) has been an effective method to support client focus on a future without the "problem." This intervention is likened to the *miracle question* used by solution-focused therapists (Macdonald, 2011) with many published variations. This chapter expands on Bertolino's (2016) variation of the activity to explain how to conduct the crystal ball intervention via teletherapy.

Rationale for Use

The crystal ball technique is helpful in working with children, adolescents, and their families to allow family members to equally contribute to the collective vision of their preferred future. Solution-focused brief therapy supports clients in achieving their self-identified goals by drawing on the client's own resources and using a strengths-based approach (Macdonald, 2011). The crystal ball technique can assist with goal development, similar to the miracle question; however, this version may increase engagement and is more inclusive by allowing non-verbal contributions. This intervention may be used during the assessment phase of treatment to ensure that both clients and therapists have a mutual understanding of what a "problem-free" future will look like. It may be helpful to include family members in this activity at the onset of treatment to instill hope and promote a strengths-based perspective that may help shift family members from blame and problem talk.

Setup

Prepare a file in PowerPoint or another computer program that can be used to compile images. Include in this file an image of a crystal ball (see Figure 14.1). Also, prepare a digital file filled with clip art and/

DOI: 10.4324/9781003330912-18

Figure 14.1 Crystal ball. Credit: Dr. Christine Walsh Borst.

or images that symbolize a variety of emotions (e.g., peace, frustration, happiness, satisfaction, sadness) and relevant contextual factors (e.g., culture, hobbies, school, faith, friendships).

Instructions

When working with families, you may have clients each complete their own crystal ball activity, or request that the family work together to create a shared vision of a preferred future.

1. ***Share your screen.*** Show the image of the blank crystal ball.
2. ***Provide the prompt.*** Say, "I want you to imagine going into the future, in a space that is familiar. This is a time when 'the problem' is no longer there. As you peer deep within the crystal ball in front of you, notice what you see. What does this crystal ball show you that will be different in this future?"

   When introducing this technique to families with younger children, you can also discuss using a magic wand or spell to connect with this age group (Gehart & Tuttle, 2003). Allow two to three minutes before asking clients to share what they have envisioned in the crystal ball.
3. ***Show images.*** If clients have a hard time envisioning their preferred future, you can show clients the images that you compiled and ask that they choose any images that they think might be fitting to place inside of the crystal ball.
4. ***Share visions.*** If clients are successfully able to envision this preferred future without assistance, ask them to share what they saw in their crystal ball. You can also ask them if they would like to

find images that might represent those things to place inside of the crystal ball. You may send a copy of the crystal ball to clients and ask that they share their screen as they search for images to place in the crystal ball. Alternatively, you can search for images using key words provided by clients and ask that they select from images that you show on a shared screen.

5. ***Save the file.*** Once clients have completed their crystal ball, ask if it's okay if you save a copy of the file so you can refer to it again in the future. If you created the crystal ball on your computer, you might also send a copy of the completed crystal ball to clients so they can keep a copy for themselves.

Some clients may prefer activities that are more physical in nature rather than digitally based activities. The following offers two variations of this activity that may be more engaging for some clients using physical drawing and inflated balloons.

Physical drawing: Ask clients if they have drawing materials available at their physical location (e.g., plain paper, crayons, colored pencils, markers). If so, ask that they bring these materials with them to the session in which you plan to conduct the activity. Also, ask if they have a printer available. If so, send a copy of the crystal ball image and ask that they print it out. If they don't have one, ask that they bring a piece of plain paper. Alternatively, you may mail required materials to clients with their permission in advance (see Chapter 8). Then, rather than having clients search for images, simply allow them to draw what they envision and show you by holding their paper up to the camera once they have completed the activity.

Inflated balloon: Ask clients if they have a latex balloon and markers available at their physical location. If so, ask that they bring these materials with them to the session in which you plan to conduct the activity. If they don't have these materials, consider doing another variation of the activity or mailing materials to clients with their permission in advance (see Chapter 8). Washable and dry-erase markers will likely smear on the balloon, though permanent markers may not be appropriate for younger children. Consider the developmental age of the clients with whom you are working, ask caregivers about their own preferences, and request adult supervision if a young child is using markers independently. Young children may also need help blowing up their balloon, so discuss the need for adults to help with this task prior to the session if necessary. Then, have clients draw what they envision on the balloon and show you by holding the balloon up to the camera once they have completed the activity.

Select the variation that you think will be most fitting for your clients and their unique needs (e.g., available materials, preferences for being on the computer vs. drawing by hand).

Processing

Upon completion of the activity, facilitate a discussion that allows clients to identify the metaphorical meaning each image has within this preferred future. If using this activity within a family session, process how each family member interprets the meaning of various images and work to build a cohesive vision of their preferred future. Example questions may include:

- What does [image] represent in your vision of the future?
- How do the [image] and [image] work together in this future?
- How do the images within this crystal ball connect with one another?
- What other people and places might be connected to your preferred future?
- What are your thoughts about how [name of person]'s [image] fits with your own vision of the future?

- What is it like for you to hear [name of person] describe their vision of this future?
- What parts of this future are already happening?
- What do you think it would take for just a little bit of this vision to actually happen?

Vignette

Nevis (45), Kingston (44), Benita (16), and Anton (14) presented in teletherapy reporting an increase in family arguments and feelings of disconnection in the last year. The crystal ball technique was introduced in the third session to assist the family in goal setting and to shift the family from problem talk to solution talk.

During the session, the therapist showed the family an image of an empty crystal ball and slowly and softly stated, "I want you to imagine going into the future, in a space that is familiar. This is a time when the problem is no longer there. As you peer deep within the crystal ball in front of you, notice what you see. What does this crystal ball show you that will be different in this future?" The therapist allowed the family a few minutes to engage in this visual imagery. The family was then asked to tell the therapist what they envisioned.

Given the ages of each member of the family, the therapist asked if they would like to search for images that might represent what they saw and place them inside the crystal ball. The family agreed, so the therapist sent the family a copy of the crystal ball while they searched for images. Anton took the lead in searching for images, asking the family what to search for next, and compiling them within the crystal ball (see Figure 14.2).

Benita volunteered to share first. She stated, "It's really important for me to be able to ask for space and to have others respect my boundaries. When dad is home, I want to spend time with him, but that doesn't mean that the rest of my life should stop. I chose the yin and yang symbol to represent the balance that I'd like to see in our family in terms of those boundaries and time spent together versus time spent apart."

Anton selected an image of a smiling father with and baby. He shared, "I feel that a lot of the communication that we have with our parents is about what we're doing wrong. I want us to also talk about what's going well. I think that will make us all happier like we used to be when Benita and I were little."

At first, Nevis and Kingston struggled to choose an image and discussed feeling conflicted because how they wanted to parent and communicate was starkly different from the communication style within their Afro Caribbean culture of origin. Nevis was Active Duty in the U.S. Army, and the family unit was adapting to their latest move. Eventually, Nevis selected an image of a ship. She shared, "I want to feel like we're going somewhere in our communication. I want us to feel connected like we do when we go on family vacations; to be a team."

Kingston selected an image of a temple on top of calm waters. He stated, "I just want the verbal exchanges to come from places of peace and not feeling like you have to walk on eggshells. I want our interactions to feel pleasant, respectful, and loving."

While everyone was sharing, others observed and listened. The therapist facilitated a discussion surrounding the connectedness of their images. At the completion of sharing, the therapist reflected, "It seems like all of you have similar themes of wanting communication as a family to be peaceful and enjoyable, but also with gentle boundaries. I wonder if there are times when you experience bits of this vision? What would it take for your family to achieve just a little bit more of what we're seeing here in the crystal ball?"

They then asked if the family might be okay with making a few edits to their crystal ball to further align their visions (see Figure 14.3). The family worked together to add images depicting Nevis as a

Figure 14.2 Completed crystal ball. Credit: Dr. Christine Walsh Borst.

strong woman at the helm of the ship alongside Anton's image of a father holding a baby to remind them to focus on what is going well. The ship appeared to be sailing in the water to the peaceful place that Kingston had described. Benita appeared as a mermaid who had the freedom and space to jump in the water while remaining close to the ship. With further processing and continued therapy, the therapist supported the family in navigating a path toward reaching their shared vision for the future.

Suggestions for Follow-Up

You may encourage clients to put a copy of their crystal ball in a place that they can see it regularly to support them in further envisioning their preferred future. Reference this activity in subsequent sessions to assess client progress toward their vision. Client visions for preferred futures may change over time. Allow clients to make edits to their crystal balls over time as they see fit.

Contraindications

The notion of peering into a crystal ball to see the future may not be a suitable metaphor for clients from all cultures and religious beliefs. Adjust language and images used for the intervention to meet the

Figure 14.3 Edited crystal ball. Credit: Dr. Christine Walsh Borst.

needs of each client. For example, rather than using a crystal ball, you may have clients create a vision board instead (Scott-Poe & Patel, 2024).

Envisioning the future may be difficult for clients in the early stages of grief, as they may envision a restoration of the loss (Macdonald, 2011). Work to directly address grief and utilize this intervention once clients have accepted their loss.

References

A.J. (2011). *Solution-focused therapy: Theory, research & practice* (2nd ed.). SAGE. https://doi.org/10.4135/9781446288764

Bertolino, B. (2016). *The therapist's notebook for families*. Routledge.

de Shazer, S. (1985). *Keys to solution in brief therapy*. W.W. Norton & Company.

Erickson, M. E. (1954). Pseudo-orientation in time as a hypnotherapeutic procedure. *Journal of Clinical and Experimental Hypnosis, 2*(4), 261–283. https://doi.org/10.1080/00207145408410117

Gehart, D. R., & Tuttle, A. R. (2003). *Theory-based treatment planning for marriage and family therapists: Integrating theory and practice*. Brooks/Cole-Thomson Learning.

Scott-Poe, D. S., & Patel, K. S. (2024). Changing narratives with virtual vision boards. In R. A. Cobb (Ed.) *The therapist's notebook for systemic teletherapy: Creative interventions for effective online therapy* (pp. 107–114). Routledge. https://doi.org/10.4324/9781003289920-23

CHAPTER 15

FAMILY PHOTOGRAPH GENOGRAMS

Rebecca A. Cobb and Emerald Niakan

Materials for Therapists: PowerPoint or another computer program that can be used to create a genogram and compile images.

Materials for Clients: Digital photographs of themselves and family members.

Objective

Photographs have been used in conjunction with genograms in in-person therapy to experientially investigate family-of-origin patterns and to enhance the therapeutic process (Cook & Poulsen, 2011). This chapter explains how to conduct family photo genograms to creatively assess family-of-origin dynamics with children, adolescents, and their families via teletherapy.

Rationale for Use

Genograms are used in individual and family therapy to assess family history and intergenerational patterns (McGoldrick et al., 2016). Digital play genograms are an adaptation of traditional in-person play genograms that support therapists in creatively engaging children, adolescents, and adults in discussion of these dynamics using clip art or other digital images (Cobb, 2024). An adaptation of this teletherapy approach is to use photographs of each member of the client's family to digitally represent them on their genogram. Clients may select preexisting photographs that best represent each member of the family, or they may take photos specifically for the purpose of this activity.

Setup

The family photograph genogram requires discussion with clients prior to the session in which you plan to conduct the activity. The following provides step-by-step instructions to prepare for it.

1. ***Discuss comfort with having photographs taken.*** Ask everyone present how they feel about having their photos taken. Also, assess members of the family who may not be present. This may generate a fruitful discussion about family roles and dynamics. Consider asking the following questions:
   - Who in your family likes taking photos?
   - Who in your family likes having their photo taken?

DOI: 10.4324/9781003330912-19

- Is there anyone in your family who dislikes taking photos?
- Is there anyone in your family who dislikes having their photo taken?
- Is there a "family photographer" in your family? If so, who?

2. ***Introduce the activity.*** Discuss with clients the possibility of conducting a family photograph genogram as a way of getting to know them better. Explain that it's kind of like a map of their family using pictures.
3. ***Discuss who will be included in the genogram.*** This will determine which family members clients need to bring photos of to the next session. You may ask that they include two or three generations. Consider the size of the family and how many photographs you can realistically include on the genogram at once while allowing it to be visible in its entirety on the computer screen. Some clients may want to include pets in their genogram. Pets can be important members of the family and their inclusion in the family photograph genogram can provide great insight into the family.
4. ***Present two options.*** Explain that they can either use preexisting photographs or take new photographs to complete the activity.
   - ***Use preexisting photographs:*** If they have photographs available of themselves and other members of their family, offer the option of using these for the activity. Explain that if they choose this option, they can have each person select one photo for each member of the family to include on the genogram. Rather than selecting the best-looking picture of each person, the photo that they select should represent that person in some way. You might provide an example such as, "If I were to include my dog, Laney, on a genogram, I would probably choose a photo of her with a ball in her mouth. She's very playful." Some clients may have printed photographs that they would like to use for the activity. Explain that they will need to scan any printed photographs that they would like to use or take pictures of them so they can later send them to you in digital format.
   - ***Take new photographs:*** Explain that if they choose this option, they can take new photos for the purpose of this activity. Each person is to take one photo of each member of the family that will be included on the genogram. Rather than taking the best-looking picture of each person, they should ask them to pose in a way that somehow represents them. You might provide an example such as, "If I were to take a photo of my dog, Laney, for this activity, I would probably give her a ball to hold in her mouth to show how playful she is." If there are members of the family that they would like to include in the genogram that live far away, they may ask them to have someone else take the photo and send it to them, or they may take a screenshot during a videocall. When taking photos of themselves, they can either take a selfie or ask someone else to take the photo for them while they pose.
5. ***Identify a strategy.*** After determining which option they would like to do, discuss a strategy for collecting the photographs. When conducting the activity with families, some may prefer to browse photographs together. Others may prefer to work alone. Younger children, whether working with them individually or in a family setting, may need the assistance of older members of the family to obtain photographs to browse through or to take photographs of other members of the family. Remind clients that they should each also include a photo of themselves.
6. ***Request photos.*** Tell clients that prior to the next session, you would like them to send you the photos that they selected. When working with a family, determine who will be in charge of collecting the photos and sending them. When working with younger children in an individual setting, you may need to collaborate with the child's legal guardian to send the photographs.

Provide whoever is in change with a way of sending or uploading their selected photographs in a way that is Health Insurance Portability and Accountability Act compliant. You might discuss any requirements regarding file size that are specific to the method with which you are having them send or upload their photographs. For example, you might explain that when emailing photos, they should send them as smaller file sizes or as a ZIP file to ensure that it comes through. Share a day and time that you need them to send the files by.

7. ***Compile photos.*** Copy and paste the photos that you receive to one file using the computer program that you plan to use to construct the genogram. For example, when using PowerPoint, you might paste the photographs around the outside edges of a PowerPoint slide. Size the images so that they can all eventually fit on the slide after the genogram has been created.
8. ***Prepare the genogram.*** If you already know the composition of the family, you can prepare the genogram prior to session. If you are uncertain, simply prepare place basic shapes necessary for genogram construction (e.g., circle, square, triangle, vertical and horizontal lines) in the file so you can easily copy, paste, and arrange them in session.

Instructions

The following provides instructions for constructing the family photograph genogram in session. Do not ask processing questions during the construction of the genogram. Rather, reflect what you hear clients say if they choose to share information about what they selected and why.

1. ***Share your screen.*** Only allow the program that you are using to create the genogram to be visible so clients can't see other windows or applications that may be open on your computer.
2. ***Create the genogram with the assistance of the family.*** You can use any computer program that allows you to make basic shapes necessary for genogram construction and to compile additional images (i.e., photographs).
3. ***Ask if the genogram needs any changes made to it.*** Make any changes necessary.
4. ***Add photographs.*** Have each member of the client system guide you in placing each image that they selected adjacent to the symbol on the genogram that represents them. You might consider starting with the youngest member present or the person who typically speaks the least. Repeat this same process until all members in the family have selected images.
5. ***Ask again to see if the genogram needs any changes made to it.*** Make any changes necessary.

Processing

After the completion of the genogram, ask processing questions about the images selected. For this activity, clients don't need to explain why they chose each photograph. Rather, keep the activity playful and engaging by asking questions about the photos themselves and the relationships between them.

This activity can be processed with many different guiding theories (e.g., Bowen's family systems theory; Platt & Skowron, 2013; solution-focused; Kuehl, 1995; Weiss et al., 2010; narrative therapy; Chrzastowski, 2011; Kuehl, 1996). Keeping a guiding theory in mind will help focus the types of questions that are asked. Regardless of your theoretical orientation, processing questions may be asked to facilitate discussion of both intrapersonal and interpersonal relationships (i.e., discussion of relationships between photographs selected for the same family member and discussion of relationships between photographs selected for different family members). Processing questions for working from a Bowenian framework are provided as an example.

Intrapersonal Processing

- What is [name of person/animal] doing here?
- How does this photograph represent [name of person/animal]?
- How [does/would] the [name of person/animal] in this photograph get along with the [name of person/animal] in this photograph?
- What might the [name of person/animal] in this photograph think of the [name of person/animal] in this photograph?
- Does the [name of person/animal] in this photograph ever disagree with the [name of person/animal] in this photograph? If so, what happens?
- What similarities are there between all the photographs that have been selected for [name of person/animal]?
- What differences are there between the photographs that have been selected for [name of person/animal]?

Interpersonal Processing

- How [does/would] the [name of person/animal] in this photograph get along with the [name of person/animal] in this photograph?
- What might the [name of person/animal] in this photograph think of the [name of person/animal] in this photograph?
- When do [name of person/animal] feel [closest to/most distant from] one another?
- What happens when the [name of person/animal] in this photograph disagrees with the [name of person/animal] in this photograph?
- What do the others [do/feel] when the [name of person/animal] in this photograph feels [angry/happy/lonely/sad]?

Vignette

Misha (31/female), Ali (43/male), and Eve (8/female) presented in teletherapy after a recent argument where Misha expressed that she was seriously considering a divorce from Ali. Around this same time, Eve began frequently experiencing stomach aches and constipation. Misha initiated therapy, reporting that she had hit her "line in the sand" after years of feeling alone in an "asymmetrical" relationship. Misha shared that she had tried to leave Ali when Eve was nine months old but stayed in an attempt to work through their issues. Once again, she was seriously considering a divorce from Ali and felt overwhelmed with how to address her marital concerns and Eve's wellness simultaneously.

Through initial conversations, the therapist learned that Misha was a white, stay-at-home mom who was raised in a rural conservative Christian town of Texarkana, Texas. Ali was an Iranian used car salesman who immigrated to the United States at 18 when he was the chosen family member to come to the United States in hopes of the "American Dream." They shared about the importance of their extended family and the ways in which they had intentionally maintained connections to Ali's family and culture while they raised Eve in the United States.

At the end of the session, the therapist introduced the family photograph genogram as a way of getting to know the family better and facilitating discussion among family members. Misha and Eve both perked up at the idea of looking through old photographs, which was one of their special pastimes. Misha also shared that she had previously created a genogram in her personal therapy and sent it to the therapist to facilitate the process.

Between sessions, the therapist recommended couples therapy to Misha and Ali and sent several recommendations for therapists. They shared that while family therapy seemed appropriate to address concerns regarding Eve's wellness, couples therapy would be a more appropriate place to address their conflict to protect Eve from conversations that she didn't need to be a part of. Misha and Ali shared that they understood the need to keep certain things between them and agreed to investigate the options that had been provided to them.

In the following session, the therapist opened the genogram and photographs that Misha had sent. Though the therapist had requested that each person select one photo for each member of the family that represents that person in some way, members of the family explained that they only sent one photo of each person that they chose to represent. For some members of the family, they only had one photograph available. For others, they ended up collaboratively selecting photographs that represented their most fond memories and cherished times with one another. Surprisingly, they all agreed on these and appeared to be getting along much better than they had the week prior.

The therapist asked the family to guide them in placing the photographs that they sent to the correct places on the genogram. As each photo was selected, the therapist placed it on the shape representing the person (or animal) that the image was selected for (see Figure 15.1). Without prompting, the placement of each photograph often elicited a description of why that photograph was selected or a story behind the photo.

While processing the photographs selected, the therapist learned that Eve's best friend was the family's dog, Toosh, and that he was a great source of comfort for her when her parents fought. Misha shared that she experienced a painful childhood. Her parents were divorced, her father was an alcoholic, and she witnessed emotional and physical violence in her home until she moved out at the age of 18. Though her family lived nearby and Ali's family was physically very distant, she felt closer to Ali's family than her own. Ali was still the only family member from his very large family to live in the United States, and while he missed them, Misha took on the greatest responsibility in keeping the family connected with his side of the family and their Iranian culture.

Through this process, Eve's stomach aches, constipation, and anxiety emerged not just as individual symptoms but as a "wake-up call" for the family's shared experience. Rather than seeking only medical relief for Eve, Ali and Misha began to explore their roles in shaping the tension that she had internalized.

As they examined the genogram and discussed the stories contained within each photograph, Ali and Misha recognized a powerful and painful pattern. Both had experienced "isolation" within and from their families of origin. It became strikingly clear that Eve, too, had absorbed this familial undercurrent of isolation, seeking comfort and connection primarily through Toosh, their beloved dog. The genogram revealed a generational thread of cutoff and disconnection, woven through both sides of the family, manifesting in their current relational struggles. Beneath this pattern of isolation, however, was something deeper—a longing to be seen, to belong, and to be loved.

This recognition also brought new insight into Eve's physical symptoms. The family began to see her constipation as more than a medical issue, but as an energetic and emotional "stuckness"—a

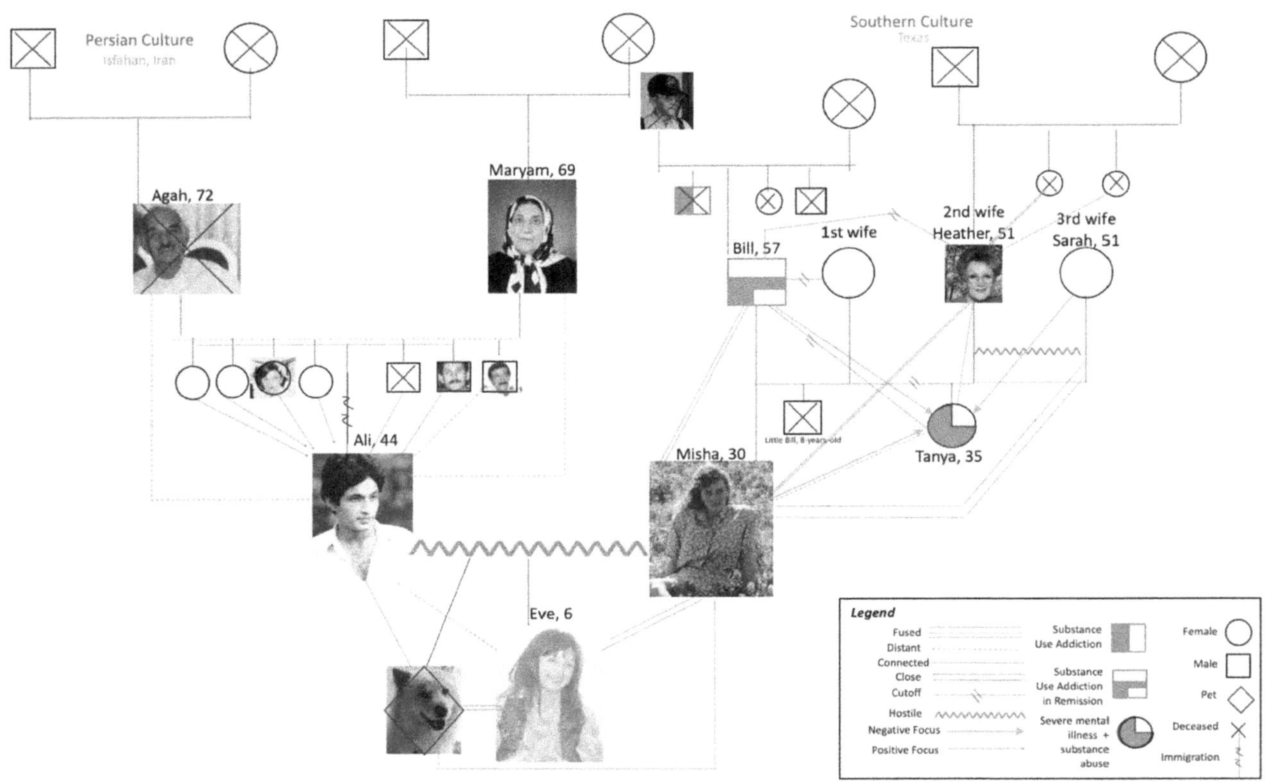

Figure 15.1 Family photograph genogram. Credit: Emerald Niakan.

somatic reflection of the unresolved tension in their home. They came to understand that, just as Eve struggled with elimination, their family was struggling with holding on to pain and discord rather than finding a way to release and transform it. This shift in perspective reframed Eve's symptoms as not just hers alone, but as a family symptom—one that could begin to shift at the very heart of Ali and Misha's relationship.

With this new awareness, the family began to reimagine their narrative. They saw the possibility of moving from a story of isolation to one of connection, mutual support, and love. In this emerging narrative, their relationships could become spaces of belonging rather than distance, allowing them to cultivate a more secure and nurturing foundation—not just for Eve, but for their family as a whole.

Suggestions for Follow-Up

One of the benefits of doing genograms via teletherapy is the ability to save it for future use. Keep a copy of the genogram in the client's file to use in future discussion. Note which clients select which photos for each family member to facilitate further processing (Gil, 2015). To assess client progress and change over time, ask clients if they would like to change any of the photographs that they selected to better represent them and their current relationships. When doing this, save a copy of the original genogram and then cut and paste new photographs. Rather than simply processing the new genogram, compare similarities and differences between the old and new genogram to track progress toward identified goals and changes over time.

Contraindications

Consider culture, spirituality, and personal preferences as they relate to access to family photographs and comfort with having photos taken. Photographs may be associated with wealth and privilege, especially for older clients who had less accessibility to cameras when they were younger. Some clients may have lost photographs in natural disasters, during migration, or by other means. Others may simply be uncomfortable having their photo taken or using personal photographs for the purpose of this activity. Respect each client's personal values and preferences and provide alternative options or variations to the activity as needed.

References

Chrzastowski, S. K. (2011). A narrative perspective on genograms: Revisiting classical family therapy models. *Clinical Child Psychology and Psychiatry, 16*(4), 635–644. https://doi.org/10.1177/1359104511400966

Cobb, R. A. (2024). Digital play genograms. In R. A. Cobb (Ed.), *The therapist's notebook for systemic teletherapy: Creative interventions for effective online therapy* (pp. 189–194). Routledge. https://doi.org/10.4324/9781003289920-36

Cook, J. M., & Poulsen, S. S. (2011). Utilizing photographs with the genogram: A technique for enhancing couple therapy. *Journal of Systemic Therapies, 30*(1), 14–23. https://doi.org/10.1521/jsyt.2011.30.1.14

Gil, E. (2015). Individual and family play genograms. In C. S. Sori, L. L. Hecker, M. E. Bachenberg (Eds.), *The therapist's notebook for children and adolescents* (2nd ed., pp. 13–20). Routledge.

Kuehl, B. P. (1995). The solution-oriented genogram: A collaborative approach. *Journal of Marital and Family Therapy, 21*(3), 239–250. https://doi.org/10.1111/j.1752-0606.1995.tb00159.x

Kuehl, B. P. (1996). The use of genograms with solution-based and narrative therapies. *The Family Journal, 4*(1), 5–11. https://doi.org/10.1177/1066480796041002

McGoldrick, M., Gerson, R., & Petry, S. (2016). *Genograms: Assessment and treatment* (4th ed.). Norton.

Platt, L. F., & Skowron, E. A. (2013). The family genogram interview: Reliability and validity of a new interview protocol. *The Family Journal, 21*(1), 35–45. https://doi.org/10.1177/1066480712456817

Weiss, E. L., Coll, J. E., Gerbauer, J., Smiley, K., & Carillo, E. (2010). The military genogram: A solution-focused approach for building resiliency in service members and their families. *The Family Journal, 18*(4), 395–406. https://doi.org/10.1177/1066480710378479

CHAPTER 16

DIGITAL PHOTO TREE OF LIFE

Hailee Hughston, Tiffany Alexis Leal, and Rebecca A. Cobb

Materials for Therapists: PowerPoint and images of a tree with visible roots, leaves, fruit, flowers, and seeds (included as supplemental materials to this book).

Materials for Clients: Ten to twelve digital photos.

Objective

The tree of life activity is a creative narrative therapy intervention in which clients draw a tree with roots, branches, leaves, fruit, seeds, and a compost heap and write narrative responses representing details of their lives onto the tree. This activity assists clients in conceptualizing their personal strengths, supports, hopes for the future, and other meaningful aspects of their lives through metaphor (Lock, 2016; Ncube, 2006). In this chapter, an alternative version of the tree of life exercise is presented in which clients use digital photos rather than written labels on their tree of life as a visually stimulating and engaging teletherapy intervention.

Rationale for Use

Narrative therapy is grounded in the idea that the stories people tell about themselves and that others tell them shape the way that they make meaning in their lives. Narrative therapists work with clients to deconstruct these stories, map and externalize problems, and identify unique outcomes in which the problem either doesn't exist or isn't as much of a problem as it usually is, with the ultimate goal of changing problem-saturated stories into preferred ones (White & Epston, 1990).

The tree of life activity utilizes a storytelling lens characteristic of narrative therapy (White & Epston, 1990) that emphasizes client strengths identified through elements of their story. The exercise was originally developed to help children in Southern Africa identify their unique values, strengths, and community supports (Ncube, 2006). However, it is a flexible approach meant to fit the needs of a variety of systems (Weller, 2024). The origin and purpose of the activity's development naturally embraces the ideologies of non-Western cultures, thereby expanding its potential reach and positive impact for diverse populations (Ncube, 2006). Moreover, tree symbology is a relevant visualization tool that represents life in various cultures and religious traditions, which can be organically integrated into the therapy process for many clients.

In the original version of this activity, clients draw the ground and a tree with roots, a trunk, branches, leaves, fruit, flowers, seeds, and a compost heap. The therapist then guides them in identifying and writing on the tree things that each part of the tree represents (see Table 16.1).

DOI: 10.4324/9781003330912-20

Table 16.1 Parts of the tree of life

Roots	Where you came from/core aspects of identity (e.g., culture, people, places, traditions, favorite books, colors, songs)
Ground	Where you currently live and things you choose to do on a regular basis
Trunk	Personal values, qualities, abilities
Branches	Hopes, dreams, and wishes
Leaves	Important people or pets that have had a positive impact on you
Fruit	Gifts, legacies, and impacts passed down to you from others
Flowers/Seeds	Legacies and impacts that you want to pass down to others
Compost	Experiences that no longer serve you and that you would like to leave behind

This activity is an effective assessment and intervention tool for children and families in any phase of therapy (Ncube, 2006). This visual representation of one's story helps clients experience a greater sense of clarity and self-trust (Weller, 2024) and assists clients in identifying past, present, and future elements of self. With the therapist, clients share their narrative, discover and rediscover aspects of self, and identify alternative story paths by reauthoring their narrative.

The following describes a variation of the tree of life intervention in which the therapist provides pre-drawn elements of the tree of life, which clients can piece together in digital form. Then, rather than adding written labels, clients are guided in adding digital photographs that represent each of the elements of the tree of life. The personal photo element provides an opportunity for enhanced meaning-making and adds visual simulation to help with client engagement via teletherapy.

Setup

The following specifies the steps required for setting up the digital photo tree of life for teletherapy intervention. These steps may be taken prior to the session in which you plan to conduct the activity.

1. ***Open the digital tree images.*** These can be found in the supplemental materials that accompany this book (see Figure 16.1).
2. ***Introduce the idea of collaboratively creating a digital photo tree of life.*** Start by telling clients about the activity and explain that they would be assembling and arranging meaningful photos on a digital tree diagram to represent key aspects of their lives. Guide the family through each part of the tree, sharing what each part represents. Table 16.1 is included in the supplemental materials that accompany this book to facilitate this discussion.
3. ***Invite clients to gather digital photos that represent each part of the tree.*** Consider sending clients a list of the different elements of the tree with a description of what each part of the tree represents. When working with individuals, ask that they choose one to five photos for each part of the tree. When working with families, ask that each member choose one to three photos for each part of the tree. If clients bring more or less, tell them that it's okay, but to start with the most important photographs for each part of the tree in case they run out of room. If personal photos are not readily accessible, clients can find and save photos that resonate with them through an internet search.

Figure 16.1 Digital tree images. Credit: Dr. Christine Walsh Borst.

Instructions

The following specifies steps for completing the digital photo tree of life activity in the next session with clients. These instructions have been adapted from Weller (2024).

1. ***Share your screen.*** Show the file with the elements of the tree of life on it.
2. ***Introduce the parts of the tree again.*** Explain what each part represents (see Table 16.1). When describing the compost, you might say "Experiences that no longer serve you and that you would like to *leaf* behind," while emphasizing the word leaf as a playful pun to engage clients while talking about a more difficult topic.
3. ***Invite clients to create their digital tree image.*** When working with older children and adolescents, you may email them a copy of the PowerPoint file with the digital tree images in it so that they can add their images directly to the file. When working with younger clients or those who are less technologically savvy, you may ask that they email you their photos in advance so they can guide you in placing each photo in the appropriate place on the tree.
4. ***Save the digital tree image.*** Once clients have finished their tree, either save it in the client's file or ask them to save it to their device. If clients have the file on their own device, ask if they would be willing to share the file with you so you can save it to their file for use in future sessions. If the tree was created on your own device, ask if they would like you to send it to them. Share the file with them if requested.
5. ***Review the tree and its accompanying images.*** Ask clients to describe each photo that they selected and how it represents each part of the tree of life.

Processing

The main goal of narrative techniques is to reframe stories into alternative perspectives with potential for actionable change (White & Epston, 1990). Conclude the activity by prompting insights from clients about their chosen photos, then ask specific reflection questions. These questions should encourage clients to find connections, patterns, and themes between the chosen photos. Use processing to support in identifying goals of therapy and in creating a preferred narrative.

When discussing images placed in the compost, consider ways in which these images may be related to the client's presenting problem(s) and how you might discuss these images in a way that externalizes the client's problem(s).

The following example questions can be used with individuals and families.

- Tell me more about your chosen photos.
- What patterns do you notice among the photos on the [roots/ground/trunk/branches/leaves/fruits/flowers/seeds/compost]?
- What does this tell you about your values?
- Which parts of the tree came easily to you?
- Which parts of the tree were challenging to identify?
- Did any stories or narratives emerge in the creation of your tree that surprised you?
- Did any memories emerge in the creation of your tree that you had forgotten about?
- Did you learn anything new about yourself or others from this activity? If so, what?
- Which parts of your tree feel most connected to your sense of family?
- What story does this tree tell? How is that story different from the story you tell yourself?
- What is the preferred narrative the tree tells?
- Is there anything about the tree that you would like to change? If so, what?
- How did it feel to create the tree?
- What did it feel like to see the completed tree?
- How do you and other people respond to [externalized problem/compost]?
- How would you like to respond to [externalized problem/compost]?
- How would you like others to respond to [externalized problem/compost]?

Vignette

Trevor (14), his mother Melinda (32), and stepfather Jeff (40) presented in teletherapy to work through the process of Trevor returning home from a three-month stay at a residential facility. It was disclosed that Jeff had a biological nonbinary child named Kai (17), who was close with Trevor, but was away at a science camp at the time of the session. Trevor stated in session that among the few personal possessions he could have at the facility, his photos of family, friends from home, and dog Scooter helped him the most to get through tough days. After reflecting and validating this information, the therapist proposed creating a family photo tree during the next session. The therapist briefly explained the tree of life activity and what each part of the tree represented. They also emailed a list of these parts and what each part represents for reference in gathering photographs. They shared that they would like each person to collect one to three photos to place on each part of the tree of life in the following session. The therapist explained that by completing the activity, the family would better understand each family member's individual stories and how these stories can come together in the photos as one shared story, which would provide a good starting point for creating shared goals as Trevor reassimilated into family life. The family agreed to assemble some of their most meaningful photos and create their photo tree in the following session.

At the start of the next session, the family came prepared with a file of their photos ready on Melinda's laptop. The therapist emailed the family a copy of a PowerPoint file with the tree diagram (see Figure 16.1) and asked that they share their screen once they opened it. The therapist then instructed the family to decorate the tree with the images that they had selected and the additional images of leaves, flowers, and fruit as they saw fit. The therapist asked that they start by placing their selected images representing where they were from and core aspects of their identity among the roots. They then guided them through each subsequent part of the tree of life, briefly reminding them what each part of tree represents along the way.

As each family member took turns placing their photos, they shared details without prompting from the therapist (see Figure 16.2). For the branches, the therapist noticed that Melinda and Jeff both chose family photos. Melinda's picture showed her with Jeff holding Trevor as a small child, and Jeff's showed the four (including Kai) on a camping trip before Trevor was admitted to the facility. Jeff stated, "It was really nice when we could just go out and spend time together. I'd like to get back to that at some point." Trevor placed a photo of himself with his friend group on the branches, saying that he really hoped to spend more time with them now that he was back home. It also was of note to the therapist that Trevor had placed a picture of his ID card to the residential facility on the compost pile.

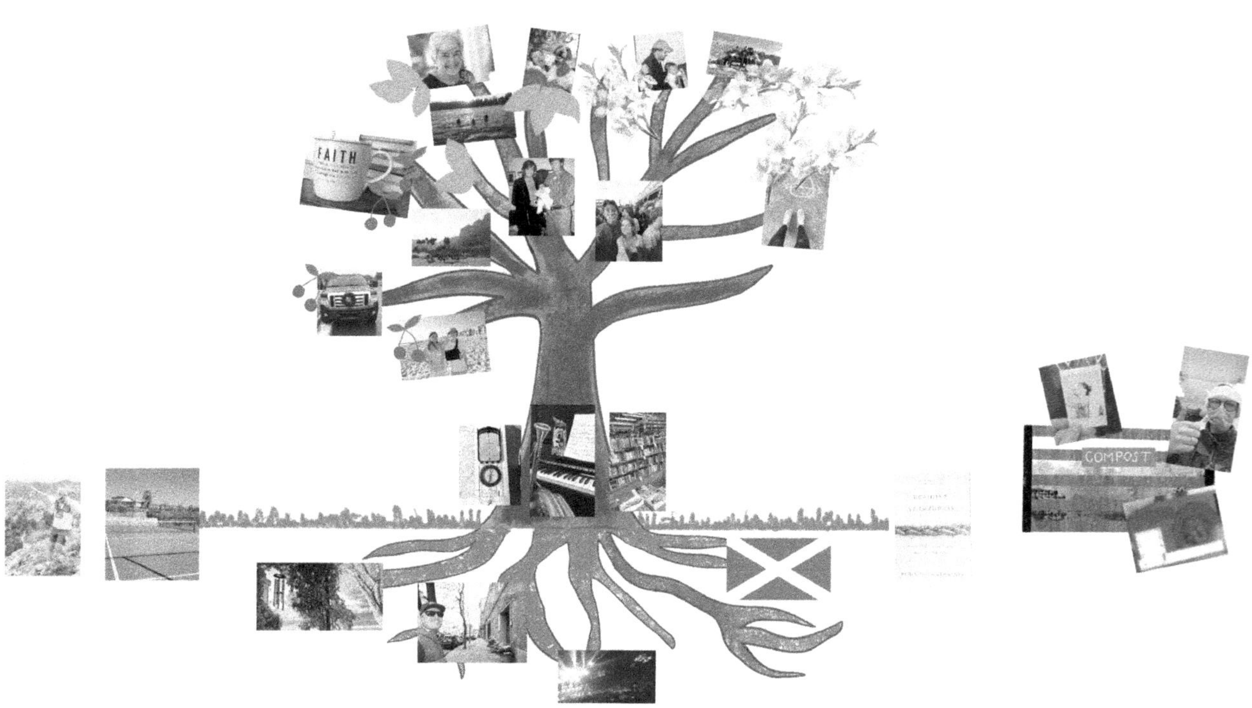

Figure 16.2 Tree of life. Credit: Hailee Hughston and Dr. Christine Walsh Borst.

After the last photos were placed near the flowers, the therapist gently asked each family member to share some insights about the photos they placed on the tree. After this was done, the therapist reflected dominant themes that emerged through each section of the tree. For Jeff and Melinda's photos, the therapist noted a theme of appreciation and commitment to maintaining loving family relationships. Trevor's choices suggested a desire to return to meaningful friendships and activities as he moved past his residential stay. The therapist hypothesized aloud that the underlying narrative of these themes was that despite the previous hardships, the family wanted to return to a state of mutual love and trust that was enjoyed before the experiences that brought Trevor to the facility. They processed the tree and its creation with the family and asked the family how they responded to Trevor's ID being on the compost pile. In turn, the family processed and shared their desire to support Trevor in his transition back home. When asked what story the tree told, the family shared that it told the story of a strong family coming together and moving forward toward recovery. The therapist worked with the family in processing the emotions that the family felt as they shared about each part of the tree and the photos attached to those pieces. At the end of the session, Jeff mentioned that seeing how the meaning of the images from the ground affected the meaning of the roots, then the trunk, then the branches, leaves, fruit, and flowers really "helped to connect the dots" and provide a way to include the perspectives of the whole family. Although Melinda, Jeff, and Trevor each had their own interpretation of the tree, seeing images that represented their collective strengths and legacies allowed them to begin leaving behind externalized problems placed in the compost pile and co-create preferred stories.

Suggestions for Follow-Up

Make note of themes and patterns in the photo content chosen by each person and keep a copy of the tree of life in the clients' records to discuss in future sessions. With time, clients may choose to add to or alter their tree of life as subjugated narratives become a greater part of their dominant story.

Contraindications

This activity may be difficult for young children or those with limited cognitive abilities, though younger children may be able to participate with their families with simpler prompts and example images from which to choose. When working with clients with visual impairments, the original version of the tree of life activity may be more appropriate, as it is based on written words, rather than images.

References

Lock, S. (2016). The tree of life: A review of the collective narrative approach. *Educational Psychology Research and Practice*, 2(1), 2–20. https://doi.org/10.15123/uel.88582

Ncube, N. (2006). The tree of life project – Using narrative ideas in work with vulnerable children in South Africa. *The International Journal of Narrative Therapy and Community Work*, *5*(1), 3–16.

Weller, N. B. (2024). The tree of life: A simple exercise for reclaiming your identity and direction in life through story. Nathan B. Weller. https://nathanbweller.com/tree-life-simple-exercise-reclaiming-identity-direction-life-story/

White, M., & Epston, D. (1990). *Narrative means to therapeutic ends*. Norton.

CHAPTER 17

DIGITAL COLLAGE

SHARING STORIES THROUGH PICTURES

Kimberly Riley, Rebecca A. Cobb, and Tiffany Alexis Leal

Materials for Therapists: None.

Materials for Clients: Computer program or application that allows for the compilation of images (e.g., Canva, PowerPoint).

Objective

Collages are used in therapy with children, adolescents, and families for both assessment and intervention. With increased use of digital tools, software applications have been used for the purpose of making therapeutic collages in therapy (Diggs et al., 2015). This chapter provides instructions on how to support children, adolescents, and their families in creating therapeutic collages in online therapy for assessment and intervention using a narrative approach.

Rationale for Use

Collage making in therapy is effective for treating presenting concerns such as anxiety, grief, and trauma (Diggs et al., 2015; Stallings, 2015). Collage making engages clients the physical senses and utilizes aspects of free association and play while allowing clients to verbally or non-verbally express themselves (Diggs et al., 2015; Keisari et al., 2021). This contributes to an embodied sensory experience which fosters the working through of emotions which are rooted in the somatic experience (Keisari et al., 2021).

Traditionally, collages have been created using magazines, scissors, glue, and other physical objects. More recently, software applications have been used to overcome barriers, such as lack of resources, in the creation of collages (Diggs et al., 2015). Digital collages have been found to achieve many of the same therapeutic goals as paper collages. Research indicates that the use of digital collage making in therapy can expand upon current therapeutic interventions while increasing comfort and engagement in therapy (Diggs et al., 2015). The use of digital collages as a therapeutic approach can help individuals of all ages and populations create meaning, achieve insight, express emotions and thoughts, and increase their sense of well-being (Diggs et al., 2015). In addition, when specific prompts are provided, it can serve as an excellent tool for therapy assessment and the identification of therapeutic goals.

DOI: 10.4324/9781003330912-21

The use of digital collages in therapy can be applied with most theoretical approaches, though it may be particularly fitting with narrative therapy. Collage making can help clients to tell a story about who they are and how they came to be the person that they are today (Van Schalkwyk, 2010). Collages may help therapists assess dominant stories and help clients identify unique outcomes and preferred stories. The use of collage in narrative therapy may also help clients visually depict and externalize problems and visually share subjugated narratives with others as a form of outsider witnessing.

The following describes setup and instructions for creating collages in teletherapy with children, adolescents, and families.

Setup

1. ***Inquire about the client's knowledge of and experience with making collages.*** If clients are unfamiliar with collages, explain that collages are created by compiling images, words, phrases, or other objects in one place, like on a piece of paper, poster board, or even on a computer program.
2. ***Describe the therapeutic use of collages in therapy.*** Collages can be used to help clients express complex emotions, access unconscious thoughts, and gain self-awareness through visually representing their lived experiences through images. Clients are empowered to share their stories through visual storytelling, assisting clients in processing trauma, working through difficult emotions, and in treating anxiety, depression, and other presenting concerns.
3. ***Discuss the possibility of creating a collage in therapy.*** Inquire about the client's interest in conducting this activity.
4. ***Identify the client's collage medium preferences.*** Clients may create their collage using tangible objects available to them (e.g., magazines, scissors, glue, tape) or they may create a digital collage using digital photographs or other images found on the internet and compiling them in one place using a computer program or an application. Alternatively, clients may create a mixed-media collage using a combination of tangible and virtual objects. For example, the cover of this book was created by first making a collage from cut and torn images from magazines and other sources. That collage was then photographed and transferred to a digital format. Text and additional digital images were then overlaid onto that collage to create a mixed-media collage depicting the sense of hope, playfulness, and creativity that this book is intended to inspire. Allow clients to create the collage using their preferred medium.
5. ***Ensure that clients have all necessary materials.*** For those who wish to create a collage using physical materials, work with adults to ensure that all necessary materials will be available and make sure that it's okay to cut and/or tear any paper materials being used. If clients have limited access to physical resources, a digital collage may be ideal. For the creation of digital collages, inquire about computer programs or applications that clients may already have that would allow them to compile images (e.g., Canva, PowerPoint). If clients don't have access to a relevant computer program or application, they may need to download one.
6. ***Discuss any limitations to HIPAA compliance.*** Help clients understand any limitations to confidentiality using online apps and support them in choosing the program or application that they are most comfortable using for the purpose of the activity.

7. ***Discuss when the collage will be created.*** Collages may be created in or between sessions. Discuss with clients when they would like to create their collage and help them to consider any additional support that they might need in the creation of their collage. For example, younger clients may need the support of an adult to use glue and scissors. Others who are less comfortable with technology platforms may need support from others in navigating computer programs and applications necessary for digital collage creation. If clients need emotional/therapeutic support while creating their collage, encourage them to create the collage in session.

Instructions

1. ***Provide a prompt.*** Select a prompt that is fitting for the unique needs of each client and their presenting problems. The following are examples of prompts that you may provide to help identify dominant stories and preferred narratives:
   - Create a collage that shows your world.
   - Create a collage that represents your life story (Van Schalkwyk, 2010).
   - Create a collage that represents significant or important experiences in your life (Van Schalkwyk, 2010).
   - Create a collage that represents your relationship with [one another/name of person].
   - Create a collage the represents your relationship with [presenting problem].
   - Create a collage that depicts your overcoming [presenting problem].
2. ***Provide instructions.*** Explain to clients how to create their collage. These instructions will differ depending on the chosen medium for collage creation.
   - ***Physical collage:*** For those using physical objects, explain that they should cut and/or tear images from magazines or catalogues and glue or tape them onto a piece of paper or poster board any way that they would like.
   - ***Digital collage:*** For those creating a digital collage, instruct clients to create a folder on their computer where they can save images that they would like to use in their collage. Then, they can search the internet for relevant images. You may provide guidance on where and how to search for images so clients are only exposed to age-appropriate content. For example, you might provide a list of age-appropriate websites that clients can search, instruct them to use a search engine designed for kids (e.g., Kiddle), or ensure that an adult is present while children search for their images. Clients may also save photographs that they have taken to a file for use in their collage. They can even take new pictures of objects around them for use in their collage if they would like! Then, instruct clients to save each image that they would like to use in their collage to the file that they created. Finally, they can then transfer the images to the computer program or application that they are using to create their collage. Instructions for this will vary depending on the program/app being used. Alternatively, for some software (e.g., PowerPoint), clients may simply copy and paste the images that they find directly into the program in which they intend to create their collage. Support clients in saving their collage to a location where they will be able to find it easily and with a file name that they can easily identify. Remind clients to save their collage periodically to avoid losing progress if the program were to close or the computer were to freeze.

- ***Mixed-media collage:*** For those creating a mixed-media collage, provide the aforementioned instructions for both physical collage and digital collage creation. Explain that clients may take a digital photograph of their physical collage and then use that photograph in the creation of a digital collage to create a mixed-media collage.

3. ***Create the collage.*** If clients create the collage in session, ask that they share their screen during its creation so you can observe their process.
4. ***Provide support as needed.*** Clients may need varying levels of support in creating their collage. This will be dependent on age, experience conducting internet searches, and familiarity with the software used to create the collage. If clients appear to be struggling to find an image(s), you can send links to websites with images through the chat function of the teletherapy platform. For younger children, those less technologically savvy, or those otherwise unable to create the collage themselves, you can have clients guide you in creating a digital collage for them while sharing your screen. Most importantly, provide any emotional support that may be needed.
5. ***Save the collage.*** Upon completion of digital collages, ask clients to save them. Ask if they (or a family member) could email you a copy of the collage so you can save it to their file for future reference. Though you may take a screenshot of the collage, having the actual file for future use may allow you to support clients in editing their collage in future sessions. Having a copy of the file will avoid any situations in which clients can't find or has lost access to their file.

Processing

Dependent on your approach to therapy, you may ask processing questions while clients are creating their collage and/or after its completion. The main goal of narrative techniques is to reframe stories into alternate perspectives with potential for actionable change (Epston & White, 1990). Conclude the activity by prompting insights from clients about their chosen photos. Continue processing and ask specific reflection questions. The goal behind these questions is to encourage clients to find connections, patterns, and themes between the chosen photos.

When using a narrative approach, identify unique outcomes by discussing ways in which the images on the collage relate to the client's goals of therapy. Support in the process of externalization by discussing the client's problems, depicted by images in the collage, as things that are separate from them – things that they can fight against! Systemic processing questions may also be asked to support clients in sharing their collage and accompanying story with others and in thickening the plot of their preferred story. The processing questions that follow can be used to support in externalizing problems, identifying unique outcomes, creating preferred narratives, and supporting the process of outsider witnessing.

Externalizing the Problem

- What is it like to see [the problem] in your collage in this way?
- How does this collage help you see yourself as separate from [the problem]?
- In what ways does this collage help you see [your/your family's] connection to the problem in a new way?

Unique Outcomes and Preferred Stories

- How did your collage help you notice times in the past when [the problem] did not exist?
- What do you think you could do to overcome [the problem]?
- What might your collage look like if [the problem] no longer existed?

Outsider Witnessing

- What is it like to look at [name of person]'s collage?
- What is it like to have others see your collage?
- How does this collage help your family understand you better?
- How do you think others might respond to seeing your collage?
- Is there anyone else that you might want to share your collage with?
- Is there somewhere that you might want to put your collage on display so you or others can see it?

Vignette

George (40), Angie (38), and their daughter, Rainy (15), presented in teletherapy to work through concerns regarding the establishment of agreed-upon family rules that everyone would follow. George and Angie reported that since moving to Washington from California, Rainy had struggled with staying on task, completing her homework, and following rules. Her grades had started to fall, but she said she didn't care because she hated her new school.

After reflecting and validating the information previously shared, the therapist proposed creating a collage during the next session and provided the prompt to "show me your world" to help the family in creating a representation of their life. The therapist briefly explained that the collage might help them to unpack the family's story and identify preferred narratives that the family might agree upon. The family agreed that they would like to do this activity together, and that they would be a good excuse to go through old family photographs. They shared that most of their photographs were in digital format, so it made the most sense to create a digital collage.

During the next session, the family came prepared with a file of their photos ready on Rainy's laptop. The therapist invited the whole family to participate in the digital collage to assist with expressing what their world looks like. The therapist explained that they could add any images that they would like, including those found on the internet if they didn't have photos readily available that depicted something that they wanted to share.

Rainy shared her screen with the therapist and opened Canva on her laptop. The family then took turns uploading their selected photos onto Canva to make their digital collage. As each family member took turns placing their photos in the collage, they shared details without prompting from the therapist. Rainy shared that a lot of the photos on the screen were from their "old world in California." Angie's picture showed her with George holding Rainy as a baby, and George's showed the family on a walk in San Francisco. Rainy stated, "I remember when we used to go on adventures back home. I really miss California. We were so happy then." Rainy included a picture of her and her friends from California next to a picture of her at her current school where she was standing alone. Angie reflected to Rainy, "I guess it's been pretty lonely since we moved."

Once the collage was completed, the therapist asked each person to share some of their insights about the photos they placed within the collage. Family members each reflected that they all missed California and each had recently felt like they didn't belong, but they hadn't noticed until now that others were feeling the same way. The therapist asked, "In what ways does this collage help you see your family's connection to the problem in a new way?" Angie reflected that while they had initially thought that the problem was Rainy's engagement in school, it actually seemed that everyone was having a problem adapting to their new community. George agreed. The therapist reflected, "It seems that maybe loneliness is the problem that you're all up against. I wonder how you might be able to unite against "loneliness" and to help each other transition to your new life in Washington." The therapist worked with the family in processing what had emerged as their newly identified problem and supported them in brainstorming ways to combat "loneliness." Seeing images that represented their collective stories had allowed them to identify their current dominant story in a new way and eventually co-create preferred narratives.

Suggestions for Follow-Up

A benefit of creating digital collages is the ability to save the collage for future use. In future sessions, clients may add to or alter their digital collage as subjugated narratives become a greater part of their dominant story. You may encourage clients to make any changes to their collage that they see fit. Alternatively, you may provide a new prompt that may help them to thicken the plot of unique outcomes or preferred stories. For example, you might ask clients to make edits to their collage that demonstrate their fighting against externalized problems. Clients may respond to this by covering up images that represent their presenting problem or removing them completely to create a new collage in which the problem isn't so much of a problem anymore.

Contraindications

Utilizing digital platforms for the creation of collages takes away from the tactile therapeutic process of using tangible objects when making traditional collages, such as flipping through magazines, ripping, tearing, and cutting paper (Diggs et al., 2015). When offering collage as a potential therapeutic intervention, allow clients to use tangible objects if this is their preferred medium and all necessary materials are available to them.

References

Diggs, L. A., Lubas, M., & De Leo, G. (2014). Use of technology and software applications for therapeutic collage making. *International Journal of Art Therapy, 20*(1), 2–13. https://doi.org/10.1080/17454832.2014.961493

Epston, D., & White, M. (1990). *Narrative means to therapeutic ends*. Norton.

Keisari, S., Piol, S., Elkarif, T., Mola, G., & Testoni, I. (2021). Crafting life stories in Photocollage: An online creative art-based intervention for older adults. *Behavioral Sciences, 12*(1), 1–23. https://doi.org/10.3390/bs12010001

Stallings, J. W. (2015). Collage as an expressive medium in art therapy. In D. E. Gussak & M. L. Rosal (Eds.), *The Wiley handbook of art therapy* (pp. 163–170). John Wiley & Sons. https://doi.org/10.1002/9781118306543.ch16

Turns, B., & Macey, P. (2015). Cinema narrative therapy: Utilizing family films to externalize children's 'problems.' *Journal of Family Therapy, 37*(4), 590–606. https://doi.org/10.1111/1467-6427.12098

Van Schalkwyk, G. J. (2010). Collage Life Story Elicitation Technique: A representational technique for scaffolding autobiographical memories. *Qualitative Report, 15*(3), 675–695. https://doi.org/10.46743/2160-3715/2010.1170

CHAPTER 18

MIXED-MEDIA AQUARIUM

Rebecca A. Cobb with Eliana Gil

Materials for Therapists: PowerPoint or another computer program and clip art or other digital images. Some preliminary images are included in the supplemental materials that accompany this book.

Materials for Clients: Paper (plain and/or construction), crayons, markers, and/or colored pencils, scissors, and digital camera or smartphone. Glue and/or tape, googly eyes, pom poms, craft pipe cleaners, and/or yarn are optional.

Objective

The family aquarium is a creative activity for engaging families in in-person therapy where therapists have crafting materials readily available in the therapy room (Gil, 1994, 2014; Gil & Sobol 2005). This chapter describes how to conduct a mixed-media variation of this activity via teletherapy in two or three sessions. For this intervention, family members each draw and decorate their own water creature. They then collaborate to make an aquarium where their creations can live and place them in the aquarium. This chapter ends with reflections by Eliana Gil, who initially created the family aquarium for in-person intervention.

Rationale for Use

The family aquarium can be used to assess family dynamics and serves as an intervention to stimulate conversation about these dynamics and family functioning. Though this intervention can be conducted with many theories, it is particularly fitting for structural theory and is well suited for assessment and intervention regarding boundaries and hierarchies within families.

By engaging families in the act of creating water creatures with physical objects, this activity maintains the attention of a wide age range of clients. Through collaboration between adults and the therapist, these objects are transformed into digital format, further engaging clients in an online platform. With guidance from the therapist, the family then collaborates to create a habitat for their creatures and engages in metaphorical discussion about their creatures and their home. Discussion via the metaphor of the aquarium and its inhabitants reduces client resistance (Gil, 1994; Schaefer, 1993) and makes the activity more engaging for younger and less verbal clients.

DOI: 10.4324/9781003330912-22

Setup

The following steps will prepare you to conduct this activity.

1. ***Choose a computer program.*** You will need a program that allows for cropping and the compilation of images. PowerPoint is a great option for this activity. In PowerPoint, a slide serves as the aquarium. You may then zoom out on the slide and place images around the outside edges of the slide that clients can select from when creating the environment for their water creatures.
2. ***Select images for the base of the scene.*** You could set the stage with a plain blue background to represent water or select an image of an aquarium, ocean, lake, or pond (Gil & Sobol, 2005). In some instances, it is appropriate to let the family choose. Allowing the family to choose their environment allows for assessment of dynamics that may not be as readily apparent when you select the environment. In other instances, it may be preferable for you to select the base of the scene. For example, it may be best to use an image of an aquarium with some families because it has more permanent boundaries, which may be of symbolic significance. A family with disengaged boundaries might benefit from the representation of an environment that requires a higher degree of closeness. Alternatively, an ocean or lake scene that depicts space both above and below the water may allow clients who feel like a "fish out of water" to place their object above the waterline. This scene may also allow more amphibious water creatures to create their own spaces on islands, boats, lily pads, or other objects. A family with enmeshed boundaries might benefit from the representation of an environment that allows separate spaces for each member of the family. Consider the specific family with which you are working and choose your approach accordingly.
3. ***Place other images.*** Place aquatic objects (e.g., cave, coral, island, lily pad, seaweed, sunken ship) and images of any other objects that may be of potential significance (e.g., heart, headstone) around the edges of the digital file that can be used to decorate the aquarium (see Figure 18.1 for

Figure 18.1 Aquarium setup created in PowerPoint. Credit: Dr. Christine Walsh Borst.

basic aquarium setup created in PowerPoint). A PowerPoint slide with some preliminary images is included in the supplemental materials that accompany this book. You may add to them based on your own preferences and the needs of your clients.

4. ***Discuss access to crafting materials with an adult in the family.*** If available, ask that the family gather necessary materials prior to the session in which you plan to conduct the activity. Alternatively, you may send clients the materials in a therapeutic care package (see Chapter 8).

Instructions

The following specifies instructions for this activity.

1. ***Create a fish or other water creature.*** Instruct each member of the family system to "create any fish or other water creature." Rather than requiring family members to create fish, as instructed in the original variation of this activity (Gil & Sobol, 2005), allowing a "water creature" allows for the creation of other living things that might be found in the water. Again, you may strategically choose whether you want to require a fish or allow more variation, depending on the needs of the family. Even when provided specific instructions to create a fish, some members of the family may create something else regardless of instructions provided. When this occurs, take note of these differences for processing. During this part of the activity, encourage each member of the family to decorate their creation any way that they wish. Gil and Sobol (2005) suggest that the therapist observe family interactions and avoid taking on the role of the helper during this part of the activity. Young children may require assistance from an adult or other family member when creating their creature. To assess dynamics, make note of who asks who for help, how resources are shared, and who appears to be in charge if and when disagreements take place. This part of the activity typically takes one session.
2. ***Send images.*** After each family member has finished the previous step, ask an adult in the family to take a photograph of each creation. Each creation should be placed on a surface with a solid, contrasting color. For example, a black fish could be photographed on a white countertop, but not on a black countertop. Each creature may need to be photographed in different locations. It could be a fun activity for each family member to try to find the best place to photograph their creature as a collaborative effort with the photographer. These specific instructions allow you to successfully crop each image for insertion in the aquarium. Once all photographs have been taken, they should be sent to you via a Health Insurance Portability and Accountability Act (HIPAA)-consistent platform.
3. ***Crop images.*** Between sessions, place all images into a file on a computer program that allows you to crop them. PowerPoint is a great place to crop images, especially if you choose this platform to set up the aquarium. Simply select one of the images, click on the tab for "picture format," and select the option to "remove background." If you are cropping the images in PowerPoint, place them above the slide in which the environment will be created. Once the background has been successfully removed from each image, save the file in a HIPAA-compliant location.
4. ***Share your screen.*** During the next therapy session, share your screen with options for the living environment and objects that can be placed in that environment. Before you share your screen, position the slide so that the creatures that clients created are not yet visible. This may mean zooming in on the slide more or scrolling down so they are under the PowerPoint toolbar.
5. ***Create the environment.*** Instruct clients to collaboratively create an environment in which to place their water creatures. Upon instruction by the family, organize the objects to help create the

environment. Consider starting with the youngest member present or the person who typically speaks least and having each member of the family make one change at a time in sequential order by age. Throughout the process, check in with the family to see if you've placed the objects in the right place and adjust as needed. At this point in time, the family may engage in discussion about their preferred environment and will need to work through any potential disagreements to successfully guide you. Again, primarily observe family interactions and avoid taking on the role of the helper during this part of the activity. If the family is having difficulty collaborating, you may intervene to maintain appropriate therapeutic structure.

6. ***Reveal the creatures.*** Change the positioning or zoom of the slide so that the creatures that clients created are now visible above the environment. This helps to create a fun element of surprise for clients to see the creatures that they created with physical materials suddenly appear in virtual format on the screen.
7. ***Place creatures in the environment.*** Invite each family member to instruct you on where to place the image of the creature that they made. Again, consider starting with the youngest member present or the person who typically speaks least and having each member of the family make one change at a time in sequential order by age. Throughout the process, check in with the family to see if you've placed their creatures in the right place and adjust as needed. Once each member of the family has placed their creature, ask if everyone is happy with the placement of their creature, or if anything needs to be changed. Follow the guidance of the family to make any necessary changes until the family is satisfied. During this stage, avoid asking processing questions. You may, however, reflect what you're hearing clients say if they choose to share information about why they want something placed in a particular location or why they want to move it.
8. ***Save the file.*** Save the completed file to a HIPAA-compliant location for use in future sessions.

Processing

At the start of processing, share your screen with the completed image of the water creatures in the living environment created by the family. The image should be as large as possible and should not show any remaining images that were not placed into the environment. Maintain visuals of both the environment and clients while processing if possible.

Then, ask a series of questions similar to those presented by Gil and Sobol (2005). While processing, ask questions that are in the metaphor of the images/objects within the environment and use the family's language and labels for each creature. For this activity, clients don't need to explain why they chose or created each object. Rather, by focusing on metaphors, the activity remains playful and engaging, and allows right-brain creative processing. For example, you might ask:

- How do the [creature] and the [creature] get along?
- What do you think it's like for the [creature] to be swimming [all alone/along with the other creatures]?
- What might the [creature] think of the [creature]?
- How do you think the creatures like living together in this space?

Again, this activity can be processed with many different guiding theories. Keeping a guiding theory in mind helps to focus the types of questions that are asked. The following vignette will demonstrate the use of structural theory in conceptualizing and processing this activity.

Vignette

Manuel (38), Blanca (37), José (17), Monica (15), Jasmine (12), Marcello (8), Vincent (6), and Sandra (5) presented in teletherapy reporting difficulty adjusting after moving the youngest three children into the household for temporary care while their mom, Maria (27; Manuel's sister) was out of the country caring for their terminally ill grandmother.

At the end of the first session, after hearing a bit about the family and why they came to therapy, the therapist introduced the idea of doing the aquarium activity as a fun way of getting to know them more over the next two sessions. The youngest children enthusiastically agreed that they would like to participate in this activity, while the others agreed to doing it with them. The therapist asked Manuel and Blanca if they had arts and crafts supplies and a cell phone with the ability to take photographs available for use in the next session. They said that they did and agreed to have them ready to use the following week. Knowing that the family was using a laptop to attend therapy, the therapist instructed them to find a spot in the house with enough room for all eight of them to gather to work on an arts and crafts project together and to find a find a good spot to set up their laptop where the therapist could see them all as they worked on it. The youngest children jumped at the idea of knowing just where to do this.

At the start of the second session, the therapist instructed the family to use the supplies that they had gathered to each "create a water creature." The family spent the remainder of the session creating their creatures and talking with one another about what each was doing. Meanwhile, the therapist observed patterns of interaction and communication styles within the family. At the end of the session, the therapist asked the family to find a good place to photograph each creature, explaining that each creation should be placed on a surface with a solid, contrasting color, and that each creature may need to be photographed in different locations. The therapist asked that each person participate in finding a good place to photograph their own creature and that Blanca and Monica assist the others by taking photographs on their phones. Once all members had found a good location and photographs had been taken, the therapist instructed Manuel and Blanca on how to send the photos via a HIPAA-consistent platform.

Between sessions, the therapist created a PowerPoint slide with the following images around the sides of the slide: an aquarium, an ocean scene, a cave, an island, a sunken ship, seaweed, coral, waves, a treasure chest, a fishing pole, and a fishing lure (see Figure 18.1). Knowing a bit about the family and their history, the therapist strategically selected a headstone to include in the images that might be used to represent the deceased father of the youngest children or the impending death of their grandmother. The therapist also cropped photographs of the eight creatures created by the family and added them to the PowerPoint file above the slide, attempting to make each creation about the same size as the others.

At the start of the next session, the therapist explained that the family would be working together to create a place for all their creatures to live. Before sharing their screen, the therapist positioned the slide so the creatures weren't visible just yet, but the slide and all other objects that might be used in the creation of the environment were visible along the sides of the slide. They then shared their screen and told the family that they could use any of the images on the screen to create a place for their creatures to live. The therapist instructed the family to start by choosing the background (i.e., aquarium or ocean scene). After some discussion and going back and forth between two options, the family eventually agreed on using an ocean scene. The therapist expanded this image to cover the entire slide.

The therapist then instructed the family to choose from the objects on the sides of the slide to place in their environment. The therapist explained that they would take turns selecting objects, starting with Sandra, the youngest, and making their way up to the oldest in the family. One by one, each member selected an object that they wanted to put into the scene, instructing the therapist on what size to make the image and where to put it. Once everyone had a turn, the therapist asked if there was anything else that the family wanted to add, leaving it open for anyone to participate in no particular order. On occasion, members disagreed, but were generally able to come to consensus. Once the conversation came to a lull, the therapist asked what the family thought of the environment, if everyone was happy with what they had created, or if there were any changes that needed to be made before putting their creatures in the environment. Everyone agreed that they liked the scene and were ready for the next step.

The therapist then scrolled the PowerPoint slide down to reveal the eight creatures that they had created come to life on the screen in front of them. The youngest children, especially, were excited to see their creations in their new digital form and ran to get the physical versions that they had created the week before to participate in the festivities.

The therapist explained that they would take turns telling the therapist where they wanted to place their creatures within the environment that they had created, this time starting with Jasmine, who had been the least verbal in sessions, and letting others join in any order after that. One by one, each member told the therapist where they wanted to place their creature, telling the therapist if they wanted it bigger or smaller or facing a different direction.

- Jasmine shared that she had made the "octopus" and instructed the therapist to place it near the bottom of the scene.
- Sandra shared her "pom pom fish" and asked the therapist to place it near the bottom of the slide near the treasure and the octopus. She shared that her fish wanted to explore the ocean.
- Vincent explained that his fish had two sides, and therefore had two images to be placed in the scene. He instructed the therapist to place the "blue fish" near the bottom next to the pom pom fish and the octopus. The "colorful fish" was then placed swimming away from the others and up toward the top of the ocean.
- Marcello shared that he wanted his "jellyfish" hiding behind the seaweed, next to the treasure, but near the other fish.
- José shared his "nudibranch" with the therapist, showing the physical representation of it in a brilliantly colored three-dimensional form. After a few questions from other members of the family, José educated the family on the nudibranch and its real-life role as a mollusk that sheds its shell after its larval stage, also known as a "sea slug," "clown," or "dragon." He stated that he wanted the nudibranch to be on top of the water and that a wave needed to be added so it could surf.
- Monica then asked to place her "mermaid" halfway in the water and halfway out, sitting on the island.
- Blanca and Manuel went last. Blanca asked the therapist to place her "clown fish" at the bottom of the scene looking at the octopus, blue fish, pom pom fish, and jellyfish. Manuel's "sponge" was to be placed to the side of all the other creatures, "soaking it all in."

Throughout the activity, the therapist made note of which creature had been created by which person and any comments or observation of significance that might be brought back up during discussion.

The therapist then asked what everyone thought of the placement of each of their creatures and if anything needed to be moved or changed.

- Jasmine asked the therapist to add the cave to the scene and to put her octopus inside of it. She then requested that the octopus be made smaller and move to the back of the cave.
- Monica asked the therapist to add a fishing pole to the mermaid's hand and place a lure at the end of the string going into the water.
- Vincent requested that his blue fish move a little closer to the entrance of the cave and that the colorful fish move a little closer to the surface of the water, near where the nudibranch was surfing.
- The others indicated that their creatures were fine where they were and everyone agreed to leave everything else as it was (Figure 18.2).

The therapist thanked the family for the work that they had done together and proceeded to ask questions in the metaphor of the images on the screen. Though the therapist's attention was drawn to the octopus hiding in the cave and the jellyfish hiding behind the seaweed, they began asking questions about other creatures first so as to not immediately draw too much attention to the two creatures that appeared to be in hiding. Example processing questions included the following:

- What do you think it was like for the nudibranch to shed its shell? What does it think about having so many different nicknames? What might it feel like for him to be surfing above the water?
- What's it like for the mermaid to be halfway in the water and halfway out? What does the mermaid see below in the water? What do you think the mermaid is fishing for?
- What might the pom pom fish hope to find as it explores the ocean? How does it feel being surrounded by so many other fish?

Figure 18.2 Completed mixed-media aquarium. Credit: Dr. Christine Walsh Borst, Erin Dierickx, Spencer Erwin, Nicole Ma, Mikaela Quintinita, Addison, Charlie, and Rebecca A. Cobb.

- What's it like for the blue fish and the colorful fish to be in two different places at once? How does this fish choose when to show its blue side and when to show its colorful side?
- What do you think the jellyfish is hiding from? What might the jellyfish find in the treasure chest?
- How does it feel for the sponge to be floating around by itself? What might it be thinking as it looks on at the others?
- What does the clownfish think about the nudibranch and its nicknames? In what ways are the nudibranch and the clownfish alike? How are they different? What does it feel like for the clownfish to be so close to the octopus but to have it hiding in the cave?
- What do you think it's like for the octopus to be surrounded by so many fish that want it to come out of its cave? What might it take for the octopus to come out of its cave? Might the mermaid have a special lure that could bring it out of the cave just a little bit?

Responses to these questions revealed the following:

- The nudibranch appreciated its multifaceted identity and was enjoying its newfound freedom, though it still liked going down to swim with the other creatures.
- The mermaid liked spending her time halfway in and halfway out of the water. She hoped to lure the octopus out of its cave and hoped that maybe it could play up at the top of the water with her but wasn't sure what kind of bait to use when fishing for an octopus.
- The pom pom fish liked being around the other fish and wished that the octopus and jellyfish would come out to play more often. It hoped to find more friends.
- The blue fish and the colorful fish wanted to be close with the pom pom fish and the octopus, but it also wanted to go off and have fun. Usually, the blue fish would stay with the pom pom fish and the octopus if it thought that it needed them. When it wasn't needed, the colorful fish would go have fun.
- The jellyfish wasn't in hiding as much as it was feeling a little lonely and missing its mom.
- The sponge was also feeling a little lonely. He missed the nudibranch, the mermaid, and the octopus, and similar to the blue fish and colorful fish, wished that he knew how to be everywhere at once.
- The clownfish was proud of the nudibranch for finding its own identify, and especially loved that one of its nicknames was "clown." This made the clownfish feel connected to the nudibranch even when he was far away, though she still missed him being around more often. The clownfish also missed the mermaid and the octopus, though she was mostly worried about the octopus hiding in its cave since the mermaid still came down to play. She wasn't sure why the octopus was in hiding but wanted to ask it.
- The octopus revealed that it was also feeling a little lonely now that the nudibranch and the mermaid were away so much. It liked having the fish around, but also felt that it needed its own space from them since octopi like to do different things than fish. The octopus thought that maybe it could use one of its arms to reach up to play with the mermaid if it could still be touching its cave. The octopus also realized that it had eight arms and that there were eight other creatures in the ocean with it. It wasn't quite sure what that meant, but it seemed significant.

Hypothesizing, but not assuming, that the images in the aquarium were metaphors for this family's current dynamics, the therapist deducted the following:

- José, the oldest son, was demonstrating developmentally appropriate steps in gaining independence from his family as he prepared to leave home and go to college in a different state. Though he still very much saw himself as part of the family and had an especially close relationship with his mom, he was ready to begin asserting his independence from the rest of the family.
- Likewise, Monica was on her own developmentally appropriate path to gaining independence from the rest of the family and felt as though she was straddling two worlds – one with her family and one with her friends.
- The increased independence of both José and Monica was at times difficult for the others in adjusting to a new structure that didn't involve them in family activities as much as it used to. As a result, it appeared that Jasmine, the youngest of Manuel and Blanca's three children, was feeling left behind, especially as their three younger cousins joined the household, taking over the role of the youngest in the family and some of the attention that was normally paid to her. Though they all wanted to spend time with her, this appeared to leave her wanting to retreat even more, feeling like she didn't quite fit in.
- Marcello, the oldest of the three younger children, appeared to be having the hardest time being away from his mom. Within this new household structure, Marcello was now a middle child, as opposed to the oldest, and appeared to be having a difficult time finding his place.
- Vincent appeared to be taking on a caretaking role with his little sister. His concern for Jasmine also indicated a tendency for him to take on this role in relationships. Encouragement from adults in the family to play and have fun, and assurance that they would care for Sandra and Jasmine, could allow Vincent the freedom stop worrying about others as much or feel the need to be in two places at once.
- Sandra appeared to be adjusting well and might benefit from spending time with friends, Manuel, and Blanca, to give Jasmine more space and to allow Vincent to not have to worry about caring for her as much.
- Manuel and Blanca both appeared to be missing the structure that their family once had before their children began gaining greater independence but seemed understanding and supportive of them in these transitions. Though unsure of how to help the younger children, they appeared to want to help in whatever ways they could.

In this instance, the family followed the therapist's lead in discussing in the metaphor of the family's aquarium and did not discuss their own identities or relationships as they related to the creatures in the scene. Yet, the activity appeared to be felt on a deeply personal and intimate level that allowed them to process thoughts, feelings, and relational dynamics that had not been previously attended to.

Following the activity, José moved away to college and Jasmine moved into José's old room, allowing her increased independence and space from the rest of the family when needed. Manuel and Blanca made a point of spending extra time with Jasmine doing things that she wanted without the younger children around. They also paid extra attention to Marcello, who remained shy, but happier, and arranged playdates for Sandra, which appeared to remove pressure from both Vincent and Jasmine in terms of needing to care for and entertain the youngest of the bunch. Vincent still helped his little sister and others in the family as needed but was more likely to follow his own interests and appeared

Figure 18.3 Mixed-media aquarium follow-up. Credit: Dr. Christine Walsh Borst, Erin Dierickx, Spencer Erwin, Nicole Ma, Cary Plewka, Mikaela Quintinita, Addison, Charlie, and Rebecca A. Cobb.

more carefree in his interactions with the family. Jasmine began to engage more in family activities again, and especially began to enjoy spending more time with Monica.

Several months after the initial aquarium activity took place, Maria returned home and moved in with the rest of the family. The family returned to therapy and the therapist revisited the aquarium, this time with Maria present.

Before revisiting the aquarium activity, the therapist made a copy of the initial scene to preserve the image of the initial aquarium and afford the opportunity to make changes and to create an altered scene. The therapist brought up the image of the final aquarium scene and shared it with the family. After explaining the activity to Maria, the therapist asked Maria if she would like to create her own character to add to the aquarium. She agreed, quickly made a starfish in the session, and sent the therapist a photo of it. The therapist asked Maria where she would like to place the starfish and added it to the aquarium. The therapist then told the family that sometimes things change within aquariums and asked them if there was anything that they thought should be different.

In this altered scene (see Figure 18.3), two headstones were added near the sunken ship. The starfish was placed halfway in and out of the water, above the headstones. The jellyfish came out of hiding near the surface of the water, next to the starfish. The pom pom fish joined closely behind, but near the treasure. The colorful fish lost its blue fish counterpart, allowing the octopus to still have enough arms to reach each creature in the ocean. The nudibranch and mermaid remained in the same positions, but the mermaid was happy to play with the octopus, who had come out of its cave. Finally, the clownfish and sponge moved more central to the scene where they could stay close to everyone in it.

Suggestions for Follow-Up

Gil and Sobol (2005) suggest taking photographs of the family's work and sharing them in follow-up sessions. Because the outcome of this activity is finalized in digital form, you can keep a digital copy of the aquarium in the clients' file and return to the aquarium in follow-up sessions for continued assessment and further discussion. Hypothesizing, but not assuming, that the images and creatures in the aquarium are metaphors for the family's dynamics, you can use information gathered from this activity to engage in further discussion with the family, both in and out of the metaphor of the aquarium. You might ask the clients if they would like to make any changes to the aquarium. If this is the case, save the original aquarium to a separate file so that the original aquarium can still be accessed after changes have been made. Alternatively, you might give the family the option of creating a new aquarium (e.g., Gil & Sobol, 2005) to allow the opportunity to create and share something entirely different. In either case, both aquariums might then be compared in a discussion about what's changed and what has stayed the same.

Contraindications

Clients may not have access to resources suggested for conducting this activity. Because this activity relies on clients having physical materials, first consider the family's ability to acquire prerequisite materials prior to introducing the activity. Ask adults in the family what crafting materials they have in the home. For clients with the means to do so, you could ask adults in the family to purchase necessary materials. For families who can't afford this, you might consider sending materials to adults in the family ahead of time, with permission (see Chapter 8). Alternatively, you could introduce the activity with fewer required materials (e.g., paper and pen/pencil). For families without access to a digital camera or smartphone, families could take photographs with their computer cameras.

Reflections by Eliana Gil

It was wonderful to learn about this virtual adaptation of the aquarium project, initially done exclusively in person. Dr. Cobb aptly describes the rationale for using this art activity both during assessment and treatment; what technology is required to transform it from in-person to virtual; and illustrates how the technique can be processed by showing pictures of completed work. I have always encouraged clinicians to use these activities as a springboard for the integration of other ways of working, other priorities, etc. I read with interest as Dr. Cobb made adjustments in a thoughtful and successful manner.

Having used this activity for decades, I will offer some observations designed to further elicit discussion.

1. I like to see what emerges when everyone receives the same directive to "draw a fish," as opposed to the directive that they "create a fish or other water creature," because a client's choice to deviate from the directive could include a meaningful communication. When asked to "draw a fish, any fish at all," I discovered that sometimes family members show their perception of feeling different from others by drawing something other than a fish. Sometimes people draw sea creatures spontaneously and this interests and inspires others. I have seen people make sea urchins, starfish, turtles, seahorses, etc. in response to the directive to draw a fish. My assumption is that whatever is drawn will have a projective component. I believe that few images are drawn by accident and usually have some relevance to the artist.
2. Dr. Cobb, likewise, discusses the option of expanding the directive so that clients have the choice of making an aquarium or another body of water. Interestingly, when I was first developing and testing this activity with families, I gave people the option of making "a body of water," and sometimes families wanted oceans, lakes, ponds, or streams. One especially splintered family had half of the family members creating a fresh water option and the other half creating an ocean, thus

highlighting their differences and lack of connection. As mentioned in the directive about drawing fish versus water creatures, I encourage everyone to consider the aquarium project rather than specify a different option. Aquariums are a well-known physical structure that serves as a home for a variety of fish, and thus, can serve as an organizing principle for this activity. Most individuals are familiar with how aquariums run, that is, that you have to figure out how to feed the fish, what the temperature of the water will be, how much light will descend into the tank, what fish can get along, etc. In addition, most aquariums have objects where fish feel camouflaged, where they can play, and where small particles of food gather. Thus, I prefer the aquarium metaphor for families to use as a basic structure.

3. One of my initial reactions when I learned the aquarium project could be virtual was bemoaning the lack of a sensory or kinesthetic experience. So often, using art materials, glue, cutting things out, or touching other objects such as puff balls or feathers can interact with the individual's nervous system, causing a sense of relaxation or triggering warm memories. I was interested to read that Dr. Cobb's clients are instructed to make the art at home, which still provides this touch component, photograph what they create, and then send back to the therapist for cropping and filing. A shared screen online allows clients to collaboratively pick the objects they want for their environment. A final task is for clients to ensure that the therapist can place their fish or water creatures precisely where they want them to be. It appears that selecting images and creating virtual aquariums still possesses the possibility of using creative imagination, and the clients' ability to direct the therapist on the screen could provide a sense of mastery.

This activity has endless possibilities for family discussion and it was wonderful to read Dr. Cobb's clinical example and have her discuss both her interpretations and how she would approach the metaphors that the family built. This example is rich and powerful and clearly demonstrates how invested families can become in this project, how clinicians and families can interact to help them reflect and gain insight based on their artwork, and how valuable it can be to collaborate on a project like this, which provides an alternative language for communicating, decreases ambivalence about participating in therapy, and offers a shared experience that feels constructive and valuable.

References

Gil, E. (1994). *Play in family therapy.* Guilford Press.
Gil, E. (2014). *Play in family therapy* (2nd ed.). Guilford Press.
Gil, E., & Sobol, B. (2005). Engaging families in therapeutic play. In C. E. Bailey (Ed.), *Children in therapy: Using the family as a resource* (pp. 341–382). Norton.
Schaefer, C. E. (Ed.). (1993). *The therapeutic powers of play.* Jason Aronson.

CHAPTER 19

ONLINE CHILD OUTCOME RATING SCALE

THE PARTNERS FOR CHANGE OUTCOME MANAGEMENT SYSTEM

Lisa René Reynolds and Barry L. Duncan [1]

Materials for Therapists and Clients: Child Outcome Rating Scale (CORS). Paper-and-pencil versions and oral scripts can be downloaded in 36 languages at https://betteroutcomesnow.com. A Young Child Outcome Rating Scale is also available for children under six but is not scored or available digitally.

Objective

Validated for use with children 6–12 years of age (Duncan et al., 2006), the CORS is a four-item self-report instrument that assesses a child's perspective of progress in therapy as well as that of their caregivers. While paper-and-pencil versions of the measure and oral scripts are available, this chapter offers instructions on how to use online versions of the CORS using the Partners for Change Outcome Management System (PCOMS; Duncan & Reese, 2015) when working with children via teletherapy.

Rationale for Use

The CORS (Duncan et al., 2003) is the first of two measures of PCOMS (Duncan & Reese, 2015). PCOMS is an evidence-based practice supported by ten randomized clinical trials that report significantly improved outcomes and reduced dropouts in therapy (Duncan & Sparks, 2024). Collaborative monitoring of outcomes using the CORS increases client engagement, tailors services to client preferences, heightens hope for improvement, and enhances the therapeutic alliance (Duncan, 2014). Routinely requesting, documenting, and responding to client feedback also transforms power relations by privileging client beliefs and goals over potentially culturally biased and insensitive practices (Sparks & Duncan, 2018).

Setup

The PCOMS employs two four-item scales intended for use in every session. The CORS focuses on outcome and the Child Session Rating Scale (see Chapter 20) assesses the therapeutic alliance. It includes

DOI: 10.4324/9781003330912-23

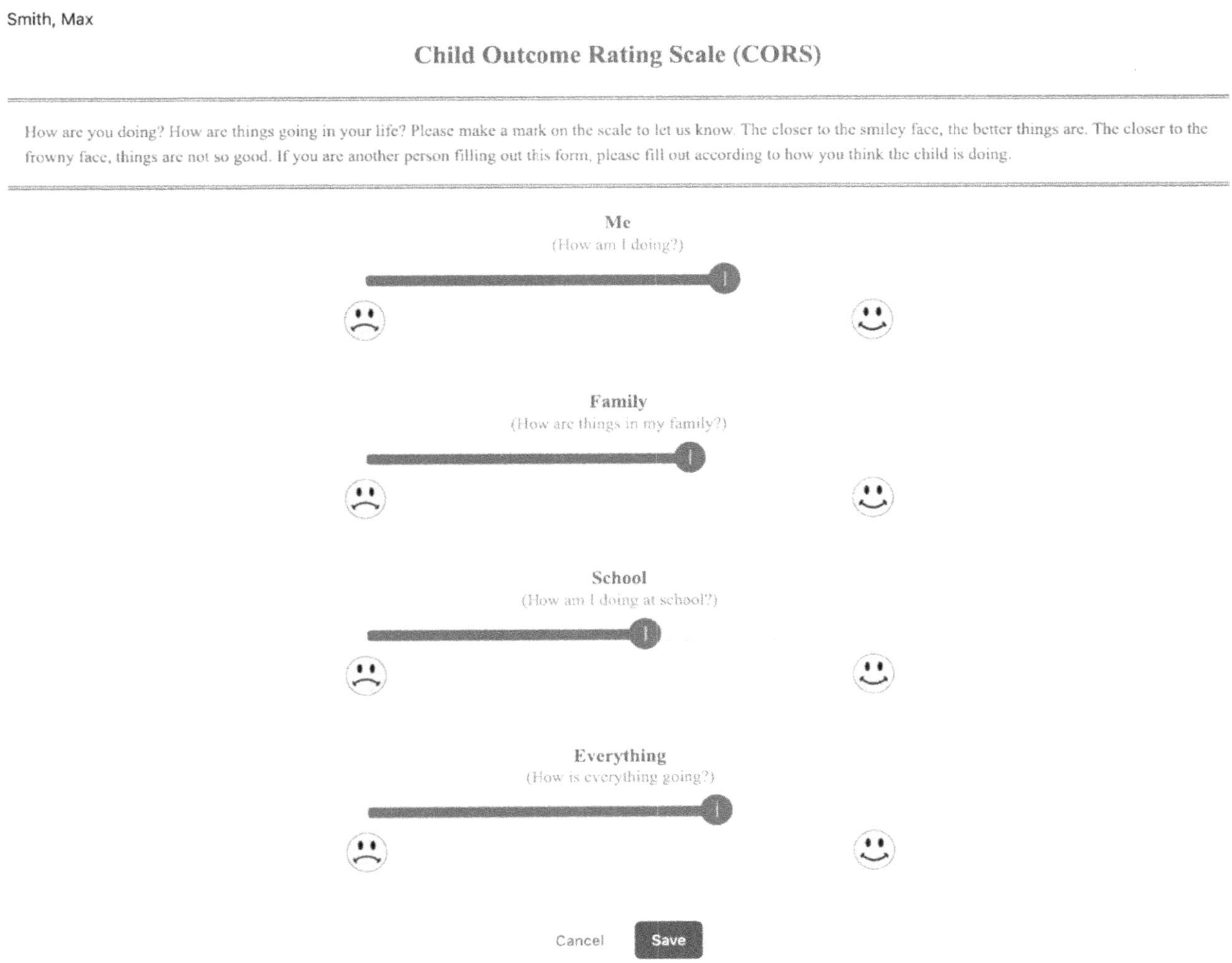

Figure 19.1 CORS in Better Outcomes Now.

a real-time collaborative comparison of client views of outcome with an expected treatment response (ETR) that serves as a yardstick for gauging client progress and signaling when change is not occurring as predicted. With this alert, therapists and clients have an opportunity to shift focus, re-visit goals, or alter interventions before deterioration or dropout. PCOMS is a checking-in process that usually takes about five to ten minutes to administer and integrate into therapy, depending on the number of clients involved. The CORS provides a mutually understood reference point for reasons for seeking service, progress, and engagement.

An inspection of Figure 19.1 reveals that rather than a symptom checklist on a Likert scale, the CORS is a visual analog scale consisting of four 10 cm lines, corresponding to four domains (i.e., me, family, school, everything), allowing for the client's idiosyncratic rendering of their life circumstance, including concerns like discrimination and deportation (Duncan & Reese, 2024). Smiley and frowny faces provide useful endpoints for this age group. Adolescents use the adult Outcome Rating Scale (Miller et al., 2003). Clients place a touch or a click on an iPad or phone on each 0–10 scale. A maximum score is 40 with lower scores reflecting more distress.

When a family enters services because of a problem related to a child, the parent scores the CORS based on their perception of how the child is doing as well as the child. When the family presents with a shared problem (e.g., divorce, illness), everyone takes their own age-appropriate measure. When the child is presented as the problem, the differences between parent ratings and child ratings (and others like teachers) offer additional insight and are very helpful for generating solutions. Teachers and other significant people in the child's life are assessed as often as practical but at least once per month of service.

While the use of paper-and-pencil measures and oral scripts is possible for teletherapy, online versions offer a more practical way of using the CORS, tracking results, and hosting discussions.

Instructions

Accessing the online CORS for teletherapy requires a paid subscription to Better Outcomes Now (BON) or another software system. Investigate available options and find the best fit for your practices. The online CORS enables a seamless way to replicate face-to-face encounters during teletherapy as well as the convenience of automatic scoring, graphing, and analysis.

Specific teletherapy instructions vary by software system. To administer the CORS in BON in one of eleven available languages, first provide login details to clients so that they can create their own accounts, using either the web or the available app. You can share your screen from the web version of BON or clients can access the measures through their own account via the web or an accompanying app. Children and parents both have accounts allowing flexibility for how teletherapy sessions are provided, including individual sessions with one family member. Once the measures are completed, you can share the screen of the graph with all the scores (see Figure 19.3). Clients can complete the measures independently and review their results, although collaborative administration is preferred and discussion of client progress is critical to the evidence based, PCOMS protocol. Families can take turns and complete the CORS on the same device, or each can use their own device.

It is important that clients understand two points: (1) the CORS is used to track progress in every session to ensure benefit and (2) the CORS ensures that the client's voice about progress is not only heard but also remains central. Introducing the CORS to families requires tailoring language according to the age and cognitive capabilities of multiple family members.

Processing

In the first meeting, the CORS pinpoints where the client sees themselves, allowing for an ongoing comparison in later sessions. The CORS allows everything to be totally upfront right from the beginning—the agreements and disagreements that everyone knows about, except the therapist, until now. Graphs provided by online software promote a visual catalyst for discussion, illustrating differences in responses of family members and trends over time. Clients can view the graphs independently as well as with their therapist.

The individual graph (see Figure 19.2) helps everyone understand what their score means and how the scores reflect their reason for seeking therapy. Toggle to each family member, sharing the screen of the graph, and comment on clients' scores in relation to the cutoff and the domains. Twenty-eight is the cutoff for children and caretakers, meaning that, on average, persons seeking clinical services will fall below that, and those not typically seeking counseling will score above. Let each person know, in everyday language, whether they are above or below the cutoff. For those showing below cutoff scores, assure them that they made a good decision to come to therapy, that their score suggests they are looking for a change. For those scoring above the cutoff, simply validate their score by saying that it looks like things are going pretty well, which leads to the next logical question, "What are the reasons for meeting at this time?"

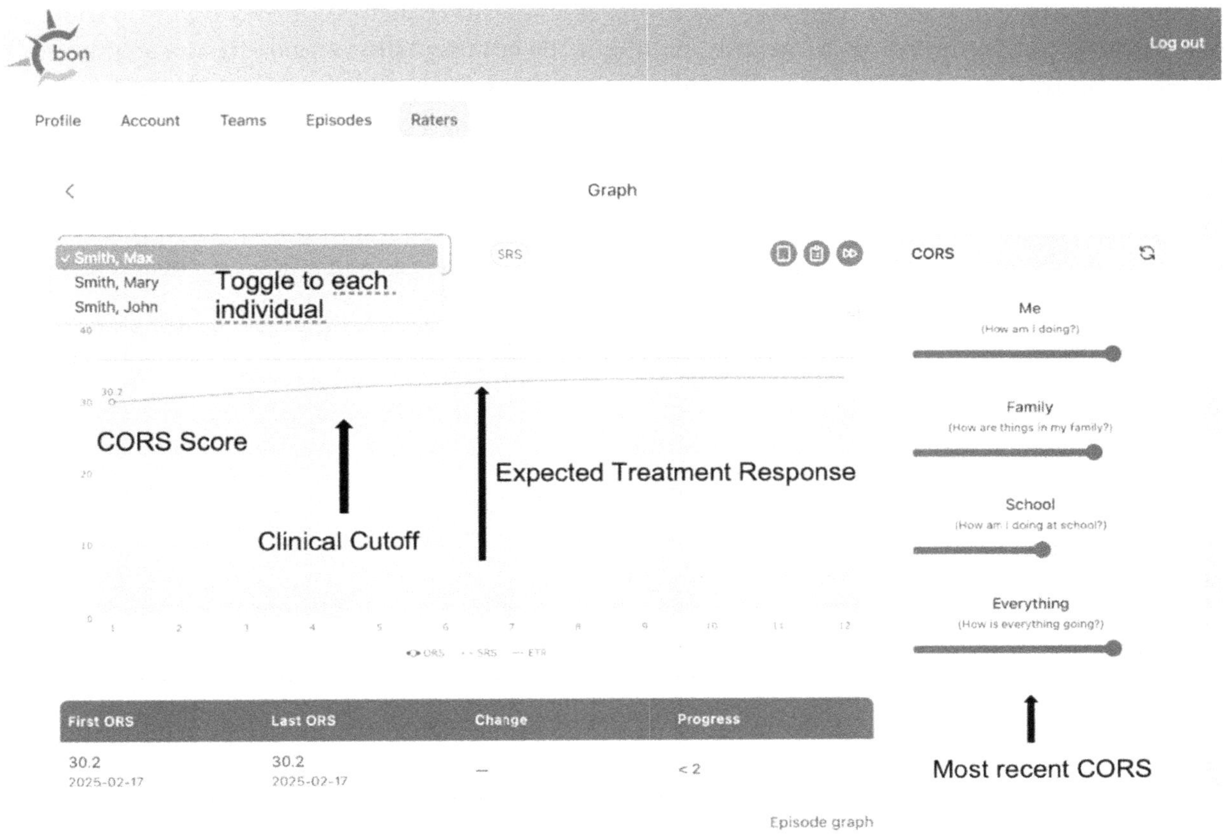

Figure 19.2 Graph allowing toggle of family member CORS scores, clinical cutoff, and ETR in Better Outcomes Now.

When this is done well, the CORS is no longer a disembodied, pro forma exercise. Instead, it becomes a graphic link to real feelings and events occurring in clients' lives. This process is the beginning of creating a shared understanding of the reason for service and what they hope to achieve. Comments about the cutoff also teach clients about what their scores mean in terms of the instrument (not the substance behind it which only can be learned from clients). Clients learn to understand the significance of the ETR as a yardstick, based in two million administrations, for being on or off-track as therapy progresses. The ETR is explained as "what we hope will happen if our work together is successful." Again, the online graph visually illustrates and reinforces what the scores mean as well as the expected or hoped-for change.

Clients usually score the domain that reflects the reason for service lower than the rest (see Figure 19.1). Of note, when a child scores above the cutoff, they will often still provide a clue to what is troubling them by placing one mark lower than others. The domain scores also offer a glimpse of what is going well in a person's life. Simply seeing which domain or domains are scored lower allows the therapist to focus on the most distressed dimension. You can comment on this area and ask if the score on that lowest domain represents the reason for seeking counseling. Or you can allow the conversation to reveal the reason for service and then make the connection to the lowest domain. Once that is established, there is a shared understanding regarding which domain is the focal point for tracking change. The moment clients connect the marks on the CORS with the situations that prompt their seeking help, the CORS becomes a meaningful measure of progress and a potent clinical tool. And that moment facilitates the next question, "What do you think it will take to move your mark just one cm to the right?"

Families either agree about their views of the level and areas of distress or they do not. When they agree, you can comment on it as a strength, highlight the commonality, and use it as a steppingstone to establish mutual goals. Different scores are to be expected and simply represent the complexity of working with more than one in the room as well as generational perspectives. For starters, different scores are concrete and visible, allowing therapists to inquire early on about everyone's unique perceptions and beliefs. The sooner this is done, the quicker goals for each person can be identified and efforts made to link these into a common strategy and mutually desired endpoint. Alternatively, discrepant scores may persist, and you can successfully validate those differences and still work toward a positive outcome.

The instrument puts those differences front and center in the first minutes of the session. Children, who are often "mandated" to therapy, may score higher on the CORS (indicating less distress) than their caregiver's rating. The discussion of distress via the CORS scores shines a light on these important issues, allowing open discussion and subsequent planning for how therapy can meet each individual's needs.

Vignette

Max (8) and his mother and father presented in teletherapy after Max's school reached out several times regarding his "acting out." After providing instructions about the telehealth process and online software, the therapist introduced the family to the CORS to facilitate a more complete understanding of each family member's experience and perceptions of improvement.

In the first session, the father scored Max well within the distressed range, the mother scored him slightly below the cutoff, and Max scored himself well above the cutoff. The therapist shared her screen and displayed the family graph with all three scores, opening the door for a discussion of divergent and congruent viewpoints. The father described being called regularly by the school because of his son's defiant behavior. To the mother, whose work required her to travel frequently, these calls were concerning but less urgent. When home, she and her son enjoyed going to the park, playing games, and watching movies together. Max was asked how he thought his teacher might score him, and he admitted it would be lower on the school domain. When the therapist asked each member of the family if that domain would need to improve for them to feel therapy was successful, they all agreed. In a parent meeting, the therapist's inquiry about differences in the parents' scores prompted Max's father to reveal his isolation as a parent, leading to goals of better communication and joint involvement in disciplining.

A major value of CORS is its capacity to initiate conversations about discrepant views in objective, non-blaming ways. The therapist's inquiry about the differences in CORS scores set the stage for developing mutual goals and a means to measure success. The transparency of the PCOMS process establishes a space where all views are respected and meanings are co-explored. Continuous responsiveness to clients' unique views, grounded in valid, objective data, fosters dialogue, the emergence of mutual solutions, and a built-in safety net for avoiding treatment failure.

Suggestions for Follow-Up

After the first session, PCOMS simply asks: Are things better or not? The CORS scores engage the individual child and/or family in a discussion about progress, and more importantly, what should be done differently if progress has not been made. While there may be agreement regarding the two possible change scenarios, it may be that there are different views. This is, of course, the challenge—to create

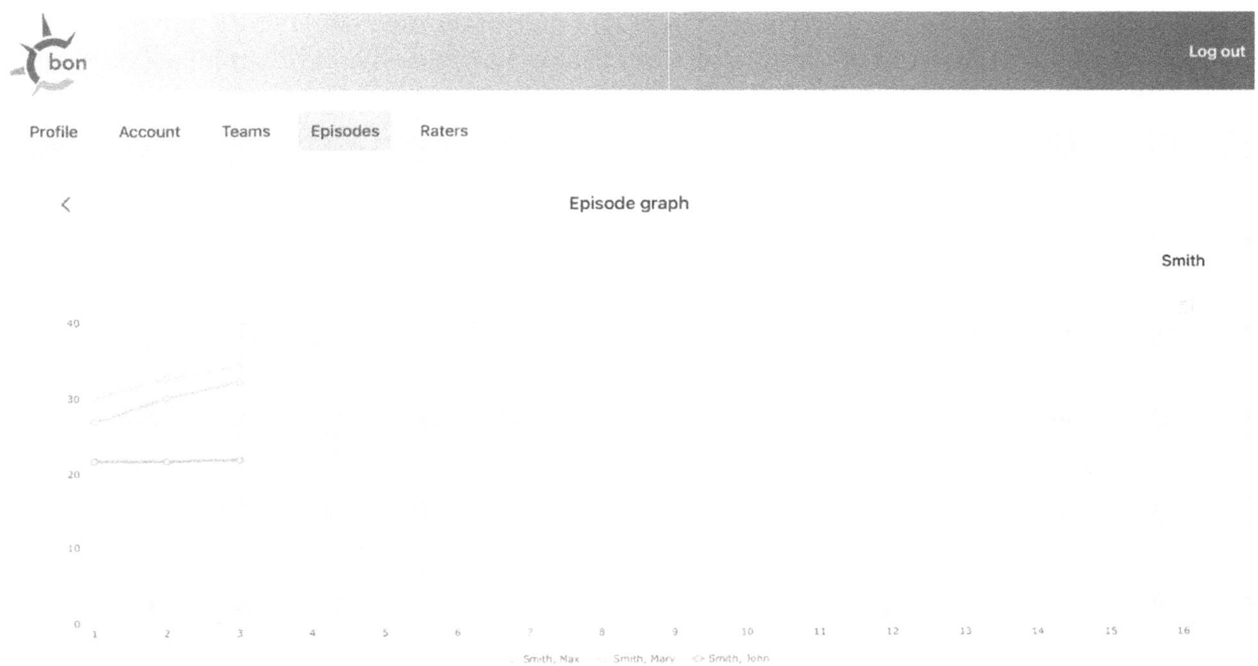

Figure 19.3 Family graph depicting three family members, one not benefitting, in Better Outcomes Now.

a therapeutic context where everyone, different views and all, benefits. While you may continue to toggle and share the individual graphs of the family members (see Figure 19.2), the family graph of all members (see Figure 19.3) visually depicts agreements and disagreements, stimulating important discussions.

Regardless of the congruence or discrepancy between client scores, the task of the therapist throughout treatment is to identify client perceptions of progress and respond appropriately. When CORS scores increase, a crucial step to empower change is to help clients see any gains as a consequence of their own efforts. Reliable and clinically significant change provides useful metrics to gauge noted gains. Reliable change is six points or more on the CORS; clinically significant change is a change of six points or more and crossing the clinical cutoff. The ETR also provides a quick visual representation, comparing achieved versus expected or hoped-for change.

A more important discussion occurs when CORS scores are not increasing. The longer therapy continues without measurable change, the greater the likelihood of dropout and/or poor outcome. PCOMS stimulates all interested parties to reflect on the implications of continuing a process that is yielding little or no benefit. Although addressed in each meeting in which it is apparent no change is occurring, later sessions gain increasing significance and warrant additional action—so-called checkpoint conversations and last-chance discussions. Online software provides a more sophisticated identification of clients at risk by comparing the client's progress to the ETR.

Checkpoint conversations are conducted at the third to sixth session and last-chance discussions are initiated in the sixth to ninth meetings. The trajectories observed in outpatient settings suggest that most clients who benefit usually show it in three to six sessions (Duncan 2014). If change is not noted by then, the client is at risk for a negative outcome. The same goes for sessions six through nine, except that the urgency is increased, hence the term "last chance."

The progression of the conversation with clients who are not benefiting goes from talking about whether something different should be done, to identifying what can be done differently, to doing something different. Doing something different can include inviting others from the client's support system, using a team, developing a different conceptualization of the problem, trying another approach, or referring to another therapist or venue of service such as a religious advisor or self-help group, whatever seems to be of value to the client.

Sharing the online graphs spotlights the lack of change, making it impossible to ignore, and often ignites both therapist and the family into action—to consider other treatment options and evaluate whether another provider may offer a different set of options and perhaps a better match with client preferences, culture, and frame of reference.

Contraindications

Although the paper-and-pencil version of the PCOMS measures can be downloaded for free for individual use, web-based applications require annual paid subscriptions, which may not be affordable for some.

Note

1 Barry L. Duncan is a coholder of the copyright of PCOMS instruments. The measures are free for individuals, but Duncan receives royalties from licenses issued to groups and organizations. In addition, the web-based application of PCOMS, https://betteroutcomesnow.com, is a commercial product, and he receives profits based on sales.

References

Duncan, B. L. (2014). *On becoming a better therapist: Evidence based practice one client at a time* (2nd ed.). American Psychological Association.

Duncan, B., Miller, S., & Sparks, J. (2003). *The child outcome rating scale*. Author. https://betteroutcomesnow.com/download-ors-srs/

Duncan, B. L., & Reese, R. J. (2015). The Partners for Change Outcome Management System (PCOMS) revisiting the client's frame of reference. *Psychotherapy, 52*(4), 391–401. https://doi.org/10.1037/pst0000026

Duncan, B. L., & Reese, R. J. (2024). The evolution of feedback: Toward a multicultural orientation. *Psychotherapy, 61*(2), 101–109. https://doi.org/10.1037/pst0000524

Duncan, B. L., & Sparks, J. A. (2024). *The Partners for Change Outcome Management System Manual* (4th ed.). Author.

Duncan, B. L., Sparks, J., Miller, S., Bohanske, R., & Claud, D. (2006). Giving youth a voice: A preliminary study of the reliability and validity of a brief outcome measure for children, adolescents, and caretakers. *Journal of Brief Therapy, 5*, 71–87.

Miller, S. D., Duncan, B. L., Brown, J., Sparks, J. A., & Claud, D. A. (2003). The outcome rating scale: A preliminary study of the reliability, validity, and feasibility of a brief visual analog measure. *Journal of Brief Therapy, 2*(2), 91–100.

Sparks, J. A., & Duncan, B. L. (2018). The Partners for Change Outcome Management System: A both/and system for collaborative practice. *Family Process, 57*(3), 800–816. https://doi.org/10.1111/famp.12345

CHAPTER 20

ONLINE CHILD SESSION RATING SCALE

THE PARTNERS FOR CHANGE OUTCOME MANAGEMENT SYSTEM

Lisa René Reynolds and Barry L. Duncan[1]

Materials for Therapists and Clients: Child Session Rating Scale (CSRS; Duncan et al., 2003a). Paper-and-pencil measures and oral scripts are free for individual use and can be downloaded in 36 languages at https://betteroutcomesnow.com. A Young Child Session Rating Scale is available for children under six but is not scored and only available in paper and pencil.

Objective

The CSRS (Duncan et al., 2003b) is the second of two measures of the evidence-based, measurement-based care system, the Partners for Change Outcome Management System (PCOMS). Designed for use with children 6–12 years of age, the four-item CSRS assesses a child's experience of the therapeutic alliance, while the Session Rating Scale (SRS) gives voice to the parent's experience. Although paper-and-pencil versions of the measure and oral scripts are available, this chapter provides instructions for using the online CSRS with children in teletherapy.

Rationale for Use

See Chapter 19 for the rationales for PCOMS (the evidence-based use of the Child Outcome Rating Scale [CORS] and CSRS). The rationale for use of the CSRS is based in the overwhelming research demonstrating that a strong alliance, from the client's point of view, predicts engagement in therapy and ultimate outcomes (e.g., Flückiger et al., 2018), regardless of therapist model, modality, or age of client. Additionally, inviting children to collaboratively monitor the "fit" of the therapist and interventions has several benefits (Sparks & Duncan, 2018): (1) ensures that children have a structured presence in their treatment; (2) encourages collaboration with the child, increasing the chances of a sound alliance; and (3) stimulates the therapist to try new strategies or incorporate different features based on client feedback. Finally, the SRS/CSRS also allows social location differences between clients and therapists to be transparently and routinely discussed. By routinizing the asking for and receiving of client feedback

DOI: 10.4324/9781003330912-24

about their experience of therapy, the alliance measures promote openness to client perspectives, laying the foundation for cultural comfort and humility (Duncan & Reese, 2024).

Setup

The CSRS is designed to be a checking-in process that continues the culture of client privilege and feedback established by the CORS. Administering and discussing the CORS and CSRS together usually takes about five to ten minutes to administer and discuss, depending on the number of clients in the session. Alliance measures must be given from a position of really wanting the feedback, especially negative feedback. The first order of business is to include the CSRS as part of your closing ritual. For example, with a child, you may start the ritual at five minutes before the end of the session and with a family at

Figure 20.1 CSRS in Better Outcomes Now.

ten minutes. The ritual might include a summary or "take-home message," or an assignment, and then the measures and discussion.

An inspection of Figure 20.1 reveals that the CSRS is a visual analog scale consisting of four 10 cm lines, corresponding to four alliance-based domains: "Listening," "How Important," "What We Did," and "Overall," with smiley/frowny faces at each end identifying a continuum of experience. Clients place a touch or a click on an iPad or phone on each 0–10 scale. The CSRS aims to create a "safe space" for clients to voice their honest opinions and track children's views of how well they are connected to their counselor and whether they are on board with what is being talked about (goals) and what is being done (tasks/methods) in meetings. Parents rate the CORS (see Chapter 19) regarding their perspective of the child, but they use the adult SRS to give their own view of the alliance. Adolescents also use the adult SRS.

Clients will often indicate a concern on the CSRS/SRS long before they would have brought it up otherwise. The CSRS requires therapist comfortability about asking for feedback and a graceful response that accommodates the work to the feedback—an authentic desire for a frank discussion about client preferences regarding the alliance.

While paper-and-pencil versions of the measure and oral scripts are available, online versions offer a more convenient option for teletherapy with automatic scoring, graphing, and tracking of results, as well as greater visibility of client responses to stimulate discussion.

Accessing the CSRS electronically for teletherapy requires a paid subscription to Better Outcomes Now (BON) or other software services. Investigate available options and find the best fit for your practices.

Instructions

Specific teletherapy instructions vary by software system. To administer the CSRS in BON in one of eleven available languages, first provide login details to clients so that they can create their own accounts, using either the web or available app. You can share your screen from the web version of BON or clients can access the measures through their own account via the web or an accompanying app. Children and parents both have accounts allowing flexibility for how the teletherapy sessions are provided, including individual sessions with one family member. Once the measures are completed, you can share the screen of the graph and toggle the family member scores for comparison. Clients can complete the measures independently and review their results, although collaborative administration is preferred and discussion of the alliance is critical to the evidence-based, PCOMS protocol. Families can take turns and complete the CSRS on the same device, or each can use their own device.

Consider who will participate in the session and who will take the measures. You may use the CSRS with all children in the session for joining and inclusion purposes and then exclude the data that seem irrelevant. Leave enough time for clients to fill out the alliance measures and process their scores. A closing ritual that fits your therapeutic style and includes the CSRS is a way to ensure that time is set aside.

For clients to feel comfortable giving alliance feedback, it must be clear that there is no "bad news" on the alliance measure and that you truly want to know how you can improve the client experience of therapy—and are not looking for compliments or are fearful about receiving feedback. Here are samples of how to introduce the CSRS and SRS to a child and parent.

To a child: Before we end today, I would like to ask you to fill out another form that has faces on it. This one is about how our meeting went for you today. It's kind of like you are grading me! It's very important for me to make sure that this is going well for you. Do you want to help me with that?

To a parent: This is the other short form that we will be doing at the end of every meeting. This helps us stay on track so we can make our work together as beneficial to you as possible. It's kind of like taking the temperature of our meeting so I can adjust the thermostat if necessary. Would that be okay?

Processing

Clients tend to score all alliance measures high and the SRS/CSRS are no exception. Hence, the cutoff is 36 out of a possible 40. For the CSRS and SRS, the conversation is far more important than the numbers. Seemingly paradoxical to many, therapists should strive for lower scores because they represent the client's comfort with the counselor and the therapeutic process. Graphs provided by online software promote a visual catalyst for discussion, illustrating differences in responses of family members and trends over time.

Any scale lower than the rest is an opportunity for discussion as is any scale less than 9 cm. For clients scoring above 36, the therapist needs only to thank the client, inquire about what the client found particularly helpful, and invite the client to please inform the therapist if anything can improve the therapy. For clients scoring below 36, the conversation is similar but also attempts to explore what can be done to improve the therapy. The SRS/CSRS provides a structure to address the alliance, allows an opportunity to fix any problems, and demonstrates that you want to form good relationships. The individual graph (see Figure 20.2) helps everyone understand their score as well as how other family members are experiencing the alliance.

Children love completing the CSRS and the way they give unfiltered feedback is both wonderful and entertaining. Adults will very rarely rate below 32, regardless of how much they dislike the therapist, the session, or both. But not children. They may give all zeros! Remember that all feedback is good feedback, and graceful acceptance and exploration will further engage clients in treatment.

The "What We Did" section often leads to suggestions by children about what can make therapy a better experience for them. It is important to ask children about a lower mark on this line

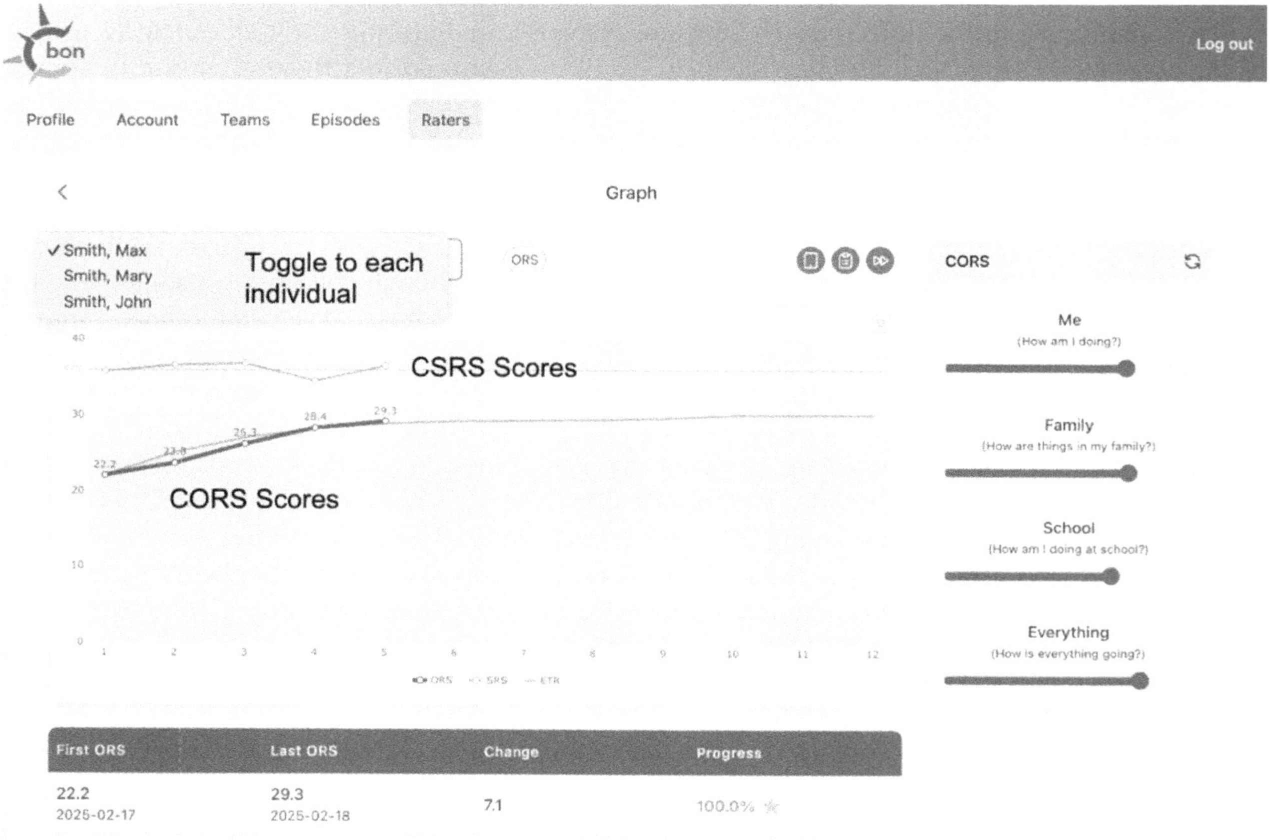

Figure 20.2 Graph depicting CSRS scores and allowing toggle of family members in Better Outcomes Now.

and to take their response seriously. While some young people might be the dream client and say something like "I really don't think we talked enough about my feelings about the divorce," many children are more likely to say something like, "I wanted to play that game we played the last time" or "I want to make some more slime." It may be tempting to keep trying to woo children to do more talking and less playing, but savvy counselors know that, for most children, talk and play go hand in hand. The point is that CSRS gives counselors a guidepost for finding out what exactly will engage clients.

Vignette

Aria (9) was in third grade and presented in teletherapy with her parents following a sudden decline in her grades at school. Her teacher reported that she seemed more withdrawn and often refused to do work in class. Her parents reported that at home she was also more withdrawn and seemed quicker to anger with her two younger sisters. The parents added that although it was amicable, they were beginning the process of divorce.

The therapist gave the parents login instructions and the parents followed Aria's request to have her own account on her tablet. The parents took the CORS and SRS on their laptop while Aria completed the CORS and CSRS on her iPad. With some guidance, Aria completed the measures. The therapist shared her screen and discussed the different CORS scores, all of which were in the distressed area of the graph (see Chapter 19). While the parents scored the SRS as completely satisfied, Aria scored the CSRS quite low, 12.3. When the therapist explored the score with her, she only said that she was bored and her parents were mean.

Consequently, the therapist saw Aria alone for the next two sessions to try to build a better alliance with her and further explore her thoughts and feelings about the pending divorce. The strategy worked. CSRS scores improved substantially and the CORS scores of both Aria and her parents increased coinciding with teacher reports of better work completion. The therapist decided it was time to involve the parents again especially since Aria shared some anger toward her parents for "being harder on me than on my sisters."

At the end of the family session, Aria was again asked to rate the CSRS. This time, Aria's rating was to the far left of the continuum, close to the frowny faces, with a total score of 6.3. Aria seemed very angry and refused to discuss her ratings. She simply said she didn't want to go to therapy anymore. Her parents, however, convinced Aria to return to another session. At the next meeting, the therapist noticed Aria's continued angry demeanor and asked again about the frowny face score that Aria had chosen at the end of the last session. Finally, Aria looked up at the therapist and said, "I'm mad at you for inviting my parents into our session last week without telling me. I don't want them to be here with me. I hate how they always make me out to be the problem and you let them do that in the session. It's their fault everything is changing because they're getting divorced."

Armed with vital feedback from Aria, the therapist restructured how she planned to work with Aria and her parents moving forward, making sure Aria had her personal time with the therapist in each family session, carefully noting the CSRS feedback. The therapist met with the parents separately within the family sessions to help them with best practices for talking with the children about their divorce, as well as continuing their strategies to encourage Aria's school performance and calmer behavior with her sisters. The therapist brought the family together at the end to administer the alliance measures.

The restructuring paid off. Aria's CSRS scores improved and her anger diminished toward her parents. After 15 sessions, Aria's and her parents' CORS scores increased reliably (>6 points), reflecting Aria's grade improvement, better relationships with her sisters, and more acceptance of the divorce.

Suggestions for Follow-Up

Once children and their caregivers understand what they are being asked to do and why, and they do it once or twice, they tend to go straight to the measure on their device as soon as the online meeting winds down. Briefly reminding adults and children of the purpose of the alliance as well as reassurance that the therapist really wants the feedback is never a bad idea. But therapist behavior is far more important than words. If the therapist is afraid of feedback or believes that the CSRS and SRS are measures of their competence, then that anxiety may shine through and clients may not share their experience.

CSRS scores engage clients in a discussion about their experience of therapy. While toggling between family members may reveal agreement or disagreement about family member perspectives of the alliance, this is of course the challenge of family work—to create a therapeutic context for everyone.

Starting meetings with CORS/ORS and ending with CSRS/SRS forms procedural boundaries for the session, beginning and endpoints of a shared experience. The ritual of collecting SRSs and CSRSs is a natural transition out of counseling and back into a summarizing, "checking-in" conversation. Your appreciation of any negative feedback is a powerful alliance builder. Graceful acceptance of any problems and a willingness to be flexible speak reams to clients. Punctuating this point is the finding that clients who report alliance problems are twice as likely to achieve a successful outcome. Lower scores on the CSRS or SRS, therefore, are good news and should be celebrated.

Contraindications

Although the paper-and-pencil version of the PCOMS measures can be downloaded for free for individual use, web-based applications require an annual paid subscription, which may not be affordable for some.

Note

1 Barry L. Duncan is a coholder of the copyright of PCOMS instruments. The measures are free for individuals, but Duncan receives royalties from licenses issued to groups and organizations. In addition, the web-based application of PCOMS, https://betteroutcomesnow.com, is a commercial product, and he receives profits based on sales.

References

Duncan, B., Miller, S., & Sparks, J. (2003a). *The child session rating scale*. Author. https://betteroutcomesnow.com/download-ors-srs/

Duncan, B. L., Miller, S. D., Sparks, J. A., Claud, D. A., Reynolds, L. R., Brown, J., & Johnson, L. D. (2003b). The session rating scale: Preliminary psychometric properties of a "working" alliance measure. *Journal of Brief Therapy, 3*(1), 3–12.

Duncan, B. L., & Reese, R. J. (2024). The evolution of feedback: Toward a multicultural orientation. *Psychotherapy*. Advance online publication. https://doi.org/10.1037/pst0000524

Flückiger, C., Del Re, A. C., Wampold, B. E., & Horvath, A. O. (2018). The alliance in adult psychotherapy: A meta-analytic synthesis. *Psychotherapy, 55*(4), 316–340. https://doi.org/10.1037/pst0000172

Sparks, J. A., & Duncan, B. L. (2018). The partners for change outcome management system: A both/and system for collaborative practice. *Family Process, 57*(3), 800–816. https://doi.org/10.1111/famp.12345.

Part 5

Interventions for Use with Multiple Presenting Problems

CHAPTER 21

INCREASING CONNECTION THROUGH BIBLIOTHERAPY IN A DIGITAL WORLD

Sarah Moran

Materials for Therapists: Children's book(s).

Materials for Clients: None.

Objective

Books have the ability to connect, enliven, develop, and validate a child's experience. In addition, shared reading with children promotes the development of empathy, theory of mind, and social-emotional skills (Gurdon, 2019). This chapter describes how to conduct bibliotherapy to increase connection between therapists and their clients via teletherapy.

Rationale for Use

Bibliotherapy is reading a book with a client to validate, normalize, and/or support the processing of the client's thoughts, feelings, and concerns. It can be used with individual clients, sibling groups, and families. Bibliotherapy is appropriate for working with children and adolescents of all ages because it can be adapted to meet individual preferences and developmental needs (Vetri et al., 2022). It can also be used in working with clients with many different presenting problems. Research demonstrates the efficacy of using bibliotherapy with children and adolescents struggling with anxiety, depression, trauma, having a parent with mental illness, coping with the death of a parent by suicide, and coping with a parent's deployment (Aydin & Basoglu, 2021; Tubbs et al., 2019; Vetri et al., 2022; Yuan et al., 2018). With bibliotherapy, children can listen to a story and just be; there is no pressure to perform. Yet connection is built in the space where a child and adult come together to share in the experience of reading out loud (Gurdon, 2019). Stories invite the listener to validate their experiences, confront their own problems, understand feelings, develop empathy, identify practical solutions, and find hope in knowing that their experience has been understood by others (Aydin & Basoglu, 2021; Gurdon, 2019).

When working with children and their caregivers, bibliotherapy supports joint attention, allowing both the child and caregivers to be present with one another, observing the brightly colored illustrations of a stationary object (Gurdon, 2019). Children often resent the competition of technology for their parents' attention. Reading together has the power to create intimacy and safety within the

DOI: 10.4324/9781003330912-26

parent-child relationship (Gurdon, 2019; Tubbs et al., 2019). With this approach, children and caregivers do not have to try to connect with one another, they just have to be present and participate in passive listening.

Bibliotherapy also provides therapists with the unique opportunity to provide psychoeducation to families in ways that meet the youngest participants where they are at developmentally and open a safe dialogue about difficult topics or experiences (Tubbs et al., 2019). Therapists provide guidance by modeling the use of appropriate language to have difficult conversations. This encourages caregivers to develop their own skills for conversing with their children, strengthening their bond.

Bibliotherapy is particularly helpful in teletherapy intervention. While telehealth occurs through a screen, treatment doesn't have to be screen focused. Bibliotherapy in telehealth provides children and adolescents with respite from the sensory overload of screens and moves clients toward regulation based in the rhythm of the spoken word (Gurdon, 2019). In addition, reading aloud can increase connection whether people are in the same room or in different physical locations (Aydin & Basoghu, 2021; Gurdon, 2019; Tubbs et al., 2019). Bibliotherapy works well via telehealth to strengthen and maintain connection between clients and therapists, despite physical distance (Tubbs et al., 2019; Yuan et al., 2018).

Bibliotherapy is fitting for most theoretical orientations and therapeutic approaches. It pairs particularly well with solution-focused therapy because it is non-pathologizing and has the power to meet children and their families where they are at without focusing on the etiology of the problem (Nelson & Thomas, 2007). The following describes a solution-focused approach to processing bibliotherapy, though you may alter the intervention to align with your own approach to therapy.

Setup

1. ***Build a library.*** Compile a collection of books that you can use for the purpose of bibliotherapy so that the financial burden is not placed on clients for owning copies of any books. Research indicates that children benefit more from reading physical books out loud than from tablets, due to the increased verbal interactions between caregivers and children during this shared activity (Gurdon, 2019; Munzer et al., 2021). In addition, young children learn vocabulary and concepts best from the interpersonal interaction aspect of reading out loud, more than through passive video watching (Munzer et al., 2021). For these reasons, written word books, whether physically printed or in e-book format, are recommended for the purposes of bibliotherapy. This maintains the focus of the bibliotherapy intervention on the value of interactively reading aloud to children, which is favorable to playing a pre-recorded video of a book reading.

   However, if you are limited in your own resources and have a library card, you can check books out of the library or reserve a digital book online and then screen share it with clients. Though printed books are preferred, this can provide a cost-effective way for children and families to visually engage with storybook pictures, while you read aloud to them.

2. ***Choose two books to offer your client(s).*** Early interventions of bibliotherapy should target general psychoeducation for emotional literacy. Consider the breadth of emotional language words described in the book and the relatability of the examples chosen to depict each feeling. Later interventions may focus more on the client's particular presenting problem. When choosing books, consider the intersection of client factors and characteristics of the book or its main character(s). Select books that align with the client's developmental level and focus the storyline on issues related to the client's presenting problem(s). Also consider the client's personal interests and social

location of main characters from the books (e.g., age, culture, ethnicity, family composition, gender, race, religious beliefs, spirituality). For example, some books about adoption, grief/loss, or death incorporate references to God or religion, which might not be a good fit for a family who has expressed that this is not aligned with their beliefs. Books may not always be available that perfectly align developmental level, presenting problem(s), personal interests, and social location, but when options are available, select books that allow clients to identify themselves in the story as much as possible (Tubbs et al., 2019; Vetri et al., 2022).

3. ***Read the books.*** Before offering book options to clients, read them in their entirety. Ensure that they are appropriate for clients prior to reading them in session. Be attuned to the details and ways in which each client and family might receive the book. Consider your client's developmental level, gender, culture, and family structure.
4. ***Address literacy abilities in the family system.*** Before offering bibliotherapy in session, inquire with clients about their practice of reading to identify which members of the household can read and their experience of reading books. By not assuming that everyone in the household can read, this helps to avoid situations in which people in the client's system feel shamed for differing abilities.
5. ***Discuss the intervention with caregivers as needed.*** For particularly challenging topics, present the idea of bibliotherapy to caregivers prior to introducing it to children. Even if children don't explicitly want to discuss the book outside of session, themes and topics from books read in session may come up outside of session that may need to be addressed by caregivers or other people within the family system. If caregivers are not present in the session in which the bibliotherapy intervention is conducted, it can be helpful to read the books you have chosen to caregivers in advance of offering them to children to ensure caregivers can appropriately support the child's processing. If caregivers are unable to attend the session or meet beforehand, it may be helpful to send them the title and a summary of the book, or a link to a pre-recorded reading of it if possible.

Instructions

1. ***Introduce bibliotherapy as a possible teletherapy activity.*** You might say, "Sometimes books are a helpful way to start talking about hard topics. I have many books that I'd like to share with you during our work together. Would you like to read a book today or next session?" Providing a choice about when to read the book offers younger clients a sense of control.
2. ***Offer two books to choose from.*** Read the title of each book and show its cover on screen. Ask the child which book they would like for you to read to them. When parents are present, clearly state that it is up to the child to choose. This offers child clients a sense of control in the therapeutic setting and affirms that bibliotherapy focuses on the child with their parents in the role of supplemental support. If more than one child is present, then you can delegate one child to pick this time, and another to pick the following book. Inviting the youngest child to pick first is often a way to engage the family in listening to bibliotherapy books starting at the most basic concepts and working upward developmentally to integrate information.
3. ***Invite clients to get comfortable.*** You may explain to children that they can bring a stuffed animal, find a cozy place to sit, and/or curl up with a family member in preparation of listening to the story. Work with clients to set up their camera to allow you to maintain visual contact throughout the activity. Likewise, ensure that the telehealth screen is placed on a sturdy surface and is visible

for everyone to see. You can do this playfully by holding up three or four fingers and asking each member to hold up the same number of fingers to ensure that everyone can see each other. When more than four people are present, an e-book shared through the telehealth platform can be an easier way for multiple people to see the pictures of the story while the therapist reads aloud.

4. ***If reading an e-book, share your screen.*** Work with clients to set up their screen so they have a good view of the e-book. It may be preferable for clients to have another screen that allows them to continue to see your face while the book is being read. This will help to increase connection between you and clients while you read aloud and demonstrate appropriate facial expressions at key points in the story. Set up your own screen so that you can read the e-book while simultaneously maintaining visual contact with your clients. If you have two computer screens, it can help to put the e-book on one screen and a visual of your clients on the other to increase visibility of both. This is particularly important when introducing difficult topics through bibliotherapy, as face-to-face engagement allows for therapist attunement to the emotional needs of each client.
5. ***Read the book.*** If reading a physical copy of a book, hold the book up to the camera. Sit far enough away from the camera so that both your face and the entirety of the book can be seen, and close enough so clients can easily see the pages and the images on them. After reading each page, take a moment to hold the book up to the camera to ensure that clients can clearly see it.

   It is natural for children to make comments while a story is being read aloud to them. You can either allow children to process throughout the story by pausing at the end of each page to allow for questions, or you can ask children to wait until the end of a story to process. When deciding how you allow each child to engage, consider the child's age, treatment goals, and your therapeutic relationship. Bibliotherapy can have the secondary benefit of allowing clients to practice skills they are working on, such as regulation, personal space, asking questions, asking for help, impulse control, taking turns, frustration tolerance, problem-solving, or trying self-relaxation techniques. For example, if a child has demonstrated difficulty asking questions, it may be of greatest therapeutic benefit to allow them to ask questions throughout the book and for you to respond immediately. Children who are working on impulse control, on the other hand, may benefit from your holding consistent boundaries around needing to wait until the end of the book to ask questions.

Processing

When working with families, begin processing with children first. If there is more than one child, begin with the youngest, or perhaps the one most interested in reading. Oftentimes, there is a child who is more excited about someone reading out loud to them, and that child can help start by bringing enthusiasm to the processing portion of the activity.

Typically, books revolve around a problem and main characters employ strategies or coping skills for managing the problem. Provide prompts to consider the problem presented in the story and the coping skills employed by characters in the book to manage the problem. Avoid discussing the client's personal experiences directly until they demonstrate that they are ready. Some children may need more time to process through the externalization of the book. If a child is ready, they will naturally shift toward talking about their own challenges. When this happens, employ the narrative technique of externalizing to help clients name their problem with a personified name, such as "The Accident," "Fighting," or "The Worry Monster." This helps children separate themselves from the problem, which can reduce defensiveness and empower children to find solutions for the problem (White & Morgan, 2006).

Processing through solution-focused strategies, including scaling questions and the miracle question, helps clients assess the intensity of the problem, understand their feelings, identify their own practical coping skills, and discover possible solutions (Nelson & Thomas, 2007). This serves as the bridge between the story and reality.

The following processing questions can be used to discuss the book and the client's experiences that relate to the story from the book. Begin with processing questions about the book. Follow the client's lead by discussing the client's experiences once they begin talking about their own challenges.

The Book

- What did the character try to make the problem go away? What worked? What didn't work?
- What else could the character have done?
- How was the character being [mean/nice/etc.]? What did they say or do?
- I wonder how the character might feel in this situation?
- How did the character know they were [anxious/happy/sad/etc.]?
- I wonder who the character could talk to about this problem?
- What do you think [thing from the story] represents?

The Client's Experiences

- On a scale of 1–10, with 1 being the worst and 10 being manageable, where would you rate this problem?
- Tell me about a time when you felt the same way as this character.
- I wonder if you have tried what the character did?
- I wonder what you would do differently than the character?
- I wonder what ways you are similar to this character?
- Imagine that while you are sleeping, [externalized problem] mysteriously disappears. When you get out of bed the next morning, what would be the first thing you notice that lets you know that it has vanished?
- If you could write the ending to your own story about [externalized problem], how would the problem change? How would it resolve?
- Tell me about a time when [externalized problem] wasn't around. When was that? What else was happening at that time?
- If I asked your [mom/dad/sister/brother/dog/cat/fish/that painting on the wall/etc.] about [externalized problem], what would they tell me?

Vignette

Jenny (7) was adopted out of foster care. Jenny's history included in-utero drug exposure, neglect, and multiple caregivers until she was adopted at the age of three. Jenny was engaged in multiple services to help her develop missed milestones. Jenny's adoptive parents brought her to teletherapy due to concerns about her impulsivity, sleep difficulties, explosive meltdowns, lying, and difficulty maintaining peer friendships. Jenny's adoptive mother often joined in sessions. When Jenny's caregiver was present, the therapist engaged both in bibliotherapy.

The therapist selected books based on Jenny's age, presenting problems, understanding of concepts discussed, and family values. Jenny's adoptive family regularly attended Catholic church and God was part of Jenny's adoption story, which was relevant to the choices selected for bibliotherapy. Bibliotherapy was appropriate for this child, due to her interest in stories and resistance to talking directly about her own adoption. This child also demonstrated a need for some structure in the tele-play therapy session, and bibliotherapy proved to maintain her interest and attention. The therapist started with general emotional intelligence books, focusing on naming feelings, worries, and anger. Gradually, more specific subjects were introduced around impulsivity, lying, and friendship. The therapist read books with Jenny's parent(s) prior to reading them with Jenny, and when possible, encouraged her parents to obtain or borrow a copy of books read in therapy for repeated reads at home.

With time, Jenny's mom reported that Jenny began asking more questions about her birth mom, biological sibling, and why her birth parents could not "keep" her. With this shift in Jenny's behavior, bibliotherapy titles were selected to focus on adoption, foster care, and early trauma. Selected bibliotherapy titles included: *Your Baby Brain is Loud Tonight, A Kids Book About Adoption, My Adopted Child, There's No One Like You, Just Because I Was Adopted*, and *Murphy's Three Homes*.

The therapist would begin the bibliotherapy portion of the session by ensuring that Jenny was comfortable and ready to start. The therapist then held up to the screen two pre-selected books for Jenny to choose from. The therapist held the books in front of the camera for about a minute, until Jenny chose which book she wanted to hear. The therapist would then set aside the other book and remind Jenny to hold onto her questions until the end of the book/section.

The therapist answered any questions asked by Jenny and/or her adoptive mother when questions arose. They provided integration of the story into Jenny's narrative through scaling questions, exception questions, and compare and contrast statements. For example, after reading *Just Because I Was Adopted*, the therapist asked:

- "I wonder how you might feel if your friends said something unkind to you about your family?"
- "Think about a time that someone said something unkind to you. How did you respond? What could be a different way to respond?"
- "What did you find helpful about the way William's dad answered the question about adoption?"
- "Who could you ask to help you if you weren't sure what to say in response?"
- "I wonder what you would tell a friend about what it means to be adopted?"
- "I wonder who you would include in your snowman family?"

Bibliotherapy was a tool that the therapist often returned to when introducing a new concept or revisiting an old one, to support Jenny's integration over time. It became comforting for Jenny and she often requested to be read aloud to in therapy and at home. Bibliotherapy gave Jenny language to talk about her feelings, her past, and her identity. Jenny demonstrated increased acceptance that all her feelings about foster care and adoption were valid, even the tough ones. With increased access to books about families separating and coming together, Jenny was able to articulate that some stories of adoption just focused on the happy endings and not the sad part of separating from a birth parent. At times, Jenny was more drawn to the characters in books about foster care, because she thought they were more realistically "sad and happy mixed together." Bibliotherapy gave Jenny validation and an understanding of how her early experiences contributed to her current behaviors of quick dysregulation, anger, and impulsivity. Jenny less frequently made up stories about her past and was more truthful in communicating her feelings and admitting to when she had made a mistake. Overall, bibliotherapy supported Jenny's increasing confidence and self-acceptance, which had a huge impact on her social relationships.

Suggestions for Follow-Up

In subsequent sessions, continue to offer bibliotherapy as a possible activity. Offering a variety of books over time is valuable, however, so is repetition. Adults often prefer not to reread books because they seek novelty and want to explore new topics, stories, and perspectives. Children, alternatively, thrive with repetition. In the same way that children demonstrate repetitive play as a way of processing their experiences, children often seek repetition in the books they read. Like play, books offer children words to articulate their experiences, and repetition can solidify and expand a child's vocabulary and a sense of self (Gurdon, 2020). When offering book options in subsequent bibliotherapy interventions, include previously read stories as one of the two options. This allows children a sense of agency and power in their processing of difficult topics. This can also help children revisit books that they were not previously ready for, or revisit ones they connected with. There are many books that focus on the hard topics addressed in therapy. If one book does not resonate with a child or strikes a particular chord that the child is not ready to work through, try another book on the same topic.

In addition, encourage caregivers to reread stories with their children outside of session. Support caregivers in finding particularly relevant books that their children have connected with at the library or in e-book format if buying copies of the books is financially burdensome. Encourage caregivers to read stories aloud to their children to strengthen their connection and attunement to one another, in addition to further integrating therapeutic information. Older children may want to read the books aloud to other members of the family. This is great too! If the family is unable to obtain a copy of the book, then an audiobook or pre-recorded reading of the book may be appropriate for repetition of information after the session.

Contraindications

Bibliotherapy is appropriate for most clients and presenting problems. However, not all books are appropriate for bibliotherapy. Older books, for example, may be less likely to portray diverse characters and may be more likely to use outdated terms and concepts (e.g., define marriage only in terms of a mom and a dad). Carefully vet books prior to sharing them with clients in session. Consider how families and their presenting problems are depicted, ways in which culture and religion are portrayed, and the diversity of characters represented in each book. Finally, review the books in your library from time to time to determine whether anything needs to be updated.

References

Aydin, E., & Basoglu, N. (2021). The approach of children's literature towards adjustmental, emotional, behavioral disorders and the bibliotherapy method. *International Online Journal of Educational Sciences, 13*(2), 502–520. https://doi.org/10.15345/iojes.2021.02.012

Gurdon, M. C. (2019). *The enchanted hour: The miraculous power of reading aloud in the age of distraction*. HarperCollins.

Munzer, T. G., Miller, A. L., Yeo, S., Wang, Y., McCaffery, H., Kaciroti, N., & Radesky, J. (2021). Parent verbalizations and toddler responses with touchscreen tablet nursery rhyme apps. *Pediatrics, 148*(6), Article e2021049964. https://doi.org/10.1542/peds.2021-049964

Nelson, T. S., & Thomas, F. N. (Eds.). (2007). *Handbook of solution-focused brief therapy: Clinical applications*. Routledge. https://doi.org/10.4324/9780203836606

Tubbs, A., Young, E. L., Heath, M. A., & Dyches, T. T. (2019). Military deployment in a family: Children's literature as a basis for counseling support. *Reading Horizons: A Journal of Literacy and Language Arts, 58*(1), 75–91. Retrieved from https://scholarworks.wmich.edu/reading_horizons/vol58/iss1/5

Vetri, K., Piché, G., & Villatte, A. (2022). An evaluation of the acceptability, appropriateness, and utility of a bibliotherapy for children of parents with mental illness. *Frontiers Psychiatry, 13,* Article 815873. https://doi.org/10.3389/fpsyt.2022.815873

White, M., & Morgan, A. (2006). *Narrative therapy with children and their families*. Dulwich Centre Publications.

Yuan, S., Zhou, X., Zhang, Y., Zhang, H., Pu, J., Yang, L., Liu, L., Jiang, X., & Xie, P. (2018). Comparative efficacy and acceptability of bibliotherapy for depression and anxiety disorders in children and adolescents: A meta-analysis of randomized clinical trials. *Neuropsychiatric Disease and Treatment, 14,* 353–365. https://doi.org/10.2147%2FNDT.S152747

CHAPTER 22

VIRTUAL DOLLHOUSE

Karen Fried

Materials for Therapists and Clients: Internet-connected desktop or laptop computer with a screen at least 13" big and access to the Online Dollhouse app, available at onlinedollhouses.com.

Objective

Dollhouses are a commonly used tool for therapeutic assessment and intervention with children, adolescents, and families (Gil, 1991). This chapter describes how to conduct this traditionally in-person technique via online therapy without the use of a physical dollhouse.

Rationale for Use

The use of dollhouses in therapy allows children, adolescents, and families to engage in self-led, ritualistic, and revelatory play to reenact real and orchestrate imaginary life events (Klem, 1992). A dollhouse should be outfitted with diverse human figures and enough varied items to exercise the child's power of making choices. Thus, it provides therapists with a relatively unguarded tour of each client's home atmosphere, family dynamics, thoughts, emotions, and experiences through "a symbolism that substitutes for words" (Oaklander, 1978, p. 160). Dollhouses have been used effectively for identifying and treating a vast range of emotional, behavioral, and relational presenting problems including life transitions and trauma.

Dollhouse play serves as both an assessment and intervention. For example, observation may reveal:

- A poor sense of self, as demonstrated by inability or difficulty choosing items for a scene
- Blocked emotions, as demonstrated by a superficial description or avoidance of reflection
- Concerns regarding safety of real or perceived support systems, as demonstrated by difficulty locating safe places in the dollhouse

As an intervention, dollhouse play enables clients to access, express, reflect on, and integrate feelings, thereby strengthening their sense of self. This work is demonstrated as clients:

- Choose figures and furnishings to create a scene
- Manipulate figures and items as they orchestrate a scene's evolution
- Judge and discuss the scene's meaning

DOI: 10.4324/9781003330912-27

Dollhouses are considered a "necessary minimum" (Gil, 1991, p. 64) material for play therapists. However, many children do not have access to a dollhouse for use in teletherapy. To allow teletherapists and clients access to this critical tool, the author of this chapter developed a virtual dollhouse that can be used for online therapy.

The virtual dollhouse contains five spaces, or rooms, that clients can use to create scenes. Next to the dollhouse are movable figures depicting dogs, cats, and people of all ages in an array of different skin tones and hair colors. Movable images of furnishings and other objects commonly found in living, cooking/eating, bathroom, bedroom, and play areas are also available.

Website records indicate that the virtual dollhouse is used monthly by approximately 5,000 people worldwide. Anecdotal data shared via email by therapists who employ this tool suggests that it is accessible and "translatable" to therapists with varied backgrounds and theoretical orientations and to clients across cultures with a variety of presenting problems.

Setup

The following specifies setup required to engage in the virtual dollhouse for online therapy assessment and intervention.

1. ***Familiarize yourself with the online platform.*** Visit onlinedollhouses.com to survey available images and features. Practice using the virtual tool so you're familiar with how it works and can guide clients in using it.
2. ***Determine whether clients have a computer that they can use to access the virtual dollhouse.*** This program runs only on computers and cannot be used with phones. If a compatible device is not available, offer alternative therapeutic interventions.
3. ***Offer options.*** Even if online dollhouse play is feasible, offer it along with other options. Acceptance or rejection of the activity allows clients to practice the self-affirming act of choosing.
4. ***Share the link.*** If the virtual dollhouse is chosen, access the online platform at onlinedollhouses.com and share the website with clients in the chat function of your Health Insurance Portability and Accountability Act (HIPAA)-compliant therapy platform. Sharing a direct link allows clients to go to the website without having to type the website address, which may be difficult and time-consuming for younger clients.
5. ***Share your screen.*** Share the browser in which onlinedollhouses.com appears on your computer. Avoid sharing your entire screen, which may contain other things that can distract clients.
6. ***Provide a visual tour.*** Show clients the virtual dollhouse and how it works. For example, you might scroll through the available figures and objects to provide a preview of what clients might use in creating their scene (see Figure 22.1). Explain, "You may choose any of these figures and objects to play with. You can change the size and position of figures and objects. You may change figures and objects any time you like. You can move them in front of or behind other figures and objects. If you'd like more rooms, you can even add things to two dollhouses by opening two tabs at once!" Multiple tabs are especially useful for work with families or groups and with prompts calling for more than one scene, such as depicting scenes before, during, and after an event.
7. ***Discuss options to save scenes.*** Explain that the online platform allows them to save an image of their completed dollhouse as a file on their device, which may be easily recreated in another session. Explain that you also have the option of taking screenshots of the dollhouse during and/or

Figure 22.1 Dollhouse from onlinedollhouses.com.

at the end of their play. These screenshots can be revisited to talk about the dollhouse after they're done playing or to help them remember where they left off if they forget to save their scene or lose access to it. Discuss with clients their preferences about saving scenes and taking screenshots. If it appears that either of these options may inhibit clients in their play or make them uncomfortable, avoid saving scenes or taking screenshots.

8. ***Share the clients' screen.*** Request that clients share their screen. If family members are participating in therapy from different locations, discuss who will share their screen.
9. ***Practice.*** Invite clients to practice selecting images to add to the dollhouse, moving them to desired locations within the dollhouse, and adjusting their sizes and positions.

Instructions

The following offers instructions on engaging clients in therapeutic play using the virtual dollhouse.

1. ***Choose a scene.*** Ask clients to think of a scene. You may take a nondirective approach by asking clients to simply, "Think of a scene." Alternatively, you may take a more directive approach at the onset of the intervention by asking clients to "Create a home that [resembles/reminds you of] your [own/mom's/dad's/etc.] in some way," "Create a(n) [ideal/safe] home," or "Create the home

you'd like to have." When working with families, each participant may create their own dollhouse scene, or they may collaborate in creating a scene together. Collaborative work may be particularly beneficial to families working toward a sense of safety in their home and offers an opportunity to envision together what that might look like.

2. ***Imagine the scene.*** Ask clients to "imagine the scene" as vividly as possible.
3. ***Make the scene.*** Invite clients to "make the scene" that they just imagined. If working with more than one client collaborating on one scene, discuss who will be responsible for physically creating the scene on the computer. If working with more than one client with each person creating a different scene, clients may work simultaneously on their scenes if they are working from different devices. Otherwise, first discuss the order in which each person will create their scene.
4. ***Be it.*** Invite clients to choose one or more figures or objects depicted in their scene to speak (e.g., "What does the _____ say?") or to act (e.g., "Where does the _____ go?"). This process of projection allows children to say something about themselves within the metaphor of the dollhouse, which helps to increase self-awareness and allow change to take place (Oaklander, 2006).
5. ***Ask clients if they would like to add or change anything in the scene.*** For example, you might ask, "Is there anyone or anything else that should be in this scene? Who or what would that be?" or "Is there anyone or anything you'd like to [remove/change/make smaller or larger] in this scene? Who or what would that be?" Allow them to add, resize, move, or remove figures or items. When working with families who disagree about desired changes, process what each person wants, how their desires are similar, how their desires differ, and how they might come to an agreement.
6. ***Save the scene.*** If clients consent to saving their scene, they can save it to their computer and refer to it or quickly recreate it to use again in future sessions. If they have consented to your taking screenshots of their scene, screenshots may be taken at any point during scene development.

Throughout the activity, offer verbal reflections on client actions using the client's terms for figures or items selected. For example, you might say, "You're moving the girl closer to the grandmother" or "You're making her much bigger now!" Often, clients will use an object to represent something that isn't available in the virtual dollhouse. Rather than correcting them, use the client's language and refer to that item with their term.

To use the activity as a form of assessment, make note of each client's:

- Selected figures and objects
- Positioning and sizing of each figure and object
- Actions, silence, or speech
- Comments made about their scene
- Interactions with others throughout the activity

Processing

Processing may occur throughout the intervention and upon its conclusion. The following are sample processing questions that address the creation of a scene by an individual, different scenes by family members, and a scene by family members working together.

Individuals Working on a Scene

- What do you like about this scene?
- What was it like for you to change the scene that you initially created?
- Is there anything about this scene you'd still like to change? If so, what is it that you'd like to change?
- What's your ideal scene? What's special about it?
- What would you change about this scene to make it more like your ideal scene?

Family Members Working on Different Scenes

- How does your scene compare with [name]'s scene?
- What did you learn about one another from your scenes?
- What might it look like if you were to create a shared scene? How might you work together to combine elements of each of your scenes? How might these scenes fit together?

Family Members Working on the Same Scene

- What was it like for you to work on creating a shared scene?
- Did you experience any disagreements in the process? If so, how did you handle them?
- What did you learn about one another from this process?

Vignette

Raquel (15) lived in a multigenerational household comprised of her father, brother, aunt, uncle, two cousins, and "Abuelita" (i.e., grandmother). Raquel began therapy to address depression and a sense of abandonment in the wake of her mother's having left the family twice when Raquel was seven. She also expressed feelings of isolation and that she didn't have many friends or connections outside of her family. She had plans to be the first in her immediate family to graduate high school and hoped to attend college but struggled to motivate herself academically.

Raquel presented as soft-spoken, introverted, and inhibited in expressing emotions, especially negative ones. She could make good emotional contact with others but needed considerable cueing. Yet she engaged warmly with family members, responded readily to prompts (even if declining), and seemed to appreciate the therapist's attention and interventions.

The central therapeutic goal was to reduce her depressive symptoms by enhancing her sense of self, which would increase her ability to make choices and to participate in activities such as schoolwork and socializing with friends. To assist in addressing her depression, the therapist had Raquel go through the 4-step Oaklander (1978) procedure in dollhouse play (i.e., imagine it; make it; be it; own it). Raquel was prompted first to "Imagine a time that was important in your home." Then, she was asked "Now make it using the dollhouse any way you'd like." Once she made her scene, Raquel was invited to enact the third prompt. The therapist invited her to "Now be it by choosing something from the scene that you'd like to be." Finally, Raquel was asked to "Own it. How does this scene fit for you in your life?"

Figure 22.2 Completed dollhouse, created at onlinedollhouses.com.

Raquel chose a past moment as an important time in her home. She populated, very sparsely furnished, and described only the lower-left-corner room of the dollhouse. In it she, her grandmother, brother, and father encircled her centrally placed newborn cousin just brought from the hospital (see Figure 22.2).

When asked about the empty spaces in the rest of the house, she said that "all their stuff" would be put in the rooms that were unused while everyone was with the baby. She then added that the baby's parents (i.e., her aunt and uncle) would have been in the kitchen, but that she hadn't placed them there.

The therapist queried, "What's the first thing you'd like to say to the baby?" She replied, "Welcome to the family, and just know that we all love you." She then volunteered that babies are annoying. Thinking she might be experiencing some anger, the therapist asked, "How's that?" Raquel returned, "Maybe because they cry." The therapist asked if she could say that to the baby. Raquel stated that she didn't want to and declined to expand on her comment.

Then the therapist next suggested that she "be" her grandmother. Raquel had her say, "I'm excited to have my fourth grandchild and happy to have him home." When asked, "How is it to be your grandmother?" Raquel answered, "It's my cousin and she's a grandmother." The therapist then invited Raquel to "be" the baby, whom the client had say, "I'm tired and confused." The therapist followed up by asking, "Why are you tired and confused?" Raquel responded as the baby by saying, "Every time I wake up, I see all these people around me." The therapist continued, "What would all these people want to say?" Raquel answered, "They're saying how cute I look." The therapist pursued the comment by asking, "How does that feel?" to which Raquel replied, "Makes me feel special." When asked to "be" anything that wasn't a person, she chose the table and said, "I'm happy to see this family coming together and happy."

Toward the end of the session, the therapist inquired, "Is there anything you would add or change in this scene?" and gave her the opportunity to do so, which she declined. Her focus remained on the baby's birth and the happiness she and the whole family felt. Finally, the therapist encouraged her to own the projections brought out by the intervention.

Therapist: Does this fit for you? Have you ever felt tired and confused?

Raquel: Yes, when my mother did not come back after the second time she left.

Therapist: Do you ever feel special, or would you like to?

Raquel: Yes; it was very lonely without my mom because Abuelita and Father work all the time.

Therapist: Does it feel good to you to see the family coming together and happy?

Raquel: Yes, since I've wanted another baby in the family.

Experiencing and processing Raquel's dollhouse play, the therapist and client learned:

- She feels proud to be part of a loving family.
- It feels good to her to state that.
- It feels good to her that she finally got a baby in the home.
- Her grandmother is a central focus in the home.
- It's hard for her to express negative emotions.

Raquel's leaving most dollhouse spaces blank suggested that it may have been difficult for her to imagine filling them herself, without family support. In subsequent sessions, the therapist asked Raquel to "make a scene that shows a memory of when you were happy" and to "create a scene recalling an unhappy time." Experiencing, depicting, and articulating diametrically differing scenes helped her integrate ambivalent feelings about the baby, metaphorically and playfully placing her annoyance into her scene. To enhance Raquel's sense of self by strengthening her contact with the range of her emotions, the therapist requested that she design scenes of when she was angry, sad, and scared. Throughout each scene creation, the therapist had her identify where in her body she felt each emotion and then describe it. These steps helped Raquel build contact between her emotions, body, and her intellect.

Suggestions for Follow-Up

Clients may benefit from playing with the dollhouse scene they created in subsequent sessions for a number of reasons. They might be working on a theme, such as a change in the household, and experience evolving feelings about it, for which you can provide a chance to make a more relevant scene. They might also revisit the dollhouse as a way to terminate therapy with a sense of accomplishment. You might invite clients to "Make a scene to show how you are in your home now that we are done with sessions. What does it look like now? What did it look like when we started?"

A unique benefit of the virtual dollhouse is the ease with which scenes can be saved for future use. Evolving stages of one or multiple dollhouse scenes saved securely on the therapist's computer may be shared for review and comparison in later sessions. When comparing different versions of the dollhouse, therapists may ask, "What changes do you see in these scenes? Which scene or scene shows best how you're feeling now? Which is farthest from how you feel today?"

Contraindications

Though therapy must take place on a HIPAA-consistent platform, onlinedollhouses.com is not HIPAA compliant, which may leave the created scenes accessible to others. Since even an anonymous scene may show private and potentially identifiable content, some clients may be uncomfortable using an online platform that is not HIPAA compliant. Discuss the use of websites that are not HIPAA consistent with caregivers and request written consent for use of non-HIPAA-consistent platforms in an informed consent document or a digital tools consent form (see Chapter 10) prior to their use as a therapeutic intervention.

Though the virtual dollhouse contains figures with varied skin tones and hair colors, the availability of culture-specific objects is limited. For example, a play therapist in Kenya shared that her clients' homes often have grass roofs, which is not depicted in the dollhouse. Though the objects available are intended to be universal, culture-specific items are not available and their absence may be a limiting factor.

Some clients or family members may reject the use of the dollhouse. Some may view it as a "girl's" toy (Saramourtsi et al., 2020) or a toy for "little kids." Some families may also prefer not to have children play with the dollhouse in therapy to avoid exhibiting their private home, even metaphorically, as this may feel invasive.

Other clients may find the use of the dollhouse difficult or painful. When working within the context of family therapy, children alternating between conflictual households may feel pressure to display preference for one home and may feel inhibited if family members are present or nearby in the household while teletherapy takes place. Clients in foster care or two custodial homes, or whose families are unhoused or subject to frequent military, diplomatic, or business relocations may experience a house-centered exercise as painful. Consider the client's culture, values, and unique circumstances as they relate to the use of the dollhouse intervention in teletherapy. Be prepared to offer alternative interventions when appropriate.

References

Gil, E. (1991). *The healing power of play: Working with abused children*. Guilford Press.

Klem, P. (1992). The use of the dollhouse as an effective disclosure technique. *International Journal of Play Therapy, 1*(1), 69–73. https://doi.org/10.1037/h0090236

Oaklander, V. (1978). *Windows to our children: A Gestalt Therapy approach to children and adolescents*. Real People Press.

Oaklander, V. (2006). *Hidden treasures: A map to the child's inner self*. Karnac Books.

Saramourtsi, E., Zafiri, M., & Pliogou, V. (2020). Gender stereotypes in children's play, pro-social and aggressive behavior in the kindergarten class: The kindergarten teachers' stance. *Universal Journal of Educational Research, 8*(12A), 7992–8009. https://doi.org/10.13189/ujer.2020.082587

CHAPTER 23

PUPPET REFLECTING TEAMS FOR TELEHEALTH FAMILY THERAPY

Chelsea L. Cheney, Megan Conrad, and Jacob B. Priest

Materials for Therapists: Puppet(s).

Material for Clients: None. Puppet(s) may optionally be used.

Objective

Puppet reflecting teams are used by therapists to playfully help clients recognize patterns of interaction, reflect on how these patterns sustain presenting issues, and generate creative shifts in those patterns (Coulehan et al., 1998; Jenkins, 1996). This chapter explains how to adapt this traditional in-person therapy intervention via teletherapy.

Rationale for Use

Reflecting teams have been used by therapists for decades (Anderson, 1987). These teams typically involve a group of therapists observing a therapy session and then sharing their observations and impressions in the presence of clients. The goal is to allow clients to hear a different perspective on their problems, without fear of judgment. Reflecting teams can be particularly useful in instances in which clients are "stuck" with an issue or problem and need additional perspectives to change their patterned behavior. Reflecting teams have also been used in teletherapy intervention (Cobb et al., 2024). However, when working with children via teletherapy a more creative approach to traditional reflecting teams may be required to capture and maintain client engagement.

Puppets are often used in play therapy and provide an opportunity for clients to see problems in new ways, including virtually in teletherapy to successfully engage children and families (Fried, 2024; Kottman, 2011). When adapted for telehealth, puppets can increase the ability for clients to suspend their disbelief, as the telehealth screen can be imagined morphing into a production screen, with puppets placed on the bottom of the screen to hide the hands that control them. Virtual backgrounds available on telehealth platforms are ideal to transport the session into an imaginative setting, whether puppets appear only on the therapist's side or additional puppets are used by clients with their own virtual backgrounds.

Using a puppet reflecting team via teletherapy intervention fuses aspects of play therapy and reflecting teams as an adaptation of the puppet reflecting teams that Brown (2009; 2013) proposed for

DOI: 10.4324/9781003330912-28

in-person therapy. Instead of the reflecting team being composed of multiple clinicians, Brown adapted the reflecting team technique for clinicians to infuse multiple voices through puppets. The puppets, animated by the therapist, reflect observations from multiple characters in a way that provides feedback in a playful way that is accessible to all clients.

For the puppet reflecting team, puppet(s) may join the therapist as "co-therapist" and part of a reflecting team to communicate observations of the client system. Alternatively, a "puppet friend" can join the session and enact issues similar to the clients' presenting problems while clients join the therapist to reflect on the puppet friend's presenting problems. This allows clients to view their patterns from a new perspective and brainstorm solutions for the puppets that can then be applied to their own life. In this chapter, instructions are provided for both approaches. Use best judgment to determine which approach best suits each client.

Though this intervention may be used with many theoretical lenses, the instructions here focus on a narrative approach in which the puppets help clients externalize their problems and imagine preferred stories in which problem-saturated narratives do not prevail (White, 2007). Though the vignette focuses on family therapy, this approach is also appropriate for individual therapy.

Setup

The following specifies the setup required to conduct a puppet reflecting team.

1. ***Gain knowledge.*** Ensure that you have good working knowledge about the client's presenting problem(s) prior to conducting the puppet reflecting team.
2. ***Develop hypotheses.*** Based on your understanding of the client's problem(s), develop hypotheses about behaviors and patterns of interaction that may be sustaining the problem(s).
3. ***Acquire and select puppets.*** You may use one or more puppets, depending on the number of different perspectives that you would like to share. If an array of puppets is available, consider the client's culture, likes, and dislikes and choose puppets that you think clients will connect with. If you do not have access to puppets, you can create your own puppets using socks or small paper bags and other crafting materials (see Chapter 7).
4. ***Select a background.*** Choose a virtual background that sets the stage for the puppets to join you in the session. This could be an image of a literal stage or something more specific to the puppets that you plan to use or the clients with whom you are working.
5. ***Develop puppet personas.*** Consider having each puppet have a different personality, voice, perspective, and backstory.
6. ***Prepare remarks.*** Develop a basic outline of what you intend to have the puppets reflect. For example, if having a puppet be a "co-therapist," you may have the puppet reflect curiosities or observations of client behaviors, patterns of interactions, strengths and resilience factors observed within the client system, and possible solutions to presenting problems. If the chosen role of the puppet is to have a "therapist's friend" join the session, create an idea of how to share the puppet's "presenting problem" so the problem is similar to, but different enough from, that of the client(s).

Instructions

The following outlines instructions for conducting a puppet reflecting team in teletherapy. First, instructions are provided for using a puppet as a "co-therapist" who can then act as part of a reflecting team with the therapist. Then, instructions are provided for using the puppet as the "therapist's friend" with a presenting problem similar to that of the client(s).

Puppet Co-therapist

For this variation of the intervention, the puppet acts as a "co-therapist" and part of the reflecting team with the therapist.

1. ***Introduce the puppet.*** Explain that you invited a helper to today's session. Say "This is [puppet's name]" and show the puppet on screen. Try to keep your arms below the view of the camera so it's not apparent that you are controlling the puppet with your hand. Explain that the puppet is also a therapist and that they'd like to join the session as your co-therapist. Then, ask if it's okay if your puppet joins you.
2. ***Facilitate a review.*** Invite clients to introduce themselves and have them each briefly describe the problem that brought them to therapy. Encourage clients to share about progress that they have made thus far in combatting that problem together and ways in which they continue to seek change.
3. ***Invite the puppet's reflection.*** Engage the puppet in a conversation so you and the puppet are talking about the client(s) and the things you've just heard discussed. When working with families, the puppet should focus on the perspective of children to help "voice" their thoughts and feelings. For example, the puppet may reflect comments children made during the session, conceptualizing what is happening for the child and reflecting their emotions. The puppet may speak directly with clients to ask questions that may provide useful material for the subsequent reflection. The following questions can be asked to gain language on externalized problems and identify alternative stories if clients do not naturally bring these up in their review.
    - I wonder, if you were to name the problem that you've been talking about, what would you call it?
    - Can you think of any stories to tell me when the problem didn't exist?

    Ensure the puppet's reflection primarily takes the form of a conversation with the therapist. The therapist or puppet may ask each other the following questions and subsequently discuss their ideas in response.

    - What do you think [name(s) of client(s)] [is/are] [thinking/feeling]?
    - What words do [name(s) of client(s)] use to separate themselves from [the problem]?
    - How do you think [name(s) of client(s)] are fighting against [the problem]?
    - Is there anything you would do differently?
    - Do you think there could be any times [the problem] isn't occurring?
    - What do you think is happening when [the problem] isn't occurring?
    - I've seen a lot of people struggle with similar things, but I'm really impressed with how [name(s) of client(s)] are banding together to make changes happen! What do you like about what you've heard [name(s) of client(s)] talk about today?
4. ***Examine and challenge.*** Invite clients to discuss with you and the puppet ways in which the externalized problem limits healthy functioning. For example, you might help clients identify the ways in which making assumptions impacts conflict with each other.

5. ***Identify solutions.*** Invite clients to discuss with you and the puppet ways to overcome the problems.
6. ***Process.*** As the therapist or puppet, explain that the puppet must leave and have it say "goodbye." Then, process the experience of having the puppet join in on their conversations. For example, you might ask the following:
   - What [thoughts/feelings] came up as you listened to [puppet's name]?
   - Was there anything that you heard me discuss with [puppet's name] that you [agreed with/didn't agree with]?
   - What do you think [puppet's name] sees as the problem?
   - What points did the puppet bring up about [the problem] that you hadn't noticed before?
   - Do you think it might be possible to make any of the changes that [puppet's name] recommended?
   - Are there any other changes that you'd like to make after having [puppet's name] visit today?

Puppet Friend

For this variation of the intervention, the therapist invites a puppet with issues similar to the clients' presenting problem(s). Clients are invited to reflect on what the puppet has shared and offer suggestions for alleviating their presenting problem(s).

1. ***Introduce the puppet.*** Explain that you invited a friend to the session. Say "This is [puppet's name]" and show the puppet on screen. Try to keep your arms below the view of the camera so it's not apparent that you are controlling the puppet with your hand. Explain that the puppet is a friend of yours experiencing some problems and that they'd like to join the session to also get some help today. Then, ask if it's okay if your friend joins the session.
2. ***Interview the puppet.*** Prompt the puppet to say hi and have the puppet explain their "problem." For example, you might say something like "Sharky, you mentioned a conflict within your family last week. Could you share that story again? I'm wondering if our friends here might be able to help." Then, have the puppet describe their problem in clear, concrete terms. When the puppet discusses their problem, have the puppet name and discuss the issue as an externalized problem. Refrain from drawing parallels between the puppet's story and the client's story unless the client does so first. Throughout the interview with the puppet, attend to the following:
   - Portray the puppet's non-verbal communication to maintain engagement (e.g., move the puppet's mouth and hands appropriately).
   - As the therapist, demonstrate active engagement with the puppet (e.g., face the puppet when the puppet is talking and use appropriate encouragement skills and reflection).
   - Note verbal and non-verbal cues from clients as the puppet shares their narrative.
3. ***Encourage client reflection.*** Ask clients for feedback on the puppet's story. For example, you might ask the following:
   - What do you think [puppet's name] is [thinking/feeling]?
   - What words does [puppet's name] use to separate themselves from [the problem]?
   - How do you think [puppet's name] is fighting against [the problem]?
   - Is there anything you would do differently?

- Do you think there could be any times [the problem] isn't occurring?
- What do you think is happening with [puppet's name] when [the problem] isn't happening?
- I've seen a lot of people struggle with similar things, but I'm really impressed with how [puppet's name] is working hard make changes happen! What do you like about what you've heard [puppet's name] talk about today?

4. ***Examine and challenge.*** As the puppet, process the client's reflections on the problem and how it affects the puppet's life. As the therapist, help the puppet identify ways in which the problem limits healthy functioning.
5. ***Identify solutions.*** Invite the puppet to discuss with you and clients ways in which they might overcome their problem.
6. ***Process.*** As the therapist or puppet, explain that the puppet must leave as it says "goodbye." Then, process the experience of having the puppet join in on their conversations for the day. For example, you might ask the following:
    - What [thoughts/feelings] came up as you listened to [puppet's name] talk about [the problem]?
    - What do you think is the most important thing for [puppet's name]to remember when [the problem] comes up?
    - How did you think of the suggestions that you made to help their situation?
    - How did it feel to work together to help [puppet's name]?

Vignette

Elaina (6), her mother, Becky (32), her stepfather, Ian (30), and their new baby, Eric (4 months) began family teletherapy after Elaina's school teacher referred them due to an increase in her absences, daily requests to go home because of tummy aches (medically cleared by her primary provider), and twice hitting other kids in class.

In the first two sessions, the therapist observed the family struggling with adjusting to the new baby, as Ian worked long hours and Becky reported symptoms of postpartum depression and episodes of intense grief over the recent loss of her mother to cancer, who previously provided daycare to Elaina.

For the third session, the therapist planned to help externalize Elaina's symptoms as a response to changes to, and issues within, the family system (e.g., grief, life cycle transitions) while attending to concerns of losing another caregiver. At the beginning of the session, the therapist asked the family if their friend, Sharky, could join the session that day. Sharky was briefly introduced, then asked to quietly listen so Elaina and her family could have their special therapy time.

As the session proceeded with the family's update on the week's events and observations of how the family was doing, it was interrupted by the baby fussing. Immediately, Elaina asked for a snack. As her parents both scrambled to sooth the baby, Elaina increased her unsuccessful bids for attention through complaining about a stomachache, attempting to show her mom a coloring page from earlier in the day, and then coloring directly on the table with markers, which received a frustrated response from Ian as Becky prepared the baby a bottle.

As the family got resettled, the therapist asked if Sharky could share his experience. Sharky was placed in front of the screen and proceeded to tell the family about his "big problem" of when he feels lonely inside, and asked if they could try to help him. Sharky described his issue, similar to Elaina's, about having a best friend that moved away and how his other best friend, Panda, spends all his time with a new student, Nemo. Sharky explained that when he feels alone, it feels like an imaginary monster named Lonely gets in his stomach and making it feel like it's tied up in knots. To help his tummy, he chews on the playground equipment, but other students accuse him of being "mean" when it damages the equipment. He lamented that he's only trying to make his tummy feel better. Sharkey then wondered aloud what computers taste like and nibbled at the screen, only to quickly make some spitting noises and say that playground equipment tastes much better. The family chuckled and appeared to have interest in what Sharkey might do next.

The therapist then asked the family to share their thoughts about the "Lonely" monster making Sharky's stomach tie in knots, if they've ever felt similar emotions, and what they thought Sharky might need. Elaina and her parents mentioned they had felt anger, sadness, and fear when they felt alone and how Sharky may need help when the "lonely monster" shows up in his tummy. The family then brainstormed ideas that might help Sharkey, including lighthearted suggestions for Sharky to "just eat Nemo!" They suggested that Sharky could find a new friend, chew on a dog bone when he wants to bite on things, invite his old friends to play at his house, or even try to become friends with Nemo. The therapist suggested talking to a parent or therapist about those feelings and worries. Sharky said that he liked these ideas and agreed to ask Panda, and maybe even Nemo, to come play video games after school.

Sharky said goodbye and exited the session. The therapist processed the activity with the family by asking questions like what they thought about Sharky feeling alone and sad, and how it felt to help Sharky find a solution together. The therapist probed into feelings that were activated when they thought about Sharky being lonely or sad and about turning to people for help when those feelings came up. Becky took the opportunity to relate to Elaina how she misses Grandma and how much cuddles and hugs help her. She also commented on how tired she had been with the baby that she sometimes forgot to make sure Elaina got cuddles too, but promised she wasn't going anywhere and she would be there whenever Elaina needed her. Ian watched quietly and suggested that maybe he'd been working so hard to get a promotion at work that he didn't realize maybe they needed his time more than a bigger paycheck. At the end of the session, a goal was created to play Grandma's favorite board game together that night to keep any "lonely monsters" at bay.

Suggestions for Follow-Up

If clients appear to respond well to the intervention, the same puppet(s) can rejoin future sessions to engage in further reflecting team conversations. Alternatively, different puppets may join future sessions to provide new perspectives.

Contraindications

Puppet reflecting teams work best for clients between the ages of two and eleven (Brown, 2013). While children typically learn and process emotion through play, some children may find it difficult to suspend disbelief due to parentification or abuse (Mann & McDermott, 1983). In this case, consider referrals to child therapy focused on re-establishing the ability to play before proceeding with puppets in session. In addition, individuals with autism spectrum disorder that have difficulty in imaginative play (American Psychiatric Association, 2022) may require adjustments to the intervention or alternatives to a puppet reflecting team. Likewise, parents may have more difficulty interacting with puppets. Consult with parents before using a puppet reflecting team and offer other options if clients appear resistant.

References

American Psychiatric Association. (2022). *Diagnostic and statistical manual of mental disorders* (5th ed., text rev.). https://doi.org/10.1176/appi.books.9780890425787

Andersen, T. (1987). The reflecting team: Dialogue and meta-dialogue in clinical work. *Family Process, 26,* 415–428. https://doi.org/10.1111/j.1545-5300.1987.00415.x

Brown, P. (2009). Reflecting puppet shows: Evoking drama through improvisation. *Context, 104,* 33–35.

Brown, P. (2013, Autumn). Reflecting puppet teams. *The Psychotherapist*, 20–22.

Cobb, R. A., Brownell, S., Camera, S. J., & Chapin, C. (2024). Virtual reflecting team: A Milan approach to teletherapy intervention. In R. A. Cobb (Ed.), *The therapist's notebook for systemic teletherapy: Creative interventions for effective online therapy* (pp. 244–250). Routledge. https://doi.org/10.4324/9781003289920-45

Coulehan, R., Friedlander, M. L., & Heatherington, L. (1998). Transforming narratives: A change event in constructivist family therapy. *Family Process, 37*(1), 13–33. https://doi.org/10.1111/j.1545-5300.1998.00017.x

Fried, K. (2024). Virtual puppet play therapy. In R. A. Cobb (Ed.), *The therapist's notebook for systemic teletherapy: Creative interventions for effective online therapy* (pp. 70–78). Routledge. https://doi.org/10.4324/9781003289920-17

Jenkins, D. (1996). A reflecting team approach to family therapy: A Delphi study. *Journal of Marital and Family Therapy, 22*(2), 219–238. https://doi.org/10.1111/j.1752-0606.1996.tb00200.x

Kottman, T. (2011). Adlerian play therapy. In C. E. Schaefer (Ed.), *Foundations of play therapy.* (pp. 87–104). John Wiley & Sons, Inc.

Mann, E., & McDermott, J. F. (1983). Play therapy for victims of child abuse and neglect. In C. E. Schaefer & K. J. O'Connor (Eds.), *Handbook of play therapy* (pp. 174–181). Wiley.

White, M. (2007). *Maps of narrative practice.* W.W. Norton.

CHAPTER 24

SCAVENGER HUNTS FOR SPECIFIC PRESENTING PROBLEMS

Aaron Norton, Jaclyn Cravens Pickens, and Tiffany Smith

Materials for Therapists and Clients: None.

Objective

Scavenger hunts have been used to support in-person therapy intervention for decades (Cavett, 2010). They are also well-suited for teletherapy due to the simplicity of instructions, lack of advanced preparation required, and lack of specific required materials. This chapter outlines ways that this intervention can be used to playfully gather critical assessment data regarding presenting problems, feelings, communication, differentiation, and culture. Through processing using prompts provided, therapists may also learn about family structure, power, roles, and other family dynamics (Lowenstein & Hertlein, 2012).

Rationale for Use

When conducting a scavenger hunt in therapy, the therapist typically provides clients with a list of three to five items that they should find in their current physical location (Lowenstein & Hertlein, 2012). The intervention is most effective if the therapist creates a list that is specific to the assessment and intervention needs of each client or family system.

A scavenger hunt is an adaptable intervention that has several benefits that make it an ideal choice for teletherapy:

- It can be used with individuals, siblings, and families, ages three and up.
- It can be used with clients from most backgrounds and with most presenting problems.
- It requires little to no materials or prior setup.
- It can be used at any stage of the therapy process.
- The "hunt" part of the process can be completed either during a therapy session or between sessions as a homework assignment.

DOI: 10.4324/9781003330912-29

Additionally, the use of scavenger hunts for therapeutic intervention is adaptable to nearly any clinical model or theoretical perspective through the prompts provided to clients and the way in which processing questions are formulated. For example, in the instructions that follow, one set of prompts provided focuses on feelings, which could easily be adapted to emotionally focused family therapy (Furrow et al., 2019). Another set of prompts focuses on items that relate to differentiation, a key concept within Bowen's family therapy model (Kerr & Bowen, 1988).

Setup

A scavenger hunt requires little to no setup. Clients need only use what is already present and readily accessible in their physical location. However, because this intervention most likely requires clients to physically move to areas outside of the therapist's field of vision, it can be helpful to understand a few critical pieces about the family's environment. First, explain to clients that you would like to do an activity that may involve physical movement outside of their current physical location and ask the following to help determine appropriate rules and boundaries:

- Are there any areas of your physical environment that may be inaccessible or forbidden to certain people?
- Are there any areas of your physical environment that are unsafe?
- Are there any areas of your physical environment that lack confidentiality?
- Are there any areas of your physical environment that lack a strong Wi-Fi connection?

Awareness of these factors should inform the therapist in making critical adaptations in the implementation of this intervention. For example, the family may have a rule that children may not go in the parents' bedroom or an older sibling's bedroom. If this is the case, when providing further instructions for the activity, specify that family members should not go into the parents' or older sibling's bedroom during the activity.

Prior to conducting the activity, determine a list of items that you would like the clients to find during the scavenger hunt. You may develop the lists of items for clients to find based on their particular presenting problem and your own theoretical orientation. The following provides example lists of items that you may ask clients to find that are aimed at assessment and intervention regarding the clients' presenting problem, feelings, communication, differentiation, and culture. Additionally, a list of questions is included that are just for fun and can be added to any type of list, though ways in which clients respond to these items can be informative as well!

Presenting Problem

- Something that represents the issue or problem that brings you to therapy
- Something that represents how the problem started
- Something that helps the problem get better
- Something that makes the problem worse
- Something that represents what life would look like if the problem disappeared

Feelings

- Something or someone that brings you comfort
- Something or someone that makes you feel [sad/happy/scared/proud/etc.]
- Something or someone that makes you laugh
- Something or someone that helps you relax
- Something or someone that makes you feel at home
- Something or someone that brings a [sad/happy/scared/proud/etc.] memory to mind
- Something that reminds you of a [sad/happy/scared/proud/etc.] memory with your [mom/dad/sister/brother/grandparent/etc.]
- Something that represents the love in your family
- Something that represents how you feel about living in your family

Communication

- Something you [disagree/fight/fought] about
- Something you agree about
- Something that represents the way your family talks with one other
- Something that makes you think of a time that you felt safe to tell the truth with one another

Differentiation

- Something of your own choice
- Something that represents each family member
- Something that is unique to you
- Something that is unique to your family
- Something that represents family togetherness
- Something that represents how the problem [affects/changes/impacts] each family member
- Something that you like that another member of the family doesn't like
- Something that another member of the family likes that you don't like
- Something you made

Culture

- Something that represents your [heritage/culture/spirituality/beliefs/values]
- Something that represents something you like about your [heritage/culture/spirituality/beliefs/values]

- Something that represents something you don't like about your [heritage/culture/spirituality/beliefs/values]
- Something that represents a change in the way that you [see/experience] your [heritage/culture/spirituality/beliefs/values]

Just for Fun

- Something that you do for fun
- Something that represents silliness in your family
- Something from nature
- Something that is loud
- Something that represents a favorite game you play with your family
- A picture or item from a family vacation or outing

The "just for fun" items can be helpful to use as filler items to break up the heavier content associated with the items of other categories.

You may use one of these exact lists in conducting the activity or you may alter items on these lists as you see fit. Alternatively, you might come up with an entirely new list based on your client's needs and therapeutic goals.

Instructions

The following outlines steps for conducting the scavenger hunt.

1. ***Provide instructions for the scavenger hunt.*** Provide clients with the list of items that you would like them to find. Indicate if you would like them to find items separately or if you would like them to collaborate in finding items together. Alternatively, you may gather additional assessment data on the decision-making process of the family by purposely leaving this part of the instruction unstated and observing whether they work separately or together on the task.

   If the intervention is introduced at the end of the session, ask clients to find the items some time prior to the next session and bring them with them the next time you meet. It can be helpful to explicitly discuss who will write the list of items down and where the list will be placed so everyone has access to it. The refrigerator is a great place for many families. It can also be helpful to email or message someone in the family with the list so they do not forget what is on it. If the scavenger hunt has been assigned as a homework assignment, clients may be more likely to complete the assignment if you send a reminder message to them at least 24 hours in advance of the next session. Start the next session by asking clients to share the items that they chose and begin processing. If clients did not complete the activity between sessions, process the reasons and underlying feelings in the family (Lowenstein & Hertlein, 2012). You can then ask them if they would like another chance to do it before the next session or do it now in the session.

   If the intervention is introduced at the beginning of the session, explain how long they will have to search for the items. The time allowed will depend on the number of items that you are asking that they find as well as the length of time remaining in the session. Five to fifteen minutes is likely an appropriate amount of time for most scavenger hunts. Also, explain that if they find the items sooner, they can return early. To assure that the family stays within the time limit, it can be helpful to ask the family to set a timer that all can hear or have a family member be responsible to keep the time. Conducting the hunt during session allows you to observe the family's interactions surrounding the activity and may provide important assessment data.

2. ***Search for the items.*** While clients are searching for the items, you have several options depending on the explicit instructions given, who is searching for items, and whether the family is using a camera that is easy to carry and move (e.g., phone vs. computer). If only the child is conducting the search, you may ask a parent to follow the child with the camera, if it is mobile, so you can observe the child's decision-making. Similarly, if the family is conducting the search together, you may ask an adult to carry the camera, if it is mobile, so you may observe the family interactions during the search. However, if none of these options are available or if clients express discomfort in response to "bringing you" with them, you may wait while the family conducts the search.
3. ***Rejoin.*** Once the allotted amount of time has passed, ask clients to return to the therapy space and display the items in a manner in which they can be seen on the camera.

Processing

Prior to having clients share the items that they found, it can be helpful to discuss the process of the scavenger hunt with the family. Ask questions that can open discussion regarding any family dynamics that may be relevant to understanding and addressing the presenting problem. For example, you might ask:

- What was it like to play this game?
- What was the [easiest/hardest] part of the scavenger hunt?
- Did anyone become [upset/frustrated/sad/etc.] during the scavenger hunt? How did the family deal with that?
- Did [presenting problem] come out during the scavenger hunt? If so, what happened?

You may also ask questions that align specifically with or your theoretical orientation. For example, if using a structural family therapy approach, the following questions might help with assessment of the family's structure, roles, boundaries, and hierarchies.

- Who initiated the scavenger hunt?
- Who led the scavenger hunt?
- Who made most of the decisions?
- How did you make decisions about which items to select?
- Did people search separately or did anyone work together on certain tasks?
- If you were a team, what roles did everyone take on?
- Was anyone left out of the scavenger hunt?

If approached from a Bowenian perspective, you might ask:

- Did anyone want to select something different? If so, what would you have chosen and why?
- How did you decide on that object?
- What would [mom/dad/brother/sister/etc.] have chosen differently for this object?
- How do you think [mom/dad/brother/sister/etc.] [thinks/feels] about your selection?
- How did [mom/dad/brother/sister/etc.] react when you selected this object?

Then, ask questions about the items that were gathered. Questions may include:

- Tell me about [selected item].
- How did you decide to select this item?
- If you were searching somewhere else, what else might you have found?

When processing, ask each member of the client system about their experiences, reasoning, and unique perspectives. Circular questioning can be an excellent way to follow up on perspectives of others throughout the process. For example, you might ask:

- If I asked [mom/dad/brother/sister/etc.], what would they say?
- What do you think [mom/dad/brother/sister/etc.] feels about [this experience/what you said]?
- If [family member who was not present] were here today, what would they have selected?
- If [family member who was not present] were here today, what would have been different about this experience?

Vignette

Aniska (30) presented for family therapy with her children, Vidia (6) and Samuel (4), after the recent death of her husband and the children's father, Jerimiah (40). Aniska was worried about how her children were coping and acknowledged that she herself was struggling with his death. She was worried about crying in front of Vidia and Samuel and wanted to remain "strong." Aniska reported not knowing how to talk to her children about the death and appeared overwhelmed with their emotions.

The therapist chose to conduct a scavenger hunt as a means of opening up conversations in a safe, playful way, integrating Satir-experiential therapy with this approach. After introducing the activity and assessing the home environment, assuring that the children were free to move around the house, the therapist directed each family member to find:

- Something that makes you happy
- Something that makes you sad
- Something that makes you laugh
- Something that reminds you of Papa

- Something that has changed since the Papa died
- Something that has stayed the same since the Pap died

Upon rejoining, the therapist asked each member of the family to share what they had found. Each person shared their items and the accompanying memories that were tied to each item. Though the therapist did not explicitly ask the family to expand on their feelings, the prompts provided in the scavenger hunt provided a natural segue for each person to share more of their emotions regarding things that made them happy and sad – particularly as it related to the loss of Jerimiah. Though Aniska appeared somewhat hesitant to openly discuss her feelings with her children at first, her children's openness appeared to naturally ease her nerves and she gradually appeared more comfortable discussing Jerimiah and his death with her children. In addition to discussing each individual item, the therapist processed with the family their overall experience of the activity to gain a greater perspective of their process of opening up with one another in this new way.

Therapist: What was it like to play this game?

Vidia: It was fun!

Therapist: You had so much fun Vidia! I saw you running so fast! What made your body move so fast?

Vidia: It was exciting to find things about Papa. I like talking about Papa.

Samuel: I like talking about him too. I miss Papa.

Therapist: Aniska, what is that like for you to hear how much Vidia likes talking about Papa?

Aniska: I didn't realize the kids might like talking about him. I was worried that bringing him up would just make them sad.

From this point, the therapist continued to process the experiences and feelings of the children, with the goal of creating a new, congruent communication for talking about Papa that broadened the experience to include positive emotions as well as grief and sadness.

Suggestions for Follow-Up

Different variations of a scavenger hunt can be completed in different sessions, depending on the needs of clients. For example, a family might complete a hunt focused on feelings in one session and differentiation in another. Alternatively, the same hunt could be completed at two different points in time to assess for therapeutic change. For example, you could ask clients to search for items related to the presenting problem in an early stage of therapy and again after a couple of months to see if clients choose the same items or if their selected items change. In this instance, help to identify the reasoning for any changes in items that were selected at this later stage of therapy. Processing questions asked in subsequent sessions for either the same or different hunts can help to identify changes in family structure, roles, power, etc.

Contraindications

Scavenger hunts may not be appropriate for clients who are in environments that are not confidential outside of the room in which they are conducting teletherapy or that may not be developmentally safe for children to explore. Carefully assess whether this intervention is appropriate prior to conducting it.

References

Cavett, A. (2010). Our family life scavenger hunt. In L. Lowenstein (Ed.), *Creative family therapy techniques: Play, art, and expressive therapies to engage children in family sessions* (pp. 55–57). Champion.

Furrow, J. Palmer, G., Johnson, S., Faller, G., & Palmer-Olsen, L. (2019). *Emotionally focused family therapy: Restoring connection and promoting resilience.* Routledge.

Kerr, M., & Bowen, M. (1988). *Family evaluation: An approach based on Bowen theory.* Norton.

Lowenstein, L., & Hertlein, K. (2012). Engaging children in family sessions: Three creative interventions. *Journal of Family Psychotherapy, 23*(1), 62–66. https://doi.org/10.1080/08975353.2012.654090

CHAPTER 25

BREAKING UP SESSIONS

Kristina Betz, Tiffany Alexis Leal, Anna Wilson, and Rebecca A. Cobb

Materials for Therapists and Clients: None.

Objective

Sitting in front of a computer for an entire therapy session can be difficult for many children and adolescents. This can be especially challenging for those who spend the majority of the day sitting in a classroom and for those who more generally struggle with sitting still and maintaining focus, such as those with attention-deficit hyperactivity disorder. This chapter presents ideas for various activities that can be utilized to "break up" sessions and actively engage children and adolescents throughout teletherapy.

Rationale for Use

To effectively engage children and adolescents in teletherapy, therapists may need to creatively engage clients in several different shorter activities or break up their sessions with playful activities that engage the senses. Sessions can be broken up with physical, mental, and emotionally regulating activities, depending on the needs of each client. The incorporation of physical movement can be particularly impactful for those who have the freedom and space available to move around the room during their teletherapy sessions. Physical activity has been shown to reduce anxiety, decrease depressive symptoms, and have a positive impact on mental health in children (Robinson & Wadsworth, 2010; Savina et al., 2016). Movement can also help children learn boundaries and develop tools for self-regulation (Furmanek, 2014; Williams, 2018). In addition, moving and learning are intrinsically intertwined. Movement stimulates the growth of new neurons which aids in learning new skills, and over time, allowing the individual to grow their behavioral skills and understanding (Stevens-Smith, 2016a, 2016b). Despite research showing the benefits of movement for children and adolescents, they are typically in sedentary positions for over 50% of their day (Pereira et al., 2019). This may make it even more difficult for children and adolescents to focus in teletherapy if they are expected to remain seated in front of a camera for nearly an hour (Stevens-Smith, 2016a). After sitting for only half an hour, over 80% of the body's blood pools in the hips, thus reducing the rate at which fresh oxygen gets introduced into the blood (Stevens-Smith, 2016a). This means that halfway through a therapy session, it is harder for new

DOI: 10.4324/9781003330912-30

learning to occur as the rate of oxygenation has decreased. Movement is crucial in allowing children and adolescents to fully process whatever they may be learning through the process of therapy.

This chapter proposes breaking up teletherapy sessions with various activities to actively engage children and adolescents throughout the therapeutic process. Though many of the activities proposed involve the use of physical movement, activities involving mental and emotionally regulating activities are also included for those who have limited space or simply need something different given their own physical, intellectual, and emotional needs. Each activity is appropriate for children and adolescents of all ages, though adaptations may be made to tailor each activity to the needs and preferences of each client.

Setup

Though no formal setup is necessary, consider the following prior to implementing activities to break up sessions.

- ***Timing of activity:*** It may be helpful to add activity breaks at natural breaking points or lulls in the conversation and before moving onto the next topic of conversation or therapeutic activity. Alternatively, you may build in regularly scheduled activities around the midpoint of sessions to maintain client engagement before it is lost. Otherwise, pay attention to instances in which clients appear to lack enthusiasm in their responses, start to fidget or become restless, appear bored or distracted, appear to have trouble focusing, or make more overt comments like, "What time is it?" or "How much longer do we have left?"
- ***Selecting an activity:*** When you notice that it's time to take a break, either provide clients with options for different activities that they can do or choose the activity for them based on the needs of each client. For example, if a child shows signs of anxiety, it may be helpful to suggest a mindfulness or breathing exercise that can calm the nervous system.
- ***Availability of space:*** Avoid assuming that clients have ample space to move around for activities that require physical movement. Inquire about the space available to them. Discuss with caregivers the use of physical movement within sessions to determine which spaces child and adolescent clients are allowed to be.
- ***Boundaries:*** Discuss the boundaries of the activity and of the physical space that clients may use during the activity. Specify if you would like them to stay in the same room as the device from which they are attending therapy or if you expect them to stay within the frame of the camera so you can maintain visual contact. If you allow clients to leave the frame of the camera, discuss when you expect them to return to the device being used for teletherapy. Devise a way in which to alert clients when it is time to return (e.g., set an alarm, play a certain song).
- ***Time allotment:*** Before having clients engage in any activity, let them know how much time they will have to do the exercise. For some activities, this may be a set amount of time. For others, you may simply explain that the activity will last for "one song" or "one breathing exercise" and that you will reengage in your discussion or begin a new activity after that. Successfully implemented activities may be as short as a minute or last as long as ten minutes. Consider the length of time left in the session, the needs of the client(s), and how long you realistically think it will take to conduct the activity. It can be helpful to provide reminders (e.g., "one minute left") as the activity is ending so clients can settle back into the session quickly and efficiently.

Instructions

The following describes activities to "break up" sessions and engage child and adolescent clients using free dance, structured dance, stretching, show and share, scavenger hunts, drawing, breathing exercises, and mindfulness activities.

Free Dance

To have clients engage in free dance, it can be helpful to play music. You might start off by asking clients if they have a favorite song that they like to dance to. Alternatively, make your own playlist to use in session. Before playing songs with children and adolescents, determine their appropriateness and consider fit for the age(s) of your client(s). Then, tell them that you'd like them to get up, move around, and show off their dance moves! If space is limited, it's okay for clients to dance while seated. Just a little movement and stimulation provided by the music may go a long way. For clients to feel they can actively participate, bring your own enthusiasm and energy into this activity. Don't be afraid to get silly and have fun with it!

Structured Dance

If free dance appears to be uncomfortable, consider playing a familiar song that incorporates instructions for dance or other forms of physical movement. The *Hokey Pokey* (as known in the United States and Canada) or the *Hokey Cokey* (as known in Ireland, the United Kingdom, and some parts of Australia and the Caribbean) is a popular children's song that is accompanied by dance in response to the lyrics. You may play your favorite version of the song, or you may simply sing it if you know the words. Other songs with "built in dance instructions" include Caspar Babypants' *Run Baby Run* and Raffi's *Shake My Sillies Out* (personal favorites of the last author's two- and four-year-old children).

Stretching

Invite clients to stretch in ways that feel good for them. Be mindful of any possible poses or movements that might be overexerting for clients. Be aware of any physical injuries or limitations of clients and attune to client cues that may indicate overexertion.

Show and Share

Tell clients that you'd like them to show you something that they would like to share with you! Give them a set amount of time to think of something, go get it, and bring it back to you. An added benefit of this activity is the possibility of gaining new information about something that is special to your clients. Once they've shown you the object, you can ask them to describe the object, how they feel about it, and what it is about that object that made them want to share it with you.

Scavenger Hunts

Scavenger hunts can be used therapeutically in numerous ways (see Chapter 24). However, they can also be used as more brief interventions to break up sessions. Ask clients to find certain objects and bring them back to show you. Provide instructions that if the objects are large, breakable, not safe to touch, or something that they are otherwise not allowed to touch, they may bring a camera with them to take a picture if one is available. Otherwise, they may simply describe the object to you once they've found it. If participating from a mobile device, clients may "bring you with them" for the hunt! The following is a list of items that you may ask clients to find:

- Something that's special to you
- Something you're proud of
- Something that has your favorite color on it
- Something that makes you laugh
- Something you enjoy doing with friends
- Something that brings back a happy memory
- Something that brings you comfort
- Something that makes you feel safe

An added benefit of this activity is that you have the possibility to gain new information about clients through the objects that they share with you. Once they've shown you each object, you can ask them to describe the object, how they feel about it, and what it is about that object that made them choose it.

Drawing

Ask clients to engage in their own free art or provide a specific prompt such as "color your current feelings or emotions." Clients may use materials available in their physical location (e.g., paper, crayons, colored pencils, markers) or they can use a whiteboard function if one is available on your teletherapy platform. Alternatively, clients may use an online drawing tool such as Mindful Draw (see Chapter 27) or Sesame Street's ArtMaker: Draw It Out! (Sesame Workshop, 2016). For clients who have difficulty being on a computer or tablet for a long time, it may be helpful to use physical materials to draw without the use of the device used to engage in teletherapy.

Breathing Exercises

Select from a variety of breathing exercises, such as bubble breathing, rainbow breathing, ocean breathing, and color breathing. Some other breathing techniques with virtual tools from Sesame Workshop (2016), a free reputable online resource, include: "Slow it Down" and "Breathe, Think, Do!" Lead clients in these breathing exercises or show the interactive breathing exercises on your computer. Encourage clients to follow along with their own breath. Participate in the breathing exercise with them to model self-regulation and deep breathing while engaging in co-regulation with clients.

Mindfulness

Select from a variety of mindfulness activities. For example, you could lead an activity from Willey's (2017) *Breathe Like a Bear.* Alternatively, you may use a website or application to help guide the activity (e.g., HeadSpace, Sesame Workshop's "Comfy Cozy Nest"). Encourage clients to find a comfortable place to sit, while still allowing them to be within view of the camera. For this activity, it's important that you be able to see clients throughout the activity in the event that they become emotionally triggered. Guide clients through the mindfulness exercise using a calming, quiet voice. This activity should not feel rushed. It may take more time for some clients to settle into their space than others.

Processing

Upon the conclusion of the activity, consider processing it using the following questions.

- What did it feel like to [dance/stretch/show me your object(s)/draw/breathe deeply/practice mindfulness]?
- What kind of emotions did you feel [before/during/after] [dancing/stretching/showing me your object(s)/drawing/breathing/doing the mindfulness activity]?
- Where in your body did you feel that emotion?
- Are there other times that you like to [dance/stretch/share objects with others/draw/breathe deeply/practice mindfulness]?
- Do you ever [dance/stretch/share objects/draw/breathe deeply/practice mindfulness] with other people?
- What might it be like to [dance/stretch/share objects/draw/breathe deeply/practice mindfulness] with your [mom/dad/family/friends/etc.]?
- When might be another good time to [dance/stretch/share objects/draw/breathe deeply/practice mindfulness]?

Contraindications and Suggestions for Follow-Up

Observe client reactions to the aforementioned activities and discuss with them their experience. Make adjustments as needed. For example, some children may become overstimulated by particular songs or more overt physical activities and may be more difficult to reengage after the activity. If this occurs, consider engaging in a mindfulness activity or breathing exercise after the conclusion of the activity.

References

Furmanek, D. (2014). Classroom choreography: Enhancing learning through movement. *Young Children, 69*(4), 80–85. https://www.jstor.org/stable/ycyoungchildren.69.4.80

Pereira, J. R., Cliff, D. P., Sousa-Sá, E., Zhang, Z., & Santos, R. (2018a). Prevalence of objectively measured sedentary behavior in early years: Systematic Review and meta-analysis. *Scandinavian Journal of Medicine & Science in Sports, 29*(3), 308–328. https://doi.org/10.1111/sms.13339

Robinson, L. E., & Wadsworth, D. D. (2010). Stepping toward physical activity requirements: Integrating pedometers into early childhood settings. *Early Childhood Education Journal, 38*(2), 95–102. https://doi.org/10.1007/s10643-010-0388-y

Savina, E., Garrity, K., Kenny, P., & Doerr, C. (2016). The benefits of movement for youth: A whole child approach. *Contemporary School Psychology, 20*(3), 282–292. https://doi.org/10.1007/s40688-016-0084-z

Sesame Workshop. (2016). *ArtMaker: Draw it out!* Sesame Street for Military Families. https://sesamestreetformilitaryfamilies.org/games/artmaker/

Stevens-Smith, D. A. (2016a). Active bodies/active brains: Practical applications using physical engagement to enhance brain development. *Strategies*, *29*(6), 3–7. https://doi.org/10.1080/08924562.2016.1231096

Stevens-Smith, D. A. (2016b). Active bodies/active brains: The relationship between physical engagement and children's brain development. *The Physical Educator*, *73*(4), 719–732. https://doi.org/10.18666/tpe-2016-v73-i4-6447

Willey, K. (2017). *Breathe like a bear*. Rodale Kids.

Williams, K. E. (2018). Moving to the beat: Using music, rhythm, and movement to enhance self-regulation in early childhood classrooms. *International Journal of Early Childhood*, *50*(1), 85–100. https://doi.org/10.1007/s13158-018-0215-y

Part 6

Working with Emotions

CHAPTER 26

CUSTOMIZABLE FEELINGS CHARTS

Kristina Betz and Rebecca A. Cobb

Materials for Therapists: PowerPoint and feelings chart template (included in the supplemental materials that accompany this book).

Materials for Clients: None. *Optional:* Printer.

Objective

Children and adolescents often need help identifying and naming the varied emotions that they experience. Feelings charts are used in therapy to aid with this task (Willcox, 1982). This chapter provides instructions for collaboratively creating customized feelings charts by asking clients to make faces to convey different emotions and taking screenshots via teletherapy. Completed feelings charts can then be printed and used outside of therapy to help express feelings with other members of the client's system.

Rationale for Use

Naming and identifying feelings are initial steps that must be taken in learning to regulate emotions and communicate them with others. Feelings charts list a varied number of different emotions that are accompanied by example images of faces portraying each of the listed emotions. This provides an accessible tool that can be used in identifying emotions both inside and outside of therapy (Willcox, 1982). In therapy, feelings charts can be used as a focal point in providing psychoeducation about emotions and in discussing them with clients. Outside of therapy, clients can use feelings charts to identify their feelings to others. Likewise, other members of the client's system may use feelings charts to initiate discussion of emotions outside of therapy sessions. Putting feelings into words reduces emotional reactivity by decreasing activity in emotion-processing brain regions like the amygdala and increasing activity in the prefrontal cortex (Lieberman et al., 2007).

A disadvantage of using premade feelings charts is that some may have an overwhelming number of feelings represented, whereas others may not convey key feelings that a client may need to practice processing. In addition, although the facial expressions that people use to convey different emotions are considered universal, people from different cultures understand and perceive emotions differently (Jack et al., 2012). Moreover, the degree to which people show their emotions on their faces can vary (Binetti et al., 2022).

DOI: 10.4324/9781003330912-32

Rather than using premade feelings charts, therapists may create customized feelings charts based on each client's age, emotional intelligence, presenting problem(s), and their own unique ways of displaying emotion. The creation of customizable feelings charts increases client engagement, supports therapists and clients in identifying and discussing feelings in session, and supports clients in identifying and discussing feelings with others outside of therapy.

Setup

The following provides step-by-step instructions to prepare for the creation of a customizable feelings chart.

1. ***Acquire guardian consent.*** Discuss with legal guardians the possibility of taking photographs of minor clients for the purpose of the activity. Alternatively, you may include the use of photographs in a digital tools consent form (see Chapter 10). If guardians do not consent to taking photographs, do not conduct the activity and use a premade feelings chart, draw facial representations of emotions, or do another activity instead.
2. ***Discuss comfort with having photographs taken.*** Talk with children and adolescent clients about how they feel having their photos taken. If they do not want their photo taken, do another activity instead.
3. ***Introduce the activity.*** Discuss with clients the possibility of creating a customizable feelings chart as a way of helping you get to know them and the ways that they show their feelings better.
4. ***Choose a template.*** If legal guardians and child/adolescent clients consent to having their photos taken and doing the activity, select one of the three feelings chart templates from the supplemental materials that accompany this book. Consider the client's age and their level of emotional intelligence. As children age, their emotional intelligence grows (Eggum et al., 2011; Lieberman et al., 2007) and the feelings that they can identify and process also grow. Therefore, it is helpful to use simpler feelings charts when working with younger children (see Figures 26.1 and 26.2) and more complex charts that list a greater number of emotions when working with adolescents with higher emotional intelligence (see Figure 26.3).
5. ***Edit the template.*** Prior to the session in which you plan to conduct the activity, make any changes that you would like to make to the template so that it will be more fitting for your client(s). You may delete feeling words to make the chart smaller, add more words to make it larger, or change words that are on the template to terms that are more fitting for your client's needs. Utilize terms that you, your client, or other members of their system use to name emotions and include any relevant words for emotions that are related to the client's presenting problem or that you hope to address in therapy. Ensure that basic emotions are represented in the chart (e.g., happiness, sadness, fear, anger). Also consider the balance between emotions. For example, it may be helpful to include words like proud, peaceful, and confident to make the experience of creating the chart and the final outcome more joyful. The inclusion of the term "silly" is also a great way to make the activity more fun and engaging. You could include the terms "silly," "sillier," and "silliest" to allow for an even more fun process and outcome! Finally, add your client's name to the chart. If you know their favorite color, you may also change the color of the chart and/or make other edits to its design.

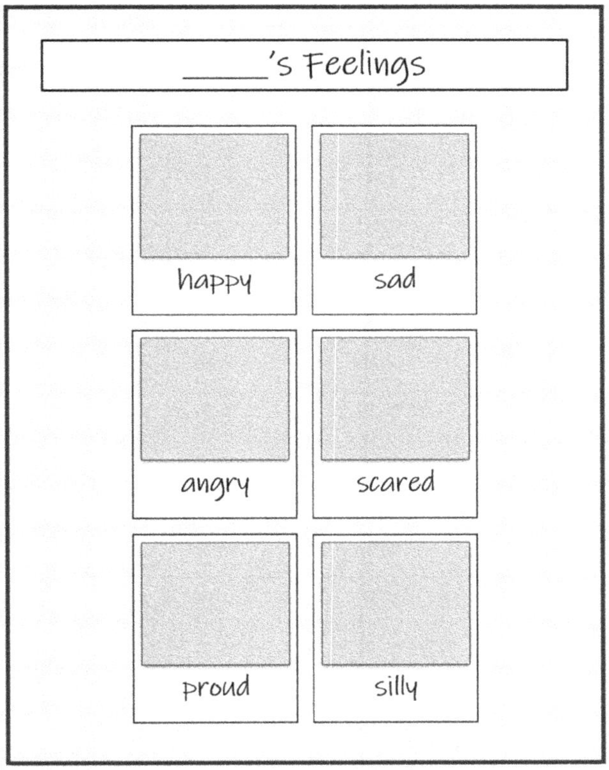

Figure 26.1 Feelings chart template with six feelings.

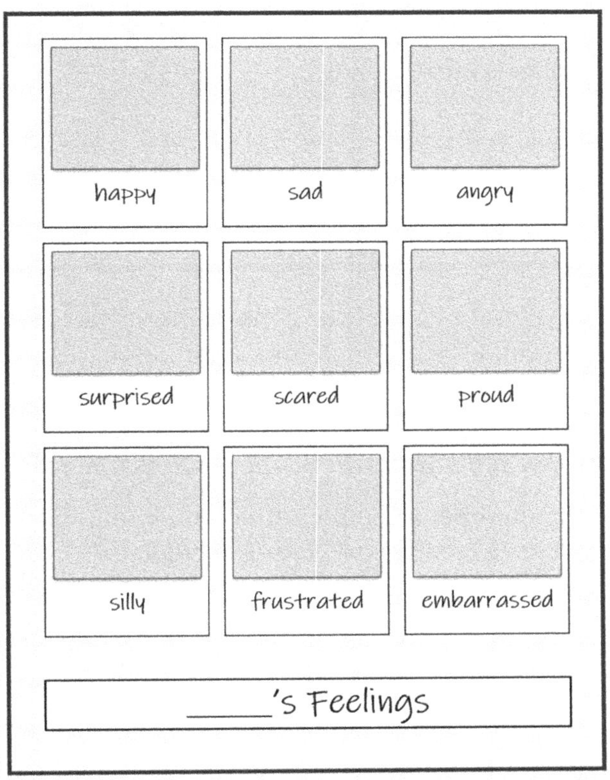

Figure 26.2 Feelings chart template with nine feelings.

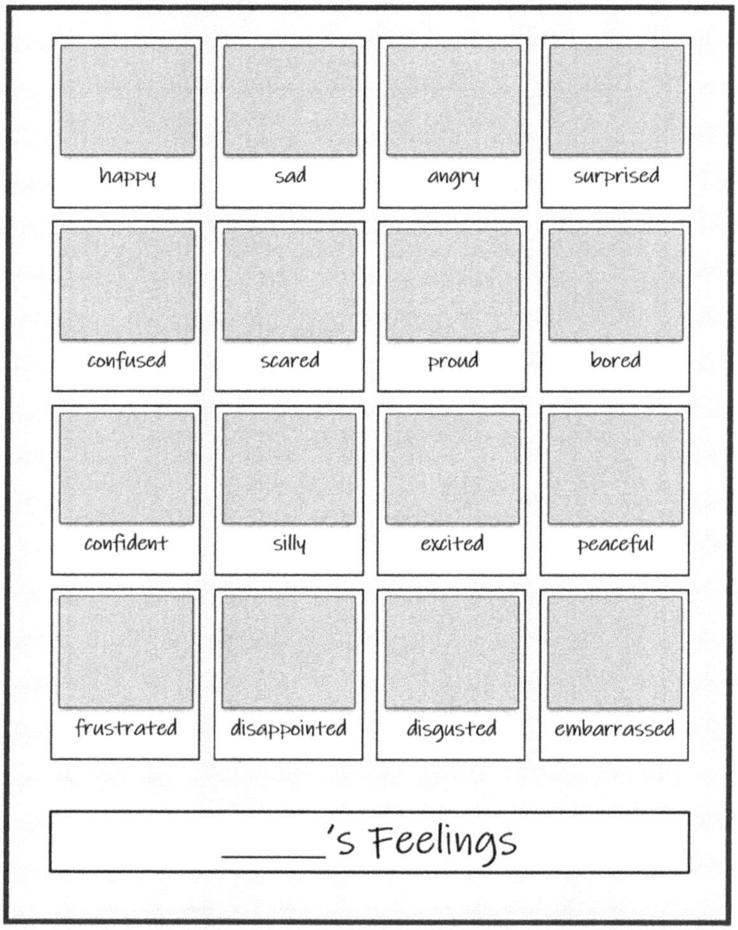

Figure 26.3 Feelings chart template with 16 feelings.

Instructions

The following provides instructions for constructing the feelings chart in session. When working with more than one person, you can create multiple charts simultaneously.

1. ***Share your screen.*** Only allow the program that you are using to edit the feelings chart to be visible so that clients can't see other windows or applications that may be open on your computer.
2. ***Review the feelings chart template.*** Explain that you would like help finishing the chart by adding a photo to illustrate each feeling word that is included.
3. ***Stop screensharing and prepare a folder.*** Make a folder in a Health Insurance Portability and Accountability Act (HIPAA)-compliant location that you can save photographs to. Ensure that this folder does not contain any other files, as it may become visible to clients through the process of reviewing photos and adding them to the chart.

4. ***Prepare to take screenshots.*** Make the image of your client as large as possible on your screen. Close or minimize any other windows so they will not be visible while taking screenshots. Ensure that no other confidential information will appear in screenshots.
5. ***Take photographs.*** Instruct the client to make faces depicting each of the emotions that are listed on the chart. For example, you might say, "What does your face look like when you feel really [happy/sad/angry/scared/proud/silly/etc.]? Can you show me? I'll take a picture!" Then take a screenshot.
6. ***Save photographs.*** Ensure that all photographs are saved in a HIPAA-compliant way. Repeat this same process until you have images for every emotion listed on the chart. It may be helpful to take several screenshots for each emotion so clients can choose from available options.
7. ***Share your screen.*** Only allow the file that contains your client's images to be visible so clients can't see other windows or applications that may be open on your computer.
8. ***Review images.*** If you took more than one screenshot for each emotion, ask the client to choose the image that they would like to include on the chart. Some clients may need to process the way that they look while expressing different emotions. Name and discuss any feelings that may come up in the process (e.g., embarrassment, frustration, happiness, pride).
9. ***Stop screen sharing.*** Though it may be therapeutic and engaging to involve clients in the process of adding each selected photo to the chart, the process of clicking on the photo icon in PowerPoint to access the folder in which you saved your client's images may take you through other folders that may contain confidential client information or other folders/files that clients should not see. Error on the side of caution to maintain confidentiality by adding photographs to the chart without sharing your screen during this process.
10. ***Add photographs to the chart.*** Add the selected photos to the chart to illustrate each feeling. While doing this, you may build anticipation by saying something like, "Oh, I can't wait for you to see the finished product!"
11. ***Share your screen.*** Once again, share your screen, only allowing the program that you used to create the feelings chart to be visible.
12. ***Review the chart.*** You might start by making an overall comment about the chart by saying something like, "Wow! This looks great! What do you think?" Then, one by one, name each feeling from the chart. You may make a comment about the photograph selected to illustrate each feeling, such as, "You really do look [happy/sad/angry/scared/etc.] here!"

Processing

You may provide a bit of psychoeducation about each feeling as you name them and/or ask a processing question about that feeling. For example, you might ask:

- When was the last time that you felt [happy/sad/angry/scared/etc.]?
- When you're feeling [happy/sad/angry/scared/etc.], where do you feel it in your body?
- What do you usually do when you're feeling [happy/sad/angry/scared/etc.]?

- What usually stops you from feeling [happy/sad/angry/scared/etc.]?
- Do you think people can usually tell when you're feeling [happy/sad/angry/scared/etc.]?
- How do you think others figure out when you're feeling [happy/sad/angry/scared/etc.]?
- How do you know when your [mom/dad/sister/brother/etc.] is feeling [happy/sad/angry/scared/etc.]?
- Who do you usually [talk/spend time] with when you're feeling [happy/sad/angry/scared/etc.]?
- What do you do for others when they're feeling [happy/sad/angry/scared/etc.]?

Finally, ask if the chart needs any changes made to it. Some clients may want to change photos and take new ones. You may also work with clients to make any changes to the aesthetics of the chart (e.g., change the font or color). Make any changes necessary.

Vignette

Jax (8) was brought to teletherapy by his mother, Shannon (26), a single mother who worked full time. Jax had been diagnosed with attention-deficit hyperactive disorder and anxiety and struggled with emotional outbursts that sometimes turned violent. Jax's teacher spoke to Shannon regarding an incident that occurred on the playground where Jax wanted to join a four-square game on the playground and when he was denied by his peers, he reacted by jumping on a boy his age and hitting him. Shannon explained she had become worried about Jax's struggle to regulate his emotions, both at school and at home. Jax shared that the other kids at school didn't want to play with him and, sometimes, he got "so mad."

At the end of the first session, the therapist introduced the idea of creating a feelings chart the following week as a way of getting to know one another better in a fun and perhaps even silly way. The therapist asked Shannon and Jax how they both felt about having their pictures taken to do this activity. Shannon and Jax both agreed that this sounded like a good idea and shared that they were comfortable having their pictures taken.

Prior to the next session, the therapist edited one of the feelings chart templates that are included with the supplemental materials that accompany this book (see Figure 26.2). The therapist wanted to use Jax's language and edited the word "angry" to "mad." The therapist also edited the chart to include the word "lonely," to allow Jax an opportunity to discuss feelings that he may have about being left out of play activities by other kids at school. The therapist wanted to include his mom in the process and edited the chart to also include "worried," a term that his mom had brought up in relation to her concerns about Jax and what was going on with him.

In the following session, the therapist guided Jax and Shannon through the process of creating a feelings chart for each of them. Both appeared to have fun throughout the process of making different faces for the therapist and commenting on one another's expressions. Upon completion of the charts, the therapist shared their screen and reviewed the final product with them (Figures 26.4 and 26.5).

The therapist began the session by asking Jax and Shannon about their experience working together on the feelings chart. Shannon shared that although it was initially awkward to make faces and have photos taken, she soon found joy in Jax's enthusiastic participation. She realized that collaborating with Jax made the process more fun and less uncomfortable. Jax mentioned that it was difficult to come up with each face, but with the support and patience from Shannon and the therapist, he found the activity fun and silly. He enjoyed making faces with his mom and appreciated seeing her expressions while practicing his own. Both Jax and Shannon felt safer exploring their emotions, recognizing that everyone experiences them.

The therapist then asked Jax how he would like Shannon to use the feelings chart. Jax suggested incorporating it into their daily routine during breakfast and dinner to discuss their feelings. They also considered how the chart could be helpful outside the home, such as on errands, vacations, and play-dates. Shannon and Jax brainstormed making multiple copies of the chart for different locations. Jax suggested placing copies on the fridge, in his backpack, with his teacher, in the car, and in Shannon's purse.

Continuing the discussion, they explored various ways to use the charts outside of therapy. They considered teaching Jax's teacher how to use the chart, having a copy with Jax during recess, and checking in weekly to see if any emotions or pictures needed updating. The therapist asked how identifying emotions could help Jax process and respond to them more effectively. Jax and Shannon agreed that the feelings chart would aid in this identification and began exploring emotional regulation tools to pair with it. Jax came up with strategies for when he feels "so mad," including telling an adult, splashing cold water on his face, and doing jumping jacks. This intervention allowed Jax and Shannon

Figure 26.4 Jax's completed feelings chart.

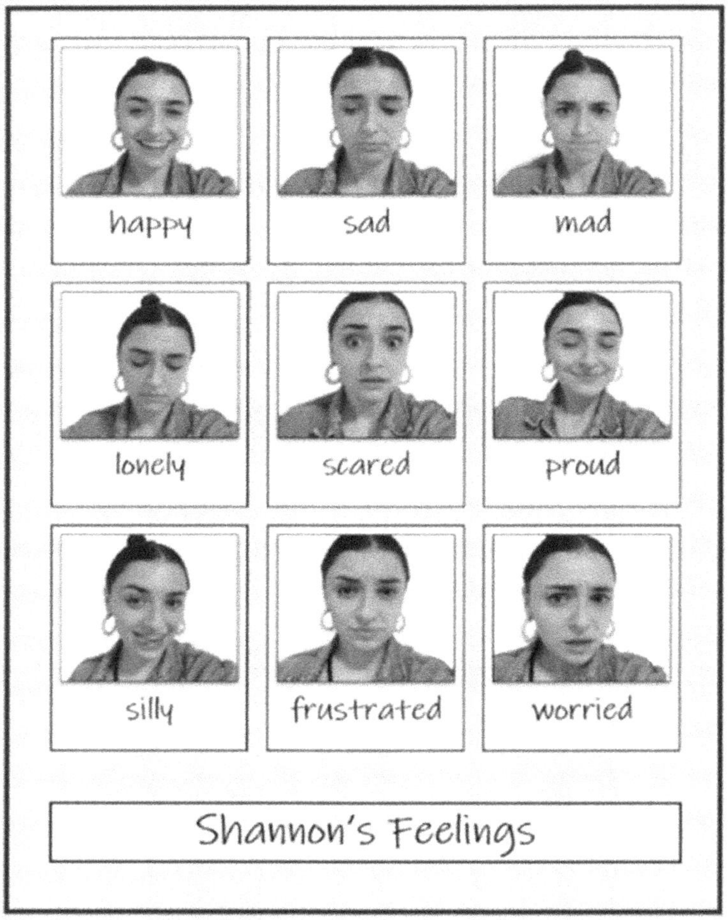

Figure 26.5 Shannon's completed feelings chart.

to connect with their feelings in a safe way, reminded them that everyone has emotions, and created a tangible support for emotional identification for them both.

Suggestions for Follow-Up

If desired, you can edit photos in Photoshop between sessions to delete the background behind your client and make it so that only the person's face is visible. You can do this for each photograph by (1) importing a photo into Photoshop, (2) using the magic wand tool to "mask," or hide/reveal parts of an image, (3) clean up the edges of the photograph, (4) save the revised file, and (5) export the file to your preferred file format (e.g., JPEG, PNG).

Completed charts can be sent to clients so they can print them and post them in a prominent location within their household. The refrigerator is a great place for this! You can then encourage clients to use the chart to communicate emotions and to facilitate further discussions outside of sessions. For example, clients may place a magnet next to the feeling that they are experiencing to communicate a felt emotion if they experience difficulty communicating this feeling verbally. By creating a chart that represents the client, everyone in the client's system may benefit from enhanced communication and clear indicators of felt experience.

In subsequent sessions, you may revisit customized feelings charts by asking about their use outside of sessions and using them to help identify, name, and discuss emotions that are experienced in sessions. As clients develop further emotional intelligence and/or experience other emotions in need of processing, you can edit completed feelings charts by adding on new terms, taking new images, and processing more complex feelings.

Contraindications

Consider culture, spirituality, and personal preferences as it relates to taking photographs and screenshots of clients. Some clients may be uncomfortable having their photo taken or using photographs for the purpose of this activity. Likewise, some guardians may be uncomfortable having their children's photos taken or using photographs for the purpose of this activity. Only conduct this activity if both clients and their guardians have consented to it. Provide alternative options or make variations to the activity as needed.

References

Binetti, N., Roubtsova, N., Carlisi, C., Cosker, D., Viding, E., & Mareschal, I. (2022). Genetic algorithms reveal profound individual differences in emotion recognition. *Proceedings of the National Academy of Sciences, 119*(45), Article e2201380119. https://doi.org/10.1073/pnas.2201380119

Eggum, D., Eisenberg, N., Kao, K., Spinrad, T., Bolnick, R., Hofer, C., Kupfer, A., & Fabricius, W. (2011). Emotion understanding, theory of mind, and prosocial orientation: Relations over time in early childhood. *The Journal of Positive Psychology, 6*(4), 101–114. https://doi.org/10.1080/17439760.2010.536776

Jack, E., Caldara, R., & Schyns, G. (2012). Internal representations reveal cultural diversity in expectations of facial expressions of emotion. *Journal of Experimental Psychology: General, 141*(1), 19–25. https://doi.org/10.1037/a0023463

Lieberman, M. D., Eisenberger, N. I., Crockett, M. J., Tom, S. M., Pfeifer, J. H., & Way, B. M. (2007). Putting feelings into words: Affect labeling disrupts amygdala activity in response to affective stimuli. *Psychological Science, 18*(5), 421–428. https://doi.org/10.1111/j.1467-9280.2007.01916.x

Willcox, G. (1982). The Feeling Wheel: A tool for expanding awareness of emotions and increasing spontaneity and intimacy. *Transactional Analysis Journal, 12*(4), 274–276. https://doi.org/10.1177/036215378201200411

CHAPTER 27

MINDFUL DRAWING IN ONLINE PLAY THERAPY

Karen Fried

Materials for Therapists and Clients: Access to the Mindful Draw app, available at mindfuldraw.com.

Objective

Mindful Draw is an online tool that allows users to create any image they want with a range of colors, brushstrokes, and even sounds. They then watch that image fade away. In a therapeutic setting, this activity benefits clients with affirmation of self through making choices, staying in the present, and metaphorically facing and coping with uncomfortable sensations. This chapter demonstrates the use of the Mindful Draw tool in facilitating the mindful expression and processing of feelings in teletherapy practice.

Rationale for Use

Research indicates that mindfulness practice improves attention, academic performance, executive functioning, and social-emotional maturation (Bostic et al., 2015; Geronimi et al., 2020; Schonert-Reichl et al., 2015). Mindfulness is an evidence-based intervention that supports the development of self-regulation and resilience in response to stress and trauma (Ortiz & Sibinga, 2017). Some advocate that mindfulness practice should be offered to all children (Substance Abuse and Mental Health Services Administration).

Drawing is an effective mode of expression and healing for children and adolescents and is also associated with mindfulness practice. Along with eliciting calm awareness, mindful drawing gives children and adolescents an age-appropriate opportunity to express their difficulties through symbolic projection. Allowing children to project their current state, and thereby experientially process, strengthens their sense of themselves as powerful and self-defining (Oaklander, 1978). Gross and Hayne (1998) found that children who drew pictures related to events in their lives were more likely to talk about them than children who did not draw such pictures.

Mindful Draw is a free online app that allows users to draw any image they want and then watch it fade. Users may select different colors, brush sizes, and brushstroke styles. They may also choose between silence and different sounds as they make their drawing. In addition, the app allows them to change the rate at which the drawing begins to fade, anywhere between 1 and 90 seconds.

The time allowed for the image to fade is based on the "90-second rule," or the 90-second chemical process that occurs in the body in response to events in the environment (TED, 2013; Siegel, 2014).

DOI: 10.4324/9781003330912-33

This chemical response results in felt experiences such as anger and anxiety. After a minute and a half, people may disengage from the feeling if they no longer think about it or they may stay in that emotional loop by revisiting the experience and thereby renewing the body's neurochemical response. By drawing something on the Mindful Draw app and being encouraged by a therapist to notice one's experience as they watch their drawing fade within 90 seconds, users practice the functional response of letting go of past experience, disengaging from thoughts and emotions when they are not productive, and remaining in the present moment.

In addition, Mindful Draw offers therapists insights that aid assessment. While clients learn about themselves, therapists learn from clients' responses to choices available in the app, which may indicate their sense of self. For example, if they appear to have difficulty deciding what to draw, what colors, brush style, sound, or fade time to pick, seem to worry about their drawing or chosen options, or struggle when expressing their experience, they may benefit from therapeutic goals aimed at enhancing their sense of self.

Mindful Draw has been applied therapeutically with clients in various parts of the world including Kenya and Ukraine. In one instance, adult refugees from genocide in their homeland participating in a citizenship course described their feelings and rated them from one to ten before using the Mindful Draw app. Many reported somatic markers of anxiety. After using the app, they were asked to revisit their feelings. Most reported a reduction in stress symptoms. This anecdotal evidence suggests that Mindful Draw provides a safe, cross-cultural tele-tool for uncovering and resolving a wide array of presenting problems including emotional dysregulation, intrusive thoughts, and test anxiety.

Setup

The following specifies the setup required to engage in the Mindful Draw app for online therapy assessment and intervention.

1. ***Familiarize yourself with the online platform.*** Visit mindfuldraw.com to survey available features. Practice using the virtual tool so you can guide clients as needed.
2. ***Determine whether clients have a computer, smartphone, or tablet they can use to access the Mindful Draw app.*** If none of these devices are available, offer alternate options for therapeutic intervention.
3. ***Offer options.*** Offer Mindful Draw as an available therapeutic activity along with other options. Acceptance or rejection of the activity allows clients to practice the self-affirming act of choosing.
4. ***Share the link.*** If Mindful Draw is chosen, access the online platform at mindfuldraw.com and share the website with clients in the chat function of your HIPAA-consistent therapy platform. Sharing a direct link allows clients to go to the website without having to type its address, which may be difficult for younger clients.
5. ***Share your screen.*** Share the browser in which mindfuldraw.com appears on your computer. Avoid sharing your entire screen, which may contain other distracting items.
6. ***Provide a visual tour.*** Show clients the Mindful Draw app and scroll through the available features including brush colors, brushstroke styles, and the speed at which their drawn image fades. They can also choose from a selection of relaxing sounds, including eye movement desensitization and reprocessing (EMDR) bilateral and bimanual pulse beats. They can further tailor their chosen sound to play in a continuous loop or for a set duration.

7. ***Discuss options to save images.*** While this app intends to normalize the fading of images, and thus the letting-go of emotions, it provides clients the option of saving drawings for later review by taking screenshots of them before they fade. It may help to discuss with clients the intention of this app to experience the fading of the image and the process of letting go. Ultimately, allow clients to decide whether they would like to save a copy of any image that they drew.
8. ***Share the clients' screen.*** Request that clients share their screen. If family members are participating in therapy from different locations, discuss who will share their screen.
9. ***Practice.*** Invite clients to play around with the app's options. If clients don't try different fade speeds on their own, encourage them to do so to see which ones feel best for them.

Instructions

The following instructions illustrate how to engage clients in therapeutic mindfulness using the Mindful Draw app and the Oaklander (1978) protocol, which intertwines prompts, responses, and processing.

1. ***Imagine it.*** Ask clients to imagine a particular event, idea, or feeling. You might consider inviting them to draw something about a theme that is relevant to the goals of therapy. For example, you might prompt clients to "think of something that makes you [angry/anxious/happy/sad/scared]" or to "imagine what [anger/anxiety/happiness/sadness/fear] might look like."
2. ***Feel it.*** Invite clients to notice how they feel when they think about this event, idea, or feeling.
3. ***Draw it.*** Invite clients to use the app to create an image of this event, idea, or feeling that will soon fade away into the background. Encourage them to practice mindfulness and being present in the moment. If clients appear to need extra encouragement, you can model steps of the activity for them as they pick, draw, let fade, and share about their own drawing.
4. ***Save it.*** If clients prefer to save their drawings for later review, save them before they fade.
5. ***Listen to it.*** Invite clients to choose one of the available sounds, such as a gentle stream, wind chimes, or EMDR beats, to play on a loop or on a timer. If chosen, encourage them to listen to the sounds while they draw.
6. ***Be it.*** Encourage clients to be the drawing or a part of the drawing before, during, or after it has faded. Ask them to speak as the drawing or the part of the drawing by asking, "What does it say?" and/or "What does it do?"
7. ***Watch it and relax.*** Encourage clients to relax their mind and body as they watch the image fade away.
8. ***Reflect on it.*** After the image fades, ask clients to notice how they feel. Ask them to report what they noticed in their mind and body before, during, and after drawing. Then, to engage more rational left-brain functioning, ask, "What is a word or a few words that go with how you're feeling about that [event/idea/feeling]?"
9. ***Repeat it.*** Ask clients to choose a color, brushstroke style, and fade time and write the word(s) on the screen. Then you may prompt clients to "Think about what you were thinking of when we started. What would you draw now? Draw it, and watch it fade." Alternatively, you may ask them to imagine what they're feeling now and to draw their current response to the event, idea, or feeling that they initially depicted. If they do so, ask them if, and how, their drawing and experience of it has changed.

Processing

Following the activity, it may help some clients to review and process the neurophysiological importance of a 90-second pause as being the length of time it takes an emotional reaction to occur. That makes this exercise especially valuable by accustoming clients to noticing how they're feeling during the 90-second fade time, and to practice pausing for 90 seconds rather than acting at the height of emotion. You might then discuss ways in which this strategy can be applied to everyday situations by asking questions such as the following.

- Does your drawing and what you noticed about it make sense for you in your life?
- How might you practice pausing for 90 seconds the next time that you're feeling [angry/anxiety/etc.] before acting on those emotions?

Vignette

Jeff (12) presented in therapy after the death of his mother. Jeff's parents had lived separately during the last 6 months of his mother's cancer treatment when financial pressure from medical expenses and his mother's inability to work forced his father to take a better-paying job out of town. Jeff struggled with reading and had previously been diagnosed with dyslexia. He had been reluctant to go to school because he thought his mother would die while he was out of the house, and his school refusal exacerbated his academic difficulties.

To address the trauma and grief brought by his mother's death, the therapist had Jeff imagine all the feelings he had about his mother dying as a "feelings soup." He was then invited to add in any other feeling "ingredients" he wanted to this "soup," including positive ones like relief or even happiness since, as he was reminded, "No feeling is bad or wrong. Put whatever feelings you want into your soup."

Jeff had played with the Mindful Draw app in the past and appeared to enjoy using it, so the therapist offered it as an activity among other choices by saying, "You can draw your soup in Mindful Draw and choose how long the image will last, or you can do a regular drawing on a piece of paper or the white board. It's your choice!" Jeff chose Mindful Draw and produced and reflected on four drawings.

After his first drawing (see Figure 27.1), Jeff explained, "This is my pot of soup and I have some feelings in it." He said he wanted to take a screenshot of it. He also said he wanted to take screenshots of all his drawings while they were fading, and that he wanted to talk about them after.

Figure 27.1 Jeff's first drawing, created at mindfuldraw.com.

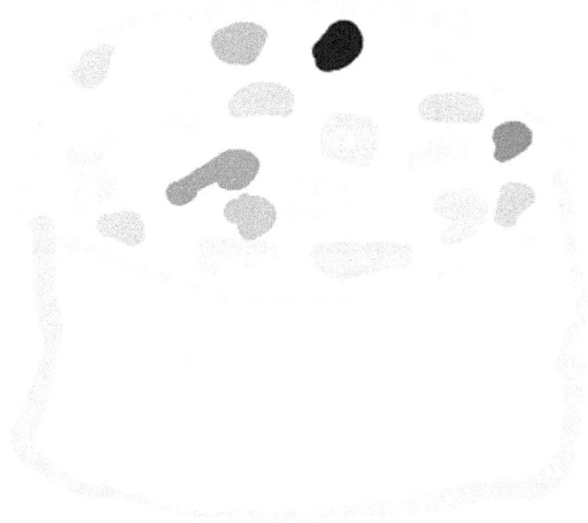

Figure 27.2 Jeff's second drawing with added emotions, created at mindfuldraw.com.

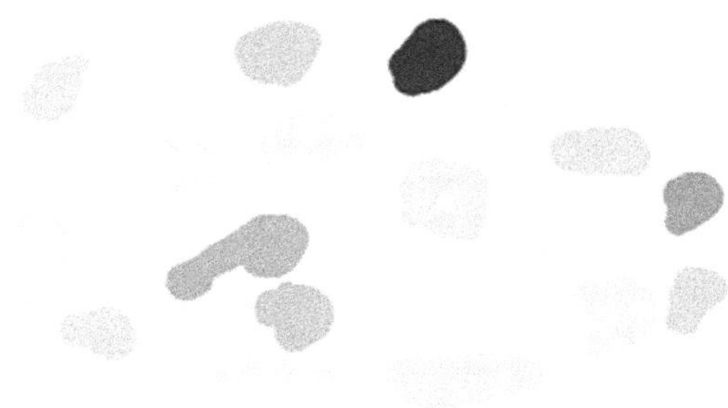

Figure 27.3 Jeff's third drawing with the pot gone, created at mindfuldraw.com.

As this drawing was fading, Jeff stated that he wanted to add more ingredients to the soup because, as he put it, "I'm feeling more as I watch the picture change." So he added more to the fading scene (see Figure 27.2).

At this point, Jeff told the therapist, "Now the pot is gone and it's just my feelings left" (see Figure 27.3).

Therapist: How is it now that just the feelings are left?

Jeff: That's how I feel right now. I only have feelings and nowhere to put them.

Therapist: Do you want to draw anything else to put your feelings somewhere?

Jeff: No. This is just what it's like right now.

They then looked at and processed what remained of his drawing (see Figure 27.4), which he also saved.

Figure 27.4 Jeff's final drawing with some emotions fading, created at mindfuldraw.com.

Therapist: How would you describe this picture?

Jeff: All my feelings have almost faded away.

Therapist: How is that for you?

Jeff: I don't want them all to fade away.

Therapist: When we look at each of these pictures – the first pot, the fuller pot, just the feelings, and the almost-all-faded pictures – is there a part that you want to be?

Jeff: Yes, the second one.

Therapist: Okay. If you were the second one, what would you say you are?

Jeff: I'm the pot of soup with feelings.

Therapist: Can you describe yourself?

Jeff: I'm filled with feelings and my pot around me is going away. But I have feelings that go away and new feelings that come.

Therapist: What is it like to be you?

Jeff: It's weird to be me. I don't think I taste very good.

Therapist: Why is that?

Jeff: Because I don't know if I'm going to spill over and I don't know if feelings taste very good.

Therapist: What would happen if you spilled over?

Jeff: Maybe I won't because my feelings are fading.

Therapist: Does it ever feel like you have a lot of feelings that might spill over like the soup?

Jeff: Yes, sometimes.

Therapist: Is there anything else you'd like to have happen in the drawing to show this?

Jeff: It's already happening because it's fading.

Therapist: Is there anything in your life that could be like the feelings fading?

Jeff: I could take this drawing home and see the feelings that are lighter.

Using Mindful Draw with the "feelings soup" prompt allowed Jeff to project, access, and process aspects of his grief and trauma. He utilized the fade feature to help him regulate feelings that seemed overwhelming, and also to add feelings with the comforting expectation that they would not spill over but would soon fade. The app also allowed him to find a sense of playfulness in processing his feelings, even joking about how bad he might taste as soup.

Screenshots of Jeff's evolving series of Mindful Draw works facilitated his strengthening of coping skills as his grief persisted. Jeff's drawings indicated mourning for his mother, as expected. They also showed his enjoyment of safely admitting new feelings into the soup, along with remarkably astute insights into the challenge of containing, yet honoring, his feelings as they faded.

In a subsequent session, the therapist reviewed the feelings in the soup. To pursue the metaphor, the therapist inquired, "What feelings faded the quickest? Which feelings lasted the longest? Does that fit for the feelings you have in your life now?"

Suggestions for Follow-Up

Following use of the Mindful Draw app, you may inquire if clients were able to let any thoughts or feelings fade in real-life experiences between sessions. You may then ask if they want to reengage the Mindful Draw app in the current session. If clients choose to revisit the Mindful Draw app, invite them to notice similarities and differences between their prior experiences using the app and their experiences using it now.

Many therapists also find the Mindful Draw app very healing for themselves. If you have a few moments between sessions, you might use the app to help relax and reset for your next session or to engage in your own mindfulness practice at the end of your workday.

Contraindications

Some clients don't feel comfortable drawing. Though the fading of their images in the app may decrease resistance, unyielding distaste for drawing may preclude the use of this intervention. Be prepared to offer alternative therapeutic activities.

Though therapy must take place on an HIPAA-consistent platform, mindfuldraw.com is not HIPAA consistent, and may leave created images accessible to others. Images may show private content and some clients may be uncomfortable using an online platform that is not HIPAA consistent. Discuss the use of websites that are not HIPAA consistent with caregivers and request written consent for use of non-HIPAA-consistent platforms in an informed consent document or a digital tools consent form (see Chapter 10) prior to their use as a therapeutic intervention.

References

Bostic, J. Q., Nevarez, M. D., Potter, M. P., Prince, J. B., Benningfield, M. M., & Aguirre, B. A. (2015). Being present at school: Implementing mindfulness in schools. *Child and Adolescent Psychiatry Clinics of North America, 24*(2), 245–259. https://doi.org/10.1016/j.chc.2014.11.010

Geronimi, E. M. C., Arellano, B., & Woodruff-Borden, J. (2020). Relating mindfulness and executive function in children. *Clinical Child Psychology and Psychiatry, 25*(2), 435–445. https://doi.org/10.1177/1359104519833737.

Gross, J., & Hayne, H. (1998). Drawing facilitates children's verbal reports of emotionally laden events. *Journal of Experimental Psychology: Applied*, 4(2), 163–179. https://doi.org/10.1037/1076-898X.4.2.163

Oaklander, V. (1978). *Windows to our children.* Real People Press.

Ortiz, R., & Sibinga, E. M. (2017, February 28). The tole of mindfulness in reducing the adverse effects of childhood stress and trauma. *Children (Basel), 4*(3), 16.

Schonert-Reichl, K. A., Oberle, E., Lawlor, M. S., Abbott, D., Thomson, K., Oberlander, T. F., & Diamond, A. (2015). Enhancing cognitive and social-emotional development through a simple-to-administer mindfulness-based school program for elementary school children: A randomized controlled trial. *Developmental Psychology, 51*(1), 52–66. https://doi.org/10.1037/a0038454

Siegel, D. (2014). *Brainstorm: The power and purpose of the teenage brain.* TarcherPerigee. https://drdansiegel.com/book/brainstorm/

TED. (2013, February 13). Jill Bolte Taylor: The neuroanatomical transformation of the teenage brain TEDxYouth@Indianapolis [Video]. YouTube. https://youtu.be/PzT_SBl31-s

CHAPTER 28

SCHOOL-BASED MINDFULNESS PROGRAM FOR TELETHERAPY

Deborah J. Buttitta, Teddy Goyer, Shyrea Minton, Jacob Kajiwara, and Dana J. Stone

Materials for Therapists: Chime sound. Additional materials may be required for particular lesson plans.

Materials for Clients: Internet, video conferencing system, and smartboard or projector for each classroom in which lessons will be provided. Additional materials may be required for particular lesson plans.

Objective

Mindfulness, or the practice of cultivating non-judgmental awareness of feelings, thoughts, and sensations, is increasingly valued by schools and integrated into school curriculums (Meiklejohn et al., 2012; Sibinga et al., 2016). The following provides instructions for the implementation of a school-based mindfulness program that may be delivered via teletherapy. Suggestions on how to include teachers and families in online mindfulness programs are also offered.

Rationale for Use

Mindfulness has been practiced in therapy since the late 1970s, though it has more recently gained popularity and widespread recognition for therapeutic benefits such as the enhancement of positive emotions, attention, self-regulation, and relationships (Harnett & Dawe, 2012; Lawlor, 2014). For children and adolescents, mindfulness can also help to reduce depression and anxiety (Meiklejohn et al., 2012; Sibinga et al., 2016). More recently, clinicians have begun delivering mindfulness interventions effectively via teletherapy (Behan, 2020; Tang et al., 2021).

School-based mindfulness interventions via teletherapy offer a unique opportunity for holistic learning and practice among children, adolescents, and their various systems (Zenner et al., 2014). Researchers suggest that students benefit when teachers incorporate mindfulness on a consistent basis (Carro et al., 2020; Harnett & Dawe, 2012; Meiklejohn et al., 2012), making mindfulness part of the classroom culture. Informed by the multi-tiered systems of support framework, school-based

DOI: 10.4324/9781003330912-34

mindfulness interventions recognize schools and classrooms as interconnected systems, facilitating accessibility and flexibility for both schools and clinicians (Goodman-Scott et al., 2019).

Setup

The following describes the setup necessary for implementation of school-based mindfulness interventions via teletherapy.

1. ***Receive training.*** The training of the mindfulness facilitator has an impact on successful outcomes of mindfulness programming in schools (Lawlor, 2014). Quality training includes continuing education or certification for teaching mindfulness. In addition, some research shows that those who are practitioners themselves are better able to lead students through example by embodying the practices throughout their interactions (Meiklejohn et al., 2012).
2. ***Select a chime sound.*** At the end of the practice portion of each session, it is helpful to ring a bell or chime to help guide students back to their mindfulness practice. You may find a digital sound that works well for this using an app or a video. In teletherapy, this tends to work better than a physical chime.
3. ***Collaborate with schools.*** To best meet the needs of each school, work collaboratively with administrators, teachers, and caregivers to conceptualize individual classroom and school-wide needs and develop a plan for implementation. This can be done through brief surveys, interviews, or focus groups. School personnel may have limited time. Try to remain non-intrusive as you gradually integrate into the larger system. However, teacher participation in in-class mindfulness lessons with students can lead to less stress and curb overall psychological distress (Harnett & Dawe, 2012). Therefore, request that teachers be available to participate and support students during scheduled meetings.
4. ***Set up a schedule.*** Work with school administrators to decide over how many weeks lessons will be delivered, how often they will be delivered, and the length of time of each lesson. Also discuss any additional supports that you may provide (e.g., family mindfulness groups, teacher and staff drop-in meetings, teacher support groups). Delivering school-wide lessons at an assembly or to all classrooms via a livestream webinar has some advantages related to scheduling. However, individual classroom lessons are typically more effective. Meeting with each classroom separately allows you to get to know the unique needs of each student and teacher and to adapt lesson plans to specific developmental needs.

   Schedule mindfulness lessons at a consistent, predictable time that accommodates the teachers' curriculum and minimizes classroom interruptions. Depending on the size of the school, the number of classrooms participating, and the number of therapists involved, mindfulness lessons can be delivered over the course of one to two days each week. It is recommended that a co-therapist team is utilized in each classroom, with therapists alternating between delivering lessons and processing the experience. Ideal schedules allow for 15-minute lessons and 5-minute breaks to transition to the next classroom. See Table 28.1 for a sample schedule.

   Provide each teacher with their own separate HIPAA-compliant link for their scheduled time to ensure privacy and minimize disruption.

Table 28.1 Sample schedule

Time	Group
7:00 am	Family Mindfulness
8:10 am	Ms. Smith's K Class
8:30 am	Mr. Clark's K Class
8:50 am	Break
9:10 am	Mr. Collins' 1st Grade Class
9:30 am	Mrs. Lopez's 1st Grade Class
9:50 am	Mr. Wilson's 2nd Grade Class
10:10 am	Ms. Terry's 2nd Grade Class
10:30 am	Mx. Shaw's 3rd Grade Class
10:50 am	Break
11:10 am	Miss. Uhlenhopp's 3rd Grade Class
11:30 am	Mrs. Bank's 4th Grade Class
12:00 pm	Teacher and Staff Drop-in
1:00 pm	Lunch Break
2:20 pm	Mrs. Istanbul's 4th Grade Class
2:50 pm	Mrs. Ross's 5th Grade Class
3:10 pm	Mrs. Ryburn's 5th Grade Class
3:30 pm	Teacher Support Group

5. ***Discuss technology.*** Meet in advance with each teacher to discuss what technology they have in their classroom and any specific needs of students. The following outlines an ideal setup for each lesson:

    - The camera captures the entire classroom of students
    - Therapists are projected onto a large screen or smartboard in front of the classroom
    - Both the classroom camera and therapists remain unmuted the entire time
    - When a student wants to share, the teacher can take a microphone (handheld or laptop) to that student or a student can walk up to the microphone source

6. ***Develop a curriculum.*** Between eight and fifteen lessons works well for a school-based mindfulness curriculum. With eight lessons, the curriculum can cover foundational mindfulness skills to help students, teachers, and caregivers develop an ongoing mindfulness practice (see Table 28.2). Additional lessons allow for the application of mindfulness-based activities to more specific topics based on the needs of the school, students, and their families (see Table 28.3).

7. ***Set a structure.*** While the content of each lesson will vary, use the same basic structure each week to establish a routine and familiarity with the lessons. This structure includes (1) checking technology, (2) a brief check-in, (3) psychoeducation about the week's topic and its relationship to mindfulness, (4) practice, and (5) discussion and suggestions for how that day's activity can be incorporated into the week both at home and at school.

Table 28.2 Eight-week schedule for teaching foundational mindfulness skills

Week	Topic
Week 1	Mindful breathing
Week 2	Finding mindfulness anchors
Week 3	Mindfulness using your senses
Week 4	Mindfulness of thoughts
Week 5	Mindfulness of emotions
Week 6	Mindful compassion for self
Week 7	Mindful compassion for others
Week 8	Mindful learning

Table 28.3 Extended schedule of mindfulness-based topics

Week	Topic
Week 9	Grounding
Week 10	Emotion identification and regulation
Week 11	Self-compassion
Week 12	Peer relationships
Week 13	Enhanced focus
Week 14	Test anxiety
Week 15	Difficulty sleeping

Sample Lesson: Emotion Identification and Regulation

The following sample lesson applies mindfulness skills to emotion identification and regulation (i.e., week 10) with elementary-age students. The lesson and language can be adapted for students of different ages. To conduct this lesson, acquire an emotions chart of your choosing to share with the class and provide the teacher with a handout of the outline of six people on the same page (see Figure 28.1; also provided in the supplemental materials that accompany this book). Ask the teacher to print a copy of the handout for each student and ensure that coloring supplies are available during the lesson.

1. ***Check technology.*** "Hi everyone! Can you hear me?"
   Have the teacher respond and make sure all two-way communication is working.
2. ***Check in.*** "It's great to see you all today. Did anyone have a chance to practice your mindfulness over the week?"
   Allow a few students to share about their practice. Provide encouragement and appreciation for ongoing practice.
3. ***Provide psychoeducation.*** "Today's mindfulness lesson is about emotions. Let's start by listing six basic emotions, which are happy, sad, mad, worried, surprised, and calm. There are many others."
   Screenshare an emotions chart.

"We are going to explore a few emotions today, starting with surprised. We can probably all think of a time when we felt surprised. What happens in our bodies when we are surprised? Our heart might go fast, our eyes get big, we might jump up and down. What happens when you get surprised?"

Allow a few students to share their experience and validate their responses.

"Yes! We feel something in our bodies and often we do something. Emotions are how our bodies and brains respond to the world around us. Emotions aren't good or bad; they are a normal part of being a human and everyone has them. But sometimes when we have a really big emotion, like when we're angry or mad, we might do something we later realize we didn't want to do. Can anyone think of an example of what happens in your body when you get angry?"

Allow one student to share an example and thank them for sharing.

"Do you ever do something when you feel that way?"

Allow the same student to respond and thank them for sharing.

"Mindfulness is going to help us with two things today. First, we're going to use mindfulness to help us be more aware of our emotions, by noticing what happens in our bodies when we have different emotions. Some of us might notice feelings or sensations in our bodies before we can identify the emotion. Second, we're going to practice using mindfulness to help us slow down, pause, and check in with our bodies and our minds. Mindfulness helps us use the wise part of our brains and helps us make smart choices when we have really big emotions. We have an exercise to help us identify what we feel in our bodies with different emotions. We're going to learn how to use color as an anchor to help us be mindful with our emotions. Remember when we talked about mindful anchors last week? Now, take out your coloring supplies. Your teacher is going to pass out a worksheet with outlines of people."

Screenshare a sample handout with outlines of six people on the same page (see Figure 28.1). Make sure everyone has their handout and is ready before resuming.

"We're going to start with the emotion of being calm. Let's take three mindful breaths and see if you can imagine being calm. Think about what happens in your body when you're calm."

Wait a minute before moving on.

"What did you notice in your body?"

Allow a couple of students to share.

"Now ask yourself, 'When I think of calm, the color I think of is _____.' You're going to select a color for calm and color in where you feel calm in your body. Let me show you my calm color."

Demonstrate an example through screen share or using the whiteboard function on your teletherapy platform.

"Everyone take a minute to color one person on the page and show where you feel calm in your body. Now let's try the same thing with the emotion of anger, what color would anger be and where do you feel anger in your body?"

Figure 28.1 Body outline handout for emotion identification. Credit: Grace Alfaro.

Work with the class to complete this exercise with at least calm and anger. Include more emotions if time permits. The outcome will be an emotions chart that represents each student's subjective experience of emotions.

4. ***Practice***. "Now it's time to practice using our mindfulness skills with our emotions. Find a comfortable position in your chair. If you feel comfortable, you can close your eyes."

   Play a chime sound to begin the practice session. Shift your presence from teacher to mindfulness practitioner. Facilitate the practice portion of the lesson in a slow and well-paced manner, allowing for breathing, guided visualization, and transitioning to the next step.

   > "Let's begin with our three mindful breaths. We're going to practice with two emotions today – calm and anger, but you can practice this with all emotions. Let's see if we can help ourselves find calm when anger takes over. I want you to imagine that something happens that makes you feel a little angry. For example, maybe someone takes something from you that you were playing with and they run off. Notice where in your body you feel anger and how you might respond. Now imagine that instead of acting right away, you take five mindful breaths and allow your body to slow down. Let's do that now."

   Count slowly from one to five to facilitate mindful breathing.

   > "Now imagine your calm color and keep using your mindful breaths to help you focus and hold onto the calm color. Imagine your calm color surrounding and filling your body, from the top of your head to your toes. With each mindful breath the calm color grows and becomes especially bright in those areas where your body usually feels calm. You notice that your calm color and mindful breaths help you pause. Your body begins to feel calmer, and most importantly you can now think about what action you would like to take. Do you want to talk to the person who took your toy, do you want to play with something else, or do you want to get an adult to help? Take three more mindful breaths and appreciate your ability to be mindful today."

   Count slowly from one to three. Play a chime sound to indicate the end of practice.

5. ***Discuss***. "What did you notice when you used mindfulness to pause after having a big emotion?" *Allow a few students to share.*

   > "How do you think this might be a helpful tool for you?"

   Allow a few students to share. As time permits, repeat the practice and discussion with other feelings.

   > "How can you be mindful of your emotions this week?"

   Allow a few students to share.

   > "Use your emotions chart to help notice what you might be feeling throughout the week. And keep practicing with the idea of using color as a mindful anchor. Thank you for your participation today. See you next week!"

Suggestions for Follow-Up

Mindfulness is a practice that becomes stronger over time. To ensure a cohesive mindfulness program is delivered over the course of eight weeks, scaffold the learning each week and encourage ongoing practice, both in the classroom and at home. Collaborate with teachers to incorporate brief mindful moments as part of the daily classroom schedule. Also, identify and communicate with teachers and other school administers any concerns observed in classroom settings, such as school-wide patterns that call for intervention or individual students who may need additional support.

Likewise, collaborate with teachers to support them in their own mindfulness journey. Teacher social-emotional competence is a contributing factor to how students engage in the classroom (Jones et al., 2014). Students are heavily influenced by their teacher's levels of emotional support, as manifested through their social-emotional competence. Emotional support from teachers can positively influence peer relationships between students and contribute to overall improved student outcomes. The use of mindfulness practice increases teachers' emotion regulation and social-emotional competence, thereby positively affecting the classroom environment.

Schedule five to ten-minute teacher and staff drop-in sessions around lunch periods to allow teachers and staff to be present with the focus solely placed on them. Offer after-school teacher support groups that involve psychoeducation, group sharing, and mindfulness skills to further enhance teacher wellbeing (see Table 28.1 for a sample schedule).

Mindfulness is more effective when skills learned at school are practiced at home (Sciutto et al., 2021). Involve parents and caregivers in psychoeducation and mindfulness practices to boost benefits and enhance parent-child relationships (Carro et al., 2020; Harnett & Dawe, 2012; Meiklejohn et al., 2012). Delivering mindfulness through a teletherapy platform increases accessibility for busy families and caregivers to be involved in this process. Brief, ten-minute family mindfulness sessions before school can help parents, caregivers, and students have a chance to be present at the start of the day (see Table 28.1 for sample schedule).

Contraindications

Contraindications for mindfulness therapy practices may arise in cases where individuals exhibit challenges or reluctance in engaging with present-moment experiences, particularly evident among children with pronounced attention deficits or individuals undergoing acute distress that could potentially be exacerbated by mindfulness exercises. Furthermore, the presence of cultural or religious beliefs conflicting with mindfulness principles necessitates careful consideration and sensitivity prior to implementation. Lastly, if substantial disruptions or adversities persist within the home environment, the introduction of mindfulness practices may be impractical or ineffective until a semblance of stability is attained.

References

Behan, C. (2020). The benefits of meditation and mindfulness practices during times of crisis such as covid-19. *Irish Journal of Psychological Medicine, 37*(4), 256–258. https://doi.org/10.1017/ipm.2020.38

Carro, N., D'Adamo, P., & Lozada, M. (2021). A school intervention helps decrease daily stress while enhancing social integration in children. *Behavioral Medicine (Washington, D.C.), 47*(3), 1–258. https://doi.org/10.1080/08964289.2020.1738319

Goodman-Scott, E., Betters-Bubon, J., & Donohue, P. (2019). *The school counselor's guide to multi-tiered systems of support*. Routledge.

Harnett, P. H., & Dawe, S. (2012). The contribution of mindfulness-based therapies for children and families and proposed conceptual integration. *Child and Adolescent Mental Health, 17*(4), 195–208. https://doi.org/10.1111/j.1475-3588.2011.00643.x

Jones, S. M., Bailey, R., & Jacob, R. (2014). Social-emotional learning is essential to classroom management. *Phi Delta Kappan, 96*(2), 19–24. https://doi.org/10.1177/0031721714553405

Lawlor, M. S. (2014). Mindfulness in practice: Considerations for implementation of mindfulness-based programming for adolescents in school contexts. *New Directions for Youth Development, 2014*(142), 83–95. https://doi.org/10.1002/yd.20098

Meiklejohn, J., Phillips, C., Freedman, M. L., Griffin, M. L., Biegel, G., Roach, A., Frank, J., Burke, C., Pinger, L., Soloway, G., Isberg, R., Sibinga, E., Grossman, L., & Saltzman, A. (2012). Integrating mindfulness training into K-12 education: Fostering the resilience of teachers and students. *Mindfulness, 3*(4), 291–307. https://doi.org/10.1007/s12671-012-0094-5

Sciutto, M. J., Veres, D. A., Marinstein, T. L., Bailey, B. F., & Cehelyk, S. K. (2021). Effects of a school-based mindfulness program for young children. *Journal of Child and Family Studies*. 30(6), 1516–1527. https://doi.org/10.1007/s10826-021-01955-x

Sibinga, E. M. S., Webb, L., Ghazarian, S. R., & Ellen, J. M. (2016). School-based mindfulness instruction: An RCT. *Pediatrics, 137*(1), Article e20152532. https://doi.org/10.1542/peds.2015-2532

Tang, D.-F., Mo, L.-Q., Zhou, X.-C., Shu, J.-H., Wu, L., Wang, D., & Dai, F. (2021). Effects of mindfulness-based intervention on adolescents emotional disorders. *Medicine, 100*(51), Article e28295. https://doi.org/10.1097/md.0000000000028295

Zenner, C., Herrnleben-Kurz, S., & Walach, H. (2014). Mindfulness-based interventions in schools-a systematic review and meta-analysis. *Frontiers in Psychology, 5,* Article 603. https://doi.org/10.3389/fpsyg.2014.00603

Part 7

Strengthening Attachment

CHAPTER 29

VIRTUAL CONJOINT FAMILY DRAWING

Krupali S. Joshi and Christie Eppler

Materials for Therapists: Whiteboard function on a teletherapy platform.

Materials for Clients: None.

Objective

The conjoint family drawing is a projective and interactive assessment tool that involves asking a family to collaboratively draw a picture of their family (Bing, 1970). The art that clients create and the process through which they create it serve as a playful way of assessing family functioning. This chapter explains how to adapt the conjoint family drawing in teletherapy assessment and intervention applying a narrative family therapy approach.

Rationale for Use

Conjoint family drawings have been used in in-person therapy assessment for decades (Bing, 1970). The activity requires that clients work together to draw a picture of their family. It allows clients to creatively and playfully express themselves and their relationship dynamics through drawing. It also offers an accessible space for self-expression and helps circumvent linguistic challenges often inherent to youth in articulating complex emotions and thoughts. While the family is drawing, the therapist observes the family's interactions and relational dynamics to assess family functioning.

While the conjoint family drawing is typically used as a moment-in-time assessment in the initial stage of therapy, it can be incorporated throughout early, middle, and late stages of therapy. Gennari and Tamanza (2014, 2022) outline a standardized and structured use of the tool through empirical studies. Traditionally used in working with families, the conjoint family drawing can also be adapted for use with siblings or other client system compositions.

A virtual adaptation of the conjoint family drawing offers convenience and accessibility for teletherapy intervention. It requires no physical materials, making it a viable activity for clients who don't have access to art supplies. It also allows for sharing and archiving of drawings. Perhaps most importantly, families attending sessions from different locations can easily collaborate in a shared activity despite physical distance. This benefit in and of itself can make this activity powerfully therapeutic for client systems who are otherwise unable to engage with one another in the same physical space.

This assessment can be utilized with many different theories, though it is particularly well suited for a narrative approach. In narrative family therapy, asking a family to collaborate on a family picture

DOI: 10.4324/9781003330912-36

can help assess the existing problem-saturated story, identify unique outcomes and preferred realities, and suggest metaphors for externalization (Serneels, 2013). The following offers guidance on how to set up and conduct this activity via teletherapy.

Setup

Prior to introducing the conjoint family drawing in session with clients, familiarize yourself with the whiteboard function on your teletherapy platform. If one isn't available, you may explore online applications, websites, or common computer programs that allow digital drawings. If you need to use an online application or website, discuss with clients any limitations as it relates to HIPAA compliance. If you need clients to use a computer program available on their own computer, this may limit the activity to clients who are all in one shared physical location. Consider unique client needs in selecting the platform used for the activity.

Instructions

1. ***Introduce the activity.*** Ask clients if they would be willing to work together as a team to draw their family doing something. Explain that creating a conjoint family drawing gives them an opportunity to see their family in a different way, through art. Share that no art skills are necessary.
2. ***Show the whiteboard function.*** If clients agree to the activity, open the whiteboard function on your teletherapy platform and provide a brief tour of the application. Demonstrate the different tools that are available for drawing and how to select different colors.
3. ***Select colors.*** Instruct clients to each choose one color that they will use to draw with for the entire session (Gennari & Tamanza, 2014). Because virtual whiteboards offer a great variety of colors, ensure that the chosen colors are different enough for you to distinguish between them. However, a benefit of this virtual approach is that clients may be able to choose from more colors than may otherwise be available in a box of colored pencils, crayons, or markers. Similarities and differences in chosen colors may provide a unique method of assessment (Snir et al., 2020).
4. ***Provide instructions.*** Ask clients to make a drawing of their family doing something (Bing, 1970). Explain that they will each take turns drawing one small part of the picture before giving someone else a turn to draw. Inform them that they will each have several turns to draw, and that it's up to them to decide the order in which they draw and when their drawing is complete. Remind them that they are each only to use their chosen color throughout the activity (Gennari & Tamanza, 2014).
5. ***Decide what to draw.*** Provide time for clients to decide what they want to draw. Observe family dynamics and interactions through this process.
6. ***Draw the picture.*** Once the family has decided what they want to draw, invite them to begin the drawing. Avoid redirecting behaviors or asking questions throughout the process. Provide support only as needed.
7. ***Analyze the process.*** As clients work together to create their drawing, observe verbal and non-verbal interactions (Bing, 1970). For example, you may consider the following:
    - What role does each family member play in the process?

- In what order do family members contribute to the drawing?
- Who is engaged or disengaged?
- Does someone give copious directions?
- What happens when there is a disagreement about what should be included in the picture?
- Does one member fix what another family member has drawn?

Interactions between the members, such as completing, enhancing, opposing, disrupting, or assisting may parallel relational dynamics. How the family works on the drawing can also provide insights into the family's decision-making process. Observe how the decisions are made, which members weigh in, who ultimately makes the decisions, and the overall emotional climate of the family during the process (Gennari & Tamanza, 2022).

Working from a narrative approach, observe how the interactions mimic the family's landscapes, such as their emotional climate, strength or problem-based communication patterns, and their ability to resolve conflict. Note any metaphors that may be used in externalizations. Remain curious about how larger social patterns are being replicated as the family works together on the drawing.

8. ***Save the drawing.*** Once clients have indicated that their drawing is complete, ask them if it's okay if you take a screenshot of their completed drawing. If they agree, save the image to the client's file for use in future sessions.
9. ***Analyze the drawing.*** Conduct a brief analysis of the completed drawing. While Bing (1970) instructs therapists to consider composition and realism, a narrative approach suggests focusing on the themes and topic(s) represented within the drawing (Gennari & Tamanza, 2022). Look for the presence of symbols that hint at preferred stories, unique outcomes, externalizations, or content for social deconstruction. For example, consider the following:
   - What barriers or challenges does the drawing depict?
   - What solutions are indicated?
   - Metaphorically, how was the problem drawn? Was it big or small? Was it colorful or monotone?
   - How were family members' positions drawn and does this align with the system's dynamics?

   Collectively, these elements offer a window into the family's internal world and relational intricacies.

Processing

Avoid sharing your own analyses of the activity. Instead, approach the activity with curiosity and inquire about the picture and client interactions using observations and prompts such as, "I noticed" or "I saw."

When processing the procedure of creating the drawing, you might ask:

- What is one feeling that arose as you were drawing?
- What did you enjoy about creating a drawing of your family together?
- What was challenging about creating a drawing of your family together?
- What surprised you about the activity?

Then ask open-ended questions about the drawing itself. For example, you might ask:

- Tell me about your drawing.
- What parts of this drawing stand out to you? What makes them stand out?

Then, deepen the collaborative exploration and re-authorship of family narratives (Freedman & Combs, 1996; White & Epston, 1994). If it appears that the family is depicted in the drawing in a way that demonstrates hardship or a challenge of some sort, ask questions to uncover the problem-saturated dominant narrative and help the family to externalize any presenting problems. For example:

- Tell me about [object/externalized problem]. What does it do? What does it sound like?
- How does [object/externalized problem] affect your relationships with others in the family?
- How does [object/externalized problem] affect your relationship with between your [mom/dad/sister/brother/etc.] and your [mom/dad/sister/brother/etc.]?

Explore preferred narratives by asking:

- What changes would you like to see in this picture?
- How might your relationships with one another be different if this picture were to change?

Vignette

Bhavesh (39), Neeta (37), Aarav (8), and Maya (5) presented in teletherapy with concerns about Aarav's recent behavioral issues. The family had immigrated five years ago from Gujarat, India, to a suburban area in Washington state. In the past year, Bhavesh had been traveling a lot for work and Aarav had been finding it increasingly difficult to concentrate on schoolwork. Aarav's teacher shared that Aarav often doodled and daydreamed in class and was disengaged from group activities. The school counselor informed the parents that Aarav had been experiencing anger outbursts. Aarav got into two physical fights with classmates and would throw things on the floor when he made mistakes during assigned tasks. Aarav's behavior had been a topic of increasing tension and conflict in their household.

Bhavesh also raised concerns about Maya's adjustment to kindergarten. He worried about her making friends and had concerns about how shy she was around her peers. Neeta, on the other hand, believed that Maya was simply taking her time to get comfortable with the environment and wasn't too worried about her.

Because the family had indicated Aarav's interest in doodling at school, the therapist thought that the conjoint family drawing might be a fitting activity to help assess the family's functioning and bring them together in therapy in a way that might pique Aarav's interest. At the start of the second family session, the therapist introduced the idea of the conjoint family drawing. Aarav immediately became more engaged just at the mention of the family drawing something together.

After the therapist explained the details of the activity, each member of the family took turns selecting a color that they would use for the drawing. They then self-determined a system of taking turns to draw their own figures using the whiteboard function of the teletherapy platform. They took about 15 minutes to complete the activity.

At one point, Aarav became frustrated after multiple attempts at drawing a certain part. He let out a growl and threw his water bottle across the floor with an angry expression. Neeta intervened

Figure 29.1 First conjoint family drawing.

by asking him what was wrong, telling him to pick his water bottle back up, and helping him with the drawing.

Once they had finished, the therapist asked the family to describe their drawing (see Figure 29.1). They took turns explaining that they had drawn themselves in their living room, with Bhavesh watching television, Aarav sitting by the window playing phone games, and Neeta building a magnetic tile castle with Maya. The family explained that the drawing also showed objects like a torn piece of paper beside Aarav, an open laptop on the dining table close to where Neeta and Maya sat, and a canned beverage on the center table close to Bhavesh.

During the discussion, the therapist asked Aarav more about the torn piece of paper.

Therapist: Aarav, tell me about the paper.

Aarav: It's my English homework. I ripped it up.

Therapist: I see, you were doing English homework! What happened?

Aarav: I tore it. It was hard and it made me frustrated!

Therapist: It's okay to feel frustrated when things are difficult.

Aarav: Yeah.

Therapist: So, the English homework was hard, and that brought Frustration into the room. It sounds like Frustration was strong enough to make you tear the paper. When else have you noticed Frustration showing up?

The therapist continued to explore how the family experienced Frustration, discussing Frustration as if it were its own character to help with the process of externalization. The therapist was cautious not to name it "his frustration" or attribute it only to Aarav. This aligns with the narrative stance that the problem is the problem, not the person. They collaboratively externalized Frustration as a red fireball that grew hotter when a family member experienced embarrassment due to perceived failure. Aarav quietly added a squiggly orange ball to the family's drawing.

> **Therapist:** Ah! There is it! There's Frustration! Mom, I noticed you helped Aarav when the fireball showed up when you were drawing. What do you think might have been going on for him at the time?
>
> **Neeta:** I saw that he erased a part multiple times and got frustrated when he couldn't draw it how he wanted. The fireball was hot then!
>
> **Therapist:** Right! And how do you respond when the fireball is hot? Dad, how do you respond? What about you, Maya?

Upon further processing of the drawing, the family identified several important factors that either contributed to or maintained the presenting problem. Aarav expressed that he wanted to do things well but was cautious about asking for support when he knew his mom was busy, especially when his dad was out of town. While talking about the laptop shown in the drawing, Bhavesh and Neeta discussed the pattern of receiving emails from Aarav's teacher before the fireball grew bright. Neeta explained that she was building a magnetic tile castle with Maya as a way of encouraging social skills and collaborative play to support Maya's adjustment to kindergarten. She disclosed that she wanted this play time to go well to help alleviate her concerns about the success of the children in a new country and her own self-worth as a mother. Bhavesh expressed his feelings of guilt and shame for not knowing Neeta's struggles and stated that he often was distant – both physically while he was away for work, and metaphorically watching television. He identified his narrative of fatherhood as stemming from his family of origin, which was a thin story limited to providing for and protecting the family without being actively involved.

There were, however, some remarkable exceptions to these problem-saturated narratives. Neeta recalled their move to the United States, emphasizing Bhavesh's support in setting up the household and caring for Maya while she was a baby. Aarav laughed at some of his mistakes without feeling frustrated, such as in dance class at school. The therapist and family collaborated to reauthor failure to growth, incorporating experiences of learning through mistakes as "trial and error" and highlighted their resilience and relational support. Bhavesh and Neeta shared their own stories of embracing failure, which supported Aarav in redefining his relationship to the problem. Their focus shifted from a narrative of inadequacy and pressure to one of resilience, mutual support, and growth.

In the following session, Bhavesh was in Oregon for work. He was able to join the family in teletherapy, however, because the therapist was dually licensed in both Washington and Oregon. As a way of continuing their last discussion of preferred narratives and engaging the family together in a playful way despite their distance, the therapist invited the family to create another conjoint family drawing (see Figure 29.2). This time, the family drew themselves building the magnetic tile castle together. Bhavesh was looking at the structure with determination, Aarav was sitting by Bhavesh trying to put a tile on a precarious tower, and Neeta and Maya were working together to build a path to the castle lined with all sorts of animals and flowers. When the family talked about the picture, they noted that building the castle was difficult and it often tumbled. But they were not going to give up easily.

Figure 29.2 Second conjoint family drawing.

Suggestions for Follow-Up

This activity can be used multiple times during treatment. Subsequent drawings can be used to elicit preferred narratives by asking the family to draw a scene depicting how they envision their ideal family dynamic. Subsequent drawings may also reflect the family's reauthored story. Another iteration of this technique may involve encouraging the client system to create the drawing without verbally communicating throughout the process (Landgarten, 1987). If used more than once, observe changes in family dynamics and differences between the pictures created. Process changes observed between the experiences.

Contraindications

The virtual conjoint family drawing should be approached with caution in instances where there are signs of domestic violence, child abuse, or other forms of trauma within the family system. Apply a trauma-informed approach when processing this activity and provide alternative therapeutic assessments and interventions when appropriate.

Using virtual means for drawing may not be best suited for large groups or for very young children or for clients who are not tech savvy. Gennari and Tamanza (2022) were guarded about using this technique virtually. If clients do not resonate with creating an online drawing, suggest using physical tools and sharing via sending a picture or holding the drawing up to the screen. Ask the family to create their conjoint family drawing using a large piece of paper and crayons, colored pencils, or markers if clients have access to these materials and it appears to be a more well-suited option. Work with clients to set up the camera to allow continued visual contact throughout the activity when offering this option.

References

Bing, E. (1970). The conjoint family drawing. *Family Process, 9*(2), 173–194. https://doi.org/10.1111/j.1545-5300.1970.00173.x

Freedman, J., & Combs, G. (1996). *Doing narrative therapy.* WW Norton & Company.

Gennari, M., & Tamanza, G. (2014). Conjoint family drawing: A technique for family clinical assessment. *Procedia – Social and Behavioral Sciences, 113,* 91–110. https://doi.org/10.1016/j.sbspro.2014.01.015

Gennari, M., & Tamanza, G. (2022). The conjoint family drawing: A tool to explore about family relationships. *Frontiers in Psychology, 13,* Article 884686. https://doi.org/10.3389/fpsyg.2022.884686

Landgarten, H. B. (2013). *Family art psychotherapy: A clinical guide and casebook.* Routledge. https://doi.org/10.4324/9780203776377

Serneels, A. (2013). Picturing stories: Drawings in narrative family therapy with children. *International Journal of Narrative Therapy & Community Work, 4,* 21–29. https://search.informit.org/doi/10.3316/informit.813909373078649

Snir, S., Gavron, T., Maor, Y., Haim, N., & Sharabany, R. (2020). Friends' closeness and intimacy from adolescence to adulthood: Art captures implicit relational representations in joint drawing: A longitudinal study. *Frontiers in Psychology, 11,* Article 2842. https://doi.org/10.3389/fpsyg.2020.573140

White, M., & Epston, D. (1994). *Narrative means to therapeutic ends.* Norton.

CHAPTER 30

VIRTUAL THERAPEUTIC GAMING

Rachel A. Altvater and Fiona Hill

Materials for Therapists and Clients: Hardware and software for gameplay.

Objective

Virtual therapeutic gaming is applicable for both virtual and in-person therapy with individuals and families. This chapter aims to assist, educate, and inspire therapists in utilizing gaming as an additive to their teletherapy intervention repertoire.

Rationale for Use

Gaming has swiftly increased in popularity for leisure, social connectedness, and personal achievement. Play habits of children and adolescents are often intertwined and immersed in the digital realm. They frequently consume gaming content in various ways, such as YouTube, streaming services, and their own play interactions. Likewise, for children and adolescents who spend much of their time playing video games, joining them within this digital world greatly abets the therapeutic process (Altvater, 2021; Stone, 2022). Gaming offers a platform to project internal and external experiences from a safe distance. This aids clients in processing, expressing, and releasing psychological distress in safe spaces where they feel a greater sense of power, control, and mastery (Schaefer & Drewes, 2014).

To truly encapsulate the benefit of virtual gaming, therapists must first understand the benefit of play. Play is a child's first language (Axline, 1947; Landreth, 2023; Ray, 2016), and it is the method that children use to conceptualize and process the world around them (Garwood, 1982). Play affords children the ability to communicate their thoughts and feelings in ways that are developmentally suitable. This is particularly powerful when they do not have the verbal abilities to fully articulate their experiences. When utilizing play in therapy, therapists carefully select therapeutic toys (Landreth, 2023) to aid children with a variety of presenting concerns in processing, healing, and reaching therapeutic goals.

The core tenets of play therapy serve as the foundation for therapeutic gaming. Play therapy is an evidence-based treatment approach (Ray, 2025). While gaming itself is a relatively newer intervention, thus in its infancy of research, the foundational components are play-based and research-informed. There is a long history of gaming across disciplines for a variety of mental, emotional, social, and physical concerns (Griffiths et al., 2017). Gaming continues to be studied with a variety of populations and clinical presentations.

DOI: 10.4324/9781003330912-37

The theoretical lenses that are reflected throughout this intervention are humanistic and systemic. A play therapy framework that encompasses both approaches is filial therapy. This method of treatment teaches caregivers how to engage in child-centered play through modeling and parent coaching. Goals of filial play therapy include improving relationships between the child and caregivers and building trust (VanFleet, 2005). Family collaboration and connection within a gaming space honors the play therapy principles of helping digital native (Prensky, 2001) children and adolescents feel seen, heard, understood, and valued (Stone, 2022).

Additionally, aiding families and caregivers in co-play within this gaming space benefits healing and connectedness for the entire system (Chua et al., 2013). Stepping inside the virtual world together broadens understanding and deepens relationships. As family members connect further in these spaces, they gain amplified opportunities to bond, collaborate, engage in healthy competition, experience opportunities for perspective taking, enhance understanding of one another, and coregulate.

Setup

Gaming is a broad category that encompasses a vast amount of hardware and software options. Hardware is equipment that processes digital information so that the game can be utilized. Examples of hardware include computers, smart devices (e.g., tablets, phones), and gaming consoles (e.g., Nintendo, Xbox, PlayStation, virtual reality headsets). Software is the actual game experienced through the hardware equipment (Stone, 2022).

The following steps are essential for setting up in-session gameplay.

1. ***Explore gaming options that you might provide to clients.*** Consider what you feel comfortable with and are competent in offering. Knowledge and understanding can be enhanced through personal exploration and by engaging in additional research about potential gaming options. Specific gaming options are ever-changing. It can be helpful to learn more about trending games. For example, from 2019 to 2025, some of the most popular commercially available games included *Roblox*, *Fortnite*, and *Minecraft*. In working with children and adolescents, it is common for these digital tools to organically emerge in session as a preferred play option.
2. ***Determine which games from those that you've selected are single-player or multiplayer games.*** Single-player games only allow one person to play. Multiplayer games offer the ability to join another person in the game directly and allow therapists to engage in virtual games with clients. These are also often referred to as live games, where the play is transpiring in real time with others. For single-player games, clients can screen share games played on their computer or cast the content from a virtual reality headset to an app or website to allow the therapist to witness the digital space.
3. ***Gather and prepare any necessary equipment.*** The gaming system(s) available to clients and their compatibility with those available to you will determine the games that you may play with each client. Cross-platform play occurs when players using differing hardware systems join each other in gameplay. For example, *Roblox*, a popular multiplayer game, can be accessed by installing the *Roblox* player on a personal computer via their website or downloading an application on a smart device, though it can also be accessed on Xbox and PlayStation. While some hardware systems allow for cross-platform play, others do not. Having hardware that allows for cross-platform play increases accessibility and inclusion, thus enhancing the likelihood that clients will have what they need to be able to play with you.

4. ***Discuss gaming with caregivers.*** Caregivers are vital members of the therapy team. Including them from the start of treatment sets the tone for ongoing care (Stone, 2022). Inquire about the family's use of video games, expectations regarding their use, parental controls, screen time tendencies and limits, and any other relevant information about the digital space at home. Caregivers who are hesitant to invite digital tools in sessions are typically unaware, anxious, unsure about their efficacy, and/or concerned about their child's use of them. Provide information about the use of virtual games in therapy, differentiating between leisure and therapeutic gaming. You may explain that virtual therapeutic gaming affords an opportunity for children to project their own experiences onto externalized objects, such as gaming avatars. This form of distancing often offers a felt sense of safety for therapeutic material to be processed in a manner that is emotionally and mentally accessible to children. Also, explain how virtual therapeutic gaming may be used to support families in working toward the identified goals of therapy when caregivers join their children within this space.
5. ***Address any necessary ethical and legal implications of virtual therapeutic gaming.*** When implementing games that are not created for therapy, safeguard client-protected health information, discuss any limitations to confidentiality regarding the use of online games, and use a digital tools consent form (see Chapter 10) to allow legal guardians to consent to their use prior to introducing them to children and adolescents in therapy.
6. ***Establish a routine for making sure equipment is ready at the time of session.*** This may include charging hardware and updating software prior to session. Also, work with clients to ensure that their hardware is fully charged and any new software updates have been downloaded prior to sessions. Develop a consistent routine for recharging your own equipment between sessions for devices that have limited power. Consider which clients prefer to utilize virtual therapeutic gaming. For back-to-back sessions in which gaming hardware needs to be used, use a docking station or have extra chargers or batteries available to ensure that you have what you need available for each client. In the event you are unable to use certain hardware or software during sessions due to updates or other delays, have a backup plan and work with clients to manage any emotions that may come up as a result.

Instructions

1. ***Determine whether child and adolescent clients will play with or without caregivers or other family members.*** Assess therapeutic goals and client and family needs to determine if the virtual therapeutic gaming session will focus on systemic co-play or individual processing.
2. ***Determine if the session will be client-led or therapist-led.*** Operate from your chosen theoretical model, as it informs and guides your therapeutic direction. If the session will be client-led, provide gaming options for the client to choose from. If the session will be therapist-led, choose a particular game and offer it as a possible activity for that day's session.
3. ***Provide gaming option(s) for clients to choose from.*** Search the Entertainment Software Rating Board's (ESRB) website for video game rating summaries that include information on age appropriateness. Consider each client's developmental needs, abilities, interests, and the goals of therapy when choosing which games to offer.
4. ***Engage in gameplay.*** If the game is a single-player game and is accessible to the therapist, client, and family (if applicable), parallel play (i.e., simultaneous solo gaming) can be a powerful way to

incorporate gameplay into session. If the game is a multiplayer game and is accessible to everyone, you may play the game together for individual and family sessions. In many cases, everyone will join from a separate device and account. If a game is on a console, however, players might only require separate controllers. Identify themes that emerge during gaming to assist in recognizing and addressing the client's clinical needs (Stone, 2022).

With child-centered and filial therapies, reflect on the content of play, expressed emotions, and provide tracking statements (Landreth, 2023; VanFleet, 2005). Avoid asking questions that are outside of the metaphor of play. You may, however, express curiosity about something by wondering out loud (e.g., "I wonder what [avatar's name] feels when their parent takes care of them"). When appropriate, offer commentary about play themes and other relevant therapeutic material that transpires. Provide insight and guidance to family members about these child-directed interventions and encourage them to follow your modeling. Scheduling a separate caregiver appointment to provide these insights ahead of time can help to avoid disrupting the play process during the session.

5. ***End gameplay.*** Leave enough time at the end of the session to wrap up with any necessary topics of discussion (e.g., checking in with caregivers, scheduling). Provide time reminders, either verbally, visually (e.g., through use of parental controls), and/or auditorily (e.g., with an alarm), ten minutes, five minutes, and one minute before gameplay needs to end to support a smooth transition. If the game can be saved, ask clients if they would like to save the game before they exit it.

Processing

Processing questions explore information about the game to enhance connection and uncover how the themes that emerge through gameplay are related to the client's life experiences. To assist with conceptualization and ongoing therapeutic processing, the following questions/prompts are provided to serve as a starting point from a humanistic and systems lens.

Individual Processing

- Tell me as much as you'd like about this game.
- Tell me about your avatar.
- Who is your [favorite/least favorite] character? What do you [like/dislike] about them?
- What character would you say you identify most closely with? What are their [strengths/areas for growth]?
- If you could create an avatar for [name of family member], what features would you choose? How come?
- What character in the game most reminds you of [name of family member]?

Family Processing

- Share each of your roles in this gaming space. How did you make these selections?
- How did it feel for each character to experience the game in the manner that they experienced it?
- Name one thing you noticed about each [avatar/family member] during gameplay.

- How have some of your [relationships/interactions/communication patterns] changed as you have begun playing this game together?
- What have you discovered about one another that surprised you?
- What was your [favorite/least favorite] aspect of the gaming experience? What would make this better next time?

Vignette

Sammy (9) and his family sought therapy services for Sammy's anger outbursts, defiant behaviors, and hitting his sister Maria (2). According to teachers, there were no issues in the classroom or with peers. However, his parents reported that Sammy was having two to three 'tantrums' at home daily and had recently begun hitting his sister when he became angry.

Sammy's favorite game was *Adopt Me!* (*Roblox*; Uplift Games, 2017). *Adopt Me!* is a live, multiplayer, role-playing game. The purpose of the game is to assume the role of a baby or parent, and then raise, trade, and collect pets and build a home. The therapist invited this as an option for play during virtual therapy services.

After six sessions, Sammy mentioned to the therapist that 'no one listens' to him and 'no one loves' him since his sister was born. During the seventh session, the therapist met with both parents to discuss observations and make plans to involve the Sammy's parents in virtual therapeutic gaming in the next session.

Since the game *Adopt Me!* aligns with filial therapy, in that it mirrors systems dynamics, it is an appropriate game to implement for in-game session play with others. The game offers an opportunity for co-play and the client to experience nurturance (e.g., feeding, bathing), therefore building trust and a sense of felt-safety within the family system. The therapist provided psychoeducation to Sammy's parents related to the upcoming family session, including information about virtual therapeutic gaming and guidance for how to interact with Sammy in this space (e.g., follow his lead).

In the following session, the therapist met with Sammy and his parents. At the start of the session, the therapist and each family member joined the *Roblox* platform from their own account on their own personal computer. The therapist did not play the game this session and simply observed to witness the family's interactions and in-gameplay.

The therapist gave Sammy the option of role-playing as a baby or a parent. This let Sammy have agency to play the role that he felt that he needed to play with his parents and allowed the therapist to assess family roles and dynamics. Sammy chose to be a baby and requested that his parents play as his parents. During this gameplay, Sammy's parents attended to his every need. They fed him, bathed him, put him down for a nap, and carried him when he was too tired. The therapist made tracking and reflective statements throughout the session and provided them with time warnings to signal when the session was nearing an end. When the session ended, Sammy commented how much he loved his parents and knew his parents loved him. No processing questions occurred this session to align with the filial model that encourages verbal processing with caregivers in a separate session.

A subsequent parent consultation was conducted in which the therapist asked Sammy's parents the following questions:

- What was your most and least favorite experience in the game?
- What came easily to you and what was more difficult?

- What did you notice about Sammy's demeanor and your family interactions before, during, and after the session?
- What insights were gained from the co-play?

The therapist facilitated further discussion about the play themes, the therapeutic powers of play that were observed in the session, and how to apply therapeutic content outside of therapy. Sammy's parents remarked on their enjoyment with Sammy's positive, connected feelings. They expressed challenges with perspective-taking, particularly in regard to recognizing and meeting Sammy's needs in the gaming space. They acknowledged the pleasurable feelings and interactions within the session, resulting in a felt sense of enhanced connection and committed to ongoing co-play to mitigate some of Sammy's emotional, relational, and behavioral challenges.

Suggestions for Follow-Up

You may recommend that family members engage in gaming co-play together between sessions. Encourage caregivers to process between-session gaming experiences with one another and to share their experience with you in subsequent sessions to support in tracking therapeutic progress. When clients provide feedback on between-session gameplay, consider what aspects of the system may need additional support and provide guidance as needed.

Contraindications

A common concern for gaming is addiction. The World Health Organization (2019) lists 'gaming disorder' in the 11th Revision of the International Classification of Diseases. The research, however, has produced mixed results about gaming being a diagnosable behavioral disorder (Aarseth et al., 2017; Bean, 2019) and deep engagement in a gaming space is not necessarily a problem. There can, however, be unhealthy methods to gaming. When unhealthy technology usage is a concern, uncover more about the reasons behind the level of engagement in this space.

The following are examples of questions that you might ask to preliminarily assess the function of unhealthy technology usage with clients and their caregivers (Altvater, 2021):

- What purpose does this game serve for you?
- In what ways does this [game/digital world] result in an increased sense of [purpose/connection/accomplishment]?
- Describe in [words/images/play] the [emotional/social/physical] experiences within this space.
- How does this digital world compare to experiences off-screen?
- Share your perspectives about your connection to and use of the digital realm.

Then, assist clients and their caregivers in setting appropriate limits on screen time when needed. The American Academy of Pediatrics (2016) created a personalized Family Media Use Plan which may be helpful in working with families to establish limits that work within their values, obligations, and expectations. The calculator offers an estimated time that children and adolescents can engage with screens after considering various individualized factors, including age, time needed for sleep, meals, family and free time, and all academic, extracurricular, and household obligations.

By establishing a deeper awareness of the client's connection to the gaming space, you can identify possibilities for future therapeutic intervention and aid families in finding a healthy balance of gaming outside of sessions.

References

Aarseth, E., Bean, A. M., Boonen, H., Colder Carras, M., Coulson, M, Das, D., ...Van Rooij, A., J. (2017). Scholars' open debate paper on the world health organization icd-11 gaming disorder proposal. *Journal of Behavioral Addictions, 6*(3), 267–270. https://doi.org/10.1556/2006.5.2016.088

Altvater, R. A. (2021). The culture of technology and play therapy. In E. Gil & A. Drewes (Eds.), *Cultural issues in play therapy* (2nd ed., pp. 172–190). Guilford Press.

American Academy of Pediatrics. (2016). *Family media plan.* Healthy Children. https://www.healthychildren.org/English/fmp/Pages/MediaPlan.aspx

Axline, V. M. (1947). *Play therapy: The inner dynamics of childhood.* Houghton Mifflin.

Bean, A. (2019). I am my avatar and my avatar is me: Utilizing video games as therapeutic tools. In J. Stone (Ed.), *Integrating technology into modern therapies: A clinician's guide to developments and interventions* (pp. 94–106). Routledge.

Chua, P., Jung, Y., Lwin, M. O., & Theng, Y. (2013). Let's play together: Effects of video-game play on intergenerational perceptions among youth and elderly participants. *Computers in Human Behavior, 29*(6), 2303–2311. https://doi.org/10.1016/j.chb.2013.04.037

Garwood, S. G. (1982). Piaget and play: Translating theory into practice. *Topics in Early Childhood Special Education, 2*(3), 1–13. https://doi.org/10.1177/027112148200200305

Griffiths, M. D., Kuss, D. J., & De Gortari, A. B. O. (2017). Videogames as therapy. *International Journal of Privacy and Health Information Management, 5*(2), 71–96. https://doi.org/10.4018/ijphim.2017070105

Landreth, G. (2023). *Play therapy: The art of the relationship* (4th ed.). Routledge.

Prensky, M. (2001). Digital natives, digital immigrants. *On the Horizon, 9*(5), 1–6. https://doi.org/10.1108/10748120110424816

Ray, D. C. (Ed.). (2016). *A therapist's guide to child development: The extraordinary normal years.* Routledge.

Ray, D. (2025). Research in play therapy. In D. Crenshaw, A. Stewart, and D. Ray (Eds.), *Play therapy: A comprehensive guide to theory and practice* (2nd ed.). Guilford Press.

Schaefer, C. E., & Drewes, A. A. (Eds.). (2014). *The therapeutic powers of play: 20 core agents of change* (2nd ed.). Wiley.

Stone, J. (2022). *Digital play therapy: A clinician's guide to comfort and competence* (2nd ed.). Routledge.

Uplift Games. (2017). *Adopt Me!* (online version) [video game]. https://www.roblox.com/games/920587237/Adopt-Me

VanFleet, R. (2005). *Filial therapy: Strengthening parent-child relationships through play* (2nd ed.). Professional Resource Press.

World Health Organization. (2019). *ICD-11: International classification of diseases* (11th revision). Retrieved from https://icd.who.int/

CHAPTER 31

THE FAMILY GIFT

AN EXPERIENTIAL TELETHERAPY INTERVENTION FOR FAMILIES LIVING APART

Amy A. Morgan and Kayla Sellers

Materials for Therapists and Clients: None. Writing materials, art materials, or the whiteboard function on a teletherapy platform are optional.

Objective

The family gift intervention, originally designed for in-person therapy, engages family members in collaboratively creating a shared gift that benefits everyone in the family (Lowenstein, 2006). This activity promotes active listening, problem-solving, and communication skills while providing the therapist with real-time insights into family dynamics and relational processes. Its experiential nature fosters play and bonding, which are especially valuable in the context of physical separation. Adaptable for teletherapy, the intervention suits families separated by living arrangements, travel, migration, deployment, incarceration, or other circumstances, offering a meaningful way to maintain connection. This chapter outlines steps for implementing a teletherapy-specific variation of the family gift intervention for families engaging from different locations.

Rationale for Use

Separation from family members can create significant hardship (Rodriguez & Margolin, 2015). The circumstances surrounding the separation shape the family's emotional and social experiences. For example, a military deployment may be predictable, accompanied by pride for the service member, but also fraught with concern for their loved one's safety (Mulholland et al., 2020). In contrast, forced separations, such as those caused by deportation (Boado & Ferrer, 2021) or incarceration (Mowen & Visher, 2016), may involve stigma, uncertainty about reunification, and anxiety over the risks of migration or life in carceral settings (Rodriguez & Margolin, 2015).

Regardless of the cause, separation – except in cases of safety or to prevent violence – can lead to emotional distress, attachment disruptions, caregiver strain, academic struggles, economic hardship,

DOI: 10.4324/9781003330912-38

and behavioral challenges (Morgan et al., 2021; Rodriguez & Margolin, 2015). The impact of the separation is influenced by factors such as its duration and frequency, social acceptability, expectedness (e.g., sudden or traumatic events), perceptions of danger to the absent family member, secondary economic impacts, cultural norms (e.g., whether separation is seen as typical or exceptional), and family characteristics (e.g., age, social support; Rodriguez & Margolin, 2015).

Maintaining connection during separation can help mitigate its negative effects. Regular, high-quality communication between separated family members fosters a sense of connection and family cohesion (Zentgraf & Chinchilla, 2012) while also alleviating the effects of "ambiguous loss," in which a parent is psychologically present but physically absent (Boss, 1999). With the growing use of telehealth, teletherapy provides a valuable tool for families experiencing the burden of separation and living apart.

The family gift intervention, originally developed as an assessment tool for families undergoing divorce (Lowenstein, 2006), is an art-based experiential activity that fosters meaningful insights for both clients and therapists. In this intervention, family members collaborate to create a "gift" that everyone agrees on and benefits from using common writing tools and/or art supplies. The gift can be either literal or metaphorical, and family members are encouraged to be as creative as possible. Although initially designed for in-person use, the family gift can be easily and effectively adapted for teletherapy, particularly for families experiencing separation. By guiding the family to collaboratively create a gift, the therapist fosters a safe space for family members to share emotions, desires, and needs in an approachable way, offering valuable insights into family dynamics.

While this intervention can be used with various theoretical approaches, it is particularly well-suited for experiential therapy (Satir, 1983; Whitaker & Bumberry, 1988). By encouraging family members to describe their feelings, expectations, needs, and desires, the intervention fosters emotional exploration and connection, helping families come together in the context of physical separation.

Setup

Prior to implementing the intervention, assess for the availability of writing and/or art supplies. When working with clients who are physically separated, especially due to circumstances such as travel, military deployment, incarceration, or forced migration, anticipate limited access to resources. Although access to common writing or art materials is ideal, the intervention can be successfully conducted without physical supplies. For instance, if clients desire to draw the family gift, this can be done using the whiteboard function available on most teletherapy platforms.

Instructions

1. ***Introduce the activity.*** To ensure there is adequate time for both completing the activity and processing its outcomes, introduce the intervention early in the session. Share that clients will work together to create an imaginative gift for the entire family. This gift should not require monetary resources to acquire it and may not even be a physical object. Explain that they may use the whiteboard function of the teletherapy platform or any writing and/or art supplies that they have available in the creation of their gift. Emphasize that the goal is to collaboratively design a single gift that everyone in the family both agrees on and desires, including how it

will be used within the family. Encourage creativity and reassure them that there are no right or wrong answers.

Let clients know they will have 15–30 minutes to complete the task, but additional time can be provided if needed. Larger families or those with diverse processing styles may require more time. Be flexible and, if necessary, extend the intervention over multiple sessions. The priority is to preserve the experiential nature of the activity and facilitate family connection and therapist observation, rather than adhering strictly to a specific timeframe.

Mention that you will observe and may chime in if appropriate, and you will remain available to answer questions.

2. ***Ensure understanding.*** Confirm that all participants understand the instructions and address any questions they may have. If the family chooses to use the teletherapy whiteboard function, provide a brief demonstration to ensure they feel comfortable using it.

3. ***Provide examples if appropriate.*** Providing examples of family gifts may be helpful for some clients who have difficulty conceptualizing their own family gift. Examples may also reduce the likelihood of innovative ideas if clients are inclined to simply use or build on examples that you have provided. Use best judgment in determining whether it is in the client's best interest to provide examples. If you decide that examples would be helpful, examples of family gifts may include the following:

    - A toolbox that the family can collaboratively fill over time in therapy, with skills for connection, communication, or emotional coping
    - A playlist where each person adds meaningful songs that evoke shared connection
    - A vision board or mission statement to articulate shared values, goals, and aspirations
    - A memory or gratitude jar, where each family member writes down favorite memories with or expressions of gratitude for one another

4. ***Facilitate the activity.*** Observe the family's engagement throughout the activity, taking note of their verbal and nonverbal communication, interaction patterns, decision-making processes, family roles, and dynamics. Pay attention to any underlying themes or meanings associated with the gift they create.

    As you observe, consider cultural and contextual factors and adapt the intervention to align with the family's values and preferred ways of interacting. For some families, the concept of a "family gift" may resonate with shared values, while other families may need guidance to focus on a collective goal. Allow families to interpret the idea of a "gift" in ways that align with their values, whether as a practical resource, symbolic gesture, or shared experience. In addition, be mindful of cultural norms around separation, as some families may view separation as a sacrifice for the greater good, while others may experience it as deeply challenging or traumatic.

    If a client insists the family gift should be an unrealistic gift (e.g., new puppy or toy), observe how the family responds. Unless clarification is needed, avoid intervening so you can authentically observe the family's dynamics. If necessary, you can repeat the activity with a different prompt, such as, "Last time, the family chose a wonderful 'want-to-have' gift – a puppy. This time, let's focus on a 'helpful-to-have' gift. Can you collaborate to create a gift that would benefit the entire family in addressing [presenting problem or adjacent issue]?"

5. ***Conclude the activity.*** Monitor for signs that the family is naturally concluding the task. If the session is ending and they need more time, communicate that they can revisit the activity during

the next session. As with any intervention, end the activity early if interactions become, or are approaching, inappropriate or harmful.

Processing

The following prompts, grounded in experiential family therapy principles, can help guide post-intervention discussion (Gehart & Tuttle, 2003). These prompts are organized by Satir's (1983) six levels of experience: behavior, coping, feelings, perceptions, expectations, and yearnings.

Behavior

- How did your family decide on the gift?
- What roles did each person take in the activity?
- What did you notice about your own behavior, and the behavior of others during the activity?

Coping

- Did you encounter any difficulties or disagreements while creating the gift? If so, how were they resolved?
- How did you cope with any challenging moments?

Feelings

- What emotions came up for you during the activity? For example, how did it feel when your gift idea was chosen—or not chosen?
- To what extent did your emotions feel validated by others during this activity?
- When did you feel empathy for others during the activity?

Perceptions

- How do you think the current [travel/deployment/incarceration/physical distance] influenced the gift your family chose?
- How did you think others perceived you in this activity?
- How did you perceive yourself?

Expectations

- To what extent did your experience match your expectations of how this activity would go?
- In what ways were you surprised by the process of creating the family gift?
- In what ways were you surprised by the gift that you came up with?

Yearnings

- How might the gift that you created help your family?
- How does the gift that you chose [address/not address] things that your family is longing for?

Vignette

The Berkley family sought therapy to cope with Aaron's (32) incarceration. During the initial call, Karrie (29) shared concerns about their oldest daughter, Emily (7), who was struggling academically, socially, and emotionally, with frequent outbursts at home. Aaron, incarcerated for nine months with a three-year sentence, had no prior legal history, leaving the family shocked and overwhelmed. Karrie noted that Brooke (5) had become emotionally withdrawn, and Mila (3) seemed confused, raising concerns about her relationship with Aaron and her sisters.

Aaron had pleaded guilty to charges related to a hit-and-run accident and accepted a plea deal for a reduced sentence. He had been approved for family teletherapy due to the family's expressed needs and his lack of prior history of abuse or danger toward his family. After an initial session with just Aaron and Karrie, and a second session involving the entire family, it became evident that their once close-knit bond had been strained, particularly when discussing their feelings about the incarceration. For the third session, the therapist introduced the family gift intervention as a playful and approachable way to help the family share their needs and emotions.

As the session began, the therapist explained the activity. The family would work together to create a single gift that everyone agreed they would want and would benefit the family. The therapist observed as Emily immediately took charge, sternly instructing her younger siblings to "be serious" so they could finish on time. Her sense of urgency grew when Mila and Brooke interrupted each other with ideas, and she became visibly upset. When Aaron gently asked for Emily's suggestions, she snapped, saying there was no point in sharing because no one was listening. Karrie attempted to soothe Emily, reassuring her that "it's just an activity," but Emily erupted, shouting that if they didn't follow the rules, "everything could go seriously wrong, and people could get hurt." She began crying, prompting Brooke to retreat to the floor, while Aaron became quiet and withdrawn.

Mila then asked Aaron if he could come home to help them "feel better." Karrie responded, saying, "You know dad can't come home for a few years." Brooke, speaking softly, said she wished for a time machine so her dad could go back and stay home the night of the accident. Karrie, avoiding further discussion of these emotional statements, redirected the girls to focus on the gift. Mila quietly stated that they would need a superhero to help. Once the idea of a family superhero was agreed upon, family members began to rapidly brainstorm ways the superhero could help. Brooke exclaimed, "She could visit us when we feel sad!" Aaron solemnly shared, "She can remind us of good memories." Although initially withdrawn, Emily quietly suggested, "Maybe she can help us figure out how to communicate when things are hard." The girls appeared to enjoy collaborating on the superhero's name, uniform, and superhero tools, while Karrie and Aaron complimented the girls' ideas.

As they developed their family gift, the therapist noticed several dynamics at play. Emily's sense of urgency and fear of making mistakes seemed tied to some anxiety, possibly reflecting fears that errors could result in serious harm or further separation. The therapist wondered if this anxiety stemmed from internalized concerns about her father's incarceration. Brooke, on the other hand, appeared to withdraw when emotions escalated, sharing during processing that she worried about her family but tried to stay quiet to avoid adding to the tension. Mila's suggestion of a playful gift reflected her developmental need for security and joy, but her question about Aaron coming home revealed her awareness of the family's struggles.

The therapist also observed Karrie's difficulty processing her emotions, as she focused on managing the activity rather than engaging with her own feelings. This pattern is reflective of the many burdens and challenges that primary caregivers tend to experience while a partner is incarcerated, illuminating how Karrie may benefit from additional support. The therapist wondered if Karrie feeling overwhelmed may have made it harder for her to help the girls process their emotions, especially Emily's heightened anxiety and Brooke's withdrawal. Aaron's quiet withdrawal during the activity suggested unresolved guilt or sadness, which could be explored further in future sessions.

The therapist also noted the wonderful strengths displayed as the family decided on and developed their family gift. The family's collaboration demonstrated creativity, imagination, and a capacity to work together.

To help the family reflect, the therapist used processing questions rooted in experiential family therapy. The therapist asked Emily about her emotions and perceptions during the activity, exploring her fear that "doing things wrong" could lead to harm. The therapist then asked Brooke how it felt to see Emily struggle and explored her tendency to stay quiet to avoid being "too different." The therapist invited Mila to share her perception of the changes in the family, ensuring her voice was heard despite her young age. Turning to Aaron, the therapist inquired about his emotions regarding his incarceration, and they asked Karrie how managing the activity, and so much at home, impacted her ability to connect emotionally with the family. The therapist also asked about everyone's roles in the activity, inquiring about yearnings for cohesion and emotional connection.

As the processing continued, the therapist helped the family identify themes in their struggles, such as their difficulty having fun or staying connected without Aaron, collective emotional distress about the family separation, and their shared desire for him to come home. They also highlighted the family's strengths, noting that despite the challenges, they collaborated to complete the activity, demonstrating their ability to harness play and imagination in working together toward a common desire. The therapist shared these observations and encouraged the family to use this resilience to support one another while Aaron remained incarcerated. This led to a discussion about therapeutic goals, helping the family identify steps to improve communication, manage emotions, and strengthen their bond during the challenging experience of family separation. Throughout the family's therapy journey, the therapist consistently referred to the family superhero as a unifying symbol. As the family developed emotion regulation and communication skills, they collaboratively created new superhero tools to represent each skill. The superhero served as a reminder of their shared hopes and goals, a prompt to practice learned techniques, a source of encouragement during difficult moments, and a way to foster connection through imaginative shared experiences.

Suggestions for Follow-Up

The family's gift can serve as a meaningful metaphor throughout future sessions, acting as a touchpoint for how the family perceives their progress in addressing the needs and desires that inspired the gift. Track the family's progress by discussing whether they feel closer to "receiving" or achieving the benefits of the imagined gift. You might also encourage the family to build on their original idea by asking, "If you could add one more characteristic to the gift, what would it be?" This question can uncover new or emerging needs as the family adapts to ongoing challenges. Revisiting the activity later in therapy can provide a valuable comparison between gifts created at different times, illustrating the family's evolving priorities and relationships.

Contraindications

The family gift intervention is contraindicated for families with a history of abuse, neglect, or harm by any family member present toward any other family member that is present. The family gift intervention is also not recommended for families displaying persistent hostile communication or tension, overt conflict, or unresolved disagreements between parents or other family members, especially if such dynamics are likely to cause distress for children. If you anticipate that the activity may create distress, prioritize interventions focused on building emotional safety, communication, or conflict resolution.

Additionally, this intervention may need to be adapted to be more inclusive for families with members who approach imaginative play, collaboration, or sustained focus differently due to neurodivergence or developmental considerations. For example, consider structured prompts, shorter activity durations, and multisensory engagement options to ensure everyone can participate meaningfully.

References

Boado, H. C., & Ferrer, A. G. (2021). The impact of physical separation from parents on the mental wellbeing of the children of migrants. *Journal of Ethnic and Migration Studies, 10,* 2436–2454. https://doi.org/10.1080/1369183X.2021.1935670

Boss, P. (1999). *Ambiguous loss: Learning to live with unresolved grief.* Harvard University Press.

Gehart, D. R., & Tuttle, A. R., (2003). *Theory-based treatment planning for marriage and family therapists.* Brooks/Cole, Cengage Learning.

Lowenstein, L. (2006). *Creative interventions for children of divorce.* Champion Press.

Morgan, A. A., Arditti, J. A., Dennison, S., & Frederiksen, S. (2021) Against the odds: A structural equation analysis of family resilience processes during paternal incarceration. *International Journal of Environmental Research and Public Health, 18*(21), Article 11592. https://doi.org/10.3390/ijerph182111592.

Mowen, T. J., & Visher, C. A. (2016). Changing the ties that bind: How incarceration impacts family relationships. *Criminology & Public Policy, 15*(2), 503–528. https://doi.org/10.1111/1745-9133.12207

Mulholland, E., Dahlberg, D., & McDowell, L. (2020). A two-front war: Exploring military families' battle with parental deployment. *Journal of Pediatric Nursing, 54,* 34–41. https://doi.org/10.1016/j.pedn.2020.05.019

Rodriguez, A. J., & Margolin, G. (2015). Parental incarceration, transnational migration, and military deployment: Family process mechanisms of youth adjustment to temporary parental absence. *Clinical Child and Family Psychology Review, 18*(1), 24–49. https://doi.org/10.1007/s10567-014-0176-0

Satir, V. M. (1983). *Conjoint family therapy* (3rd ed.) Science and Behavior Books.

Whitaker, C. A., & Bumberry, W. M. (1988). *Dancing with the family: A symbolic-experiential approach.* Routledge.

Zentgraf, K. M., & Chinchilla, N. S. (2012). Transnational family separation: A framework for analysis. *Journal of Ethnic and Migration Studies, 38*(2), 345–366. https://doi.org/10.1080/1369183X.2011.646431

CHAPTER 32

ONLINE CHILD-PARENT RELATIONSHIP THERAPY

Michael R. Whitehead

Materials for Therapists: List of toys to provide parents and a diagram of the way in which parents should set up the space for play sessions (included in the supplemental materials that accompany this book).

Materials for Clients: Video camera, an object that can be used to create a boundary (e.g., masking tape, twin-size blanket, sheet), and toys (see handout for suggested toys).

Objective

Child-parent relationship therapy (CPRT; Landreth & Bratton, 2005) is an evidence-based filial therapy approach designed to strengthen the connection between parents and their children. In CPRT, parents learn how to use child-centered play therapy (CCPT; Axline, 1981) skills to attend to their children in much the same way a play therapist would. CPRT was originally facilitated in in-person group therapy sessions. This chapter outlines how to use CPRT as a teletherapy intervention.

Rationale for Use

CPRT engages parents as change agents for their children (Cornett & Bratton, 2014) while the therapist acts as a coach/supervisor. Teaching parents how to use CCPT skills with their children on a daily basis is a long-term solution for a variety of concerns (Edwards et al., 2010). In addition, CPRT can also be used when working with families where one parent does not consent to mental health treatment. For instance, if one parent attends CPRT training and implements play sessions with a child, the child can still benefit from that parent's utilization of CCPT skills even if the child can't attend therapy. It can also be used for families in very rural communities with limited child mental health resources. Parents in rural communities can attend CPRT sessions via telehealth, implement the skills from each session, and both the children and parents benefit from the skills learned.

Research for CPRT indicates that it is an effective intervention for internalizing disorders (Karami & Zabet, 2015), externalizing disorders (Costas & Landreth, 1999; Kale & Landreth, 1999; Rennie & Landreth, 2000), attachment difficulties (Opiola & Bratton, 2018), and behavioral and social-emotional problems at school (Smith & Landreth, 2004). CPRT is recommended for children ages 18 months to 12 years old. There are adaptations and adjustments required for younger and older age groups; however, overall concepts and skills are beneficial for children of all ages. CPRT has been successfully implemented via teletherapy with some additional instruction/guidance on the part of the therapist

DOI: 10.4324/9781003330912-39

(Agarwal et al., 2022; Chau & Baggerly, 2024; Hicks & Baggerly, 2017). An advantage to implementing CPRT via teletherapy is that the therapist can see the parents set up the play area in the home and provide real-time coaching and troubleshooting throughout the setup.

Landreth and Bratton (2005) originally designed CPRT to be completed in ten weekly group sessions. The following describes an adaptation to this original format that allows sessions to be completed either in individual or group appointments tailored to a teletherapy environment.

Setup

Most therapists with a background in child development and a familiarity with CCPT should be able to utilize this intervention with little additional training. Therapists not familiar with CCPT should review the following materials before using this intervention:

- *Play Therapy* (Axline, 1981)
- *Child Parent Relationship Therapy (CPRT): A 10-Session Filial Therapy Model* (Landreth & Bratton, 2005)
- *Child-Centered Play Therapy* (VanFleet et al., 2011)

Have training materials available to show parents. Prepare a list of CPRT play session toys (see handout) and a diagram of the way in which parents should set up their space for play sessions. Figure 32.1

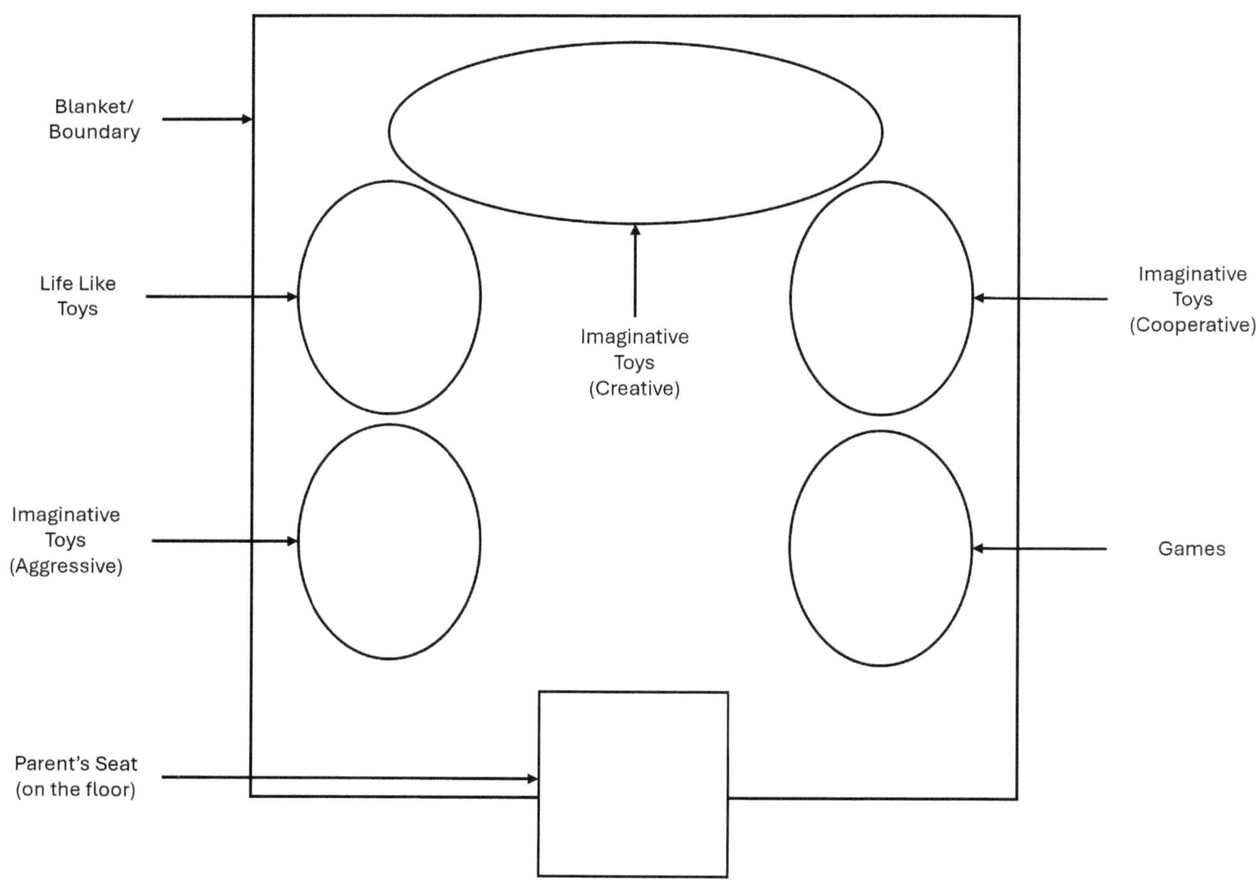

Figure 32.1 Diagram of room setup for CPRT play sessions.

provides an example that you may show parents. This diagram is also available in the supplemental materials that accompany this book, so you may edit the diagram and work with clients to design a setup that will work for the unique space in which they plan to conduct play sessions.

Instructions

Unlike parent-child interaction therapy (McNeil & Hembree-Kigin, 2010), where parents attend with children and are instructed live while a therapist watches, CPRT focuses solely on training parents and coaching through videotaped play sessions. Therefore, only parents should attend these sessions. This format allows parents and therapists to talk openly about children without worrying about what they might hear. It also focuses the attention on the parents as the change agents with the therapist giving live feedback. It is best when all active parents who regularly interact with children participate so all parents can learn the skills. For example, a child who lives half of the time with their biological dad and stepmom and half time with their biological mom and other stepmom may have all four parents involved in treatment. If this is not feasible, involve as many parents as possible. Each session builds upon the last, wherein the therapist provides didactic teaching, gives examples from their own experiences, engages parents in role-plays, and typically ends with homework for the parents to complete. Later sessions typically involve video feedback of play sessions, coaching, and building on earlier skills. An outline of each session follows.

Session 1: Introduction to Child-Centered Play

1. ***Introduce CPRT.*** Briefly explain to parents the concepts of parent-child attachment. Explain the differences between insecure attachment and secure attachment (Siegel & Bryson, 2020). Discuss child emotional and behavioral problems as an outgrowth of parent-child attachment and family systems dynamics (Landreth & Bratton, 2005). Introduce the concept that CPRT will strengthen the relationship between parent and child, will teach parents a different way to be with their child, and provide skills to both them and their child in ways that other more direct forms of therapy cannot. Explain that using the parents as change agents is more beneficial and longer lasting than having the child only work with a therapist (Cornett & Bratton, 2014).
2. ***Share materials.*** Find a video or explain the concept of the Still Face Experiment. A video is more powerful and can be easily found by using the following search terms: "Ed Tronic, Still Face Experiment." If a video cannot be utilized, describe the experiment as found in the article, *"Infant Affective Reactions to the Resumption of Maternal Interaction After the Still-Face"* (Weinberg & Tronick, 1996). Discuss with parents their emotional reactions to either the video or the experiment as you described it.
3. ***Teach skills.*** Introduce parents to the concept of play as a behavioral health intervention. Introduce the idea of being child-led. Review the basic principles of child development and why children respond better to play. For instance, you might say

    > Children utilize play to explore their world and understand how things work. They also use play to process their emotions and to overcome difficulties they are facing. An important way to think about this is that play is a child's language, and toys are the words they use to express their language.

4. ***Assign homework.*** Encourage parents to spend five minutes of undivided time with their child this week. Encourage them to just be observant of what they notice.

Session 2: Play Materials and Setup

1. ***Review homework.*** Process with parents using the following questions:
   - What did you notice about your child that you didn't notice before?
   - What did you like about this experience?
   - What was most difficult about this experience?
   - How did you feel when your child did or said something and you couldn't respond?
2. ***Share materials.*** Introduce the concept of child-led play either by explaining CCPT (Axline, 1981) and the concept of "being vs. doing" as discussed by Siegel and Bryson (2020) in Chapter 1 of *The Power of Showing Up* or show videos that you find to explain these concepts. Discuss with parents what they felt as you discussed these concepts or as they watched the videos you showed.

   Also, provide a list of play materials that will be required for future homework assignments (see handout). Inform parents that these toys should not be the child's favorite toys. They should only be used during play sessions. Parents may work with children to identify toys to set aside for the purpose of special play time, or they may acquire toys for this purpose. A more cost-effective means of acquiring toys for this purpose is to purchase them used, though many children will willingly set toys aside for this activity.
3. ***Teach skills.*** Teach parents the basics of play sessions. Explain that the play session is to be child-led and that the parents are not to teach, correct, or criticize the child or their play. The parent should avoid setting limits unless absolutely necessary. Instruct them on how to introduce the play session and how to set limits at the beginning of the session. Provide the following example of what the parent might say when introducing play sessions:

   > Right now is our special play time. For the next 30 minutes you and I will play with these toys in a lot of the ways that you want to. The only rules are that I am not for hurting, you are not for hurting, and the toys are not for breaking. Please take a minute to explore the toys to decide what you would like to do first.

   Then, teach parents reflecting skills. Parents should be enthusiastic announcers of the child's play, much like a sports announcer. However, they should not label any item until the child has labeled it. For example, if a child is playing with a toy dog, the parent should not refer to the toy as a dog unless the child has first labeled it as such. Explain that parents are often surprised to see that the toys that children use frequently represent things in their play that they might not expect. For instance, the toy "dog" may represent a cat, horse, or even a piece of cake!

   Instruct parents to use a timer to keep track of the time. Request that they provide three warnings before the play time is up. These warnings should take place where there are five minutes, three minutes, and one minute left. The warnings should be stated in a similar format as the following:

   > "We now have [five/three/one] minute(s) left in our playtime."
   >
   > "Our play time is now over. You may go [identify a pre-determined activity for them to do after the playtime] while I clean up."

   Children may want to help clean, but it is important for the parent to clean without the child so their play is not limited in anticipation that they will have to clean afterwards.

4. ***Role-play.*** Role-play with parents each step of play sessions and reflecting skills. When providing feedback regarding role-plays or attempts to use reflecting skills, highlight the things they do well first, then add any corrective feedback that may be needed. For instance, "I can feel the enthusiasm you bring to your reflections! Some kids will get overwhelmed with too much reflection. Use that same enthusiasm but try spreading your reflections out more over time."
5. ***Assign homework***. Instruct parents to gather play materials and schedule a time where they can dedicate 30 minutes of undivided play time at the same time once per week with their child. They will start this 30-minute play time after the next session, in the meantime, encourage parents to practice reflecting their child's play during another 5 minutes of undivided time with child.

Session 3: Limit Setting

1. ***Review homework.*** Process with parents using the following questions:
   - What was the experience of your play time like this last week?
   - How did your child respond?
   - What came easily to you when reflecting?
   - What challenges did you experience when reflecting your child's play?
   - How did you feel when your child did or said something and you couldn't respond?
2. ***Share materials.*** Introduce the idea that limit setting can happen without saying "no" or "stop." Explain why this style of limit setting increases a child's feeling autonomy, and self-regulation, as well as maintaining a positive parent-child relationship. Discuss with parents what they felt as you discussed these concepts.
3. ***Teach skills.*** Teach ACT limit-setting skills. Teaching parents how to set limits can often be challenging. Using the ACT acronym to help parents remember this skill allows parents to implement it while at the same time attending to their child's emotional needs. For instance, if a child wants to shoot a parent with a dart gun, this would be an appropriate time for the parent to set limits.

   A stands for *acknowledge*. When a child does something that is not allowed, or needs a limit, first acknowledge their internal thought process, emotions, and desires.

   C stands for *communicate*. After acknowledging the desire of the child, communicate what limit that you are setting.

   T stands for *target*. A target is an appropriate alternative behavior/activity that the child can do.

   Using the example of the dart gun, the parent might say something like:

   A: "I know you would like to shoot dad with the dart gun…"

   C: "however, dad is not for shooting."

   T: "If you'd like to shoot something, you can shoot the ground."

   This formula for limit setting can be used both in the play session and out of the play session. For example, if a child wants to jump on the couch and this is not permissible in your home, you could use the following statement:

   A: "You think it would be fun to jump on the couch…"

C: "but the couch is not for jumping on."

T: "You can jump on your bed or the grass outside."

4. ***Role-play.*** Role-play with parents allowing them to practice the reflecting skills from session two, and the ACT limit-setting skills that you just taught them.
5. ***Assign homework.*** Hold and record the first 30-minute play session.

Sessions 4–5: Supervision and Coaching of Play Sessions

1. ***Review homework.*** Reflect on the play session. Process with parents using the following questions:
   - What did you enjoy most about the play session?
   - Share three things you did well in the play session.
   - What was most difficult about the play session?
   - What skill was hardest to use, reflecting or limit setting?
   - Answer any questions that come up from the discussion on the play session.
2. ***Coach.*** Watch the play session together, you can either have them share their recorded session with you before meeting using a secure file-sharing system or have them share their screen with you on the teletherapy platform while they play the video. If you view the video together, stop and comment on the video when you see successful skills demonstrated and when you see major deviations or concerns.
3. ***Teach skills.*** Re-teach any skills from the previous sessions that seemed to be difficult for them to grasp in the recorded play session.
4. ***Role-play.*** Role-play with parents any skills that need adjusting as evidenced by the videotaped session.
5. ***Assign homework***. Continue 30-minute play sessions.

Session 6: Choice Giving

1. ***Review homework.*** Reflect on the play session. Process with parents using the following questions:
   - What did you enjoy most about the play session?
   - Share three things your child enjoyed about the play session.
   - What was most difficult about the play session?
   - What skill was hardest to use, reflecting or limit setting?
2. ***Coach.*** Watch the play session together. Stop and comment when you see successful skills demonstrated and when you see major deviations or concerns.
3. ***Share materials.*** Find a video about Garry Landreth's Oreo Cookie Choice analogy (Play Therapy Institute, 1996) or discuss the concepts with the parents. Answer any questions that come up about choice giving.
4. ***Teach skills.*** Teach parents the choice-giving intervention. This intervention is often difficult for parents to master because it requires a longer phrase than is typically used in CPRT. Essentially, we

want parents and children to know that the choices they make (both in the play sessions and out of play sessions) lead to other "choices." For example, if after using the ACT limit setting, the child does not comply, use the following format for choice giving:

> "If you *choose* to continue pointing the dart gun at me, you *choose* to have the gun put away during the rest of the play session. Which *choice* do you *choose*?"

As with all the other skills, this can be used at any time outside of play sessions. For instance, if a child wants to have five cookies after dinner, you can use this phrase to help them make a better choice:

> "You can *choose* to have one cookie now, or you may *choose* to have no cookies. Which *choice* do you *choose*?"

The importance of using this exact phraseology comes down to helping children understand that they are making the choice of both the action and the potential consequences. This allows them to better see the connection between their actions and any aftermath that may follow.

5. ***Role-play.*** Role-play with parents in a way that allows them to practice choice giving and any other skills that need adjusting as evidenced by the videotaped session.
6. ***Assign homework.*** Continue 30-minute play sessions.

Session 7: Encouragement vs. Praise

1. ***Review homework.*** Reflect on the play session. Process with parents using the following questions:
   - What did you enjoy most about the play session?
   - What was most difficult about the play session?
   - What skills were hardest to use, reflecting, limit setting, or choice giving?
2. ***Coach.*** Watch the play session together. Stop and comment when you see successful skills demonstrated and when you see major deviations or concerns.
3. ***Share materials.*** Find a video or discuss the concepts of Carol Dweck's (2016) research regarding growth vs. fixed mindsets, specifically mentioning the impact of praise on children.
4. ***Teach skills.*** Teach parents encouragement skills and explain the problems with praise. Explain that encouragement allows children to discover for themselves how to find solutions to problems. It also helps children develop a positive self-regard and help them discover their many capacities and strengths.

   The essential hallmarks of encouragement are as follows:

   - ***Focus on what the child did.*** For example, "Wow, you cut that paper pretty fast." Avoid focusing on any imperfections or opportunities for growth (e.g., paper is cut crooked).
   - ***Encourage children to find solutions rather than doing things for the child.*** For example, you might say, "How would you like me to help?"
   - ***Celebrate their successes.*** For example, "You found a way to do that!"

   Most importantly, do not express any evaluative statement on their work (i.e., "that looks pretty," "I like blue," "you are so strong/smart/helpful").

5. ***Role-play.*** Role-play in a way that allows parents to practice encouragement skills and any other skills that need adjusting as evidenced by the videotaped session.
6. ***Assign homework.*** Continue 30-minute play sessions.

Sessions 8–10: Supervision and Coaching

1. ***Review homework.*** Reflect on the play session. Process with parents using the following questions:
   - What did you enjoy most about the play session?
   - What was most difficult about the play session?
   - What skills were hardest to use, reflecting, limit setting, choice giving, or encouragement?
2. ***Coach.*** Watch the play session together. Stop and comment when you see successful skills demonstrated and when you see major deviations or concerns.
3. ***Teach skills.*** Re-teach any skills from the previous sessions that seemed to be difficult for parents.
4. ***Role-play.*** Role-play with parents any skills that need improvement.
5. ***Assign homework.*** Continue play sessions and schedule a follow-up appointment for one to two months after this last session.

Vignette

Jessica (45) contacted a therapist seeking therapy for her son, Luke (7), who was struggling adjusting to a recent high-conflict divorce. Jessica reported that Luke was experiencing intense anxiety regarding exchanges, as exhibited by telling Jessica that they were experiencing stomach aches when they thought about having to visit their other parent. Jessica also reported that Luke experienced massive behavioral outbursts for two to three days upon returning to Jessica's home after visiting with Jessica's former partner. When the therapist sought consent from Jessica's former partner, they refused to allow Luke to participate in therapy. Believing that Luke could benefit indirectly from the therapist's services with Jessica, it was confirmed with Jessica's lawyer and the therapist's liability attorney that CPRT to Jessica alone would not violate the other parent's parental rights to refuse therapy treatment. Legal counsel also indicated that therapy could make use of recorded play sessions with Jessica and Luke.

Due to the two-hour drive from Jessica's home to the therapist's office, it was decided that sessions would be conducted via telehealth. This was the best set up for Jessica and her family since they lived in a rural community, the other parent wouldn't consent to therapy, and the therapist believed that strengthening the relationship between Luke and Jessica would decrease Luke's anxiety when visiting his other parent, increase Jessica's ability to set appropriate limits, and increase her non-anxious presence when Luke experienced disruptive behaviors.

Jessica was a quick learner and eagerly applied the CCPT skills when interacting with Luke during play sessions. Luke challenged Jessica in the first play session by throwing toys and refusing to play. The supervision/coaching feedback in the fourth session allowed the therapist to role-play with Jessica how to respond to instances like this in the future.

Jessica utilized the feedback effectively and set limits appropriately. Luke responded to this limit setting with compliance and cooperation. Jessica struggled to understand and effectively implement the encouragement skill over praise. She wanted to praise Luke in her play sessions because she felt a need to build him up due to the intensity of the conflict that was taking place in the divorce. The therapist worked with Jessica on this skill each week until she began to praise less and encourage more.

By the seventh session, Jessica was alarmed by Luke's reduction of behavioral outbursts upon returning from visitation with his other parent. After processing this, Jessica reported that she did not think playing with Luke once a week could have as big of an impact on his behavior as she was seeing. Jessica and the therapist agreed to keep track of this as a possible anomaly and address any potential regression if necessary. When his behavior continued to improve, she was convinced that regular play sessions were allowing her and Luke the time to build trust and relational capital to protect against behavioral regressions after visitations.

By the tenth session, Luke reported less anxiety and worry about visiting his other parent. Even teachers reported that they were noticing a difference in his "calm presence."

The therapist continued to work with Jessica once a month for another 10 sessions to support any concerns that might come up. Jessica continued to engage in regular play sessions and Luke continued to improve.

Suggestions for Follow-Up

Check in with clients to see how play sessions outside of therapy are going. Provide continued coaching as needed.

Contraindications

The use of CPRT may be contraindicated with clients experiencing abuse or neglect, or where a parent is not emotionally, psychologically, or developmentally capable of exercising CCPT skills effectively. To apply CPRT with clients experiencing high-conflict divorce, therapist may need additional training, supervision, and oversight.

References

Agarwal, S. M., Rodríguez Delgado, M., & Tapia-Fuselier Jr., J. L. (2022). Meeting the needs of children through telemental health: Application for rural mental health using child–parent relationship therapy. *International Journal of Play Therapy, 31*(4), 216–227. https://doi.org/10.1037/pla0000178

Axline, V. (1981). *Play therapy*. Ballantine Books.

Chau, I., & Baggerly, J. (2024). Online child–parent relationship therapy in Hong Kong during COVID-19: Results of a pilot study. *International Journal of Play Therapy, 33*(1), 12–23. https://doi.org/10.1037/pla0000210

Cornett, N., & Bratton, S. C. (2014). Examining the impact of child parent relationship therapy (CPRT) on family functioning. *Journal Of Marital and Family Therapy, 40*(3), 302–318. https://doi.org/10.1111/jmft.12014

Costas, M., & Landreth, G. (1999). Filial therapy with nonoffending parents of children who have been sexually abused. *International Journal of Play Therapy, 8*(1), 43–66. https://doi.org/10.1037/h0089427

Dweck, C. S. (2016). The perils and promises of praise. In M. Scherer (Ed.), *On formative assessment: Readings from educational leadership (EL Essentials)* (pp. 66–75). ASCD.

Edwards, N. A., Sullivan, J. M., Meany-Walen, K., & Kantor, K. R. (2010). Child parent relationship training: Parents' perceptions of process and outcome. *International Journal of Play Therapy, 19*(3), 159–173. https://doi.org/10.1037/a0019409

Hicks, B., & Baggerly, J. (2017). The effectiveness of child parent relationship therapy in an online format. *International Journal of Play Therapy, 26*(3), 138–150. https://doi.org/10.1037/pla0000033

Kale, A. L., & Landreth, G. L. (1999). Filial therapy with parents of children experiencing learning difficulties. *International Journal of Play Therapy, 8*(2), 35–56. https://doi.org/10.1037/h0089430

Karami, J., & Zabet, M. (2015). Efficacy of child-parent relationship therapy in reducing anxiety syndrome in preschool children. *Quarterly Journal of Child Mental Health, 2*(3), 39–47.

Landreth, G. L., & Bratton, S. C. (2005). *Child Parent Relationship Therapy (CPRT): A 10-session filial therapy model.* Taylor & Francis.

McNeil, C. B., & Hembree-Kigin, T. L. (2010). *Parent-child interaction therapy.* Springer. https://doi.org/10.1007/978-0-387-88639-8

Opiola, K. K., & Bratton, S. C. (2018). The efficacy of child parent relationship therapy for adoptive families: A replication study. *Journal of Counseling & Development, 96*(2), 155–166. https://doi.org/10.1002/jcad.12189

Play Therapy Institute. (1996). *Choices, cookies, & kids: A creative approach to discipline.* [Streaming]. https://prolearning.unt.edu/unt/course/course.aspx?C=122&pc=9&mc=32&sc=42

Rennie, R., & Landreth, G. (2000). Effects of filial therapy on parent and child behaviors. *International Journal of Play Therapy, 9*(2), 19–37. https://doi.org/10.1037/h0089434

Siegel, D. J., & Bryson, T. P. (2020). *The power of showing up: How parental presence shapes who our kids become and how their brains get wired.* Ballantine Books.

Smith, D. M., & Landreth, G. L. (2004). Filial therapy with teachers of deaf and hard of hearing preschool children. *International Journal of Play Therapy, 13*(1), 13–33. https://doi.org/10.1037/h0088883

VanFleet, R., Sywulak, A. E., & Sniscak, C. C. (with Guerney, L. F.). (2011). *Child-centered play therapy.* Guilford Press.

Weinberg, M. K., & Tronick, E. Z. (1996). Infant affective reactions to the resumption of maternal interaction after the still-face. *Child Development, 67*(3), 905–914. https://doi.org/10.1111/j.1467-8624.1996.tb01772.x

CPRT Play Session Toys

Lifelike Toys

- One or two baby dolls (with gender specific and gender-neutral clothing)
- A baby bottle (real or toy)
- Figurines or dolls sufficient in number and type so they can be used to represent your family
- Toy animals including a variety of domestic and wild types
- Toy cars and/or trucks
- Toy kitchen supplies (e.g., plates, bowls, spoons, forks, food)
- Play money (e.g., coins, bills)
- Play phones
- Play doctor kit

Imaginative Toys (Aggressive)

- Army men toy
- Toy dart/nerf gun
- Costume mask
- Toy handcuffs with key
- Bendable, toy knife
- Short rope

Imaginative Toys (Creative)

- 3-1 oz. containers of dough (e.g., Play-doh) in a variety of colors
- 1–8 count crayon set
- 3 sheets of plain white paper
- 2 blunt tipped scissors
- 1 roll of transparent tape
- 3 balloons of moderate size that have not been inflated
- 4 sheets of origami sized paper

Imaginative Toys (Cooperative)

- Ball (e.g., tennis ball or ball of similar size)
- Small 100 count set of blocks (e.g., LEGO®)
- Easy 50–100-piece puzzle

Games (2)

- Playing cards
- Uno
- Phase 10
- Checkers
- Other similar games

Part 8

Anxiety and Trauma

CHAPTER 33

TEDDY GOES TO THE DOCTOR

Adrian Knauss, Taylor Young, and Jennifer L. Hodgson

Materials for Therapists: PowerPoint file with images of a teddy bear or another animal and basic medical supplies commonly encountered in a pediatrician's office or hospital setting (included in the supplemental materials that accompany this book).

Materials for Clients: None.

Objective

The teddy bear check-up, also known as the teddy bear clinic, is an intervention that has been used worldwide to engage children in medical roleplay with stuffed animals to increase understanding of upcoming medical procedures, increase familiarity with medical settings, and decrease fear of medical personnel (Bloch & Toker, 2008; Dalley & McMurtry, 2016; Santen & Feldman, 1994; van Sommeren & Ottenheim, 2018). This may be particularly beneficial for children who have been affected by past medical trauma. This chapter outlines how to conduct this traditionally in-person intervention via teletherapy.

Rationale for Use

For many children, medical interventions, such as office visits, hospitalizations, and invasive medical procedures, can be frightening (Chrisler et al., 2021). If previous experiences with medical systems have been traumatic, there is oftentimes increased fear and anxiety when receiving medical care. Unfamiliar healthcare environments and the physical discomfort associated with them may contribute to increased feelings of anxiety or fear.

Medical play explores medical themes and equipment and aims at decreasing anxiety and increasing resilience when working with children (McCue, 1988). Medical play is different from preparation in that preparation is a direct intervention that is led by a caregiver or therapist that psychologically prepares a child for interactions with the healthcare system (Bolig et al, 1991). Medical play is nondirective and is led by the child for them to explore on their own terms. Therapists can have a pivotal role in promoting medical play and preparation for children and their families through play therapy interventions such as the teddy bear check-up (Beyers et al., 2017; Dalley & McMurtry, 2016). The teddy bear check-up allows children to explore upcoming healthcare visits by telling a story about a teddy bear. This is done by the therapist and family developing the parameters of the story (i.e., teddy

DOI: 10.4324/9781003330912-41

goes to the doctor) and allowing the child to create a story within those parameters. Therapy sessions can be structured to encompass non-directive medical play and preparation and to process these activities upon their conclusion.

The following provides instructions for conducting a virtual teddy bear check-up with children between the ages of four and twelve. Adaptations can be made for younger or older children.

Setup

Setup for the virtual teddy bear check-up should include collaboration with caregivers and medical providers whenever possible.

1. ***Assess the client's experience.*** This will inform you on the who, what, when, where, how, and why of the backstory that you will create for "Teddy Goes to The Doctor." It will also inform the utilization of medical play and preparation throughout the session. Inquire about the following:
   - What is the family's history with the healthcare system? Have there been any traumatic or distressing experiences?
   - How does the child react to interactions with the healthcare system?
   - Have they expressed fear or anxiety around a certain object (i.e., needles, blood pressure cuffs)?
   - Is there a certain part in the doctor's appointment where the child expresses fear or anxiety?
   - Is there a certain point where any of the child's caregivers feel anxiety or fear?
   - Who usually goes to doctor's appointments?

   If you are able to receive a release of information to collaborate with medical providers, ask the following:
   - What are some challenges children and their families commonly face during this experience (i.e., office visits, specific procedures)?
   - What are important elements to include in the teddy bear story to best prepare the child and their family?
2. ***Create a backstory.*** Using the responses provided by the aforementioned assessment, create a backstory for why "Teddy," or another stuffed animal that the child connects with, may need to visit the doctor. For example, if a child was recently diagnosed with type 1 diabetes, the child might be anxious about blood sugar checks and administrating insulin due to fear of needles. The therapist can tell a story about "Teddy" receiving the same diagnosis and having the same fear of needles. However, "Teddy" knows he needs to do these things and uses support from his mom when he gets scared.
3. ***Establish a timeframe.*** Create a loose plan for the time allotted for medical play, preparation, and processing. Consider the number of sessions available before the child's next doctor's appointment or anticipated procedure and how much play time in each session you plan to be child-led, therapist-led, and caregiver-led.
4. ***Provide psychoeducation.*** Inform the family about play therapy and the difference between medical play and preparation. Educate caregivers on the parameters of play therapy and medical

play and its non-directive nature. Ascertain how long the caregivers observe and how/when they should join in the session.

5. ***Introduce the activity to caregivers***. Explain to caregivers your intention to conduct a teletherapy intervention in which their child will use medical play to explore medical interventions in a safe, nonthreatening environment. To facilitate this play, caregivers are encouraged to utilize available toys and objects that are similar to what a child might encounter during a medical intervention.
6. ***Assess availability of supplies.*** Ask caregivers if they have any supplies available that may be used for the intervention. If possible, it can be helpful to conduct the intervention using physical materials that are available in the client's environment. Some children may have a toy doctor bag, which may prove useful in conducting the intervention. Provide a list of items that you wish to use and ask which items are available. The following items are ideal:
   - Teddy bear or another stuffed animal
   - Available first aid supplies:
     - Adhesive bandages (various colors and designs)
     - Thermometer
     - Tongue depressor
     - Blood pressure cuff
     - Syringes (no needles attached)
     - Scale for weight and height
     - Empty prescription bottles
     - Alcohol pads
     - Cotton ball swabs
     - Rubber gloves
     - Masks
   - Available medical toys:
     - Toy stethoscope
     - Toy syringe
     - Toy doctor bag
   - Reward supplies:
     - Lollipops
     - Stickers

If physical materials are not available, you may use digital images that are available in the supplemental materials that accompany this book. You may even ask caregivers to provide a photograph of the child's favorite stuffed animal to crop and display on screen with these materials to make a beloved friend come to life on screen! Digital materials may be ideal when caregivers are not able to easily acquire physical materials or for children that are particularly interested in the digital realm. Digital materials also allow the therapist to play along through the screen.

Instructions

The following instructions should be followed to implement the activity with children. Include caregivers when possible.

1. ***Share your screen.*** If you will be conducting the activity using digital images, open the PowerPoint file that contains the images for this activity and share your screen, first showing only the digital "stuffed animals" (see Figure 33.1). You may provide several options from which the child may choose for the activity. Alternatively, if a caregiver shared with you an image of the child's stuffed animal, display this image.

2. ***Encourage the child to retrieve one of their own stuffed animals to participate.*** Regardless of whether or not you are using virtual materials for this activity, it can be helpful for children to have a tangible item in their hands to play with during the experience that they can then continue medical play with post-session. If caregivers shared that they have medical toys or supplies available, request that they bring these out at this time as well so that the child can play with them if they choose.
3. ***Introduce the teddy bear.*** Ask the child to introduce their stuffed animal to you. If you will be using additional virtual materials, tell the child that there is someone you would like to introduce them to and show them the teddy bear or another virtual "stuffed animal." If you are showing an image of their own stuffed animal, you may say something like, "look who wanted to join us today!" Explain that they are going to be the main character of a story that you will create together with their family. In this story, the teddy bear must go to the doctor to get better. Use an appropriate backstory that is either specific to the child's situation (e.g., they are going to have a procedure done at the hospital) or more general about medical care visits (e.g., they will be seeing the doctor soon).

Figure 33.1 Digital "stuffed animals." Credit: Dr. Christine Walsh Borst.

4. ***Invite the client(s) into the story.*** Encourage the child and family to contribute their ideas to the story. For example, the child can name the teddy bear and provide more details about them. Allow the child to take their time, be creative, and build on the character as much or as little as they would like.
5. ***Engage in open play.*** Encourage the child to play out the story. Open play may take place with a physical toy the child possesses, digital materials (see Figure 33.2), or a combination of the two. Observe and reflect on how the teddy bear is doing during the story. Family members may also have reflections to contribute to the story. Encourage the child to stay within view of the computer so you are able to observe and participate. Some children may be very comfortable telling and acting out a story about a healthcare visit with their stuffed animal. Other children may require more encouragement and participation. If everyone is safe, there is no one right way to play. You can choose to set a specific amount of time to allow for play or leave it open. You can play along by acting out the child's story or narrative with the digital images. This step may occur in one session or across multiple sessions.
6. ***Prepare.*** If there is a specific medical visit that is coming up, you can follow open play with storylines that are consistent with the child's situation. Do not provide specific medical advice or provide information outside of your knowledge about medical interventions. However, you may be able to give the child an idea of what to expect, especially if you have received additional information from the family or healthcare team. This may also be a time to correct any misconceptions or inaccurate information the child demonstrated during open play. Using the teddy bear, tell a story about them going to the doctor. Demonstrate how the teddy bear experiences the healthcare visit and encourage the child to share their ideas about how the teddy bear is thinking, feeling, and behaving. Ask the child if they have any ideas about what the teddy bear can do to feel safer and calmer during the experience.

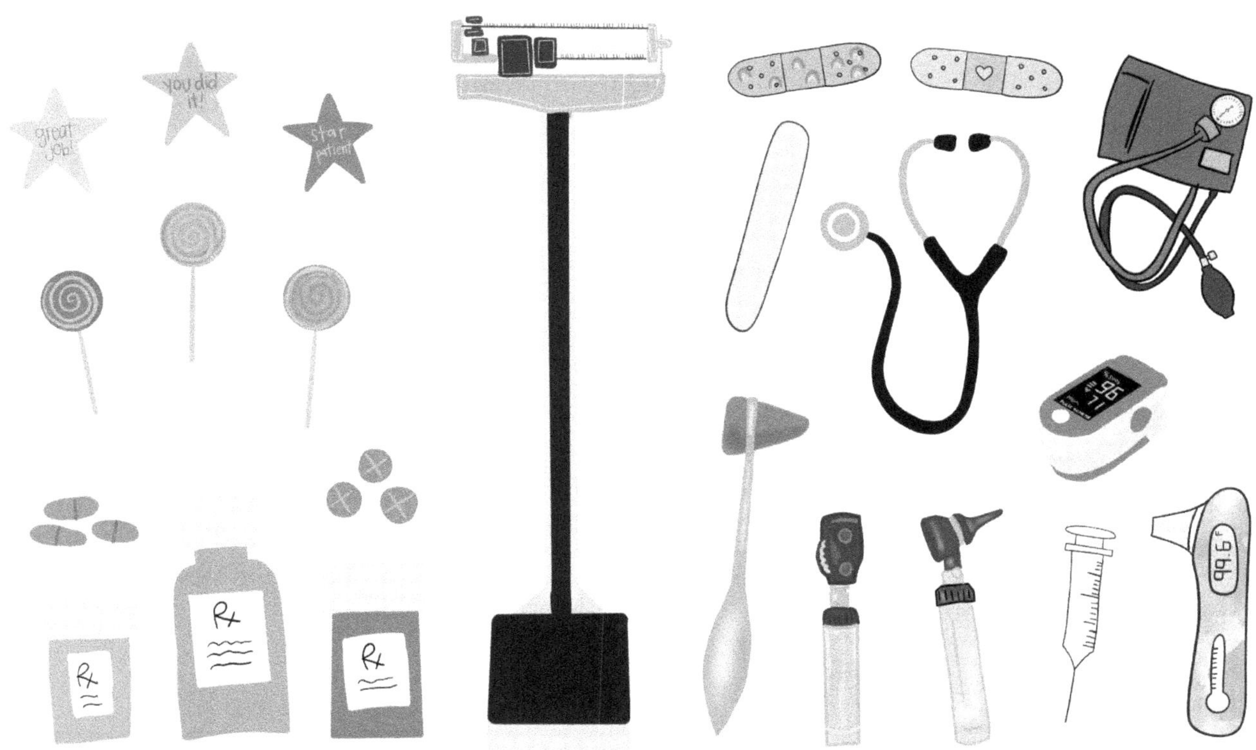

Figure 33.2 Digital medical supplies. Credit: Dr. Christine Walsh Borst.

Processing

Within the play therapy model, it is common to process with children and caregivers in the act of playing. For the therapist, processing includes reflecting the child's actions and experiences back to the child (O'Connor et al., 2016). Observe themes and patterns that emerge from the child's play and recognize how the play may reflect the child's inner experiences (Cuschieri, 2019). Example reflection statements for the Teddy Bear Check-Up include the following:

- "It looks like putting that band-aid on Teddy helped protect the area that hurts."
- "Teddy seems to like the doctor. The doctor in this story seems friendly."

After the open medical play and during preparation, you may also ask processing questions about the child and family's experience. It is important to note that children's answers may not always be direct responses to questions. Rather, consider how the child's play may be metaphorical and reflective of their thought processes (Cuschieri, 2019). The following is a list of questions that you might ask children and their caregivers.

Children

- What was your favorite part of playtime today?
- Why is it important for the teddy bear to go to the doctor?
- Why is it important for you to go to the doctor?
- What was the teddy bear feeling during their doctor's visit?
- What do you feel during a doctor's visit?
- Would you like to take [name of the child's stuffed animal] with you to your next doctor's appointment?

Caregivers

- How did it feel to let your child control the medical play? Is this reflective of your experience with the healthcare environment?
- What stood out to you during the activity?
- What do you think could have gone differently?
- What were your thoughts and feelings seeing your child play out a doctor's visit?
- What else do we need to do to prepare your child for their next doctor's appointment?
- Do you think it would help your child if they brought [name of the child's stuffed animal] to their next appointment?

Vignette

Maria (6) was brought to therapy by her mother, Ana (26), and grandmother, Luisa (58). Maria lived with her mother and grandmother, who were her primary caretakers. Maria's biological father was not in the home and had no contact with Maria, Ana, or Luisa. Ana helped care for Luisa who had undergone multiple surgeries on her knees and back and experienced chronic pain. Ana reported being overwhelmed in caring for both Maria and Luisa, though Maria often helped care for Luisa as well. Maria had accompanied Ana to Luisa's last two doctor's appointments. Maria appeared uncomfortable during these appointments but was not overly distressed.

Maria's pediatrician, Dr. Long, referred the family to therapy after a recent incident at the doctor's office. The mother reported that at an annual check-up, Maria was visibly distraught, and her mother had a difficult time getting her into the office. Neither Ana nor Luisa were able to calm her down during the visit. In a consultation with Dr. Long, he explained that Maria exhibited high anxiety during the office visit, beyond what is typical for a child at this age. They were unable to complete the appointment and all parties were concerned about Maria's reaction to another upcoming appointment where lab work needed to be completed. Ana reported that Maria needed help managing her anxiety. Luisa expressed that Ana was not strict enough with Maria and should not allow Maria to throw "tantrums" like the one at the doctor's office.

During the session with the family, the therapist introduced the teddy bear check-up to the family. The therapist provided psychoeducation about medical play therapy to Ana and Luisa. Ana confirmed that Maria had a stuffed animal she could have with her during the virtual session. Luisa also agreed to gather some household supplies that Maria could use as medical supplies during play.

The therapist and family discussed the backstory that would be appropriate for Maria. Ana and Luisa explained that there is a family history of type 1 diabetes on Maria's father's side of the family. After Ana and pediatrician noticed some symptoms of pre-diabetes, Dr. Long ordered blood work to be completed to test hemoglobin A1C at the next visit.

During the session with Maria, the therapist shared her screen to show Maria the digital images of a teddy bear, named Teddy, at the doctor office. She encouraged Maria to introduce her stuffed animal too. Maria introduced her stuffed elephant, Trunkie, to the therapist. Maria described her friend to the therapist by explaining their likes, dislikes, and personality (i.e., a friendly elephant who likes popcorn the best). The therapist explained that the stuffed animals (i.e., Teddy and Trunkie) are going to the doctor soon. The therapist asked Maria to continue the story of what happens to Teddy and Trunkie at the doctor's office.

For the next 30 minutes, Maria told the story of Teddy and Trunkie's doctor's visit. The therapist played alongside Maria, using the digital images to act out Maria's story. Maria used her animal, along with cotton balls, bandages, and other items she found around the house to represent medical tools. At times, the therapist had to remind Maria of the backstory (e.g., going to the doctor), but other than these gentle reminders, Maria was able to direct most of the play herself. Throughout the medical play, the therapist used reflective statements such as:

- "It looks like Teddy is especially nervous waiting for the doctor but Trunkie doesn't seem as nervous."
- "You were very kind to Trunkie after his shot. You even gave him a superhero band aid."

The therapist also paid special attention to themes that emerged from the non-directive play. The therapist noticed that when the doctor gave shots to Trunkie and Teddy, it seemed to be associated with intense pain that lasted a long time. Maria acted out exaggerated emotions and behaviors, including loud exclamations, crying, and trying to run away from the needle. At one point, Maria had Trunkie break the pretend syringe, which they found funny.

At the next session, the therapist shared a story with Maria, Ana, and Luisa about Teddy getting lab work done. The therapist used the digital images of Teddy and their medical supplies to show the different steps, including arriving at the doctor's office, checking in, waiting for the nurse, cleaning Teddy's arm with an alcohol swab, using the syringe to take blood (see Figure 33.3), and bandaging the arm (see Figure 33.4). The therapist was even able to find a picture of Dr. Long from the website that they included. The therapist was careful to set realistic expectations of what to expect from the needle stick. The therapist showed that the prick hurt Teddy a little, but it was not that painful and over really quickly. Maria played along with Trunkie as the therapist and family acted out the story. At the end, Maria chose a sticker to give to Trunkie for doing well.

Throughout the story, the therapist and the family asked different questions and processed Teddy and Trunkie's experience. Process questions included:

- "What were Teddy and Trunkie feeling as they waited for the doctor? What were they feeling when their blood was drawn?"
- "What could we do to make them feel better? What makes you feel better during appointments?"
- "Ana and Luisa, what stood out to you from playtime with Maria?"

Figure 33.3 Teddy during blood draw. Credit: Dr. Christine Walsh Borst.

Figure 33.4 Teddy getting bandaged. Credit: Dr. Christine Walsh Borst.

Together, the family and therapist were able to solidify different coping skills that Maria could use during the doctor's appointment. For example, Maria said Trunkie might feel better if they could hold Mama's hand when they see the needle. Subsequently, Ana asked Maria if she could hold her hand at the next appointment and Maria said she would like that. Maria also asked Luisa to pray for Trunkie. Luisa promised to keep Trunkie and Maria in her prayers. At the end of the session, the family created a plan to bring Trunkie with them to the doctor's appointment and set up a follow-up therapy session after the appointment.

Suggestions for Follow-Up

The activity can take place during one session or throughout multiple sessions. For children with chronic illnesses who frequently receive medical care, you may revisit this activity to prepare for subsequent encounters with healthcare systems. Additionally, you can follow up with caregivers, medical professionals, and other persons involved in the child's care to collaborate using comforting language, rituals, and interactions that emerged during the medical roleplay. For example, children may develop their own term for medical equipment or procedures that feel less threatening to them. If appropriate, medical personnel and families can adopt this terminology. You can also talk with caregivers about allowing children to bring their stuffed animals to the next doctor's appointment. This may increase comfort, provide continuity to the "Teddy Goes to the Doctor" story, and aid in processing in follow-up sessions.

Contraindications

Exposure to medical supplies and/or discussions of medical procedures may evoke strong emotional responses in children, especially if they have experienced medical trauma. Monitor how clients respond during the activity and take breaks when necessary. Follow safe practices when interacting with medical tools and providing age-appropriate education to children about being safe with real-world medical supplies.

References

Beyers, L., Phipps, W. D., & Vorster, C. (2017). An introduction to teddy bear therapy: A systems family therapy approach to child psychotherapy. *Journal of Family Psychotherapy, 28*(4), 317–332. https://doi.org/10.1080/08975353.2017.1301156

Bloch, T. H., & Toker, A. (2008). Doctor, is my teddy bear okay? The "Teddy Bear Hospital" as a method to reduce children's fear of hospitalization. *The Israel Medical Association Journal, 10*(8–9), 597–599.

Bolig, R., Yolton, K. A., & Nissen, H. L. (1991). Medical play and preparation: Questions and issues. *Children's Health Care, 20*(4), 225–229. https://doi.org/10.1207/s15326888chc2004_5

Chrisler, A. J., Claridge, A. M., Staab, J., Daniels, S. R., Vaden, V., & McTaggart, D. (2021). Current evidence for the effectiveness of psychosocial interventions for children undergoing medical procedures. *Child: Care, Health and Development, 47*(6), 782–793. https://doi.org/10.1111/cch.12900

Cuschieri, E. (2019). Play therapy: An introduction to theory and practice. In P. K. Smith & J. L. Roopnarine (Eds.), *The Cambridge handbook of play: Developmental and disciplinary perspectives* (pp. 630–648). Cambridge University Press.

Dalley, J. S., & McMurtry, C. M. (2016). Teddy and I get a check-up: A pilot educational intervention teaching children coping strategies for managing procedure-related pain and fear. *Pain Research and Management, 2016*, Article 4383967. https://doi.org/10.1155/2016/4383967

McCue, K. (1988). Medical play: An expanded perspective. *Children's Health Care, 16*(3), 157–161. https://doi.org/10.1207/s15326888chc1603_5

O'Connor, K. J., Schaefer, C. E., & Braverman, L. D. (2016). *Handbook of play therapy*. John Wiley & Sons, Inc.

Santen, L., & Feldman, T. (1994). Teddy bear clinics: a huge community project. *MCN. The American Journal of Maternal Child Nursing, 19*(2), 102–106. https://doi.org/10.1097/00005721-199403000-00011

van Sommeren, R., & Ottenheim, M. (2018). The teddy bear hospital: How to influence the attitude of kindergarten children towards doctors, hospitals and falling ill? *Journal of the European Teacher Education Network, 13*, 106–116.

CHAPTER 34

EXTENDED REALITY-BASED EXPOSURE THERAPY

Richard Lamb and Jason Perry

Materials for Therapists: Timing device. Optionally, a second computer monitor and extended reality (XR) headset may be used to join clients directly in the XR environment. If using a headset, you will also need a minimum of 4 square feet in a seated position or 6.5 square feet for room-scale settings to move around.

Materials for Clients: XR hardware and a minimum of 4 square feet in a seated position or 6.5 square feet for room-scale settings to move around.

Objective

XR-based exposure therapy in telehealth settings offers several advantages over traditional in vivo and imaginative exposure methods. The objective of this chapter is to explain how teletherapy-based XR exposure therapy can be used in treating post-traumatic stress disorder, phobias, and anxiety for children and adolescents.

Rationale for Use

In-person treatments for post-traumatic stress disorder, phobias, and anxiety include medication, cognitive behavioral therapy, talk therapy, and imaginative and in vivo exposure approaches (Reeves et al., 2022). Of these approaches, exposure therapy is most effective (Butler & Heimberg, 2020).

Unlike traditional therapy or exposure therapies using flat displays, XR-based exposure therapy integrates computer graphics and various input technologies to immerse users in authentic environments to help generate responses. To accomplish this, clients wear head-mounted displays featuring a separate screen for each eye, along with integrated stereo earphones, and head-tracking devices. This combination of technologies generates immersion in a virtual reality in which therapists create customized virtual environments that tailor exposure scenarios to client-specific phobias or triggers and then create gradual exposure assignments that enhance treatment effectiveness over time (Lamb et al., 2020). Through processes such as habituation and extinction, the triggering stimuli gradually diminish their impact, leading to the reassociation of memories as non-threatening. This, in turn, diminishes phobic, anxious, or traumatic responses.

DOI: 10.4324/9781003330912-42

As early as 1995, Rothbaum illustrated that the use of XR-based environments in the treatment of psychological disorders, specifically acrophobia (i.e., fear of heights), has significant positive effects (Kothgassner & Felnhofer, 2021). Within the Rothbaum (1995) study, participants were repeatedly exposed to XR environments which included locations like bridges of varying heights from the ground and differing levels of stability, outdoor balconies, and elevators. Results from this study illustrate that XR significantly decreased phobic responses and improved attitudes toward heights (Huang et al., 2022).

XR-based telehealth exposure therapy offers several advantages over traditional in vivo and imaginative exposure methods. XR-based exposure therapy incorporates a combination of imaginal techniques and in vivo techniques, striking a balance between safety and vividness in an immersive yet controlled environment. Unlike imaginative exposure, where clients simply imagine a feared scenario, XR consistently triggers client responses, offering the chance to confront underlying negative thoughts directly and with in-the-moment guidance, which is typically very difficult to accomplish in traditional exposure therapy.

XR illustrates significant potential in its application for diagnostic purposes as well (Lamb & Etopio, 2019). In most approaches, diagnostics consist of questionnaires, interviews, and tracking of avoidance behaviors. XR-based environments offer a potential means to aid in identifying stimuli useful for exposure therapy both within real-life exposure and XR environments.

Setup

Prior to using XR in therapy with clients, prepare clients and caregivers with coping strategies for facing any feared stimuli that you intend to expose them to in the XR environment. In addition, familiarize yourself with XR equipment and technology. Practice using XR on your own so you are well versed in both technical procedures and the virtual experience itself. The following describes the steps necessary for setup in an initial therapy session and between sessions.

First, involve children and adolescents, along with caregivers, in the following conversations regarding the use of XR-based exposure therapy in teletherapy.

1. ***Discuss how XR works in therapy.*** Explain the use of XR in exposure-based therapy approaches and the perceived benefits of XR in helping clients progress toward the client's goals of therapy.
2. ***Assess the availability of XR equipment, physical space, and caregiver involvement.*** A minimum of 4 square feet in a seated position or 6.5 square feet for room-scale settings is required for clients to physically move around while they are immersed within the virtual environment. In your assessment, ensure that the space available will allow you to maintain visual contact with clients during the activity through the teletherapy platform and that the client's physical environment is safe (e.g., no nearby stairs or breakable objects). Explain that a caregiver must be available during all XR exposure-based therapy sessions to monitor physical safety and to provide immediate support should the child become too fearful during the activity. If XR equipment, required space, or caregiver involvement are not available, consider other options for therapeutic intervention.
3. ***Discuss the length of treatment and time typically spent in the XR environment.*** XR-based exposure therapy typically requires 10–15 weekly sessions (Lamb et al., 2024). XR sessions typically last between 10 and 30 minutes per session.
4. ***Explain potential harm which can occur due to the use of the XR environment, identify ways in which to mitigate these barriers, and discuss what clients and caregivers***

should do if they occur. XR-based playrooms generate digital data related to each client's psychological and physiological state. Discuss potential limitations to client confidentiality. In addition, explain that simulation sickness is a potential barrier to treatment. Discuss how clients can exit the augmented reality environment any time that this occurs by simply removing the XR headset.

To prevent simulation sickness, use a timing device to limit the client's headset usage to the recommended 10- to 30-minute timespan. Some clients may need tolerance training prior to intervention to mitigate simulation sickness. Begin with shorter immersive experiences until clients have demonstrated the ability to withstand longer periods of involvement. Should simulation sickness occur, you can (a) suggest they get fresh air or have a fan blow cool air on them; (b) ask the client to redirect their gaze to a distant object or the horizon; or (c) have the client lie on their back. Continue to monitor them until the symptoms resolve. If the symptoms do not resolve within 10–20 minutes, refer them to their primary care provider and reassess the use of XR for this client.

Explain that the client may experience fear, associated physiological responses such as increased heart rate, and simulation sickness. Discuss how clients can exit the XR environment any time these things occur by simply removing the XR headset.

Prior to XR intervention, work with clients and caregivers to develop coping techniques to use when they face anxiety-provoking stimuli. Work together to identify how caregivers can successfully support child and adolescent clients when this does occur. Then, provide in-the-moment coaching for child and adolescent clients and their caregivers when the need arises.

5. ***Discuss how the XR system works.*** If clients have access to their own XR equipment and are familiar with their system, this may require little explaining. If caregivers are familiar with the system and child or adolescent clients are not, support caregivers in providing a tutorial. Then, explain how the XR system will be used in subsequent sessions to help them overcome their fears!

6. ***Practice.*** Allow children and adolescents the opportunity to try using XR equipment without exposing them to anxiety-provoking stimuli. This may be done in the initial session in which XR is discussed, or in a subsequent session prior to the XR exposure-based therapy intervention. Caregivers may also support with this endeavor outside of session.

   Following practice, inquire about the client's experience and assess for any possible simulation sickness that may have occurred. Provide tolerance training as needed by having clients practice being in the virtual environment for shorter periods of time and then increasing time spent in the virtual environment until they can withstand longer periods of time without simulation sickness.

7. ***Assess the client's willingness to participate.*** If clients appear fearful or unwilling, you may suggest simply playing with XR in session without exposure to any fearful stimulus to help clients increase comfort with the equipment and then later reassess their interest in the intervention. Avoid forcing clients to participate in XR exposure-based treatment and identify alternative interventions as needed. Then, if clients appear willing to participate, complete the following steps between sessions.

8. ***Review client history***. Identify the object or scenario that elicits fear or anxiety for the client. Consider caregiver and client assessment, as well as your own.

9. ***Select a virtual environment***. XR environments can be downloaded through the headset application store of via online websites from the software developer. Select an environment that contains an element of the client's fear, anxiety, or phobia. Initial triggering stimuli should start as low level triggers and gradually increase intensity and exposure length over the totality of the

sessions. Ensure that the environment will not be too anxiety provoking but will likely elicit some sort of a response. Also, ensure the environment has an "escape" button so the client can remove themselves to a safe environment. For example, a child who is fearful of spiders may first be immersed into an XR environment in which there is a picture of a small, friendly looking cartoon spider. Once the client has gained comfort with this scenario, increase the intensity of the stimulus. For example, more realistic environments may be chosen that depict an image of a real spider, and over the course of multiple sessions possibly even several images of real spiders.

10. ***Provide the virtual environment to caregivers.*** Virtual environments can be made available through download via a computer file transfer from the therapist's website. Provide any additional instructions that may be necessary to help caregivers upload the environment to their XR hardware.

Instructions

In the next session, conduct the following steps with clients and their caregivers both present.

1. ***Check with caregivers to ensure that the virtual environment has been uploaded to the XR hardware.*** If it hasn't been uploaded, ask that caregivers do this in session. Provide support as needed.
2. ***Mentally prepare clients by explaining what the XR environment will be like.*** Discuss how long you intend for the experience to last and what they are going to see, hear, and potentially "feel" within the environment. Discuss any concerns that the client or caregiver may have.
3. ***Reassure clients that they are in control of the experience.*** Review XR controls and the way that the client and caregiver can access a "safe" environment either by removing the headset or pressing the "escape" button on the controls. Explain that you will be able to observe their actions and provide just-in-time coaching as they negotiate the environment.
4. ***Obtain assent from clients and consent from their caregivers to begin the intervention.*** When working with younger children, caregivers may place the headset on the client's head when they are ready. Have the caregiver support in adjusting the headset as needed so the client is comfortable.
5. ***Provide instructions for any "tasks or activities."*** Ask clients to interact within the environment. For example, the client may look at, "touch" items, and move around areas which contain different triggers. In addition, clients may be asked to complete a specific task such as sitting near a feared animal, location, or object for a specific time or to touch that specific object. Provide coaching and support as needed.
6. ***Monitor clients.*** Throughout the activity, monitor clients for signs of distress and coach clients and caregivers on applying coping strategies to reduce anxiety around the phobias as needed. If the environment appears to be overwhelming and these strategies do not work while in the XR environment, calmly remind clients and caregivers that they may exit the environment using the "escape" button" and applaud them for facing their fears. Revisit coping strategies and adjust the virtual environment intensity to one that will likely be less distressing for the next session. During the initial XR session, capture baseline levels of anxiety, traumatic, or phobic responses for comparison post-intervention. In subsequent sessions, assess for any changes in the client's response to stimuli.

7. ***Prepare to exit the environment.*** Provide a 30-second to 1-minute warning to inform clients that their time in the headset is coming to an end.
8. ***Exit the environment.*** At the appointed time, have caregiver guide clients to a seated position and ask the client to press the escape button or remove the headset.
9. ***Monitor for signs of discomfort or simulation sickness.*** Observe clients for ten minutes with the aid of caregivers to ensure that they are not experiencing any negative effects associated with the environment (Lamb et al., 2021). If simulation sickness occurs, provide guidance to caregivers on steps to take to mitigate the effects. If clients are feeling well, you can begin the processing portion of the intervention during this time.

Processing

After exposure therapy, clients benefit from processing approaches that help them reflect on their experience and identify thought patterns influencing behavior and emotions. Two highly effective approaches are cognitive processing and systemic processing (Asmundson et al., 2019). During cognitive processing, clients evaluate maladaptive thoughts related to trauma, anxiety, or phobia within the context of exposure. Clients then develop strategies to address triggers and assess how these changes impact various aspects of their lives through systemic processing, including family interactions, friendships, and school relationships. Caregiver involvement provides valuable input and support during therapy, helping to leverage existing and potential support systems.

To aid in processing, discuss triggers, fears, and behaviors. Develop a list of triggers and rank their intensity from lowest to highest. This will help to guide the remaining exposures. Identify strengths and resources that may help clients achieve their goals. Additionally, ask questions to clients and caregivers to identify ways in which people in the client's support system might assist them with these strategies. Provide psychoeducation about XR-based exposure therapy and coping techniques throughout the process as needed.

The following solution-focused questions may be used to aid in cognitive and systemic processing.

- What specific thoughts were you having during the XR experience?
- What are different thoughts you can have about this experience?
- On a scale of 1–10, how would you rate your response to this trigger? A rating of 1 indicates that you experienced no distress. A rating of 5 indicates that you experienced moderately high levels of distress, but the distress was bearable. A rating of 10 indicates that you experienced the maximum level of distress you can imagine.
- Has there ever been a time when your response to this trigger was just a little lower than what you just reported? What was different when this happened?
- What do you think it would take for you to be just one point lower on this scale the next time that you enter the XR experience?
- What might your [mom/dad/caregiver] do to help you move just one point lower on this scale the next time that you enter the XR experience?
- What [qualities/skills] do you have that help you feel more grounded during times you feel anxious?
- What changes do you notice in the others and yourself when you're not feeling anxious?

Vignette

Grace (13) presented in teletherapy with her mom, Deanna (48), after several months of her refusing to go to school, often saying that she had a stomachache in the morning, which typically seemed to go away by lunch time and there was little chance of her still needing to go to school. When she attended school, Grace reported experiencing intense anxiety during routine classroom changes and teaching transitions. She also hesitantly shared that the cafeteria overwhelmed her and that she often became frustrated or embarrassed when her teacher wasn't available to let her eat in the classroom. These challenges all appeared to be hindering her school participation, friendships, and academic success. In addition, her parents reported that the discussion of school often led to withdrawal and irritability at home.

During the initial intake and assessment, the therapist identified Grace as a potential candidate for XR-based exposure therapy to help her reframe and restructure her thoughts, feelings, and behaviors around attending school and engaging in activities in her class. Though Grace did not often use XR, her family had the necessary equipment at home, which was most often used by Grace's older brother, and she was familiar with it.

During the second session, the therapist used a psychoeducational approach to explain to Grace and her parents about anxiety, cognitive processing therapy, and exposure therapy, focusing on the benefits and challenges. The therapist laid out a 15-session plan in which Grace would be placed in digital environments such as her classroom and the school cafeteria. Initially, the environments were acquired using a three-dimensional camera to record the environments within her school. The therapist then converted the 3D images to computer-generated environments using rendering software. Once fully rendered, the client could move around the environment and interact with objects to improve the realism of the experience.

The exposures started off mild with little activity where Grace could practice routines. During this time, the environments did not include other "people" and had reduced noise levels. The work slowly progressed to larger areas with more people and greater levels of noise, eventually approaching levels within a real school. The exposure culminated with Grace walking from the car to her class and then to the cafeteria with her class (see Figures 34.1 and 34.2). Within the XR environment, Grace could move around the school and interact with items in a limited fashion.

During the initial sessions, Grace spent about 10 minutes in the environment and seemed to find comfort in being able to exit the scenario at will. As sessions went on, the amount of time Grace spent in the environment was gradually increased to 30 minutes, and the amount of just-in-time coaching was reduced. For example, if Grace became fearful while ordering her lunch in the cafeteria, the therapist would remind Grace of strategies should could use to calm herself. For example, the therapist might say, "Grace, take a deep breath, close your eyes for a second, think about the next step." About 30 seconds to a minute before the specified end time, the therapist would warn Grace that the scenario was about to end. Grace's mom or dad would guide her to a seated position, remove the headset, and then monitor her while the therapist processed the experience with her. Only once during the sessions did Grace experience discomfort when she removed the headset. This was remedied by allowing Grace to sit for a few minutes and drink some water.

The remaining portion of the session consisted of processing the exposure experiences with a focus on identifying specific systemic, physical, cognitive, and emotional responses to the environment. Once these aspects were identified, Grace was asked to consider how she might react differently, how her reaction might impact others, and what that reaction might look like for her. Over time, though the experiences were intended to be more intense, Grace often rated them lower than the initial experiences. Grace also noted an overall reduction in her social anxiety related to interactions within classrooms and in new places. Below is an example of a processing conversation between Grace and her therapist.

Figure 34.1 XR cafeteria without children. Credit: University of Georgia Neurocognition Science Laboratory.

Therapist: What was it about the cafeteria environment that caused anxiety?

Grace: I felt really anxious because the room was crowded and noisy. There were too many people talking at once, and I couldn't focus on anything. The bright lights also made me feel overwhelmed.

Therapist: How were you able to overcome this?

Grace: I took a few deep breaths and tried to find a quieter corner of the room. I also put on my noise-canceling headphones, which helped block out some of the noise. It took a little while, but I started to feel more in control.

Therapist: What coping strategies were identified that helped with this?

Grace: One of the strategies that really helped was using my noise-canceling headphones. I also practiced deep breathing exercises you taught me. Another thing that helped was having a small object in my pocket that I could fidget with when I felt anxious.

Therapist: How did you feel after using your coping strategies?

Grace: I felt a lot calmer and more in control. It was like I had a toolbox to help me manage my anxiety, and knowing I had those tools made a big difference.

Therapist: What advice would you give to someone else experiencing similar anxiety?

Grace: I'd tell them to find what works best for them, whether it's deep breathing, using headphones, or having a fidget object. It's important to have a plan and to communicate with the people around you so they can support you. And remember, it's okay to take a break if you need to.

Figure 34.2 XR school hallway without children. Credit: University of Georgia Neurocognition Science Laboratory.

Suggestions for Follow-Up

Assess each client's experience with XR-based exposure therapy prior to using it again in other sessions. Ensure that the intensity and length of the exposure is appropriate and is progressing clients toward therapeutic goals. Adjust the intensity and length of exposure in subsequent interventions as needed.

Help clients integrate and transfer strategies that they applied in XR settings into the real world. Include caregivers and other key stakeholders (e.g., school personnel) to assist with this endeavor.

Contraindications

XR hardware costs can limit accessibility for clients. Additionally, physiological conditions (e.g., seizures, epilepsy) may be triggered by intense emotional experiences in XR environments. Respiratory or cardiovascular concerns could also lead to negative outcomes due to physiological stress. Psychological factors, such as emotional instability, may impact XR-based exposure therapy. In addition, clients with dissociative disorders or intellectual impairment might struggle to engage fully and could be further destabilized. Thoroughly assess clients for safety of use prior to implementing XR-based exposure therapy and provide alternative interventions as needed.

References

Asmundson, G. J., Thorisdottir, A. S., Roden-Foreman, J. W., Baird, S. O., Witcraft, S. M., Stein, A. T., ... & Powers, M. B. (2019). A meta-analytic review of cognitive processing therapy for adults with posttraumatic stress disorder. *Cognitive Behaviour Therapy, 48*(1), 1–14. https://doi.org/10.1080/16506073.2018.1522371

Butler, R. M., & Heimberg, R. G. (2020). Exposure therapy for eating disorders: A systematic review. *Clinical Psychology Review, 78,* Article 101861. https://doi.org/10.1016/j.cpr.2020.101851

Huang, T., Li, H., Tan, S., Xie, S., Cheng, Q., Xiang, Y., & Zhou, X. (2022). The efficacy and acceptability of exposure therapy for the treatment of post-traumatic stress disorder in children and adolescents: A systematic review and meta-analysis. *BMC Psychiatry, 22*(1), Article 259. https://doi.org/10.1186/s12888-022-03867-6

Kothgassner, O. D., & Felnhofer, A. (2021). Lack of research on efficacy of virtual reality exposure therapy (VRET) for anxiety disorders in children and adolescents: A systematic review. *Neuropsychiatrie, 35*(2), 68–75. https://doi.org/10.1007/s40211-020-00349-7

Lamb, R., & Etopio, E. (2019). VR has it: A framework for virtual reality integration into therapy. In J. Stone (Ed.), *Integrating technology into modern therapies* (pp. 80–93). Routledge. https://doi.org/10.4324/9781351014113

Lamb, R., Etopio, E., Firestone, J. B., Zeder, J., & Hand, B. (2020). Realism, immersion, and interactivity. In K. A. Croce & J. Firestone (Eds.), *Developing science literacy in the 21st century* (pp. 83–106). Information Age Publishing.

Lamb, R., Firestone, J., Kavner, A., Almusharraf, N., Choi, I., Owens, T., & Rodrigues, H. (2024). Machine learning prediction of mental health strategy selection in school aged children using neurocognitive data. *Computers in Human Behavior, 156,* Article 108197. https://doi.org/10.1016/j.chb.2024.108197

Lamb, R., Hand, B., & Kavner, A. (2021). Computational modeling of the effects of the science writing heuristic on student critical thinking in science using machine learning. *Journal of Science Education and Technology, 30*(2), 283–297. https://doi.org/10.1007/s10956-020-09871-3

Reeves, R., Curran, D., Gleeson, A., & Hanna, D. (2022). A meta-analysis of the efficacy of virtual reality and in vivo exposure therapy as psychological interventions for public speaking anxiety. *Behavior Modification, 46*(4), 937–965. https://doi.org/10.1177/0145445521991102

Rothbaum, B. O., Hodges, L. F., Kooper, R., Opdyke, D., Williford, J. S., & North, M. (1995). Virtual reality graded exposure in the treatment of acrophobia: A case report. *Behavior Therapy, 26*(3), 547–554. https://doi.org/10.1016/S0005-7894(05)80100-5

CHAPTER 35

SPEAKING IN CODE

USE OF SIGNALING IN TELETHERAPY

Amanda Veldorale-Griffin

Materials for Therapists: Telehealth platform with a chat feature, reaction icons/emojis, and/or virtual backgrounds.

Materials for Clients: None.

Objective

The purpose of this chapter is to assist therapists in using visual cues in teletherapy to enhance the comfort and safety of clients during these appointments. Therapists will understand ways to use a variety of visual cues and signals during teletherapy sessions and how this can help facilitate strong therapeutic relationships and build a safe space for clients, especially for those who may be from minoritized populations, connecting with their therapist from high-risk environments or situations, and/or have difficulty verbally communicating their needs for other reasons.

Rationale for Use

For therapy to be effective, there must be privacy. Confidentiality is a key part of ethical codes for therapists (e.g., American Association for Marriage and Family Therapy, 2015) and the ability to have access to that privacy promotes comfort and safety for clients. However, when conducting teletherapy, therapists cannot automatically assume that clients have access to a private space from which to attend virtual appointments. For clients whose home environments may not be emotionally or physically safe, this can be even more problematic.

For example, LGBTQIA+ children and adolescents whose parents or caregivers are non-affirming may have difficulty discussing their needs in their home environment for fear they will be overheard, punished, or even kicked out of the home (Hamnvik et al., 2022). Likewise, if a child or adolescent is in the same physical location as someone who has been abusive toward them, talking about the abuse may put them at an increased risk if what they are sharing might be overheard, and it may be particularly difficult for them to open up during teletherapy sessions. Even if their abuser is not present at the time of therapy, clients may experience a state of hypervigilance that can diminish their ability to

DOI: 10.4324/9781003330912-43

effectively engage with therapy (Aisbitt et al., 2022). Because therapists and clients can lose some of the nonverbal cues in teletherapy that would typically be picked up on in in-person sessions (Yamamoto et al., 2021), it is vital that therapists engage with clients in collaboratively shaping their own communication "code."

To address these safety needs, therapists can be creative in developing solutions with clients. This may include finding alternate locations for therapy to occur, such as in a private reading room at a library. It can also include working with clients to create their own unique language to indicate when confidentiality may be compromised or safety may be at risk. Other signals may include letting the therapist know that they don't want to discuss certain topics that day or that the client is becoming emotionally flooded and needs to engage in regulating activities. This may be especially helpful for clients with trauma history or those who need additional time to engage in auditory information processing, such as people on the autism spectrum (Williams et al., 2015). The following provides instructions for assessing confidentiality, discussing the need for signaling, identifying messages to communicate, and identifying signals to use in teletherapy.

Instructions

1. ***Assess for confidentiality.*** Ask clients if they currently have privacy. You can ask them to answer on a scale from 0 (no privacy) to 10 (complete privacy). If there appears to be any concerns about anyone else being able to overhear the conversation, consider communicating with clients via the chat function of the teletherapy platform and requesting that they respond using the chat function as well. If no one of concern can overhear the conversation, talk with clients about where they will be physically located during the session, who else may be around while they are in session, what topics may feel unsafe to discuss around others, and what may help them feel safe discussing vulnerable topics.
2. ***Discuss the need for signaling.*** Highlight any discomfort you may notice from clients when others are present within their physical location during sessions or any other issues you may notice with regard to privacy. Likewise, highlight any potential instances in which it appears difficult for clients to communicate other messages with you, such as when they don't want to talk about a particular topic. Explain the idea of using a signaling system to nonverbally communicate messages with you as needs arise.
3. ***Identify messages.*** Discuss with clients any messages that they may want to be able to communicate with you nonverbally during sessions. The following is a list of some of the messages that clients and therapists may benefit from having a signaling code for:
   - Someone else is in the room with me.
   - Someone else might be able to hear us.
   - I feel unsafe in my physical environment.
   - I'm afraid I might hurt myself.
   - I don't want to talk about tough stuff today.
   - I'm ready to talk about tough stuff today.
   - I'm feeling emotionally overwhelmed.

- I need more time to answer.
- I don't want to talk about this.

Other symbols can include simple reminders, such as displaying a timer that shows how long is left in the session or giving a visual cue that there are only five minutes left in the session.

Avoid creating codes for too many different things at once. Rather, consider your client's most pertinent needs and develop signals for a few things that clients would most benefit from being able to communicate with you. If the signaling system works well, you can add more signals over time.

4. ***Identify signals.*** Based on the earlier assessment, discuss with clients specific signals that they may want to use to communicate with you during sessions. Explore the options available on your teletherapy platform for different forms of nonverbal communication. For example, many teletherapy platforms will allow clients to do the following:

   - Use the chat function
   - Use "reactions" or emojis (e.g., clapping hands, thumbs up, heart)
   - Change the background

   Some platforms (e.g., Zoom) may allow you to add your own custom emojis or virtual. The options that you discuss with clients for this activity will be dependent on what your teletherapy platform allows.

   Come to a mutual agreement with each client on what will work best for them. It can be helpful to discuss the pros and cons of different options. For instance, the chat function allows a conversation to continue when someone may not be able to verbalize but could be seen by someone if they can view the screen. Displaying a "reaction"/emoji, such as a thumbs up or thumbs down may also be easily interpreted by others but provides a simple way for clients to communicate an emotion without having to communicate it out loud or in written form. Changing backgrounds can provide a lot of variety in terms of the messages that can be conveyed but may take longer than using a "reaction"/emoji or the chat function.

Processing

Once you've finished devising the signaling system, review the signals and their corresponding messages with clients. You may even try practicing them with clients in advance of when they're needed. Then, check in with clients to see how they feel about the signaling system that you have devised together and ask if there is anything they would like to change about it.

Vignette

Amber (40), John (45), and Laura (12) presented for therapy due to concerns about Laura recently appearing to be more withdrawn without explanation. After meeting with the family all together and gathering information about their family dynamics and why they were coming to therapy, Amber and John signed off of the teletherapy platform and the therapist met individually with Laura. Laura had relocated to her room and used her computer to rejoin the session individually. Amber remained in the house where Laura was located. During this time, the therapist observed that Laura looked frequently at her bedroom door when she was talking about her parents. The therapist inquired about this and

Laura shrugged it off, saying that it was nothing. The therapist let Laura know that they wanted to help Laura be as comfortable as possible and acknowledged that it can be difficult to talk when parents are in the house. The therapist also noted that some topics may be particularly hard to discuss when others may be around and suggested that they develop some signals to communicate with one another. Together, Laura and the therapist came up with a system of reactions that Laura would share on her screen to indicate the level of comfort with a topic.

- The thumbs-up symbol would be used when the therapist checked in and Laura was doing okay.
- The heart would be used to indicate some discomfort and need for relaxation/emotional regulation.
- The open mouth symbol would be used to indicate a need to stop the topic and engage in positive coping skills.
- The clap reaction will be used to indicate that someone else was in the room or that Laura was worried that someone else could overhear their conversation.

In the second session, the therapist again met with the family together and Laura individually. Laura pointed out the pride flag that the therapist had displayed in their physical background and asked what they knew about "LGBTQ stuff." The therapist provided a bit of information about their background and shared their affirmative stance. Laura then told the therapist that they were figuring out their gender identity and sexual orientation. Laura reported wanting to see how "he/him" pronouns might feel and described himself as "maybe [being] a straight boy." Laura said that he was very concerned about how his parents, especially his mom, would respond and wasn't ready to talk about it with them yet. During this discussion, Laura used his heart symbol to indicate a need to slow down and the therapist engaged him in some deep breathing exercises. Laura also used his clap reaction when his mom walked into the room to ask him a question. The therapist immediately stopped the discussion.

Over the next several sessions, Laura and the therapist continued to use these signals until Laura was comfortable enough to talk to his parents. During that session, Laura explained the system of symbols to his family so they could all implement it. Using this system, the therapist helped facilitate the conversation between Laura and his parents. Amber employed the heart symbol several times, as she was overwhelmed by the topic, and the therapist was able to help validate her experience and set up sessions without Laura for Amber to process her feelings. As the family further processed the discussion and their accompanying feelings in therapy with the use of signaling, Laura's symptoms of withdraw dissipated.

Suggestions for Follow-Up

Periodically check in about the use of the signals and the need for any changes. This should include continual safety assessment and discussions of any changes in who is in the home. Consider asking clients the following questions:

- What helps you feel safe and comfortable in this space?
- What has your experience of using the signaling system that [you/we] came up with been like?
- Are there any cues or signals that you would like to add?
- Are there any cues or signals that you would like to change?

When appropriate (e.g., safety is not of concern) and if child/adolescent clients are interested in sharing with others, family members can also be taught the agreed-upon signals to help facilitate family sessions. This can help to ease conflicts and give families tools to have difficult conversations in safe ways.

Contraindications

Some clients may be in situations that represent too high a risk for the use of the signaling methods discussed in this chapter. In some situations, teletherapy may not be recommended due to safety concerns. Client safety should always take precedence and appropriate reporting must occur when necessary.

References

Aisbitt, G. M., Nolte, T., & Fonagy, P. (2023). Editorial perspective: The digital divide—inequalities in remote therapy for children and adolescents. *Child and Adolescent Mental Health, 28*(1), 105–107. https://doi.org/10.1111/camh.12545

American Association for Marriage and Family Therapy (2015). *AAMFT code of ethics*. AAMFT.

Hamnvik, O. R., Agrawal, S., AhnAllen, C. G., Goldman, A. L., & Reisner, S. L. (2022). Telemedicine and inequities in health care access: The example of transgender health. *Transgender Health, 7*(2), 113–116. https://doi.org/10.1089/trgh.2020.0122

Williams, D. L., Minshew, N. J., & Goldstein, G. (2015). Further understanding of complex information processing in verbal adolescents and adults with autism spectrum disorders. *Autism, 19*(7), 859–867. https://doi.org/10.1177/1362361315586171

Yamamoto, F. R., Voida, A., & Voida, S. (2021). From therapy to teletherapy: Relocating mental health services online. *Proceedings of the ACM on Human-Computer Interaction, 5*, 364–394. https://doi.org/10.1145/3479508

Part 9
Neurodivergence

CHAPTER 36

VIRTUAL SENSORY PLAY THERAPY

Cary McAdams Hamilton and Sarah Moran

Materials for Therapists and Clients: A variety of sensory items can be found within the office and/or home.

Objective

Sensory-based regulation strategies promote overall physical and mental health for children and adolescents. Implementing sensory strategies via telemental health, however, requires modifications to approaches that are applied in in-person settings (Smith-Foley, 2020). This chapter presents ways to successfully implement sensory play activities for use with children, adolescents, and families via teletherapy intervention.

Rationale for Use

The use of sensory-based regulation strategies in therapy and outside of it may benefit most children and adolescents. Those with neurodivergence may especially benefit from sensory-based regulation strategies due to the high comorbidity of sensory sensitivities. Sensory sensitivities or stressors result when an individual is overwhelmed by one or more senses in their internal state or the environment. Sensory processing disorder is characterized by the "traffic jam" of neuronal stimuli that occurs in the brain-body connection that sends the body into hyper/hypo-arousal, resulting in limited functioning and often a "meltdown" in presentation. Sensory regulation strategies are coping skills for managing sensory overwhelm or the need for stimuli to achieve full cognitive functioning. Sensory regulation strategies are used to engage the body's communication with the brain consistently and predictably. Research has elucidated that neurodivergent diagnoses (e.g., attention-deficit/hyperactivity disorder [ADHD], autism, dyspraxia) consistently have sensory sensitivities contributing to the primary complaint that brings them into therapy (Grant, 2021).

Neurodivergent clients often elect for teletherapy to avoid the sensory overload that often presents in clinical settings (Anderson & Reyna-Vasquez, 2020; Grant, 2020; Hull, 2021). For many neurodivergent individuals, sensory stressors must be attended to in therapy before they can focus on anything else (Smith, 2021). Therefore, teletherapists should be prepared to introduce sensory-based regulation strategies when working with children and adolescents, particularly those who may be neurodivergent. Introducing sensory-based regulation strategies at the onset of therapy allows clients to utilize these strategies during moments of distress and dysregulation when discussing more difficult topics and can lead to more successful therapeutic outcomes.

DOI: 10.4324/9781003330912-45

Sensory regulation strategies practiced with caregivers activate the mirror neurons that foster attachment and downregulation required for successful treatment (Baker, 2022; Gaskill & Perry, 2014).

This neurobiological approach of co-regulation mimics the therapeutic powers of play provided in face-to-face sessions (Association for Play Therapy, 2020; Smith, 2021). The following describes the setup and instructions for psychoeducation and implementation of strategies for sensory regulation that are experiential, client-centered, and involve family systems when possible.

Setup

Initial setup for virtual sensory play therapy involves providing a psychoeducational overview of all eight senses, assessing the sensory processing profiles of each person in the client system, and explaining the trajectory of future sessions.

1. ***Provide a psychoeducational overview.*** The following provides examples of what you might say to introduce each of the eight senses.
    - ***Visual:*** Visual sensations are everything that you can see. Do you like bright colors or muted ones? Do you like overhead lights on or off? Do you get distracted when things are moving around you? Do you like to look at yourself in the camera? Do you squint when you go outside because of the sunlight?
    - ***Auditory:*** Auditory senses are everything that you can hear. Do you like loud or quiet music? Do you get started by sounds? Do you hear things others can't? Can you always hear the clock in a room? Does the sound of people chewing make you angry?
    - ***Olfactory:*** Olfactory senses are everything that you can smell. Do you walk into the house and know the trash needs to go out? Do you gag when cleaning the litter box? Do you smell smoke before others? Do you like scented items? Do you hate perfume or feel sick when you smell it? Do you avoid eating things that smell bad?
    - ***Gustatory:*** Gustatory senses are everything that you can taste. Do you prefer mild or bland foods? Do you like salty or sweet things? Do you like hot sauce? What are your comfort foods?
    - ***Tactile:*** Tactile senses are everything you can feel when something touches your skin. Do you like soft items? Do you like squishy items? Do you cut the tags out of your clothes? Do you like to wear stretchy pants or loose-fitting clothing? Do you avoid certain textures? Do you recoil when touching something sticky or scratchy? Are you easily ticklish?
    - ***Vestibular:*** Vestibular sense is about balance. Do you like to be lifted off the ground? Do you like being upside down? Do you like rollercoasters? Can you spin without getting dizzy? Do you trip a lot? Do you get carsick or seasick?
    - ***Proprioceptive:*** Proprioception is about muscles and joints or push-pull actions. Do you like to roughhouse? Do you like firm hugs? Do you slam doors and cabinets? Do you often break crayons? Do you like to carry heavy things? Are you often told to touch more gently?
    - ***Interoceptive:*** Interoception is everything you feel internally, including heartbeat, lungs, hunger, going to the bathroom, temperature, and pain. Do you often feel cold? Can you feel your heart beat fast? Do you ever feel hungry or full? Do you often wait too long to go to the bathroom? Do you feel pain easily? Do you know when you need to vomit?

2. ***Assess sensory preference profiles.*** Use the questions provided in the psychoeducational overview to make note of sensory preferences of each person present in therapy. Often, family members will have opposite sensory profiles and will need opposite regulation strategies. If members of the client's household are not present in the session, you may ask questions about perceived sensory preferences of others or assess their preferences in future sessions. This assessment informs the treatment trajectory with a focus on self-awareness, co-regulation, and relational connections for the family.
3. ***Explain the trajectory of future sessions.*** Share that in each session, you will be focusing on a different sense. Each sense will be explored through psychoeducation and the application of sensory activities that increase tolerance and regulation.

Instructions

Introduce and explore a new sense in each session using the following instructions.

1. ***Identify the sense.*** It can be helpful to start with the senses currently deemed most disruptive for the client.
2. ***Define the sense.*** Though you already defined each of the eight senses during setup, restate the definition as a reminder.
3. ***Acquire materials.*** It may be helpful to have items available that are commonly used to address sensory processing (e.g., fidget toys); however, both therapists and clients may use objects commonly found within their office and/or home without needing to acquire any specific materials. Consider having clients go on a scavenger hunt to identify or collect items they can use for the activity each session. You can make it a game and give a time limit to return as fast as possible or within three minutes. Alternatively, you may ask them to come to the session with these materials at the onset. For example, you might ask clients to search for the following items.
    - ***Visual:*** Find something that is your favorite color. Find something that makes you smile when you look at it. Find something that you dislike looking at. Find something that's too bright.
    - ***Auditory:*** Find something that makes a sound you enjoy, a sound you dislike, and a sound that a family member dislikes. Identify and play a song you enjoy.
    - ***Olfactory:*** Find something that you love to smell. Find something that you don't like the smell of. Think of a smell from a positive memory.
    - ***Gustatory:*** Identify your favorite food. Identify your least favorite food. If you could pick only one food to eat, what would it be?
    - ***Tactile:*** Show me something that you enjoy wearing. Show me something that you never want to wear again. Show me your favorite stuffed animal. Show me something that you don't like touching.
    - ***Vestibular:*** What in your home can you spin on? Did you know that you need to spin both ways equally to give equal input to both sides of your brain? Where is somewhere you can hang upside down?

- ***Proprioceptive:*** Find something heavy. Find something that tricked you because the weight surprised you. Identify something you push around a lot.
- ***Interoceptive:*** What's something that makes you feel [cold/warm]? What's your favorite [cold/warm] drink? How big of a breath can you hold? Do 10 jumping jacks and feel how fast your heart beats.

4. ***Encourage clients to actively engage in the identified sense.*** Encourage them to use the object(s) they brought or identified to facilitate this process. When working with families, you might ask them to engage with one another through their senses (e.g., look at one another's objects, listen to them, smell them).

Processing

Support clients in describing how they experience each sense after they engage it and identify ways in which they might use this sense during moments of dysregulation. Focus on practical coping skills using the strengths of each individual's sensory systems (Thomas & Nelson, 2012). Apply unconditional positive regard and curiosity throughout the activity. The following questions may be used to facilitate this process.

- What did you [like/dislike] about engaging this sense?
- What might be different if you were to engage this same sense with a different object? For example, what is it like smelling something that smells good versus something that smells bad?
- Does this activity bring you more energy or does it calm your body?
- Do you want more or less of this activity?
- Can you do this with your [mom/dad/etc.]?
- Is this something you can do in your family's daily routine?
- Is this something you can do anywhere or anytime?
- Can you verbalize your desire for this activity? If so, what might you say?
- [Mom/Dad/etc.], how might you respond to this request to support them in their attempt to regulate?

As each sense is processed, a recipe is formulated for each person in the family to support and encourage each other's sensory regulation at any time.

Vignette

Liam (9) attended therapy for explosive emotional outbursts and destruction of property with a diagnosis of ADHD. His parents reported trying behavioral programs to no avail and that academically, he was behind due to his inability to focus or stay in his seat. He had also grown in size, making behavior management challenging for the family.

Liam's parents provided a developmental history and reported that an occupational therapy referral had been made; however, access to those services in their rural hometown was limited, and telehealth-only occupational therapy options were unavailable. Upon completing the child's sensory profile, a treatment plan was established to implement sensory regulation strategies in telemental health therapy.

Liam's first session focused on meeting his proprioception needs, a common sensory need for those with ADHD with the destruction of property as a behavior problem (Panagiotidi et al., 2018). After briefly defining all eight senses, the therapist provided a more in-depth definition of the proprioceptive sense and how it works to provide information to the brain and body about where it is in space and time. The therapist described ways in which they could identify the proprioceptive sense by asking each family member to push on a couch to see how far they could move it in ten seconds in the view of the computer screen. This allowed Liam to engage his proprioception sense to move it toward regulation. The therapist then asked the family to repeat the exercise and to notice any changes or differences in how they felt after each time that they moved the couch.

The therapist then asked the family the following questions:

- How did your body feel while you were moving the couch?
- How does it feel after moving it?
- Do you now feel tired or "ready" to do more?

Following this activity, the therapist encouraged the family to identify ways in which they could further engage in proprioception regulation strategies together as a family outside of therapy. Proprioception needs can be met relationally via roughhousing or games that require push-pull actions like tug-of-war. Liam's parents identified an opportunity for Liam to "wrestle" more often with his dad, an activity that Liam loved and his dad enjoyed. Liam shared that he would play tug-of-war more often with their family dog, Luca, because Luca really liked that. Liam's mom identified these types of activities as more difficult for her to engage in given her sensitivities, but she cheered them on.

In subsequent sessions, the therapist processed the remainder of the eight senses with Liam and his family. With time, Liam was able to identify when his body was seeking a sensory need and meet this need using the coping skills developed in therapy. This helped Liam stay more regulated throughout his school day, limiting impulsive behaviors he had previously demonstrated when trying to meet these sensory needs. Additionally, through participating in sensory regulation activities together, Liam and his family increased their connections with one another and strengthened their bond as a family, including Luca the dog.

Suggestions for Follow-Up

Inquire about the use of sensory strategies utilized since the last session and the client system's ability to support one another in this endeavor. Process additional senses in subsequent sessions and identify other strategies by repeating the process as needed. Once you have reviewed all eight senses. Discuss the most helpful strategies and return to those strategies in subsequent sessions as needed.

Contraindications

Sensory processing disorder is formally treated by occupational therapists with specialized training. If no occupational therapy is engaged or available, develop a sensory plan to meet the child client's regulatory goals early in treatment. There is no harm in a therapist providing skills toward sensory regulation to meet emotion regulation needs. There is, however, a limit to what mental health professionals can achieve. This occurs when physical behaviors are not successfully mitigated or decreased with the sensory engagement tools described in this chapter. Occupational therapy is required for many for a bottom-up approach toward a more thorough body-brain integration success. Refer clients to occupational therapy when necessary. If occupational therapy occurs concurrently or has already been engaged, work with families to build repeated routines based on guidelines provided by occupational therapist assessments (Smith-Foley, 2020).

References

Anderson, C., & Reyna-Vasquez, P. (2020). Creative activities in teleplay therapy. *Play Therapy™, 17*(2), 24–27.

Association for Play Therapy (2020). *Play therapy best practices: Clinical, professional, and ethical issues.* https://cdn.ymaws.com/www.a4pt.org/resource/resmgr/publications/apt_best_ practices_-_june_20.pdf

Baker, L. (2021). Expressive therapies in telemental play. In J. Stone (Ed.), *Play therapy and telemental health: Foundations, populations, and interventions* (pp. 201–215). Taylor & Francis. https://doi.org/10.4324/9781003166498-13

Gaskill, R., & Perry, B. (2014). The neurobiological power of play: Using the Neurosequential Model of Therapeutics to guide play in the healing process. In C. A. Malchiodi & D. A. Crenshaw (Eds.), *Creative arts and play therapy for attachment problems* (pp. 178–194). Guilford Press

Grant, R. J. (2021). Autplay® Therapy and telemental health: Strategies for children with autism. In Stone, J. (Ed.), *Play therapy and telemental health: Foundations, populations, and interventions.* Routledge. https://doi.org/10.4324/9781003166498

Hull, K. B. (2021). Electronic game play therapy. In H. G., Kaduson & C. E. Schaefer (Eds.), *Play therapy with children: Modalities for change* (pp. 225–240). American Psychological Association. https://doi.org/10.1037/0000217-015

Panagiotidi, M., Overton, P. G., & Stafford, T. (2018). The relationship between ADHD traits and sensory sensitivity in the general population. *Comprehensive Psychiatry, 80,* 179–185. https://doi.org/10.1016/j.comppsych.2017.10.008

Smith, M. L. (2021). *The connected therapist: Relating through the senses.* Marti Smith Seminars.

Smith-Foley, S. (2020). Consideration when moving school-based sensory interventions to telehealth. *In the Home.* www.AOTA.org

Thomas, F. N., & Nelson, T. S. (Eds.). (2012). *Handbook of solution-focused brief therapy: Clinical applications.* Taylor & Francis.

CHAPTER 37

ANIME WITH NEURODIVERSE TEENS

Kevin B. Hull

Materials for Therapists: Access to streaming sites for anime (e.g., Crunchyroll, Netflix).

Materials for Clients: None.

Objective

Anime is a popular interest among neurodiverse teens (Rozema, 2015). This chapter will present ways in which to use anime with neurodiverse teens to increase self-acceptance and overcome environmental challenges using integrative play therapy, a collaborative, relationship-based play approach.

Rational for Use

Many neurodiverse teens struggle with the development of social functioning, self-awareness, and self-acceptance. Neurodiverse teens are likely to experience sensory overload, emotional dysregulation, and the inability to see different perspectives (Rydzewska & Pirrie, 2015). Stress responses then hamper the view of the self, and along with memory disruptions, the individual naturally compares themselves to others and often with a judging viewpoint that results in negative loops of thinking and self-rejection. This cycle may lead to avoidance of social outlets due to the perception of rejection based on how the individual views themselves, the expectation of emotional pain, and the desire to avoid that pain. Depression, anxiety, obsessive-compulsive disorder, and self-harm comorbidities (Pagni et al., 2019) are partially connected to a lack of self-understanding and self-awareness. Therefore, it is important that therapeutic interventions focus not only on behavioral and social navigation but also on self-understanding and self-acceptance.

Part of the attractiveness to anime amongst neurodiverse teens is that it can serve as a safe zone in the form of "escapism" (Sosso, 2017) which many neurodiverse teens use to manage stress and make sense of the surrounding world. Anime has rich story lines, including fantasy elements that are often attractive to neurodiverse individuals (e.g., mythology, superheroes) and reflect familiar environments such as families, friendships, homes, and schools. The artwork of anime tends to be appealing with graphic depictions, brilliant colors, and the expression of emotional content through the character's facial and body expressions.

Due to neurodevelopmental delays, neurodiverse individuals often reference others and external objects in the form of media as reference points to learn about themselves, make sense of the world around them, and attempt to fit in (Rydzewska & Pirrie, 2015). The emotional content of anime

DOI: 10.4324/9781003330912-46

deals with subjects like loneliness, anger, and social rejection, as well as themes of love, overcoming challenges, believing in oneself, and not giving up. The stories and characters from anime provide a foundation for self-understanding that can lead to increased self-acceptance. Anime is also useful for helping neurodiverse teens understand social situations and may increase prosocial behavior through the modeling of anime characters.

Common themes found in anime include the following:

- Friendship
- Sacrificing one's own comfort and safety for another person
- Navigating betrayal and rejection
- Freedom of choice
- Need to be flexible
- Self-acceptance
- Self-forgiveness

Through the analysis and observation of characters and embedded themes within anime, therapists can guide neurodiverse teens to challenge negative self-concepts and encourage greater self-awareness and self-understanding (Hull, 2022).

Setup

The following specifies the setup necessary prior to conducting the intervention in session with clients. Setup begins with conversations with clients in session and ends with your own work between sessions.

1. ***Introduce the client to the use of anime in therapy.*** Explain how its stories may be used to increase understanding of oneself and the world around them.
2. ***Inquire about the client's experience with anime.*** It is very likely that teens are familiar with anime and may have a favorite series. Encourage them to share details about their favorite anime. Investigate themes and characters.
3. ***Conduct your own research.*** If clients report having a favorite anime that you're unfamiliar with, consider watching it. Then, identify any connections between the anime and the goals of therapy.
4. ***Select anime.*** You may select something that clients have identified that is of interest to them. Alternatively, you may introduce something new that you think may be particularly relevant given the themes within the anime and the goals of therapy. Ensure that what you select is available to you to watch and show clients in therapy. See Table 37.1 for examples of anime and the themes addressed in each one.
5. ***Select a clip.*** You may not have enough time in one session to watch an entire show. Select a portion of the show that you can view with clients in session that will demonstrate relevant themes for therapy. You may also choose a variety of anime clips that relate to treatment goals and align with themes connected to the client's challenges or strengths. Make a note of the start and end times of each clip.

Table 37.1 Examples of anime with themes

Anime	Themes
Avatar the Last Airbender **(Nickelodeon, 2006)**	Friendship, forgiveness, self-development/self-acceptance/self-understanding, overcoming challenges, trusting others, asking for help, resilience
March Comes in Like a Lion **(Shaft Animation Studios, 2016)**	Navigating anxiety and depression, self-rejection/self-acceptance, abandonment, reforming attachment, perfection, pressure to perform, asking for help, friendship, overcoming challenges
My Dress-Up Darling **(CloverWorks, 2022)**	Self-understanding, introversion, romance, gender-role challenging, friendship, self-acceptance, expanding self and social world, sexual development
Naruto **(Pierrot, 2007)**	Overcoming challenges, orphans, family of origin issues, abandonment/rejection, self-development, emotional and impulse control, self-understanding/acceptance
Re:Zero **(Whitefox, 2016)**	Starting over, dealing with the unknown, building/sustaining friendships, self-acceptance, self-understanding, dealing with negative emotions

Instructions

When you meet again, conduct the following.

1. ***Review the goals of therapy and make connections with the anime that you intend to show.*** Identify the client's strengths and challenges and discuss related themes regarding anime characters, the plot, and other things related to what you will show that may bring the client enjoyment. For example, you may review the elements of self-understanding, self-acceptance, and navigating social situations and how these themes will be seen in the clips that will be shown as characters navigate their own related challenges.
2. ***Open the selected anime.*** Have this prepared in advance so you don't need to spend time searching for it with clients present.
3. ***Share your screen.*** Select the option to share only the window in which the anime is shown, rather than making your entire computer screen visible.
4. ***Play clips.*** Ensure that the sharing options that you select allow clients to hear the audio. Have clients keep their own sound on as well so you can hear any verbal responses that they may offer. As clients watch, maintain your focus on the video of the client to observe nonverbal communication and emotional responses.

Processing

The processing stage is the point that themes and metaphors found within the anime can be applied to the teen's life. Through this discussion, the teen's perspective is expanded and new meaning is created (Hull, 2022). Processing prompts may include the following.

- What did you notice going on in this clip?
- What emotions did you notice in the character(s)?
- What emotions did you notice coming up for yourself as you watched?
- What challenges did you notice for the character(s)?
- How did the character(s) overcome that/those challenge(s)?
- What similarities do you notice between the character(s) and yourself?
- What similarities do you notice between your experiences and the themes in the anime?
- What similarities do you notice between your social experiences and those in the anime?

Vignette

Roger (17) was diagnosed with autism spectrum disorder in elementary school. He lived with his mother and younger sister and had never met his father. Roger presented in teletherapy stating that he had always felt "awkward" and never felt like he fit in socially. As a boy, he reported being "obsessed" with video games and electronic devices. Roger was a gifted athlete and liked athletics of all kinds, particularly soccer. As he got older, the pressure to perform from family members and coaches created feelings of depression. He began to hate himself and his abilities, feeling depressed and isolating himself from family and social events. Like many neurodivergent youth, he struggled to understand himself and make sense of emotions. Putting thoughts and feelings into words was a challenge for Roger. His self-rejection increased in his junior year of high school, and he acknowledged suicidal feelings to his mother, which brought him to teletherapy.

Using principles of integrative play therapy, the therapist used a mixture of non-directive and directive elements and collaboratively joined with Roger to explore his challenges and strengths. Therapy focused on helping Roger better navigate social situations, express his emotions, decrease depression, and increase self-understanding and self-acceptance. Exploring Roger's feelings of depression revealed that his self-rejection beliefs led to a fear of abandonment, causing him to avoid forming close friendships. He said that he often felt confused by emotions, and even soccer was becoming a dreadful experience. For Roger, the praise and encouragement from family and teammates created a sensation of pressure to perform and he worried about letting everyone down.

Exploration of Roger's interests revealed that he liked anime, an interest that formed a few years prior when a fellow teammate introduced him to the genre. The therapist and Roger explored the various types of anime that Roger liked, and the therapist revealed that anime could be something that they discussed in therapy, which excited Roger.

The therapist introduced Roger to an anime called *March Comes in Like a Lion* (Shaft Animation Studios, 2016), an anime that explores themes of depression, isolation, performance pressure, friendship, and a main character who is an introvert. Rei Kiriyama, the main character, is a teenage, gifted shogi player who has been orphaned, and attempts to become independent. Rei battles feeling depressed, experiences self-rejection, and feels pressure to perform due to his talent as a professional shogi player. Rei is an introvert and isolates from others to avoid social situations. Rei also struggles with trusting others due to feelings of abandonment.

The therapist showed Roger several clips that revealed the aforementioned themes and that related to the goals of therapy. For example, one clip demonstrated Rei's internal struggle with self-acceptance, while another showed his anxiety regarding an upcoming shogi match. Other clips showed the theme of others in Rei's life who were available to help him, and how Rei struggled with trust and accept help.

The therapist then processed these clips with Roger by asking him to draw connections between Rei and himself. Roger identified the following connections.

- Rei was a gifted shogi player and Roger was good at playing soccer.
- Both Rei and Roger experienced pressure to perform the thing they were gifted at.
- Rei and Roger both felt loss and abandonment from parents.
- Rei and Roger both battled with depression and struggled to articulate how it feels to others.
- Both Rei and Roger felt tension between wanting to perform and wanting to hide from people.
- Rei purposely avoided those who might help him to protect himself from being hurt. As he learned to accept love and support from others, he found self-acceptance and contentment. Roger similarly avoided others and rejected advances by teammates, peers at school, and extended family members.
- Rei enjoyed shogi, a board game of strategy, and Roger also enjoyed strategy-based games.

Roger also identified that the themes presented in the show surrounding shogi were that loss is a part of life, but we do have some level of control in how we choose to represent ourselves in our lives.

Ultimately, using anime with Roger was successful in accomplishing treatment goals through providing insight and representations of internal struggles. Roger's depression lessened as his self-understanding and self-acceptance improved. He identified with the themes found within the anime, such as being able to understand emotions and put them into words. Roger's perspective of support and trust expanded as he realized that he had several sources of support around him. Watching the evolution of Rei's character helped Roger see good characteristics in himself and that his depression was connected to self-rejection. Using the themes from the show and discussing them helped Roger broaden his self-acceptance and self-understanding, as well as find ways to navigate the negative emotions he previously struggled with.

Suggestions for Follow-Up

This intervention is designed to take place over several sessions and can be built upon as clients gain insight. Anime can elicit powerful emotional reactions. Support clients in processing emotions as needed. Watching anime can also be assigned as homework once tools for processing emotions have been provided.

Contraindications

Parents should be made aware of the use of media when working with minors. Consider using a digital tools consent form (see Chapter 10) to allow legal guardians to consent to the use of anime in therapy prior to its use. This also allows you to explain how anime will be used for therapeutic purposes and may help adults understand ways in which the teen may use anime to increase their understanding of the world outside of therapy.

References

Hull, K. (2022). Neurodiverse older teens and young adults in teleplay. In J. Stone (Ed.), *Play therapy and telehealth: Foundations, populations, and interventions* (pp. 156–169). Routledge.

Pagni, B. A., Walsh, M. J. M., Foldes, E., Sebren, A., Dixon, M. V., Guerithault, N., & Braden, B. B. (2020). The neural correlates of mindfulness-induced depression reduction in adults with autism spectrum disorder: A pilot study. *Journal of Neuroscience Research, 98*(6), 1150–1161. https://doi.org/10.1002/jnr.24600

Rydzewska, E., & Pirrie, A. (2015). Risk behaviours in transition to adulthood for people with autism spectrum disorder. *Scottish Educational Review, 47*(1), 15–27. https://doi.org/10.1163/27730840-04701004

Rozema, R. (2015). Manga and the autistic mind. *English Journal, 105*(1), 60–68.

Sosso, G. (2017, July 5). *Autism and anime connection.* CARD-USF. https://cardusf.wordpress.com/2017/07/05/autism-anime-connection.

CHAPTER 38

ROLLING VIRTUAL

THERAPEUTICALLY APPLIED TABLETOP ROLE-PLAYING GAMES

Adam D. Davis

Materials for Therapists and Clients: Desktop or laptop computer with internet access, game rulebooks and reference materials, dice, and character sheets. Access to an online virtual tabletop (VTT) platform and character management system are optional.

Objective

The Game to Grow Method of therapeutically applied tabletop role-playing games (TA-TTRPG) has successfully been used in schools, inpatient and residential treatment settings, private practice, community mental health, hospitals, and other settings to address mental health issues including anxiety, depression, post-traumatic stress disorder, and substance use (Kilmer et al., 2023). This chapter provides an introduction to the Game to Grow Method and instructions on how to apply it through a virtual context.

Rationale for Use

In tabletop role-playing games (TTRPG), a group of three to six participants each role-play as a character in a collaboratively created story. A facilitator, commonly referred to as a game master (GM), develops and describes the story scenarios, often involving a large, fantastic quest. Players decide how their characters will attempt to overcome in-game challenges and progress in the story. In most TTRPGs, each character's unique skills and abilities are determined via the specific game system and are outlined on a "character sheet." Their personality and narrative characterization are determined by the player that controls that character. The structure of the game involves the GM arbitrating the rules of the game, determining player success and failure in their in-game attempts, and describing results via verbal narration. In a casual TTRPG game, the GM has an incredible impact on the level of enjoyment players experience in their gameplay sessions. In TA-TTRPG, the GM is a therapist, who leverages game mechanics and designs in-game scenarios to target real-world therapeutic goals via a modality that is safe, supportive, and fun. In this chapter, in the context of describing TA-TTRPG work, therapist and GM are used interchangeably to describe the individual leading the group.

DOI: 10.4324/9781003330912-47

The Game to Grow Method of TA-TTRPG was originally developed to support groups of neurodivergent youth in building social confidence using the tabletop role-playing game Dungeons & Dragons, though it is applicable to wider populations and does not require the specific use of that specific game. The Game to Grow Method and Critical Core, the game system developed by Game to Grow, has been used by Game to Grow trainees with participants of all ages worldwide. It incorporates therapeutic factors from drama therapy, interpersonal process group therapy, cognitive behavioral therapies, and Developmental, Individual-differences, and Relationship-based/Floortime approaches, though it is fundamentally a transtheoretical approach and is compatible with many theoretical orientations (Kilmer et al., 2023)

Gameplay prompts the development of five core capacities (i.e., regulation, collaboration, planning, perspective, pretend play; Kilmer et al., 2023), which the therapist supports throughout gameplay.

- ***Regulation:*** The regulation capacity is an individual's capacity to stay emotionally regulated in times of excitement and distress, which is stimulated by the unpredictable narrative aspects of the game and the randomness that comes with relying on dice rolls to determine success.
- ***Collaboration:*** Collaboration is harnessed and developed in a TA-TTRPG through opportunities to work directly with peers, building on others' ideas throughout gameplay.
- ***Planning:*** The planning capacity involves logical sequencing and reasoning skills, which are incorporated in gameplay when players must plan and execute a scheme, predict outcomes, and respond when plans divert from expectation.
- ***Perspective:*** The perspective capacity is developed through role-play, as players must identify, consider, and respond to the internal states of others, including the characters that they portray.
- ***Pretend play:*** Pretend play is the capacity that involves symbolic thinking and imaginative play. This capacity involves a participant's ability to experiment with aspects of their identity, try on new perspectives and behaviors, and consider alternative paths.

Ultimately, participants vicariously experience the successes of the characters they portray while the therapist supports them in building confidence and insight, focusing on the aforementioned core capacities. Because the intervention is delivered through the format of a fun and compelling narrative game, participants are eager to return to regularly scheduled sessions.

Setup

Successful application of this intervention requires significant planning and preparation.

1. ***Gather a group of clients or discuss the option of playing a TTRPG in future sessions.*** A group of four to six participants is ideal for a TA-TTRPG group. Though this depends on particular group members, a group that is too large may result in participants feeling that they have to compete for attention or may cause them to become resentful of other participants' contributions. Group members do not all need to have the same presenting problems, though it may help to have group members with similar goals participate together. As TA-TTRPG is an experiential peer-learning model, a mixed cohort may serve to benefit participants as they can share and learn from others with different knowledge and experience. Two participants with the same goal of building social confidence, one who displays impulsive behaviors and one who is risk-averse, could both benefit from regular meaningful relational exposure to each other. A 90-minute session has shown

to be a suitable session length for most participants, as it permits ample time for gameplay while also reducing potential fatigue for players with less experience and endurance for this type of social engagement.

2. ***Choose and acquire a tabletop role-playing game.*** TTRPGs vary in numerous ways. Choose a game suitable for your participants. Consider popularity, structural game design, system complexity, age-appropriateness, setting/genre, and personal taste. It can be helpful to use simple and straightforward games set in a magical fantasy setting, such as Critical Core, the game system designed by Game to Grow as a support to new TA-TTRPG facilitators. Examples of other applicable games may include Dungeons & Dragons 5th Edition, Pathfinder, Kids on Bikes, Fate, and No Thank You Evil!

3. ***Prepare materials.*** GMs will need dice, the specifics of which depend on the game being played. Many TTRPGs use a set of seven dice, with 4-, 6-, 8-, 10-, 12-, and 20-sided dice, as well as another 10-sided die that can be used in combination with the other 10-sided die to show results between 1 and 100. GM dice rolls are often kept secret from players, so they can be rolled off camera. Digital dice rollers found on websites or mobile phone apps are also an option.

   Another practical consideration is that TTRPG and TA-TTRPG sessions vary in the amount of materials used in gameplay. Some GMs use tokens and/or miniature figures on a terrain map or "battle map" to show where characters are relative to each other, especially in games that feature tactical combat. Some GMs prefer to use "theater of the mind," a gameplay style which emphasizes vivid verbal narrative description over physical representation with tokens.

   It is entirely plausible for a TA-TTRPG session to be facilitated entirely in the "theater of the mind" style, requiring only a teleconferencing platform in which participants can connect through voice and video. In such a format, players roll physical dice in their own locations and verbally share results. Online platforms, often called VTTs, simulate the physical terrains and battle maps of in-person settings. These platforms can be difficult to master but have numerous additional features that surpass their physical counterparts, such as animations, status effect markers, and automatic calculations of dice rolls to determine damage and effects. Some also digitally store character sheets and allow for rolling and sharing results from digital dice, promising an alluring one-stop opportunity for gameplay.

   While VTTs can appear promising, they can also serve as a distraction from the core social connection and narrative gameplay that makes the format so effective. The decision to use a VTT should be informed by the therapist's willingness to learn and problem-solve the platform, along with the participants' capacity to similarly navigate the technical challenges of learning the platform. Some groups in which participants are already familiar with VTTs from casual TTRPG gameplay adapt well to their use in TA-TTRPG services, while others find onboarding a VTT to be cumbersome and frustrating. Some VTTs additionally have costs to fully access.

   A hybrid can also be achieved, in which some of the benefits of a VTT can be utilized without its entire adoption by all participants. Most teleconference platforms have the ability for participants to share their screen, which allows a GM to selectively show single images or websites to participants. This can be effective for immersion and engagement, as the GM can show an image of a setting or an opponent as they introduce a narrative encounter. Similarly, a GM can use a share screen option to move tokens around on a VVT for participants to observe. Using this type of hybrid gameplay format keeps participants engaged in the teleconferencing software instead of requiring them to shift between programs and web browser windows. This reduces the likelihood they will become distracted by other online activities or become fixated on the minutiae of the VTT.

4. ***Familiarize yourself with the rules of the game.*** Prepare to answer questions about the rules of the game and navigate situations that may arise from disagreements or misunderstandings between participants regarding rules.

5. ***Plan the narrative sequence of the session.*** This may include creating your own story to set the narrative of the gameplay. Alternatively, you may familiarize yourself with a pre-written story adventure, also known as an "adventure module." Another option is to engage in more improvised and collaborative story-building processes by preparing participation structures in alignment with participants' abilities, interests, needs, and goals.

   Consider establishing narrative moments that are analogous to participants' real-life situations and plan to support them as they navigate the situation. An example of this would be a participant's character needing to interact with a character in the story that is overbearing or belittling. A participant navigating analogous real-world interactions with a parent, teacher, or employer may benefit from an opportunity to practice alternative ways of navigating the social interaction safely through make-believe. Doing so while emotionally distanced in a context of imaginative play guarantees that the participant is free from real-world consequences as they experiment with different interaction techniques.

   Similarly, if working to support the development of specific interpersonal skills, you may design in-game scenarios that allow participants to practice overcoming similar obstacles. For example, a participant may face an in-game obstacle where their character needs to learn valuable information from a character portrayed by the GM, and ideally uses friendly or pro-social tactics, as opposed to coercion or demands. The GM can scaffold and support skill acquisition, as well as provide an opportunity to practice and receive feedback on the use of a specific skill.

6. ***Prepare clients for gameplay.*** While it is usually not necessary to teach the rules of the game to participants before the first session, it can be helpful to meet individually with each participant to familiarize them with the unique asymmetric format of the game and to help them choose or create a character that they will portray in the game. This may include sending them a digital version of their character's character sheet.

7. ***Ensure participants have necessary materials.*** Players will also need dice. Physical dice rolled off camera may tempt participants to be dishonest about their results, as high dice rolls often turn into in-game triumphs. Use best judgment on whether it would be beneficial to have participants roll physical dice with an honor code or use shared digital dice that preclude lying.

8. ***Prepare online collateral.*** If you choose to use a VTT or other digital artifacts, load and log into the webpages. If you choose to use the share screen feature to share images or sounds to increase immersion, prepare them in advance and have them easily accessible. Pausing the gameplay during the session to search the computer for a specific file, or to troubleshoot VTT configurations, can negatively impact engagement, immersion, and impact.

After the initial session, subsequent sessions require less preparation. Participants generally portray the same character and continue the same story, so the therapist's preparatory labor is reduced to narrative session planning. If using a system with a narrative design structure such as that in Critical Core, plan between three and five scenes, or "encounters," for a 90-minute session.

Instructions

The structure of a TA-TTRPG session using the Game to Grow Method has a clearly established format that should be followed each session: (1) check in, (2) gameplay, and (3) check out.

1. ***Check in.*** Ask a low-stakes question such as "What's your favorite dessert?" Facilitate each group member in taking turns answering the question both for themselves and the character they portray in the game. Differentiating between their own answer and their character's answer adds distinction between the two and encourages development of a unique sense of "personhood" for their character. Therapists may also answer the check-in question to build trust and provide an opportunity for valuable modeling.

   Over time, questions can be formulated to be more thought-provoking or designed to see how participants differentiate themselves from their characters. Responses to check-in questions may inform how to structure the narrative and scaffolding of performance expectations. The following are examples of additional check-in questions that may be asked:

   - What is something you are proud of?
   - What do you look for in a friend?
   - What advice would you give your character?
   - What is something you admire about your character? Why?
   - What advice would your character give you? What would change in your life if you took that advice?

2. ***Gameplay.*** During the first session, establish how the characters are joined together and find themselves working toward a common goal. In subsequent sessions, summarize the plot of the story thus far or ask someone else from the group to offer the summary. Once players are reacclimated with the larger plot, facilitate the cycle of play as follows:

   - Narrate a description of where the characters are, including the obstacle before them in their path toward their larger goal.
   - Allow players to ask any clarifying questions to better understand the encounter.
   - Respond to any questions and provide clarification.
   - Allow players to decide what characters will do to overcome the obstacle. Players may engage in dialogue, discussion, and even debate while collaboratively weighing their options.
   - Allow players to roll dice, add any bonuses from their character sheet, and share the result.
   - Verbally narrate the results of the character's action.
   - If the character's attempt was successful, describe how the story progresses and introduce the next challenge in the story's plot if applicable. If the attempt was not successful, encourage participants to discuss and determine their next tactic.

   In a 90-minute session, players may be able to proceed through three to five cycles of the aforementioned steps. Scaffold and adjust performance demands appropriately in alignment with participant goals to provide participants a safe and fun opportunity to build transferable skills. Learning and skill-building are implicit, self-directed, and will occur organically. However, participants may benefit when you intentionally highlight growth toward stated goals. These do not need to be stated as direct references to core capacities (i.e., regulation, collaboration, planning, perspective, pretend play; Kilmer et al., 2023), but are better stated using the client's own language (e.g., "staying calm" and "thinking about others" instead of "regulation" and "perspective"). Participants may benefit from support in processing and developing skills related to each of these capacities, though acquisition of discrete skills and behaviors should never come at the cost of participants' having the opportunity to find joy in their collective experience, especially if they are challenged and frustrated by the gameplay itself.

3. ***Check out.*** Transition from gameplay to post-game processing and return to the real world by asking three check-out questions that are consistent from session to session.
   - What is a spotlight you have for someone else?
   - What is something you found challenging or something you learned?
   - What is something you predict or look forward to for the next time we play together?

   The first question, asking for a "spotlight," is an invitation to offer appreciation or a compliment to another participant. As many participants may struggle with social isolation, a word of praise from a peer may be incredibly validating and uplifting. Groups may spotlight each other for working toward their goals, such as taking risks, expressing confidence, and facing difficult challenges.

   The second question is an opportunity for participants to express a challenge, and for you to validate and even reframe the challenge as a learning opportunity. If a participant expresses frustration at a difficult in-game challenge, if appropriate, frame their facing of the challenge as a sign of their resilience or strength. This question is also an opportunity to show participants a willingness to receive feedback on the game, and an opportunity for participants to share potential requests of their peers. For example, a participant may express frustration toward other participants' lack of focus, providing an opportunity for you to support skill-building around interpersonal communication.

   The third question prompts participants to look ahead to the next session. A participant answering the question with a prediction or desired story development provides you with insight into what story or plot elements motivate participants. If a participant remarks that they are eager for their characters to confront the story's villain in melee combat, it may inspire a shift in story planning if you had originally planned a longer and more meandering plot of deduction and intrigue. Similarly, if a participant shares a prediction and it is revealed to be true in a following session, participants often feel pride and validation, even if you "borrowed" their prediction and inserted it into the story after hearing it!

To learn more about the Game to Grow Method, read *Therapeutically Applied Role-Playing Games: Game to Grow Method* (Kilmer et al., 2023) or access additional trainings at gametogrow.org.

Processing

Some processing will naturally occur mid-session. The game can be paused at any time, so as issues or concepts arise you can pause to prompt reflection and processing. Something as general as "What's happening now?" can prompt reflection and sharing. Subsequently, asking "What's *really* happening now?" can help to engage group members in reflection of core issues being explored. This is especially important when issues related to the group itself arise (e.g., interpersonal conflicts). These moments are valuable for participants to share their subjective experience, ask for remedy, and even apologize when appropriate. You may save deeper discussion for the end of the session, though there are benefits to responding to emergent challenges as they arise.

Focus on drawing correlations between in-game scenarios and real-world areas of focus, with the goal of prompting insight, not leading participants toward particular outcomes. Questions as simple as "What did you notice today?" and "What does that remind you of?" can be incredible prompts for insight and reflection. Processing questions related to specific presenting problems (e.g., anxiety, emotional regulation, social confidence) may include the following.

- Were there moments in the game where you felt similar to your character? Can you share more about that?
- Where did anxiety show up for you today?
- What emotions, if any, did you find challenging? Why do you think they were challenging?
- What strategies did your character use in the game to overcome obstacles? How might you apply similar strategies in your own life?
- Were there moments in the game where you felt particularly socially successful or confident? What contributed to those feelings?
- What support did you receive from your teammates, and how did that affect your experience?

Vignette

A group of late teens joined a TA-TTRPG group using Dungeons & Dragons to work on goals related to anxiety, emotional regulation, and social confidence. Members of the group included Caleb (Caucasian male, 19), Ashley (African American female, 18), and Willow (Caucasian female, 16). The group had been working together in the TA-TTRPG group for several years and had well-established group cohesion. They had struggled in the past with interpersonal conflict and had worked through moments of challenge with guided support from their GM. As such, they had well-established patterns of interaction.

Caleb's character was a studious wizard from a distant land who often didn't understand the social norms of the world he explored. This characterization mirrored Caleb's challenges, confusion, and sometimes frustration in social situations. Willow's character was also magically empowered, though her personality was fiery, often child-like, and reactive. Portraying her character as such allowed her to fully express and explore her emotions, which in her real life were often oscillated between repression and overwhelm. Ashley was playing a character with plant-based magic, who had been a farmer before adventuring. This character, portrayed by Ashley with a deep southern drawl, had in many ways been the party's maternal figure, caretaking and guiding the other characters (and often the players portraying them) when challenges arose. Her character allowed her some freedom to speak honestly, take a caretaker and leader role, and explore her budding confidence.

In the fantasy storyline in the game, the participants' characters were investigating an evil organization's plot for world domination. The organization was rumored to be using forbidden magic to create an army of super-powered soldiers, which would mean trouble for their heroic sensibilities. The plot had led the characters to the entrance of a towering building. The heroes believed the evil laboratory was on the top floor, and wanted to investigate, but needed to get past the guard standing at a post at the entrance. They knew that subduing the guard would not be an option due to heightened security, so they planned to convince him that they should be permitted access to the building.

After debating strategy, Caleb suggested that they should pretend to be architects and convince the guard that they were contracted to fully inspect the building. Willow, in her character's voice, spoke: "Oh come on, don't you think they'll know *you* are not an *architect?*" The session paused. Willow's comment was presumably directed to Ashley's character, a farmer with a southern drawl who was clad in torn overalls and a straw hat. However, at that moment, the narrative and Ashley's real-world experience merged. As an African American female, her real-world experience of criticism for her perceived identity and the low expectations for her capabilities were brought to the fore. Her facial experience shifted, tears swelled in her eyes, and she said, "Oh, yeah, maybe you two should go be architects, and I'll wait outside."

The therapist paused the game and reflected, "We have an opportunity here to tell a different story. What story do we want to tell?" The group unanimously decided they wanted to tell a story of Ashley's character being fully capable of being an architect and even confronting the expected bigotry of the guard if questioned. The group knew that Ashley's character would have to play the part, so they opted to do a little research, both in and out of the game, for how to best show that she was in fact an architect. Using their own internet browsers in their own locations, the players had a few minutes to freely do some research, looking up some terms Ashley's character could use, as well as the type of tools and equipment they should carry to fully play the part. After coming back together and sharing their results, Caleb's character used his magic to summon artifacts they would need, and Willow opted for her character to pay for whatever remained. Fully role-playing as their characters who were pretending to be architects, they spoke to the therapeutic GM, who was also in-character as the guard. The GM, knowing the stakes of the moment, said, "You're an architect? Really? You aren't what I expected you to look like." Ashley spoke directly and confidently, "Yes, I'm an architect. I know I may not be what you expected, but that's *your* problem. These are my assistants. We're here to inspect the building and if you don't let us in, the whole building could collapse and it'd be your fault!" The group rallied by her side, strengthening her case. The guard apologized and subdued, granting the heroes access to the building.

Before the session ended, they successfully destroyed the laboratory, defended by numerous evil super soldiers, though the post-game processing was focused entirely on surpassing the guard. The group reflected on how that moment provided an opportunity for each of them and their characters to experience something powerful. Ashley expressed how important it was for her to be the confident and intellectual team leader, not just a maternal caretaker. "It felt good." Willow expressed familiarity with speaking before thinking and not realizing the negative impact of her statements. She expressed with gratitude the ability to have a corrective experience and to have been forgiven by both Ashley and her character. Caleb expressed gratitude that he could be in a position to help out his friends.

Suggestions for Follow-Up

This intervention is designed to be applied consistently over time. It becomes richer and more impactful as group cohesion improves, trust with the therapist builds, and familiarity with the game format increases. When group members have been playing together for a longer period, encourage reflection on the group's change and development over time. For example, you may ask the following questions:

- What was it like playing together when we first started?
- What is it like playing together now?
- What changed? What caused that change?
- Is there anything we can learn from that journey?
- What else can we do to continue our progress together?

Contraindications

Use caution when using TA-TTRPGs with individuals who may have difficulty differentiating the rich immersive stories created in TA-TTRPG sessions from real-world experiences (Connell, 2023; Kilmer et al., 2023). To fully engage in TA-TTRPG, participants must have the capacity to participate in back-and-forth communication and track the basic throughline of an ongoing story. As such, participants with moderate intellectual disabilities may need additional support, accommodations, or modifications to participate. Also, identify and note participants' reading and writing capacities, as those may be occasionally incorporated into TTRPG play.

References

Connell, M. A. (2023). *Tabletop role-playing therapy: A guide for the clinician game master*. WW Norton.

Kilmer, E. D., Davis, A. D., Kilmer, J. N., & Johns, A. R. (2023). *Therapeutically applied role-playing games: The game to grow method*. Routledge.

Part 10
Gender

CHAPTER 39

THE GENDER-CELEBRATORY SAFE RELATIONSHIPS GENOGRAM

Katelyn O. Coburn, Lorin C. Kelly, Kristen E. Benson, and Paul R. Springer

Materials for Therapists: A computer program or application that can be used to create a genogram. Many telehealth platforms have a whiteboard application that can be used.

Materials for Clients: None.

Objective

The gender-celebratory safe relationships (GCSR) genogram is a therapeutic tool intended for the assessment of relationships in which the client's gender is either affirmed and celebrated or not affirmed or celebrated. Through identification of these relationships, therapists and clients may discuss and develop coping strategies to bolster self-worth and relational skills for navigating ambivalent and rejecting relationships. This chapter describes an adaptation of this in-person intervention for use through telehealth using an online whiteboard or drawing application when working with transgender and nonbinary adolescents (Duvall & Béres, 2011; Milewski-Hertlein, 2001).

Rationale for Use

The use of genograms in family therapy has traditionally focused on examining generational family of origin patterns and relationship dynamics, with family being defined by biology and marriage (McGoldrick & Gerson, 1985). The GCSR genogram shares some theoretical foundations with the socially constructed genogram, which is situated within narrative therapy, and expands on more traditional approaches to genograms by including families and relationships of choice (Duvall & Béres, 2011; Milewski-Hertlein, 2001). The GCSR genogram can include any relationship that a client considers influential to their life, as these relationships may be more supportive than kinship relationships. Processing focuses on the meaning of these relationships and invites clients to consider the significance, closeness, and distance of relationships represented by how far or close the client places the relationship in relation to themselves on the genogram (Duvall & Béres, 2011). The inclusion of families and relationships of choice can be particularly important when working with transgender and nonbinary clients due to the rejection and exclusion this population may face within the family of origin.

DOI: 10.4324/9781003330912-49

Research demonstrates clear benefits of family acceptance and support and deleterious effects of family rejection as it relates to the mental health and well-being of transgender and nonbinary adolescents (McConnell et al., 2016; Ryan et al., 2009). The GCSR genogram is aimed at the assessment of relationships in the lives of transgender and nonbinary adolescents, specifically as it relates to the support of their gender and impact on mental health and well-being.

For the purposes of the GCSR genogram, relationships are conceptualized in three different categories reflected in the scholarly literature regarding family acceptance, ambivalence, and rejection (e.g., Bhattacharya et al., 2020; Reczek, 2016; Ryan et al., 2009):

1. ***Celebratory/affirmative:*** People who unconditionally love, celebrate, respect, and honor the client's whole personhood, their gender identity, and their gender expression
2. ***Tolerant/ambivalent:*** People who demonstrate a mix of conditional acceptance, some rejection, some ambivalence, and who do not fully celebrate, respect, and honor the client, their gender identity, and their gender expression
3. ***Rejecting:*** People who are overtly harmful by choosing not to respect and honor the client, their gender identity, and their gender expression

By using the GCSR genogram at the beginning of treatment, therapists develop an understanding of the relationships in the client's life that positively and negatively contribute to their mental health. Therapists can reference the GCSR genogram to work with clients on recognizing how they feel in celebratory/affirming relationships and how these relationships bolster their self-affirmation, authenticity, and worth. Therapists can also work with clients on regulating resources to use when interacting with tolerant/ambivalent and rejecting people, as well as processing harm experienced in tolerant/ambivalent and rejecting relationships.

Setup

Prior to conducting the GCSR genogram with clients, ensure that clients are in settings in which they feel safe disclosing the nature of their relationships as celebratory/affirming, tolerant/ambivalent, or rejecting.

Instructions

The following offers step-by-step instructions on creating a GCSR genogram in session with clients.

1. ***Describe what a GCSR genogram is.*** Explain that a GCSR genogram is used for identifying and exploring the relationships in which the client feels safe to share their authentic gender identity and define the difference between celebratory/affirming, tolerant/ambivalent, and rejecting relationships.
2. ***Open a virtual whiteboard application and share your screen.*** Alternatively, you can use another computer program of your choice that can be used to create basic shapes and reorder them, or you can draw the genogram on paper and periodically show clients the drawing through the camera of the teletherapy platform as the genogram is constructed. For youth whose home environment is rejecting, avoid having clients use programs on their computer to ensure that another

family member does not locate the client's genogram or other therapy materials in files saved to their computer.

Steps 3–5 can be moved between non-linearly to construct the genogram through a collaborative conversation.

3. ***Invite clients to name people in their lives that impact their mental health and feelings of safety as a transgender and/or nonbinary person.*** This may include biological, adoptive, stepfamily, and/or extended family members, chosen family and friends, community members, and anyone else. Explain that the client can use symbols to depict each person and their gender, such as using squares for masculine people, circles for feminine people, and triangles for nonbinary people. Clients can also choose any symbol they want to represent the different people in their lives (e.g., flowers, hearts, stars).
4. ***For each relationship, have clients discuss if they experience the relationship as celebratory/affirming, tolerant/ambivalent, or rejecting and why.*** Discuss with clients where they would place each person in a visual representation on the genogram indicating how emotionally close the client is to each person and the level of impact each person has on the client. This step may be done as clients are naming people or after people have been added to the genogram in the following step.
5. ***Detail relational information on the genogram.*** In the center of the whiteboard, place an image that depicts the client. Then, draw concentric circles with the client placed in the innermost circle and other people placed in the outer circles depending on how "more" or "less" emotionally close/safe they are and how "more" or "less" impactful they are on the client (Duvall & Béres, 2011). "More" emotionally close, safe, and impactful relationships should be placed in one of the circles closer to the client. "Less" emotionally close, safe, and impactful relationships should be placed in one of the circles further away from the client. Alternatively, you can ask the client how they would like to draw the genogram in a way that makes sense to them (e.g., with symbols, pictures, tiers, lines; Swainson & Tasker, 2005). Clients can decide how they want to depict the relationships as celebratory/affirming, tolerant/ambivalent, or rejecting. For example, they may create representative color codes or symbols for each category and place a symbol by each person or draw representative lines from each person to them (e.g., celebratory relationships denoted by a solid line between the client and the person, tolerant/ambivalent relationships denoted by a wavy line, and rejecting relationships denoted by a dashed line).
6. ***Save a copy of the document in the client's file.*** Ideally, the genogram should be saved in a way that allows you to make changes to it in subsequent sessions.

Processing

Throughout the construction of the GCSR genogram and after its completion, ask processing questions to explore the nature of impactful relationships in the client's life as celebratory/affirmative, tolerant/ambivalent, or rejecting. The concepts and examples of processing questions provided here are informed by narrative therapy (Duvall & Béres, 2011), queer theory (Tilsen, 2021), and polyvagal theory understandings of how the autonomic nervous system perceives safety in relationships through the ventral vagal social engagement system (Dana, 2018).

Narrative genograms can help facilitate unique outcomes in family stories (Chrzastowski, 2011). Other narrative therapy concepts such as the Team of Life approach (Denborough, 2012) can be mapped on the genogram, allowing clients to identify people who are both alive or no longer living who have been positively influential and considered to be gender celebratory. Cisgender expectations can be externalized and preferred celebratory relationships highlighted on the GCSR.

Drawing on polyvagal theory, use these processing questions to understand the impact of the identified relationships on the client's autonomic nervous system and sense of safety (or lack thereof) in these relationships (Dana, 2018). For example, celebratory/affirming relationships may elicit feelings of calmness or excitement; tolerant/ambivalent relationships may correlate with a freeze response, feeling numb, or anxious; and experiences in rejecting relationships make evoke feelings of fear or anger and physiological symptoms such as the heart rate speeding up or short, shallow breaths.

- Who comes to mind when you think of family?
- When you think about expressing your gender identity or sharing that you are [transgender/nonbinary] with [name of person], what sensations do you notice in your body?
- What do the people who are celebratory/affirming of your gender identity mean to you?
- How do the people who are celebratory/affirming contribute to you feeling like you can be yourself?
- What might the celebratory/affirming people in your life say about you if they were here talking with us?
- How do you resist pressure to conform to binary gender norms you feel from people who are rejecting in your life?
- In what contexts is it [easier/harder] to embody your authentic gender identity?
- What would it be like to ask for support from celebratory/affirming people in your life when you experience rejection based on your [transgender/nonbinary] identity?

Discuss with clients how safe, celebratory/affirming relationships can be a regulating resource when the client is struggling and needs support. Validate the client's emotions related to not feeling supported or being rejected in the tolerant/ambivalent and rejecting relationships that they identified and include treatment goals and interventions that foster coping strategies and relational skills for navigating these relationships. If the client has few safe, celebratory/affirming people on their genogram, discuss ways they can foster those relationships.

Vignette

Ollie (15) was nonbinary and used they/them pronouns. Ollie lived with their mother and stepmom throughout the school year and with their dad and his girlfriend over the summers. Ollie's parents had divorced 14 months ago, and this was the first year that they would be spending the summer away from their mom's home. Ollie's mom and stepmom were celebratory and affirming of Ollie, but Ollie reported that at times they could be "overly supportive" as they wanted to know everything that was happening in therapy. Ollie's behavior drastically changed after the divorce, which alarmed Ollie's mom and prompted the start of therapy. In their first session, Ollie mentioned that their father and his girlfriend were members of a conservative religion. They had recently overheard their father telling their mother that they should change the custody arrangements because their mother's "sinful lifestyle [was] corrupting Ollie." They had also heard their father say that if he had custody, "She (i.e., Ollie) would be in church, wearing normal clothes, and stopping with all of this 'I'm not a girl' nonsense!" At the start of Ollie's second therapy session, the therapist constructed a GCSR genogram. The following depicts key components of their conversation during this process.

Therapist: Today I want to get to know you and your relationships better, so I want us to create a genogram that maps out celebratory/affirming, tolerant/ambivalent, and rejecting relationships in your life (see Figure 39.1). Before we begin, I want to make sure that this feels like a good time to talk about this. I'm going to send you a few things via the chat function.

Then, the therapist typed the following via the chat function in the teletherapy platform:

> I know that you said last week that your moms can sometimes hover outside of your door. Do you think that they can hear you right now? If yes, do you want to play soft music in the background? Or is it better to talk about this in the chat?

Ollie replied by typing, "Yeah, I think they're there right now! Let me go turn on my music." After doing so, they continued by speaking aloud.

Ollie: Okay that's good, but if I think they're listening or they come in I'll let you know.

Therapist: Okay sounds great! I want to give you some helpful information on what a GCSR genogram is and how it can be helpful for both of us as we continue to work together. Let me share my screen with you and pull up the whiteboard so I can draw the genogram while we discuss your relationships. Can you tell me about a person in your life who you are connected to and that you identify as family? Family can be people related to you by blood or chosen people that feel like family to you.

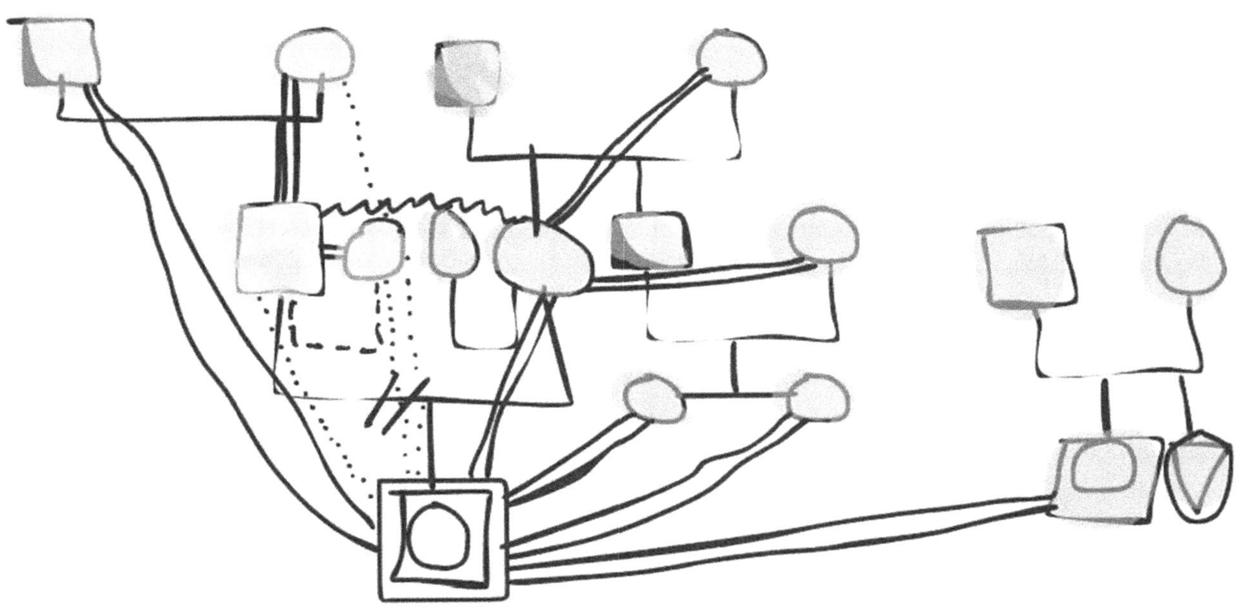

Figure 39.1 Gender-celebratory safe relationship genogram.

Ollie: My best friend Tia and their family. I always say they're my second family. I always feel loved and like I can be myself when I go to their apartment.

Therapist: It sounds like they are celebratory! How do they each identify their gender? You can see that sometimes gender is shown as a circle for feminine and a square for masculine. What symbols do you think we should use for each of these special people?

Ollie: Tia is nonbinary, so I like the circle and square combination. Their sister is bisexual. Maybe that is why their parents just seem to get it. Anyway, Tia's mom is a circle, and their dad is a square.

Therapist: Great. Since you are close with Tia, I'm going to draw these two lines connecting you to them. Can you tell me about other important relationships you have?

Ollie then proceeded to tell the therapist all of the important relationships in their life. As they described each relationship, the therapist added them to the genogram.

Therapist: Ollie, you've included several important people. Let's imagine you are going to throw a magical unicorn party where everyone there is celebrating you and your gender. When you look at this genogram, who would you invite?

Ollie: A unicorn party would be awesome! My mom and stepmom would be decorating and baking a big cake! My aunt and cousins would totally be there and would probably make the music playlist. My Nana and Pappy, my mom's parents, would come too and bring glitter. They would all be on Team Unicorn!

Therapist: Yes! Let's color in Team Unicorn. What color do you want to use for them?

Ollie: Purple, for sure.

Therapist: Who would be on the maybe list for the party? These are people who love you but maybe don't quite get your gender or don't quite understand. We might consider them to be tolerant. What color should we shade them?

Ollie: I think we should use pink for my grandpa and my uncle. They're both nice to me, but I can tell they're uncomfortable and act differently since they found out I'm nonbinary. My Grandpa tries to use the right pronouns, but he misgenders me a lot.

Therapist: It sounds like they care about you but have some work to do before you feel like they could be on Team Unicorn.

Ollie: Yeah, that's right.

Therapist: I see that your dad and his girlfriend are not purple or pink. Neither is your grandma. Can you tell me more about this?

Ollie: Yeah, I never thought of it that way but, they don't celebrate who I am. It makes me sad because I love my dad and when I was younger, we had such a good relationship.

Therapist: What do you think influences them to be that way?

Ollie: I think they have expectations about who I'm supposed to be that's about gender. And I'm not the girl they want me to be, so we fight more than we ever did before.

Therapist: It sounds like maybe they have gender expectations that get in the way of your relationship.

Ollie: Yeah.

Therapist: Is there a color you'd you like to shade these people? I'm also going to add these dotted lines to show that these relationships are challenging. Is that ok?

Ollie: Yeah. I think green would be good.

Therapist: I see that you have a lot of really loving people in your life that celebrate you! I also see that you have some relationships that make you feel sad, like the relationship with your dad, his side of the family, and his girlfriend. You mentioned that you're going to your dad's this weekend. If things get hard or you hear messages that don't honor your gender, what do you think the members of Team Unicorn would want to remind you? What would they say to you if they could whisper in your ear during those hard moments at your dad's?

Ollie: Tia would want me to remember that I'm all good just the way I am. Nana would tell me how cute I look in a bowtie and that God made me perfectly.

Therapist: It sounds like they would want you to remember you are loved and accepted, even when those gender expectations show up and try to convince your dad you need to be different than your magical unicorn self.

Ollie: Yeah. They would want me to remember those things!

Suggestions for Follow-Up

The GCSR genogram can be revisited in subsequent sessions to assess relationship changes. When revisiting the intervention, keep the original version of the genogram in its original form and make a copy of it before editing. This will allow you to display both versions of the genogram to examine changes over time. Discuss any changes with clients and assess how the changes are impacting the client's overall mental health. A GCSR genogram may also be used with parents when parents are a part of therapy (see Chapter 40).

Contraindications

You must embody celebratory, affirming, and inclusive beliefs about transgender and nonbinary identities to successfully utilize this intervention. If you are unfamiliar with or have unexplored biases regarding transgender and nonbinary identities, do self-of-the-therapist work to deconstruct the impact of cissexism on the therapeutic process before employing this intervention with clients (McGeorge et al., 2021). Further, familiarize yourself with trauma-informed practices and be able to recognize signs of trauma-related emotional dysregulation as clients with higher numbers of rejecting relationships may be likely to experience dysregulation when discussing rejecting relationships (e.g., Dana, 2018). If clients do not have regulating resources that they already use, teach grounding skills and self-compassion practices before constructing the GCSR genogram. Finally, if clients indicate they are in a location where they don't feel safe enough to discuss the GCSR genogram, avoid conducting this intervention until a confidential environment can be established.

References

Bhattacharya, N., Budge, S. L., Pantalone, D. W., & Katz-Wise, S. L. (2020). Conceptualizing relationships among transgender and gender diverse youth and their caregivers. *Journal of Family Psychology, 35*(5), 595–605. https://doi.org/10.1037/fam0000815

Chrzastowski, S. K. (2011). A narrative perspective on genograms: Revisiting classical family therapy models. *Clinical Child Psychology and Psychiatry, 16*(4), 635–644. https://doi.org/10.1177/1359104511400966

Dana, D. (2018). *The polyvagal theory in therapy: Engaging the rhythm of regulation*. W. W. Norton.

Denborough, D. (2012). The team of life with young men from refugee backgrounds. *International Journal of Narrative Therapy & Community Work, 2*(2), 44–53.

Duvall, J., & Béres, L. (2011). *Innovations in narrative therapy: Connecting practice, training, and research*. W. W. Norton & Company.

McConnell, E. A., Birkett, M., & Mustanski, B. (2016). Families matter: Social support and mental health trajectories among lesbian, gay, bisexual, and transgender youth. *Journal of Adolescent Health, 59*(6), 674–680. https://doi.org/10.1016/j.jadohealth.2016.07.026

McGeorge, C. R., Coburn, K. O., & Walsdorf, A. A. (2021). Deconstructing cissexism: The journey of becoming an affirmative family therapist for transgender and nonbinary clients. *Journal of Marital and Family Therapy, 47*(3), 785–802. https://doi.org/10.1111/jmft.12481

McGoldrick, M., & Gerson, R. (1985). *Genograms in family assessment*. W. W. Norton.

Milewski-Hertlein, K. A. (2001). The use of a socially constructed genogram in clinical practice. *American Journal of Family Therapy, 29*(1), 23–38. https://doi.org/10.1080/01926180125996

Reczek, C. (2016). Ambivalence in gay and lesbian family relationships. *Journal of Marriage and Family, 78*(3), 644–659. https://doi.org/10.1111/jomf.12308

Ryan, C., Huebner, D., Diaz, R. M., & Sanchez, J. (2009). Family rejection as a predictor of negative health outcomes in white and Latino lesbian, gay, and bisexual young adults. *Pediatrics, 123*, 346–352. https://doi.org/10.1542/peds.2007-3524

Swainson, M. & Tasker, F. (2005). Genograms redrawn: Lesbian couples define their families. *Journal of GLBT Family Studies, 1*(2), 3–27. https://doi.org/10.1300/J461v01n02_02

Tilsen, J. (2021). *Queering your therapy practice: Queer theory, narrative therapy, and imagining new identities*. Routledge.

CHAPTER 40

THE GENDER-CELEBRATORY SAFE RELATIONSHIPS GENOGRAM FOR PARENTS

Kristen E. Benson, Katelyn O. Coburn, Lorin C. Kelly, and Paul R. Springer

Materials for Therapists: A computer program or application that can be used to create a genogram. Many telehealth platforms have a whiteboard application that can be used.

Materials for Clients: None.

Objective

This chapter builds on the gender-celebratory safe relationship (GCSR) genogram intervention described in Chapter 39, by adding instructions for use with parents. Best practices indicate that as parents of transgender and nonbinary (TNB) youth address their own concerns and concerns regarding extended family, the child should not be present in sessions to shield them from negative messages about their identity (e.g., Heiden-Rootes et al., 2024). This chapter will focus on facilitating teletherapy with the parental subsystem.

Rationale for Use

Gender-celebratory parents frequently navigate relationships with adults in their extended family to determine who is safe for TNB children to continue relationships with and in what capacity. They serve as advocates for their children to ensure safety and mediate relationships that may be harmful or rejecting to their children. Informed by queer theory, narrative therapy (e.g., Tilsen, 2021), and traditional genograms (McGoldrick & Gerson, 1985), the GCSR genogram for parents can help parents to identify who in their family and social system is accepting/celebratory. It can be especially useful for parents of younger TNB children who are often in the role of disclosing the child's transgender or nonbinary gender to extended family, navigating safe relationships for their children within the family, and managing secondary stigma or the ways that they may be blamed for their children's gender identity. For example, as family members learn about a child's gender identity, the GCSR genogram can help parents identify who in the family uses correct pronouns and chosen name post-disclosure. Therapists can use this tool to explore concerns such as who parents anticipate will be accepting of their child and who would come to the youth's defense if another person acted in rejecting or un-affirming

DOI: 10.4324/9781003330912-50

ways. The GCSR genogram can help parents identify potential advocates in their relational system and facilitate conversations about how to engage loved ones in relational advocacy to increase a safe familial network.

Setup

The GCSR genogram can be utilized with parents who are seeking therapy without their children, or in conjunction with a child's therapy in individual or family settings. Therapy sessions dedicated to addressing adults in the family system should initially exclude the minor to allow adults to speak freely about challenges without causing harm to the child. For therapy with parents whose child typically participates in individual or family sessions, first engage in a conversation with the youth about what will be addressed with their parents when they are not present.

Instructions

The following offers step-by-step instructions on creating a GCSR genogram in session with parents.

1. ***Describe what a GCSR genogram is.*** Explain that a GCSR genogram is used for identifying and exploring the relationships in which it feels safe for their child to share their authentic gender identity and define the difference between celebratory/affirming, tolerant/ambivalent, and rejecting relationships.
2. ***Open a virtual whiteboard application and share your screen.*** Alternatively, you can use another computer program that can be used to create basic shapes and reorder them, or you can draw the genogram on paper and periodically show clients the drawing through video as the genogram is constructed.

You can move between steps 3 and 7 non-linearly to construct the genogram through a collaborative conversation.

3. ***Invite clients to name people in their lives that are important to them and in the life of their transgender and/or nonbinary child.*** This may include biological, adoptive, stepfamily, and/or extended family members, chosen family and friends, community members, and anyone else. This step should identify primary supports for both the adult parent clients and the TNB child.
4. ***Ask clients to identify which of the people they have identified are aware of their child's gender identity.*** Inquire about how disclosure initially occurred with each person, initial responses to disclosure, and other ways in which disclosure has been addressed in the family.
5. ***For each relationship, have clients discuss if they experience the relationship as celebratory/affirming, tolerant/ambivalent, or rejecting and why.*** Discuss with clients where they would place each person in a visual representation on the genogram indicating how emotionally close to the parents and/or the TNB child is to each person and the level of impact each person has on them. This step may be done as they are naming people or after people have been added to the genogram in the following step.
6. ***Detail relational information on the genogram.*** On the whiteboard, place images that depict parents and their TNB child. Then, ask clients how they want to depict the relationships as

celebratory/affirming, tolerant/ambivalent, or rejecting. For example, they may create representative color codes or symbols for each category and place a symbol by each person or draw representative lines from each person to them. You may also suggest expansive genogram symbols or ask clients what symbols they would like to use.

7. ***Indicate advocacy arrows to show positive influential adult relationships.*** Invite client(s) to name people in the system who might have relationships that could position them to advocate on behalf of the TNB child. For example, a celebratory person might have an advocacy arrow pointing to a tolerant person with whom they have a close relationship, in hopes that the celebratory person might be able to help the tolerant person to become more supportive.
8. ***Save a copy of the document in the client's file.*** Ideally, the genogram should be saved in a way that allows the client and therapist to make changes to it in subsequent sessions.

Processing

Throughout the construction of the GCSR genogram and after its completion, ask processing questions to explore the relationships depicted in the genogram. Processing questions will vary based on where children are in the process of gender identity disclosure within their extended and chosen family. Questions are categorized here based on whether the child is in the pre-disclosure or post-disclosure process.

Pre-disclosure

- How do you view your role as a parent to a TNB child who has yet to share this part of themselves with others?
- Who do you anticipate will be accepting of your child?
- Who do you think will support you?
- How would you like to share this information?
- How would your child like to share this information?
- Does your child plan to disclose to family, or would they prefer that you disclose on their behalf?
- How do you plan to be a buffer to any adults that don't seem to "get it"?

Post-disclosure

- How have you experienced your role as a parent to a child who has come out to others as [transgender/nonbinary]?
- Who has demonstrated support to you and/or your child? How have they indicated support?
- Of your friends and family, who uses your child's correct pronouns and name?
- Who seems willing to learn more about gender identity if this is new experience to them?
- Who is currently safe for your children to continue relationships with, and in what capacity?
- Who are you concerned might say inappropriate or invalidating comments to your child?

- Who in your relational system would come to your child's defense?
- What would need to change for tolerant family members to move to a celebratory place? How might you facilitate that process?
- Are there people in your relational system who are celebratory and have close relationships with other members who are tolerant? How can they be invited to serve as an advocate? Perhaps they can be a positive influence to share accurate information, gently address misgendering, and help to support tolerant people on their journey to being more supportive of your child.

Address potential secondary stigma of cisgender parents and identify celebratory relationships to help establish safeguards. In addition, address specific concerns for LGBTQ+ parents who face blame for their child's TNB identity.

Vignette

This chapter expands on the vignette presented in the previous chapter regarding Ollie (15), a nonbinary client who used they/them pronouns. In the initial intake session with Ollie, Alix (39/female) and Jen (42/female) discussed being supportive and affirming of Ollie. They shared, however, that Ollie's father and his girlfriend were members of a conservative religious community who invalidated Ollie's gender identity. Alix disclosed that she and her ex-husband disagreed on many issues throughout their 15-year marriage, but his refusal to affirm Ollie led to Alix filing for divorce, and subsequently marrying Jen six months ago.

In their second session, the therapist completed the GCSR genogram with Ollie (see Chapter 39), which helped to identify the people who Ollie experienced as celebratory, tolerant, or rejecting. They also described the loving messages that celebratory people would want them to remember. Following the completion of that session, the therapist discussed with Ollie the possibility of conducting a similar genogram with their mom and stepmother. The therapist explained to Ollie that this might be a way of helping them to explore ways in which to further support them in their journey of coming out as nonbinary with others. Ollie agreed that this might be a helpful activity for them and was supportive of the therapist meeting with their mom and stepmother without Ollie there in a subsequent session. The following depicts key components of their conversation during this process.

Therapist: Welcome back, Jen and Alix. Last week, Ollie and I discussed our having a meeting to create a gender-celebratory genogram to map your close relationships and further discuss the people in your life and in Ollie's that are supportive and affirming of Ollie. Ollie and I decided that it would be best to do this without them here today so you can freely share any concerns that you might have without worrying about Ollie in the process. Is this something that you would be interested in doing with me today?

Alix: Yes. We've been looking forward to this appointment. I've been worried about family members saying something that is out of line to Ollie and really want to know your thoughts about how to confront them.

Therapist: Ollie is fortunate to have such caring parents. Where are you in the process of sharing this important news about who Ollie is?

Jen: Ollie asked us to tell some of our family, and most of our friends know. We love Ollie just as they are. But we're both concerned about certain family members saying something to make them feel badly about themself.

Alix: Our custody arrangement requires Ollie to see their father regularly, which I know is a struggle. I feel terrible every time Ollie has to go there, because I know they miss the relationship they used to have with their dad. He treats Ollie differently since they told him they're nonbinary. I have to follow the custody arrangement and can't control what their dad says, but I refuse to allow my own family to say anything hateful. Ollie is a good kid.

Therapist: You have valid concerns. I hear how much you want to protect Ollie. We talked about creating a genogram, which is a relational map of people in your life. I'm going to share my screen with you which has a whiteboard app so we can draw the genogram. Here's a link if you'd like to add to the drawing, or I can do it.

Alix: Maybe you can get us started.

Therapist: Of course. I'm going to start by adding the two of you to the genogram. Genograms typically indicate each person's gender. From a binary perspective, women are drawn as circles and men are drawn as squares. We can draw nonbinary gender as well as binary gender however you'd like.

Alix: I'm good with circles and squares. Maybe Ollie can have both since they're nonbinary. They're always breaking rules to make their way in the world, and this seems fitting.

Therapist: Ok, great. Here you can see both of you are connected with a solid line to show your marriage. Can you tell me the people who you consider to be in close relationships with? This can include kinship family, chosen family, and other relationships that you think are important.

Alix, Jen, and the therapist added important relationships to the genogram (see Figure 40.1). They added a color code similar to Ollie's, with purple indicating celebratory family members, pink indicating tolerant, and green indicating rejecting or un-affirming. They also added a red heart around Ollie.

Therapist: We developed a multigenerational map of important relationships. It looks like you all have some celebratory relationships. What is it that allows you to feel supported by these people?

Alix: Well, my parents immediately started working on using they/them pronouns when we told them about Ollie. We told my brother and his family a few weeks ago. My brother tries but doesn't really understand and still misgenders quite a bit and complains that it's hard to remember. I'm close with his wife and kids, who are very supportive and try to help him.

Therapist: I see that you all would like to establish a loving and safe network for Ollie. We can add advocacy arrows to your genogram to help us mark which celebratory family members you can invite to be advocates for Ollie. They might be the folx who help more tolerant or ambivalent family members by offering gentle pronoun corrections, talking about why gender identity is important, or engaging in conversations about how important it is for Ollie to have a loving and affirming family. I added the purple arrows to show your relationship with Alix's sister-in-law and your brother. Can you add more to highlight possible advocate relationships? You can include both people you've told and how you anticipate loved ones will respond. We'll revisit this and can add updates as needed.

Jen: I added them to show my family as well, since Ollie sees them on holidays. We've made the decision to skip events when my sister plans to attend because she can't seem to stop blaming us for "brainwashing" Ollie. I tried sending her information about gender identity and kids, which she wasn't willing to look at let alone talk about. We've had a strained relationship for many years, but it seems to be worse now.

Therapist: Jen, you previously mentioned gender rules and expectations. How do you think gender expectations might be influencing your sister?

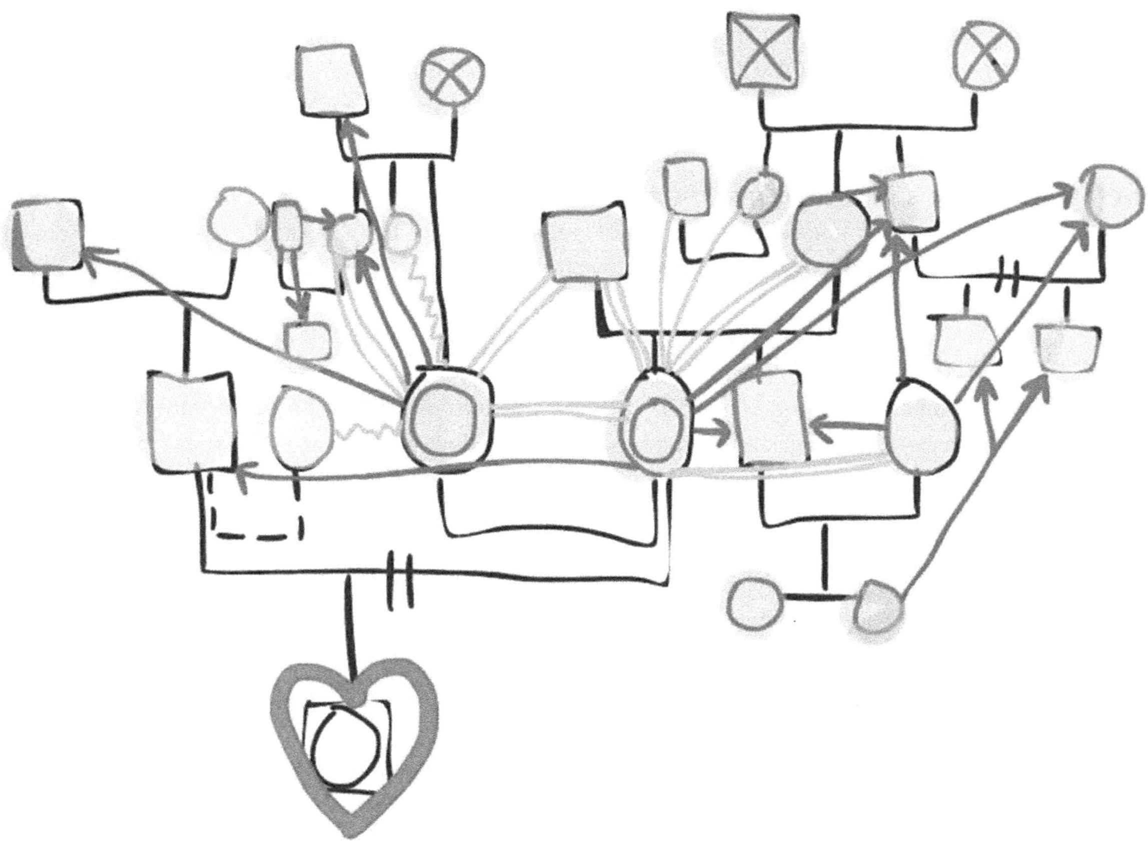

Figure 40.1 Gender-celebratory safe relationship genogram for parents.

Jen: They tell her I'm breaking gender rules and need to follow them. If I don't, there's something wrong with me and that we are ruining Ollie's life. I'm pretty sure she believes that my being queer has caused Ollie to think they're nonbinary.

Therapist: It sounds like those expectations have really convinced her that there's a right and wrong way to do gender.

Alex: We believe in love, acceptance, and inclusion. But I did blame myself when Ollie first told me. I thought that maybe I had been too indulgent with toy cars or that my pansexuality somehow caused confusion for Ollie.

Therapist: I'm curious who do you think these gender categories and rules serve? Who gets to define the gender rules for parenting?

The therapeutic conversation then focused on destabilizing the gender binary system as the norm.

Therapist: You've talked about taking a stand for love. Who do you see on your genogram that stands with you in that deep sense of love?

Alix: The purple and pink show it. I think even those who are tolerant are trying. Maybe with more love and education they can become purple.

Therapist: What changes would you need to see to feel safe to invite people into hues of purple?

Suggestions for Follow-Up

The GCSR genogram can be revisited in subsequent sessions to assess relationship changes and allow parents to further process their relational system throughout their TNB child's disclosure process. These follow-up conversations also allow parents to discuss ways in which to address intolerant family members and efforts to increase support from friends, family, and others.

When revisiting the intervention, keep the original version of the genogram in its original form and make a copy of it before editing. This will allow you to display both versions of the genogram to examine changes over time.

Contraindications

You must maintain a truly celebratory and gender-affirming stance to engage in gender-inclusive therapy practices such as utilizing this intervention. This involves participating in ongoing accountability practices to explore biases and the social impacts of living in a cisnormative culture (McGeorge et al., 2021).

References

Heiden-Rootes, K., Benson, K.E., Pedigo Carmichael, A., & Capshaw, E. (2024). Understanding transgender and non-binary youth mental health through the family resilience framework: A literature review. *Contemporary Family Therapy: An International Journal, 46*, 327–338. https://doi.org/10.1007/s10591-023-09688-3

McGeorge, C. R., Coburn, K. O., & Walsdorf, A. A. (2021). Deconstructing cissexism: The journey of becoming an affirmative family therapist for transgender and nonbinary clients. *Journal of Marital and Family Therapy, 47*(3), 785–802. https://doi.org/10.1111/jmft.12481

McGoldrick, M., & Gerson, R. (1985). *Genograms in family assessment*. W. W. Norton.

Tilsen, J. (2021). *Queering your therapy practice: Queer theory, narrative therapy, and imagining new identities*. Routledge.

CHAPTER 41

SELF-EXPRESSION TELETHERAPY INTERVENTION FOR QUEER AND GENDER DIVERSE YOUTH

Gabrielle C. Gebel

Materials for Therapists: Access to a gender-affirming website with an interactive avatar and different clothing options and accessories.

Materials for Clients: None.

Objective

This chapter provides instructions for conducting a clinical intervention aimed at empowering queer and gender diverse youth to express themselves and process gender expression through a playful format in teletherapy sessions. Using an online website that allows the user to dress up a virtual doll or avatar, clients can practice choosing preferred hairstyle and clothing options that might not otherwise be allowed, readily available, or comfortable for them to wear. Through processing questions, therapists may discuss with clients their experience of the exercise, what it would be like for them to make these changes in their life, if there are any barriers holding them back from making changes, and what it would be like to deconstruct any systems of oppression holding them back.

Rationale for Use

Gender diverse youth may present in therapy needing help increasing comfort with the expression of their gender. In addition, therapists may need to support familial relationships while adjusting to changes when a gender diverse youth expresses themselves more authentically. During in-person therapy, dress-up clothes and costumes help with self-expression and provide an opportunity for clients to try on new clothing, roles, and behaviors (Drewes, 2006).

The following describes ways in which teletherapists may empower gender diverse youth experiencing anxiety, mood disturbances, or gender dysphoria to explore their identity and self-expression and allow families to engage in exploration with their child through the use of a website-based interactive dress-up avatar. The gender diverse youth may experiment with their creativity to express themselves by trying out different clothing items, hairstyles, or accessories on an online model. In family sessions, therapists may use this intervention to strengthen family relationships by allowing youth to express themselves while family members observe and engage with the child. Using this

DOI: 10.4324/9781003330912-51

intervention, clinicians may also assess for any family dynamics that empower or disempower clients in their self-expression (Goodrich et al., 1988; Worell & Remer, 2003).

Setup

Prior to the session in which you plan to conduct the activity, search for websites that allow users to dress up a virtual doll or avatar. A keyword that you may use to search is "interactive dress up." Some examples of kid-friendly sites with an interactive avatar include PBS Kids Dress Up Games and Avatar Maker Dress up for Kids on the Google Play store. Consider the following when selecting an appropriate website:

- Are a variety of different body types, skin tones, hair styles, clothing items, and accessories available?
- Are the clothing and accessory options available appropriate given the needs of each client? For example, some sites may provide knives and guns as accessory options.
- Are hairstyles and clothing items restricted by the gender of the avatar selected?
- Does the site have ads or popups? If so, are the ads or popups appropriate?

Instructions

The following specifies instructions for this activity.

1. ***Provide an explanation of the intervention.*** For example, "If you'd like, today we can play dress up with a character. You'll get to choose a character on the computer and pick out different clothes, hairstyles, makeup, and accessories for them. We can talk while you pick stuff out."
2. ***Share your screen with the website on it.*** Show clients around the website by clicking on different options.
3. ***Send clients a link to the website.*** This step may be skipped if you think it's best to continue screen sharing and ask clients to direct you in doing the activity. If you share your screen, clients will need to ask you to choose different items, which naturally allows you a chance to ask questions and process each choice. This option may be more appropriate for younger clients or clients who are more reserved in their communication. If you send a link for clients to do the activity themselves, they naturally have more autonomy over what they choose and can play more naturally. You can simply observe, reflect, and ask questions. This option may be suited best for older clients or clients who readily share their thoughts and emotions.
4. ***Request that clients share their screen with you.*** This step may be skipped if you will be screen sharing and having clients dictate their choices.
5. ***Invite clients to select an avatar and dress it up.*** Clients will first select a character and then will add different hairstyles, clothing, and accessories to the character.
6. ***Make observations and ask processing questions throughout the activity.*** If family members are present, observe how they interact and any reactions they have. You may also encourage family members to assist in choosing items or create avatars for themselves as well.

7. ***Take a screenshot of the completed avatar.*** With the client's permission, take screenshots of the work to track progress over time. Store screenshots in a Health Insurance Portability and Accountability Act (HIPAA)-compliant file.

Processing

The following processing questions align with feminist family therapy's goal of empowerment and identifying and challenging power dynamics. Facilitate conversations to explore the real-life implications of the exercise, barriers, and/or systems of oppression that may be holding them back, and what they can do differently.

Questions for Queer or Gender Diverse Clients

- What was it like for you to choose the avatar?
- What was it like for you to dress it up?
- How did you decide to choose [clothing item/hairstyle/etc.]?
- How do you [think/feel] when you see [clothing/hairstyle/etc.]?
- How would you feel if you had [clothing item/hairstyle/etc.]?
- What would it be like if you wore this to [school/the dinner table with your family/etc.]?
    - What would you think if they [liked/didn't like] your outfit?
    - How would you feel if they [liked/didn't like] your outfit?
- How is dressing up an avatar [similar to/different than] dressing yourself?
- What was it like to share these selections with someone else?
- How might sharing your avatar with others be [similar to/different than] showing others your own [clothing/fashion] choices?
- Is there anyone you would be hesitant to share your avatar with?
    - If so, who?
    - What would need to happen for you to feel comfortable sharing your avatar with them?
- Is there anyone else that you would like to share your avatar with?
    - If so, who?
    - How do you know that you are ready to share your avatar with them?
    - Would you like to invite them to our next session to share your avatar with them?

Questions for Family Members

- What was it like for you to watch [name] go through this exercise?
- What do you think it was like for [name] to have you here to experience this exercise with them? How do you think they felt with you here?

- What meaning do you make of the fact that [name] chose to share this with you?
- What does it say about your relationship with them that they chose to share this with you?

Vignette

Casey (11) was a non-binary person who used they/them/theirs pronouns. Casey had an older brother, Aaron (14), and a younger sister, Julia (9). The three siblings lived with their parents, Jessica (41) and Matthew (43). Casey disclosed to their family about their gender identity as a non-binary person two years ago. Casey asked their family to use they/them pronouns and told them that they didn't identify as exclusively a boy or a girl, but rather a combination of them depending on the day. In the first six months of therapy, the therapist worked with Casey to empower them to express themselves both emotionally and with regard to their gender.

The self-expression telehealth intervention was utilized in therapy to allow Casey the space to safely express themselves and to assess for systems acting as barriers to Casey being able to express themselves outside of session. Given Casey's age and ability to express themselves verbally without much prompting, the therapist asked Casey to bring up the website on their screen and screen-share with the therapist. The therapist allowed Casey to pick whatever outfits or accessories they felt best represented their gender during each session. The therapist empowered Casey by asking questions like "What would it be like if you asked your sister to borrow her pink fuzzy sweater like the one you put on this model?" or "Who says you can't wear that color shirt?" Once Casey felt empowered to do so, they began asking their siblings to borrow clothes and asked everyone in their family to use they/them pronouns. The therapist encouraged Casey to take a screenshot of the avatar at the end of each session. The therapist also kept screenshots to track Casey's progress over time. In doing this, the therapist noticed that as Casey's confidence grew, they began choosing bolder colors and prints for clothing and more striking hairstyles.

With time, Casey expanded their expression of gender by wearing dresses and having their nails painted one day and wearing baggy jeans and no nail polish the next. They knew that their friends supported them in their expression of gender because their friends always complimented their outfit choices. Their friends would also ask Casey for advice in styling their own outfits.

While Jessica and Matthew accepted Casey's identity as a non-binary person, they worried about Casey being bullied later in life and about what would happen when Casey reached puberty. Julia and Aaron were also supportive of Casey. Aaron, however, had a group of friends who made fun of Casey, and Aaron struggled to stick up for Casey. Casey was in the 6th grade and would be in junior high the following year, which was in the same building with the high school where Aaron and his friends went. Casey felt rejected and hurt and was worried about being so close to Aaron's friends.

With Casey's permission, Casey's parents joined sessions, and their siblings joined soon after that. In the family sessions, the self-expression intervention was used to empower Casey to express how they felt about their gender expression, what it meant for them, and what support they needed from their family. In one session, Casey was invited to show their portfolio of screenshots of avatars to their family and allow their family to engage with them on the topic. The therapist asked questions such as:

- "Casey, what makes it important for you to be able to dress how you feel each day, like you get to dress this character during each session? What is it like for you to share that with your mom and dad here?"
- "What would you need from everyone else here to feel comfortable in expressing yourself?"
- "Julia, what would it be like if you and Casey shared a purple skirt like in the activity here?"
- "Aaron, what if Casey grew their hair out like the avatar?"

Casey was empowered to ask their parents for more support by using the self-expression intervention. With the support of their family, Casey eventually felt empowered to tell Aaron how it hurt them that Aaron didn't stick up for them with Aaron's friends. While gesturing to the screenshot of the avatar in a leopard print button-down with green cargo pants, Casey said, "Aaron, I'd like you to support me if I wore something like this around your friends."

Each family member eventually took turns creating their own avatar and experimenting with gender expression. The therapist encouraged the family members to pick something that they had a curiosity about, but that scared them to try. For example, Jessica experimented with a short hairstyle, Matthew experimented with a pair of pink socks and a cross-body bag, Aaron tried out a floral top, and Julia picked out a pair of black work boots. With time and support from the therapist, each family member examined their core beliefs about heteronormativity and cisgenderism, identified systems of oppression that held them back, and eventually reported a greater sense of empowerment to be themselves and stand up for one another in being their true authentic selves.

Suggestions for Follow-Up

The self-expression intervention may be revisited throughout the course of therapy. For example, you may have clients dress an avatar up on multiple occasions and show screenshots of previously dressed avatars to discuss differences in dress-up options over time. Another option for follow-up may be to empower the client to dress themselves like they are dressing their character and wear that outfit to a subsequent session.

Contraindications

If clients are in homes that are not accepting of their gender identity, evaluate the potential risks to emotional or physical safety before inviting family members to participate in this intervention. Further, most dress-up websites and applications are not HIPAA compliant. Discuss this limitation with clients prior to conducting the activity and take proper precautions to ensure the safety of client's protected health information.

References

Drewes, A. A. (2006). Play-based interventions. *Journal of Early Childhood and Infant Psychology, 2,* 139-157.

Goodrich, T. J., Rampage, C., Ellman, B., & Halstead, K. (1988). *Feminist family therapy: A casebook.* W. W. Norton & Company, Inc.

Worell, J., & Remer, P. (2003). *Feminist perspectives in therapy: Empowering diverse women.* John Wiley & Sons, Inc.

CHAPTER 42

CAMERAS OFF

GENDER DYSPHORIA IN TELETHERAPY

Kalen D. Zeiger

Materials for Therapists: A teletherapy platform that has a chat function.

Materials for Clients: None.

Objective

Trans and gender diverse (TGD) children and adolescents experiencing gender dysphoria may be reluctant to engage in teletherapy if they are concerned about the ways in which they appear and sound on screen. To provide a more comfortable and less anxiety-inducing teletherapy space, therapists may offer clients options regarding client visibility and use of voice during sessions. This chapter outlines ways in which to support TGD children and adolescents by giving them control over their physical and vocal visibility during teletherapy sessions, fostering new opportunities for client expression and engagement.

Rationale for Use

Gender dysphoria is a type of distress that can be experienced when an individual's gender identity does not align with their gender assumed for them at birth. TGD children and adolescents can experience gender dysphoria when it comes to either their physical and/or verbal presentation (Kameg & Nativio, 2018). Gender dysphoria can lead to a reluctance to interact in virtual settings when cameras and microphones are on due to concerns related to their experiences of gender dysphoria or the possibility of being perceived as the wrong gender (Brockbank et al., 2023; Galupo et al., 2020; Pulice-Farrow, 2020). This concern may be amplified with added reminders of their own voice and appearance as virtual therapy platforms often automatically display images of clients on their own screens and internet delays may echo back client voices.

This reluctance to engage can be counteracted by offering clients options regarding their visibility and use of voice during therapy sessions. A unique benefit of teletherapy is that clients can easily be offered control over whether they are physically seen or audibly heard. Additionally, chat functions offer the possibility of continued communication when speaking out loud is not a preferred option.

DOI: 10.4324/9781003330912-52

Using a collaborative therapeutic approach (Hoffman, 1993) regarding visibility and use of voice may improve the engagement of TGD children and adolescents in teletherapy settings.

Setup

To allow clients the option of engaging in teletherapy sessions without having to speak out loud, use a chat-capable teletherapy platform. The platform should also allow clients to turn their microphones and cameras on and off.

Instructions

At the onset of teletherapy with TGD clients, follow these steps to discuss options regarding the therapeutic experience.

- ***Provide options for being seen and heard.*** You might say something like, "I understand that being seen or heard can feel uncomfortable sometimes. You can turn your camera off or type in the chat box instead of speaking out loud if this feels more comfortable for you. Another option could be for you to turn off your own view of yourself during the session, so I can see you, but you aren't reminded that I can see you."
- ***Offer other options that may be available.*** Some teletherapy platforms may offer more playful options such as digital filters that some clients have fun using in session. Explore options that are available on your own teletherapy platform, offer these as options, and explain how to use them if they are available. For example, some filters allow people to add bunny ears, a pirate eye patch, a crown of flowers, or a silly hat to their image on screen, which may offer a playful and more comforting option. Others may allow people to soften their skin tone, minimize the appearance of "imperfections," smooth out their hair, or soften the appearance of lines or wrinkles.
- ***Inquire about your own use of the chat function.*** If typing in the chat box is more comfortable for clients, ask if they would like you to also communicate through chat. Some clients who prefer to type still like to be responded to verbally. Others prefer entirely chat-based communication.
- ***Share the benefits of being heard and seen.*** This allows clients to make an informed decision. Review the following points.
  - "Seeing and hearing you means I can recognize nonverbal cues, like body language and facial expressions, to better understand how you are feeling and respond better."
  - "Being able to see and hear you helps me monitor for signs of dissociation or emotional flooding, so I can help you regulate when we are talking about difficult experiences."
  - "When I can see and hear what's going on in your surroundings, it also lets me know if anyone else is present so I can help protect your privacy during our sessions."
- ***Explain that they can change their mind at any time.*** You might say, "You're welcome to stay entirely heard and visible one day and have your camera and mic off entirely another day. You're also welcome to switch back and forth over the course of each session, depending on what feels most comfortable for you at the time."

Processing

Check in with clients and process their experience of being seen and heard. Reflective discussions allow for ongoing co-creation, insight, and meaning-making around the reality of the client's experience (Hoffman, 1993). You may ask the following to help with this discussion:

- How does it feel knowing that you can use your [microphone/camera] as much or as little as you want?
- [How do you feel/what do you think] when I can [see/hear] you versus when I can't [see/hear] you?
- [How do you feel/what do you think] when you can see yourself on the computer versus when your view of yourself is turned off?
- How do you make the decision to be [seen/heard] when we meet?
- What does it mean for you to be [seen/heard]?
- What does it mean for you to have the choice of being [seen/heard]?
- How do you think our recent conversation might have been different if your [microphone/camera] was [on/off]?
- Is using the chat function letting you say everything you want to say? Is there anything you haven't been able to say to me that you want to?

Vignette

Sami was a 13-year-old who was assigned female at birth and had repeatedly told family and friends about really being a boy. Sami's parents were Christian and loved their child, but after talking with their church leaders were reluctant to allow Sami to transition either socially to presenting as a boy, or medically by using reversible puberty blockers to prevent further feminizing from puberty hormones. Sami had become increasingly moody, anxious, and depressed over the last couple of years. Due to Sami's increased outspoken distress over not being a girl, Sami's parents sought professional opinions about gender affirming care for Sami.

During the first teletherapy session with Sami and Sami's parents, the therapist said, "I understand that being seen or heard can sometimes be uncomfortable. You have the option to turn your camera off and use chat instead of speaking out loud, if you want to." In this first session, Sami and his family remained visible and spoke out loud. Sami appeared uncomfortable but spoke quietly when prompted.

In the next session, the therapist met alone with Sami. The therapist reminded Sami of his options regarding being seen and heard during the session. Sami kept the camera on but took a moment to adjust it so that he was visible only from their shoulders up. Sami's parents had previously expressed Sami's discomfort with his breasts, which had recently grown in size, and this allowed Sami the option of not having this part of his body seen on camera during the session. He left his microphone on, but used the chat box to type his responses, requesting that the therapist still speak aloud to him. At the end of the session, the therapist said, "We're almost out of time for today. Before we end, I wanted to check in with you to see what it means for you to have the choice of being seen and heard with me. What's that like for you?" At that point, Sami looked as though he was beginning to type in the chat box, and then paused and said aloud, "It's nice to have the choice. I feel like you get it. Not everyone gets it."

By allowing Sami the choice of being seen and heard in teletherapy, he was empowered to make choices that felt right for him in processing his experience in a way that did not provoke the additional distress of presenting as a girl. By providing options, the therapist also communicated to Sami an understanding of the difficulty of Sami's experience, which fostered the therapeutic alliance and ultimately allowed Sami a space that felt safe enough for him to speak openly with both the therapist and eventually his parents.

Suggestions for Follow-Up

The goal of this intervention is not to get clients to feel more comfortable with their presentation or to work toward clients using the camera or the microphone more. Rather, the goal is to foster a collaborative therapeutic space throughout the duration of teletherapy with TGD children and adolescents. However, increased client comfort with their presentation when using a camera or microphone can be a follow-up goal. For example, you can encourage clients to try out the microphone or the camera when clients who are transitioning share that transitioning is going well or they have reached a related transitioning milestone. For example, you might say:

- "It sounds like voice training is going well! You can use what you're learning in voice training by using the microphone in our sessions, if you want."
- "Your mom took you to cut your hair short and you really like it. That is great! If you want, you can use the camera to show me your haircut. I'd love to see it!"
- "That's great that you got a new outfit you like! If you want, you can use the camera to show it to me if you wear that outfit to a future session."

Follow the client's lead, support client efficacy, and avoid pressuring them from doing something they don't want to do.

Contraindications

There are drawbacks to clients having their cameras and microphones off. Lack of visual monitoring prevents therapists from seeing nonverbal forms of communication and other visual indicators of emotional flooding and dissociation. In addition, more serious indicators of disordered eating, trichotillomania, skin-picking disorder, and self-harm may be missed if clinicians cannot visually assess clients or visually monitor the severity of certain symptoms. This can be especially concerning given the higher instance of disordered eating in the trans population in comparison with the general population (Milano et al., 2020). Use more explicit monitoring through verbal or written communication regarding dissociation and emotional flooding during sessions. Screen for trauma responses, eating disorders, trichotillomania, skin-picking disorder, self-harm, and suicidal ideation throughout the use of this intervention.

In addition, it may be more difficult to tell if someone else is in the room during teletherapy sessions if a client's camera or microphone is turned off, which could put confidentiality at risk. Ask at the start of sessions if anyone else is present and request that clients provide an indicator if anyone else enters the room during at any point during teletherapy sessions.

References

Brockbank, M., Fujarczuk, W., Barborini, C., & Wang, Y. (2023). "At the cost of my well-being": Exploring trans, non-binary, and gender-diverse students' experiences of online learning. In D. F. Quintel & A. York (Eds.), *Privacy and safety in online learning* (pp. 19–34). Middle Tennessee State University.

Galupo, M. P., Pulice-Farrow, L., & Lindley, L. (2020). "Every time I get gendered male, I feel a pain in my chest": Understanding the social context for gender dysphoria. *Stigma and Health, 5*(2), 199–208. https://doi.org/10.1037/sah0000189

Hoffman, L. (1993). *Exchanging voices: A collaborative approach to family therapy*. Routledge.

Kameg, B. N., & Nativio, D. G. (2018). Gender dysphoria in youth: An overview for primary care providers. *Journal of the American Association of Nurse Practitioners, 30*(9), 493–498. https://doi.org/10.1097/JXX.0000000000000068

Milano, W., Ambrosio, P., Carizzone, F., De Biasio, V., Foggia, G., & Capasso, A. (2020). Gender dysphoria, eating disorders and body image: An overview. *Endocrine, Metabolic & Immune Disorders-Drug Targets, 20*(4), 518–524. https://doi.org/10.2174/1871530319666191015193120

Pulice-Farrow, L., Cusack, C. E., & Galupo, M. P. (2020). "Certain parts of my body don't belong to me": Trans individuals' descriptions of body-specific gender dysphoria. *Sexuality Research and Social Policy, 17*, 654–667. https://doi.org/10.1007/s13178-019-00423-y

Part 11

Culture

CHAPTER 43

DIGITAL CULTURAL PLAY GENOGRAMS

Kathryn McNiel, Bianca Rodriguez, Martha Hernández, and Rebecca A. Cobb

Materials for Therapists: Digital images and a computer program that can be used to create a genogram and compile images (e.g., PowerPoint). Some images are included in the supplemental materials that accompany this book.

Materials for Clients: None.

Objective

Cultural play genograms have been used in in-person therapy assessment and intervention to support clients in playfully mapping the influence of cultural identity as it relates to beliefs, values, and relationships within family systems (Gil, 2016). Play genograms can be adapted to teletherapy using computer programs and clip art or other digital images (Cobb, 2024). This chapter explains how to conduct a cultural play genogram via teletherapy using digital images.

Rationale for Use

Culture encompasses ways of living and interacting with the world that are passed down from generation to generation. Understanding and exploring one's culture in a therapeutic setting can be useful in highlighting the contextual factors that create the framework for one's behaviors, perspectives and identity formation. Genograms are an effective way to assess and learn about a client's cultural identity (Falicov, 2014; McGoldrick, 2016). Genograms can help clients and therapists gain a better understanding of family history, relationship patterns, and cultural factors that influence the family system (McGoldrick, 2016; McGoldrick et al., 2020).

Genograms are traditionally used with transgenerational theories, such as Bowen's family systems theory (Platt & Skowron, 2013), though they can be processed with many different guiding theories (Chrzastowski, 2011; Kuehl, 1995, 1996; Weiss et al., 2010). Using a Bowen family systems framework, therapists may use cultural genograms to explore intergenerational and cultural patterns that may influence the system (Brown, 1999, Gehart, 2014). A key concept from Bowen's work, differentiation of self, can be an integral part of the cultural genogram as it helps to identify themes and patterns in relationships that influence one's ability to regulate their state of being within the family system.

DOI: 10.4324/9781003330912-54

For example, therapists may explore intergenerational cultural patterns, the process of acculturation, and how they relate to the Bowenian themes of autonomy and togetherness (Brown, 1999; Erdem & Safi, 2018; Gehart, 2014).

Play genograms engage children, adolescents, and families in these discussions in a playful way that captures and maintains attention. Cultural play genograms support children, adolescents, and families in gaining insight about their cultural identity and the way in which it relates to beliefs, values, and relationships within the family system (Gil, 2016). Though toys typically used in the creation of play genograms in in-person therapy may not be available for use in teletherapy, clip art and other digital images may be used in online therapy to support a digitized version of play genograms (Cobb, 2024). The following setup and instructions are based on Cobb's (2024) digital play genogram and Gil's (2016) cultural play genogram interventions. Processing questions are grounded in Bowen's family systems theory but may be adapted for use with any approach.

Setup

1. ***Place basic shapes necessary for the creation of a genogram in a digital file.*** Basic shapes are available in a PowerPoint file that accompanies this book. PowerPoint is a convenient platform for use with this activity, though you may use any preferred software. If you already know the composition of the family, prepare the genogram prior to the session in which you plan to conduct the activity. At a minimum, the genogram should include children in the household, the children's parents, and grandparents.
2. ***Compile a digital file with a variety of images.*** Include images that represent various cultural and faith traditions, especially those that may be relevant to the family system with which you plan to do this activity. These images will be used to represent each member of the family depicted on the genogram. A unique benefit of conducting a digital genogram is that additional images may be added at no cost, and available images may easily be tailored to the needs of each client. Examples of cultural constructs may include symbols for: language/communication, rituals/traditions, cuisine, arts/literature/music, beliefs, values, religious/spiritual practices, clothing, historical/legacy traditions, and identity formation. Some images are included in the supplemental materials that accompany this book. Add to these images as you see fit.

   Alternatively, some clients could be asked to find their own images for the activity. However, this would require more left-brain cognitive processing than right-brain metaphorical/creative processing and may feel overwhelming for some people. Use best judgment in deciding whether to ask clients to search for images or simply have them choose from images that you provide.

Instructions

1. ***Explain what a genogram is.*** For example, you might say, "A genogram is a visual tool used to identify relationships across multiple generations that can help me better understand you and your family. It can be used to help you learn more about your family too!"
2. ***Share your screen.*** Show the image of the genogram that you created prior to the session. If you didn't create the genogram prior to the session, create the genogram with the assistance of the family.
3. ***Ask if the genogram needs any changes.*** Make changes as necessary.

4. ***Display images on your screen.*** You may not be able to have all images visible at once. Make as many images visible at once as you can, while still allowing clients to have a clear view of them. Scroll through additional images as needed. Alternatively, you may skip to the next step if you decide that it would be better for clients to provide their own images.
5. ***Invite clients to "pick something...that best show(s) the lessons you have learned about culture from each member of your family, including yourself"*** (Gil, 2016, p. 187). Consider starting with the youngest member present or the person who typically speaks less. You may make modifications to this prompt to explore more specific aspects of a client's culture. For example, you might ask clients to "pick something for each member of your family, including yourself, that represents ways in your family has stayed connected with the country from which your grandparents were born."
6. ***Ask the first participant to guide you on what images you should put on the genogram for each member of the family.*** As each image is selected, place the images on or adjacent to the shape representing the person that the image was selected for.
7. ***Repeat the process for each person.*** Go through the same process with the next person and continue until all members in the family have selected images.
8. ***Verify with the family that everyone had a chance to share everything that they wanted.*** Make any additions or changes as needed.
9. ***Keep a copy of the genogram in the client's file.*** Rather than simply saving an image of the genogram, save the original file so clients can make changes or add to it in subsequent sessions.

Throughout the process, reflect what you see clients select and what they say if they choose to share information about what they selected and why.

Processing

Once the genogram has been made, ask open-ended questions to explore concepts such as values, culture, identity formation, impeding family patterns, and the impact of culture on structural organization.

Begin by using the metaphor of the images. By focusing on metaphors, rather than asking clients to explain why they selected each image, the activity remains playful and allows right-brain creative processing. Then, you may consider asking about the metaphorical nature of the images selected as it relates to the family's culture.

Questions asked may also be informed by your guiding theory. The following example processing questions are grounded in Bowen's theory to support in the process of assessing differentiation and identifying transgenerational patterns.

- How do the [images selected for one generation of the family] get along with the [images selected for another generation of the family]?
- What do the [images selected for one generation of the family] [think/feel/believe] about the [images selected for another generation of the family]?
- What do the [images selected for one generation of the family] [think/feel/believe] about themselves?
- Do any of the images included here have cultural [meaning/value/significance] for you?

- How is this [meaning/value/significance] similar or different to the [meaning/value/significance] that it has for others in your family?
- How has the [meaning/value/significance] [changed/stayed the same] throughout the generations of your family?

Vignette

Julia (36), Brenda (13), Roberto (11), and Consuelo (8) presented in teletherapy following the death of Tony (38), the children's father and Julia's husband, after a tragic car accident. Following Tony's death, Julia's mother, Ms. Sanchez (59), moved from Mexico to live with the family and help with the kids, though she was not present in therapy.

Initial therapy sessions focused on the family's grief surrounding the loss of Tony, though it became apparent that the family had additional concerns about their grandmother's role in the household and her current conflict with Julia. According to the children, their mom and grandmother fought a lot and their grandmother was frequently upset about things like them not going to church enough or eating the right foods. The therapist hypothesized that the shift in family roles, paired with differences in acculturation between Ms. Sanchez and the rest of the family, may have been resulting in the conflict described by the children and asked the family if they might be open to inviting their grandmother to join them in therapy. Though they were initially hesitant to thinking anything would work, they agreed to invite her, saying that they guessed it wouldn't hurt.

The next session, Ms. Sanchez joined the family in their teletherapy session. The therapist introduced themself to her and provided psychoeducation about the use of genograms and how creating one might be helpful for getting to know their family a little better, especially since Ms. Sanchez was there that day to help. Ms. Sanchez appeared bright-eyed in response to the prospect of sharing more about her family.

The therapist proceeded to share her screen and show a basic genogram that was created prior to that day's session, given information that the therapist had already gathered. The therapist said that they would like to start with those shown on the genogram and that if they had time later they might add on more members of the family.

The therapist then displayed the images that they had prepared in advance of the session and said that they would like them to look at these images and "Each pick something that best represents the lessons you have learned about family and culture from each family member." As family members selected images for their genogram (see Figure 43.1), the therapist simply listened and placed the images where each member of the family wanted them to go. However, they often voluntarily shared information about their reasoning for why they selected certain images.

For Brenda, the family chose images of an angel, a sheep, a fish, and a cross. Ms. Sanchez explained that Brenda was her little angel and that she was reminded of the importance of doing good for one another by witnessing her granddaughter's acts of kindness toward others. Roberto and Consuelo shared that Brenda would often follow their grandmother's lead and go to church with her. Brenda agreed that she often tried to keep the peace, which she shared is important in families, and that's why she chose a dove with an olive branch for herself.

Images selected by the rest of the family for Roberto included a sailboat, a bandage with a heart on it, and two sets of hearts. The family all agreed that Roberto was willing to explore and try new things related to their family's Mexican heritage, though he also had an affinity for American culture. Roberto chose a lion for himself. He said that he was brave in that way. And yet, he was loving and wanted to care for others in the family. The family discussed that maybe they could be a little more like Roberto

Figure 43.1 Digital cultural play genogram. Credit: Dr. Christine Walsh Borst and Rebecca A. Cobb.

in the sense that they didn't have to choose one or the other. They could find ways to incorporate their Mexican heritage with their American roots in ways that felt true to them.

Images selected by the rest of the family for Consuelo included a set of hearts, glasses, a graduation cap, and an owl. The family shared that Consuelo was young, but he was an old soul. He was smart and taught them about the importance of learning more about their history and culture. Consuelo agreed that he was a bit of a bookworm, which was the image that he chose for himself, and he had become more interested in celebrating Mexican holidays since their dad had passed, especially Día de los Muertos. He shared that it helped him feel closer to their dad since he died, especially since their dad had always been the one to talk to them about the holidays when they happened. He shared that he didn't want to bring it up with their mom though because he didn't want to make her sad.

For Tony, the family chose images of hearts, candles, a gravestone, and Jesus. The family told stories about Tony's deep faith in God and his loving heart.

For Ms. Sanchez, depicted as "Abuela" on the genogram, the children chose a cross, a picture of Mary, and a phone. They shared that Abuela was a devout Catholic and that they learned about the importance of faith from her, their Abuelo, and their dad. Brenda shared that Abuela also helped them stay connected with the rest of their family by Facetiming their aunts, uncles, and cousins in Mexico so they could talk with them. Julia agreed that her mother taught her the importance staying connected with family and explained that was why she chose the glue for her. Ms. Sanchez appeared pleased to know that her family realized the importance of these things because of her and said that she chose hands in prayer for herself because she often prays for her family and for them to have strong faith and connection with one another.

The children said that they didn't know Abuelo since he had died before they were born, but Julia and Ms. Sanchez chose images of a cross and hearts for him because of his deep faith and love for their family. They shared how much he would have loved the children and how sad they were that they never got to meet him. Consuelo commented that it was nice to hear about him and that he would like to know more. Brenda and Roberto agreed.

For Julia, the children chose a watchful eye, a strong woman, and Lady Liberty for their mom. They said that she was strong and always watching out for their family and for what was right, which was important. Ms. Sanchez initially selected an image of a trash can with images of religious symbols in it, but when it came time for her to share she said that she had changed her mind and agreed with what the kids had selected for her. Julia's eyes welled with tears. She shared that she chose the apple for herself because she was a bit like Eve in the sense of pushing the boundaries of their faith and culture, but that it was important to her nonetheless. She shared that it had become increasingly hard for her to connect with their heritage in the absence of Tony because he had been the leader of the family in so many ways that related to their faith and culture, and she had been angry with God for what had happened to him.

In this session, the family took the initiative of processing much of the genogram on their own, though the therapist encouraged additional processing through the metaphor of the images on the genogram. They inquired about the ways in which the hearts were connected and how the candles continued to shine light on the others. They asked what it was like for the dove to keep the peace, wondered how the owl shared wisdom, asked if the sailboat ever took the others on adventures, asked what it was like for Lady Liberty to get help from Mary, and wondered if Mary ever gained strength from Lady Liberty.

Conversations naturally evolved to discussing ways in which the family might honor Tony in ways that he would have appreciated, which included each family member taking on different roles that he had assumed in participating in religious holidays and cultural celebrations. Though Julia was still angry with God for what had happened, she softened to the idea of participating in their old traditions as a way of honoring and remembering her husband, and Ms. Sanchez began to soften toward Julia with a greater understanding of the ways in which her grief was impacting her.

Suggestions for Follow-Up

If the genogram was conducted initially with just one member of the family, subsequent sessions including more members of the family may allow other people from the client system to add on to the genogram and participate in the activity. When this is done, ask clients who created the initial genogram and if they would like you to use the genogram that they already created as a starting point or if they would like to start over. This allows clients the option of choosing new images if they have new ideas for images that they would like to select or if they would rather not share the initial images that they chose with other members of the family. When working with more than one person, make note of which clients select which objects for each family member to facilitate further processing (Gil, 2015).

Contraindications

This activity may not be feasible for clients who attend teletherapy from a cell phone or tablet, as clients may have a hard time seeing images on a small screen.

References

Brown, J. (1999). Bowen family systems: Theory and practice: Illustration and critique. *Australian and New Zealand Journal of Family Therapy, 20*(2), 94–103. https://doi.org/10.1002/j.1467-8438.1999.tb00363.x

Chrzastowski, S. K. (2011). A narrative perspective on genograms: Revisiting classical family therapy models. *Clinical Child Psychology and Psychiatry, 16*(4), 635–644. https://doi.org/10.1177/1359104511400966

Cobb, R. A. (2024). Digital play genograms. In R. A. Cobb (Ed.), *The therapist's notebook for systemic teletherapy: Creative interventions for online therapy* (pp. 189–194). Routledge. https://doi.org/10.4324/9781003289920-36

Erdem, G., & Safi, O. A. (2018). The cultural lens approach to Bowen family systems theory: Contributions of Family Change Theory. *Journal of Family Theory and Review, 10*(2), 469–483. https://doi.org/10.1111/jftr.12258

Falicov, C. (2014). *Latino families in therapy* (2nd ed.). Guilford Press.

Gehart, D. (2014). *Mastering competencies in family therapy* (2nd ed.). Cengage.

Gil, E. (2015). Individual and family play genograms. In C. S. Sori, L. L. Hecker, & M. E. Bachenberg (Eds.) *The therapist's notebook for children and adolescents* (2nd ed., pp. 13–20). Routledge.

Gil, E. (2016). The use of the cultural play genogram. In C. S. Sori, L. L. Hecker, & M. E. Bachenberg (Eds.), *The therapist's notebook for children and adolescents* (2nd ed., pp. 186–193). Routledge.

Kuehl, B. P. (1995). The solution-oriented genogram: A collaborative approach. *Journal of Marital and Family Therapy, 21*(3), 239–250. https://doi.org/10.1111/j.1752-0606.1995.tb00159.x

Kuehl, B. P. (1996). The use of genograms with solution-based and narrative therapies. *The Family Journal, 4*(1), 5–11. https://doi.org/10.1177/1066480796041002

McGoldrick, M. (2016). *The genogram casebook: A clinical companion to genograms: Assessment and intervention.* W.W. Norton.

McGoldrick, M., Gerson, R., Petry, S., & Gil, E. (2020). Family play genograms. In M. McGoldrick, R. Gerson, & S. Petry (Eds.), *Genograms: Assessment and treatment* (4th ed., pp. 322–243). Norton.

Platt, L. F., & Skowron, E. A. (2013). The family genogram interview: Reliability and validity of a new interview protocol. *The Family Journal, 21*(1), 35–45. https://doi.org/10.1177/1066480712456817

Weiss, E. L., Coll, J. E., Gerbauer, J., Smiley, K., & Carillo, E. (2010). The military genogram: A solution-focused approach for building resiliency in service members and their families. *The Family Journal, 18*(4), 395–406. https://doi.org/10.1177/1066480710378479

CHAPTER 44

WHERE I'M FROM

A THERAPEUTIC POETIC JOURNEY ACROSS CULTURES

Tiffany Alexis Leal, Ying-Shui Wang, and Rebecca A. Cobb

Materials for Therapists and Clients: "Where I'm From" poem template.

Objective

Poetry has been used in therapeutic settings with children and adolescents to assist in identifying, expressing, and expanding on thoughts, feelings, and experiences (e.g., Leal et al., 2024). The following offers instructions on how to use the "Where I'm From" poem template in teletherapy to support clients in identifying who they are, connect with where they're from, and share this story with others. This intervention can be particularly powerful for supporting clients in the discussion of cultural and/or spiritual/religious identity.

Rationale for Use

"Where I'm From" is a poem and writing prompt created by George Ella Lyon (1999), a preeminent Appalachian poet, that encourages the creation of a poem about the people, things, and events that have been integral to the development of one's being. The prompt has been adapted to fill in the blank template formats that have allowed people across the world to easily create their own version of the poem. The "Where I'm From" poem allows people to reclaim their voices and express their own lived experiences, which can be incredibly empowering, especially for those who otherwise feel marginalized or silenced. The "Where I'm From" poem template has been utilized in refugee camps, juvenile detention centers, prisons, and in educational environments as a means to address hate crimes and discrimination, share aspects of one's culture, and celebrate diversity (Lyon, 2006).

Children and adolescents often struggle to directly express complex emotions and experiences. Writing poetry can be therapeutic and help with self-expression (Garbisch, 2020). Poetic inquiry can also be helpful in exploring identity, especially for those with complex backgrounds, like transracial adoptees (Garbisch, 2020). In teletherapy, the "Where I'm From" poem template can be used to help children and adolescents explore and express their personal histories and cultural identities in a structured, yet flexible way. Writing and reflecting on their own poem about who they are allows

DOI: 10.4324/9781003330912-55

children and adolescents to navigate identity formation and integrate their experiences into a coherent narrative. This process aids in identity development and promotes personal growth and healing. When working with families, therapists may have each member of the family create their own version of the poem and then share them with one another to facilitate connection and understanding.

The following provides guidance on how to use the "Where I'm From" poem in teletherapy with children, adolescents, and their families to help clients identify who they are, connect with where they're from, and share this story with others. This intervention fits particularly well with narrative therapy, which suggests that the stories we tell about ourselves and those we hear from others shape who we are and how we see the world, though it can be applied with many different theoretical orientations.

Setup

1. ***Identify "Where I'm From" poem templates for use in therapy.*** There are different variations of the "Where I'm From" poem template available on the internet. Some have more detailed prompts, while others leave more room for interpretation.
2. ***Adapt the template as needed.*** You can also use the template for the "Where I'm From" poem to create your own prompts to fit the needs of different clients and presenting problems. Either choose a template that feels most fitting given the needs of each client or provide clients with options. Bilingual therapists can adapt the "Where I'm From" template into different languages.

Instructions

1. ***Introduce to clients the idea of creating a poem about who they are.*** Tell clients that a template of the poem will be provided to assist them in writing their "Where I'm From" poem. This draft contains cues and prompts. They are simply to fill in the blanks. Share with clients that the prompts are only suggestions, they do not need to follow the cues, and they can respond in any way that they would like. The purpose of the cues and prompts is only to assist them in their creative writing process. Yet, poetry might not be a fitting intervention for all clients. If clients do not express interest, provide options for other activities.
2. ***Identify the preferred method of poem completion.*** Some templates of the "Where I'm From" poem are available in PDF format. Clients may print these and fill them in by hand. Alternatively, you can screen share a template on your computer and type each client's verbal responses to prompts. You can also find a "Where I'm From" or "I Am From" poem generator on the internet that clients can use. With a poem generator, clients can simply type their response to each prompt into a textbox. Once completed, the generator will display a completed version of their personalized poem that clients can then share using the screen share function on the teletherapy platform. If clients prefer to use a poem generator, explain that the website is not likely HIPAA-consistent, so there is a possibility that others can see their poem. If the generator asks for a name to be entered as one of the prompts, share that they can either leave this blank or enter a pseudonym.
3. ***Share your screen.*** Open the selected "Where I'm From" template and share your screen to provide a visual image of what clients can expect.
4. ***Send clients the template.*** If you have created your own template, email this to clients. If you are using a preexisting template available over the internet, share a link via the chat function of the teletherapy platform.

5. ***Invite clients to create their poem(s).*** Offer assistance as needed. If clients are bilingual, explain that they are welcome to write their responses in whatever language feels best for them. Some clients prefer to write their poems in a combination of more than one language. This is great too! Allow silence and provide appropriate reflections as clients create their poems.
6. ***Read the poem.*** Ask clients if they would like to read their poem aloud or if they prefer that you read the poem silently or out loud. Proceed according to each client's request. If clients write their poem in a language other than one that you are familiar with, you may ask them to read it first in the language in which they wrote it, and then in a language that you will understand. Listen with a posture of curiosity and wonder.
7. ***Save the poem(s).*** Ask clients if they are comfortable with your saving a copy of their poem to their file for use in future sessions. If clients have created their poem using a poem generator, they may save a screenshot of it and email it to you. If they printed a template and hand wrote their responses, they can take a picture of the page and email it to you. If the poem was created on your own device, save the poem to the client's file and ask them if they would like you to email it to them. Share the file with them if requested.

Processing

Once clients have shared their poem(s), process the activity using the following questions:

Individual Processing

- What prompts came easily to you?
- What prompts were challenging to identify a response to?
- Did any stories emerge in the creation of your poem that surprised you?
- Did any memories emerge in the creation of your poem that you had forgotten about?
- Did you learn anything new about yourself from this activity? If so, what?
- Which parts of your poem feel most connected to your sense of identity?
- Are there aspects of your poem that challenge how you usually think about yourself and your cultural identity?

Family Processing

- How did it feel to share and listen to each other's poems?
- What similarities do you notice between your poem and your [sister/brother/mom/dad/etc.]'s poem?
- What differences do you notice between your poem and your [sister/brother/mom/dad/etc.]'s poem?
- What new understandings or appreciations have emerged for one another after hearing their poem(s)?
- How might you create new traditions or practices that honor and integrate the diverse [cultural/religious/spiritual] backgrounds within your family?

Vignette

Feng-Yi (15) presented in teletherapy feeling disconnected from her culture and struggling with her identity. She had been adopted from Taiwan three years ago and was currently living in the United States with her adoptive family. Her sister, Martha (18), had been adopted from Mexico six years prior. The siblings reported having a close relationship. Her adoptive father, John (50), and mother, Ann (48), identified as a Caucasian, upper-middle-class, heterosexual couple who had been married for 15 years.

Ann and John strived to help each of their daughters maintain a connection to their cultural roots and identities. Feng-Yi, however, was grappling with issues of identity and belonging and was feeling disconnected from her Taiwanese heritage despite the family's best efforts. As a result, Feng-Yi expressed feelings of isolation and confusion about her identity. She reported that she struggled with integrating her Taiwanese background with her current life in the U.S. This manifested in her withdrawing from family activities and showing signs of anxiety when her cultural background was discussed. Feng-Yi, along with her family, decided to seek therapy. They corroborated Feng-Yi's presenting concerns and agreed to come to therapy as a family.

In the first session, Feng-Yi shared that she struggled with "feeling from her culture." She questioned, "Who am I now? I'm happy with my family. But I don't feel like I belong." The therapist also inquired about the cultural and religious/spiritual backgrounds of each family member as a way of getting to know each of them better.

In the second session, the therapist summarized themes from their first meeting. The therapist shared that it sounded like each of them had very different cultural backgrounds and upbringings. They introduced the idea of a poetry activity that might help to explore each of their individual identities and cultural backgrounds a bit more. The family agreed and the therapist presented the clients with several options for creating their poems.

Feng-Yi, Martha, and John created their poems using a PDF template for an "I Am From" poem available on the internet. They each printed a copy of the worksheet and filled in the blanks with pens and markers. Ann, who appeared less comfortable than the others with writing poetry, wrote her poem using a template available at freeology.com (Freeology, 2012). This allowed her to simply type her responses into a website, click a button, and have the website generate her final version of the poem. These templates provided prompts for "I Am From" poems similar to Lyon's "Where I'm From" poem, but with slightly different prompts.

The therapist invited each member to read their poems out loud to one another. Martha shared hers first, followed by Feng-Yi, John, and Ann. Family members each diligently listened, eyes welled with tears, as others read their poems.

Martha proudly shared her poem with appreciation for her cultural upbringing. Because the family lived so close to Mexico and readily had access to people, food, festivals, and other aspects of Mexican culture, this had been easier for the family to weave into daily life than some of Feng-Yi's traditions.

Martha's Poem

I am from tamales and molcajetes,
From coca and champurrado.
I am from the tropical city of Tampico,
Humid, hot, the scent of street food in the air.
I am from calla lilies and sugarcanes,
Sweet, with deep cultural roots, and immigrants like me.

I am from marigold flowers and posadas,
From Gorham Fajardo and Leal Mendoza.
I am from the hard-working and dreamers,
From "si se puede" and "que Dios te bendiga."
I am from Catholic cathedrals and daily prayers,
Church bells ringing by the hour.
I am from Mexico, mi patria,
From tortillas por kilo, menudo, y enchiladas.
From the promise of a better life al otro lado,
From the sacrifices por el Sueño Americano.
In my backpack, all my belongings I could carry,
Reminders of the pilgrimage my people make.
I hold their stories within me,
As I reach for our American Dream.

Feng-Yi quietly read her poem with a sparkle in her eye when she spoke of objects and traditions that were special to her, and she looked lovingly at her family when she spoke of her new home.

Feng-Yi's Poem

I am from chopsticks and red envelopes,
From Bubble tea and pineapple cakes.
I am from the busy streets of Taipei,
Noisy, vibrant, the scent of night markets lingering in the air.
I am from the banyan trees,
Strong, ancient roots that hold firm to the earth.
I am from Lunar New Year celebrations and midnight prayers,
From Mei-Ling and Huang.
I am from the meticulous and the hard-working,
From "Study hard" and "Be respectful."
I am from Buddhist temples,
Incense smoke curling upwards, prayers whispered softly.
I am from Taiwan, the island of my birth,
From dumplings and stinky tofu.
From the story of how my birth mother left me at the orphanage gate,
From the kind hands that cared for me.
In my new home, framed pictures rest on a wooden mantel,
Reminders of my journey, my past intertwined with my present.
I am from these memories,
Threads of my identity, weaving my Taiwanese roots with my American family.

John read his poem with confidence and appeared pleased to share this bit about himself with others in the family. Martha commented that she didn't know their dad was such a talented poet!

John's Poem

I am from surfboards and sandy flip-flops,
From Coca-Cola and Jiffy Pop.
I am from the vibrant suburbs of Los Angeles,

Warm, welcoming, the scent of jasmine in the night air.
I am from lemon trees,
Bright, fragrant fruits hanging heavy.
I am from backyard cookouts and Christmas carols,
From Michael and Linda.
I am from the driven and the nurturing,
From "Dream big" and "Love deeply."
I am from Easter egg hunts and Christmas Eve services,
The flicker of candlelight in the church.
I am from Los Angeles, with roots in England and Spain,
From tacos and lasagna.
From the tale of my grandmother's journey across the Atlantic,
From the family gatherings that stretched into the night.
On the bookshelf, albums filled with old photos,
Carefully curated, telling the story of our family.
These pictures keep our history alive,
Binding us together across generations and miles.

Ann, who had been a bit more hesitant to write a poem, began crying as she read a line about her own mom, who had struggled with alcoholism, leaving hidden notes for her to find, which she kept, but hadn't looked at since she had died.

Ann's Poem

I am from television,
From My Little Ponies and real horses.
I am from comfort,
And free roaming streets.
I am from pepper trees,
Whose arms held me high above the earth.
I am from Nintendo and Sega,
From Bill and Penny,
And from drugs and alcohol,
From lined yellow paper with smiley faces and my mom's handwriting,
Hidden in the barbeque on the back patio.
I am from sushi and TV dinners,
From suicide,
From success,
And from freedom.
I am from moments of Barbie dolls and Mille Bornes, of innocence, and of open armed love.

Other members of the family looked a little surprised to hear some of the things that Ann had written about in her poem. They each expressed gratitude for her sharing and wanted to know more.

The therapist worked with Feng-Yi and her family on processing their emotions and new understandings of each family member's identity and experience. The therapist then supported the family in discussing ways in which to help Feng-Yi feel more connected to her cultural upbringing, and ways in which they might create new traditions that honor and integrate the diverse cultural backgrounds within their family. Though they seemed like little things, Ann remembered the importance of things like note writing and began leaving little notes around the house for her daughters. She drew marigolds on Martha's notes and banyan trees on Feng-Yi's notes. The family also made a point of eating with chopsticks at dinner more often and even tried it one evening with John's mom's lasagna recipe. The family reported that it was messy, mostly because everyone ended up eating with their hands, but that they had fun trying. Acknowledging each of their own unique identities and histories, they identified the sense of belonging that they had created with one another, a unique blend of culture and tradition, all their own.

Suggestions for Follow-Up

In subsequent sessions, you can work with families to create a "We Are From" poem. This can help clients identify parts of their identities and stories that are unique to each person, and then collaboratively identify a shared story. Clients may either work together to create an entirely new poem that expresses their shared story, or they may interweave lines of each of their poems to create a shared story through the process of relational poetry (Kumsa, 2007; Taiwo, 2011).

You might also ask if clients have shared their poem(s) with others since they wrote them. If the poems contain preferred stories, sharing them with others may serve as a form of outsider witnessing (Combs & Freedman, 2012), which may help to strengthen preferred stories. When this occurs, discuss with clients their experience of sharing their poem(s) with others.

Additionally, you may offer the same activity to clients at later stages of therapy. If you save copies of original poems in client files, you can support them in comparing their poems to see what new stories have emerged with time.

Contraindications

Younger children may require more guidance and simpler prompts when engaging in this activity. The poem's complexity should match the client's developmental level. If clients cannot read, read the prompts aloud to them and support them in providing verbal responses while you write them down. After the completion of the poem, you can read it aloud to them. Alternatively, clients can use clip art, photographs, or draw on the whiteboard function of the teletherapy platform as a means of responding to prompts without written words. For very young children, visual aids or storytelling methods might be more appropriate.

References

Combs, G., & Freedman, J. (2012). Narrative, poststructuralism, and social justice: Current practices in narrative therapy. *The Counseling Psychologist, 40*(7), 1033–1060. https://doi.org/10.1177/0011000012460662

Freeology. (2012). *I am from poem.* Freeology free worksheets and more since 2001. https://freeology.com/worksheet-creator/poetry/i-am-from-poem/#google_vignette

Garbisch, A. J. (2020). Constructing identity by writing roots into life: A poetic-narrative autoethnography. *Journal of Poetry Therapy, 34*(1), 37–47. https://doi.org/10.1080/08893675.2020.1846865

Kumsa, M. K. (2007). The space between. *Qualitative Social Work, 6*(4), 489–493. https://doi.org/10.1177/1473325007083360

Leal, T. A., Downes, M. P., & Cobb, R. A. (2024). Teletherapy poetry: A narrative approach. In R. A. Cobb (Ed.), *The therapist's notebook for systemic teletherapy: Creative interventions for effective online therapy* (pp. 91–97). Routledge.

Lyon, G. E. (1999). *Where I'm from: Where poems come from*. Absey & Co.

Lyon, G. E. (2006). *Where I'm From*. George Ella Lyon, writer and teacher. http://www.georgeellalyon.com/where.html

Taiwo, A. (2011). Relational poetry in the expression of social identity: Creating interweaving dialogues. *Qualitative Social Work, 12*(2), 215–228. https://doi.org/10.1177/1473325011425892

CHAPTER 45

PUPPET PLAY TELENOVELA

Jacqueline Florian

Materials for Therapists: None.

Materials for Clients: Puppets. Alternatively, clients may create their own puppets using socks or small paper bags and other crafting materials.

Objective

Puppets have been used for therapeutic assessment and intervention with children, adolescents, and families for a variety of presenting problems (Bromfield, 1995). This chapter provides instructions for guiding clients in creating a puppet play telenovela in teletherapy to support in re-authoring problem-filled narratives into preferred stories.

Rationale for Use

Puppetry has been used in narrative therapy to support the process of externalization (Butler et al., 2009; Guterman & Martin, 2016; Nutting, 2015), allowing clients to objectify and personify problems in existing narratives (White & Epston, 1990). The use of puppets as objects representing externalized problems allows clients to give their problem life through the puppet (Butler et al., 2009) and ultimately separate themselves from the problem, rather than see it as part of their identity. As clients externalize problems, they gain freedom to fight against their problems and re-author their lives with preferred narratives (Freedman & Combs, 1996).

Telenovelas, or dramas, are popular in many cultures such as Central American/Latinx, Korean, and Turkish cultures. Telenovelas can provide a way to connect and keep in touch with family who may live far away. The following intervention applies common characteristics of telenovelas to help families engage in therapeutic puppet play in teletherapy sessions. By creating their own telenovela with the family "problem" as one of the leading characters and acting it out for the therapist using puppets, clients are offered the opportunity to re-author their problem-filled narrative and ultimately either allow the "problem" a less leading role or have it leave the "show" entirely. This intervention typically takes two sessions to complete.

DOI: 10.4324/9781003330912-56

Setup

The following specifies the setup required to implement puppet play telenovelas.

1. ***Discuss telenovelas.*** Inquire about the family's knowledge of and experience with telenovelas. If the family has an interest in this topic, engage them in a conversation regarding soap opera storylines and common themes that may be tied to their own presenting problems. In telenovelas, it is common to see themes related to blended families, family secrets, lost love, and parent-child conflict.
2. ***Introduce the intervention.*** Ask clients if they might be interested in creating their own telenovela using puppets to act out their own family's relationship with their problem. Explain that the problem gets to be its own character in the show and that this can help to gain new perspectives and help come up with new ways to fight against the problem.
3. ***Ask clients if they have access to hand puppets.*** If they do, assess the number and variety of puppets available. Having an abundance of puppets to choose from allows clients to choose at least one based on an unconscious or conscious representation of the situation at hand (Bromfield, 1995) and a puppet that will be representative of the problem. If the number of puppets available is limited or none are available, which is more likely than not, clients can create their own puppets (see Chapter 7).
4. ***Invite the family to create puppet characters.*** If the family doesn't already have enough puppets to do the show, allow them about 20 minutes to create their puppets. Alternatively, clients can create their puppets between sessions as a homework assignment. Prompt the family to think of all the characters involved in the problem and to create puppets that will embody those personalities and characters. If the family creates their puppets in session, observe how the family interacts with one another during their creation and provide support as needed. Each family member should have at least one puppet representing their own character. In addition, specify that the problem being discussed should also have its own puppet, meaning one family member will be playing the role of two puppets (i.e., their own preferred character and that of the externalized problem).
5. ***Explain the next steps.*** Tell the family that in the next session, they will be coming up with a storyline for their telenovela and that they will be acting it out for you. Request that an adult set aside the puppets that they created and bring them with them at the start of the next meeting. If anyone would like to continue working on their puppets between sessions, this is okay too!

Instructions

The following instructions should be followed in the next session.

1. ***Inform clients that they have about 15 minutes to develop a storyline for their telenovela.*** Remind the family that the storyline can follow themes like those in telenovelas if they feel that it fits their situation. Encourage the family to liken the puppet representing their problem to the villain in their story. Ensure that the villain is not likened to an actual person in their family. Rather, the villain should represent an externalization of the family's problem (e.g., fear, jealousy, anger). Explain that the family should create their telenovela based on how the villain puppet plays a role in their life. If the family would like to name their puppets, based on the storyline created, they can do so now. This can help you assess the influence of each character on the problem/villain's behavior. The first time that the family tells their story, you might leave it at that to help

assess how the family will have the other characters act in relation to one another and the problem. For a more specific prompt, or in subsequent telenovela puppet plays, you might say something like "I wonder how the other characters will join together to fight against the problem." Remind the family that in addition to the villain in the telenovela, each of them will also have at least one puppet that they will voice. One person in the family will voice both the villain and their own puppet character. Alternatively, family members may take turns voicing the villain.

2. ***Determine what language the puppets will be communicating in.*** It may be preferable for clients to act out their story in their preferred language. However, for you to have a clear understanding of what's going on while the play is being acted out, it is best that you be fluent in the language that the family will be communicating in. Alternatively, families could act out the telenovela twice, once in their preferred language, and once in a language that you will understand.
3. ***Obtain the family's permission to record the session.*** Explain that many clients enjoy seeing the play played back to them and that this can be a useful tool that the family can look back on in future sessions. Only record the telenovela if every member of the family willingly consents to recording it.
4. ***Act out the telenovela.*** Explain that the family will have about 15 minutes to act out their play. Set the scene for everyone to start and let the family know that you will be pretending to watch this telenovela on your "television." You might even say, "I can't wait to see what happens in today's episode!" As the family acts out the story, silently observe while it takes place, as if you were watching on your own streaming device. It's preferable to allow clients to act out their play without interruption. However, you may "pause" the telenovela if you notice that family members are beginning to quarrel over the direction that the story is taking or if someone has been triggered and needs to engage in coping techniques.
5. ***End the "episode."*** Once the telenovela has reached a climatic point, you can "pause" the story, reminding them that telenovelas often leave unfinished story lines at the end of an episode, and that they can continue the story next week. If you have a remote control available, you may even hold it up to the screen to playfully make the cue to pause more overt. Ensure that you save time for processing before the session ends.
6. ***Save the file.*** If the family consented to having the telenovela recorded, save it to the client's file.
7. ***Save the puppets.*** Ask an adult in the family to keep the puppets in a safe place for future therapeutic use.

Processing

After the conclusion of the telenovela and before the session has ended, ask processing questions within the metaphor of the puppets to help clients further externalize the problem, identify unique outcomes, and re-write their telenovela in their preferred manner. Questions may be asked of the clients themselves, or they may be asked directly to the puppets that were in the telenovela.

Externalizing

- Does anyone have any questions for [name of the problem puppet]?
- How do you think [name of puppet] felt about [name of the problem puppet]?
- How do you think [name of the problem puppet] impacted the relationships between other characters in the story?

Unique Outcomes

- Was there ever a time when [name of the problem puppet] wasn't present or didn't have as big of a part of the story? If so, what else was happening during those times?
- What helped [names of puppets] not let [name of the problem puppet] have control of the story?

Re-authoring

- If [name of the problem puppet] didn't have as big of a role in the story, what do you think that might look like?
- How might the other characters work together to fight against [name of the problem puppet]?
- Would you like to do another episode next week to make this happen?

Vignette

Cynthia (10) was accompanied to teletherapy by her parents, Oscar (45) and Elvia (42). Oscar and Elvia expressed concerns regarding Cynthia's behavior and anger. They were concerned that Cynthia's aggression and impulsive behaviors would escalate toward her younger sister who was one year old. They said that Cynthia was well-behaved in most settings but had instances when she got angry with other children at school. Most recently, she pushed a classmate on the playground but would not explain why she did it other than she did not like her classmate. The parents expressed that this behavior was not normal for Cynthia and that she had never been an "angry kid" before this.

The therapist explained to the family that she would like to try an intervention to understand more about what was going on. The therapist explained that this intervention would require the parents to participate and would require some creativity on their part. After hearing a brief explanation of the activity, the parents agreed to play their part and consented to recording the show. Elvia showed enthusiasm for the activity, as telenovelas were a way that she stayed connected with her own mother, aunts, and grandmother, who lived in El Salvador. The family indicated that they did not have any puppets available for use in the activity, but they did have some old socks that needed mending. Elivia offered these up for the activity and said that they had some colored markers that they could use to draw on them. The therapist requested that the family gather these materials before their next session. In their next session, they would each create one or two puppets. One of the puppets should represent "anger," though it could be named anything that they wanted, as long as it was a fictional character and didn't represent any member of their family. The other puppets should represent other characters involved in the problem.

In the next session, the family brought the puppets that they had created. The therapist gave them the instructions to "Create a telenovela together in which one of the puppets represents anger. What would it look like if anger were a villain in your story?"

After 15 minutes of discussing this scene for the telenovela, the therapist prepared the family for the start and let the family know that they would pretend to be watching this telenovela on their television and that they couldn't wait to see what happened in today's episode!

Each family member had a puppet that represented themselves. They each also had an additional puppet. Cynthia's second puppet, Rubí, was angry with everyone. Elvia's and Oscar's puppets were named after other children at Cynthia's school. In the family's story, the puppet that represented Cynthia tried playing with the friend puppets, but they often ignored her, saying things like, "No; I won't play with you!" Whenever this happened, Rubí began yelling at all the other puppets and hitting them on the head. This only made the other puppets retreat more. By the end of the story, Rubí was left all alone in one corner of the screen. Cynthia's other puppet was left crying in the other corner of the screen. Although initially unscripted, Oscar's puppet that represented himself approached Cynthi's puppet to comfort her. Elvia's puppet soon joined. Elivia and Oscar then reached out to Cynthia to embrace her, and the show came to an end.

After allowing the family a moment to sit with their emotions, the therapist checked in to see how everyone was doing. They then engaged everyone in a discussion processing their experience with the goal of further externalizing "anger" and figuring out how to help Rubí not take on such a leading role anymore.

Therapist: "I wonder. Does anyone have any questions for Rubí or for Cynthia's other puppet?"

Oscar: "I noticed that any time the friends didn't want to play with Cynthia, Rubí appeared. What makes Rubí appear in those moments?"

Therapist: "Rubí would you be able to tell us what happens for you when others don't want to play with Cynthia?"

Cynthia (as Rubí): "I don't like it when they leave her out! Then she has to play by herself. And I don't think she likes that very much."

Therapist: "Thank you for sharing that with us, Rubí. That must be hard to see Cynthia looking so lonely. Elvia, do you have any questions for Rubí?"

Elvia: "How often does this happen?"

Cynthia (as Rubí): "It happens all the time."

Therapist: "I'm sorry to hear that Cynthia is being left out so often. You know, I also noticed that whenever Rubí appeared and started yelling and hitting the others, the others ran away, and Cynthia was left all alone. I wonder what would be different if Rubí maybe still appeared, was able to keep from yelling and hitting."

Cynthia: "I think the other kids probably wouldn't run away."

Therapist: "I wonder if next week you could put on another show, kind of like the one you did today, but with this slight change to it. How does that sound?"

Cynthia: "I'd like that."

Therapist: "Me too. I can't wait to see what happens in next week's episode!"

In this example, the therapist gave the family an opportunity to externalize anger and talk about anger's influence over the situation. The following week, the family acted out the second episode of their telenovela, and Rubí took on a slightly less leading role as she was able to show herself without scaring off the other characters. As this occurred, Cynthia appeared less lonely, and a friend began to play with her. The family was also able to develop insight into how Cynthia was feeling and find ways in which to support her both emotionally and behaviorally. With time, as anger dissipated, Cynthia began to play more with friends at school and got along better with her family at home, and the family began to re-author their story as a preferred narrative in which anger no longer controlled the situation.

Suggestions for Follow-Up

In future sessions, clients may continue their telenovela, much like chapters from a book or episodes on television. They may use the same puppets and may also create new ones as their story evolves and is re-authored with time. You may begin subsequent sessions with a recap of what happened in the telenovela from the previous week, much like the start of an actual telenovela. Alternatively, if clients consented to recording their telenovela, you may watch the recording of the previous week's telenovela, or parts from it to highlight important points. Help clients notice changes over time by asking questions about character development. Your focus should be to strengthen the preferred alternative narrative so that clients can solidify it. Validate changes that clients and puppets have made over time by providing concrete details of the changes.

Contraindications

Some clients, such as older adolescents and adults, may not resonate with the use of puppetry. Others may not be familiar with or drawn to the idea of telenovelas. In addition, necessary materials may not be available to clients. Offer alternative ideas for intervention when appropriate. For example, if clients demonstrate resistance to the use of puppets or materials are unavailable, you may alter the activity to a storytelling format and clients may draw pictures on the whiteboard function of the teletherapy platform to illustrate their story.

References

Bromfield, R. (1995). The use of puppets in play therapy. *Child and Adolescent Social Work Journal, 12*(6), 435–444. https://doi.org/10.1007/BF01875812

Butler, S., Guterman, J. T., & Rudes, J. (2009). Using puppets with children in narrative therapy to externalize the problem. *Journal of Mental Health Counseling, 31*(3), 225–233. https://doi.org/10.17744/mehc.31.3.f255m86472577522

Freedman, J., & Combs, G. (1996). *Narrative therapy: The social construction of preferred realities*. W. W. Norton & Company.

Guterman, J. T., & Martin, C. V. (2016). Using puppets with aggressive children to externalize the problem in narrative therapy. In A. A. Drewes & C. E. Schaefer (Eds.), *Play therapy in middle childhood* (pp. 135–151). American Psychological Association. https://doi.org/10.1037/14776-008

Nutting, R. (2015). The strength of children in externalizing the effects of chronic illness through narrative puppetry. *Journal of Family Psychotherapy, 26*(9), 9–14. https://doi.org/10.1080/08975353.2015.1002736

White, M., & Epston, D. (1990). *Narrative means to therapeutic ends*. W. W. Norton & Company.

CHAPTER 46

MOKSHA PATAM

INTEGRATION OF AN ANCIENT INDIAN BOARD GAME INTO CULTURALLY RELEVANT TELETHERAPY

Simran K. Uppal and Rebecca A. Cobb

Materials for Therapists: A digital version of Moksha Patam, Snakes and Ladders, or Chutes and Ladders (available at various websites). Alternatively, a photograph of the gameboard for one of these games can be copied and pasted onto a PowerPoint slide to make a customized version of the game and digital dice may be used. One is also included in the supplemental materials that accompany this book.

Materials for Clients: None.

Objective

Moksha Patam is an ancient Indian game also known as Snakes and Ladders. Drawing upon its rich cultural and spiritual significance, this chapter examines how Moksha Patam can be adapted as a teletherapy intervention for children, adolescents, and families to address various therapeutic goals, cultural identity exploration, and the navigation of everyday challenges.

Rationale for Use

Moksha Patam is a traditional Indian board game that serves as a metaphor for the journey of life, illustrating the concept of karma. Unlike its Western adaptation as Snakes and Ladders, which is primarily a racing game ending in the final square, the Indian versions are deeply rooted in moral and spiritual lessons. The game's squares represent moral actions reflecting the karmic journey. Other versions of the game, like the 128-square Vaishnav Gyan Chaupar, span various religious traditions, including Hindu, Jain, and Sufism. Another version known as the "Paramapada Sopanam Pata," is played in Southern Indian states such as Telangana, Andhra Pradesh, Karnataka, and Tamil Nadu (Mukherjee, 2020). These versions emphasize the cyclical nature of life and the importance of virtues, with players navigating through rebirths until they achieve spiritual liberation, or Vaikuntha.

Moksha Patam is played by a minimum of two players. Although there is no strict maximum number of players, the game is most enjoyable with up to four players. The game's overall goal is to ascend from the bottom of the gameboard to the top by taking turns rolling dice and moving game pieces that

DOI: 10.4324/9781003330912-57

represent each player of the game. Ladders depicted on the gameboard symbolize strengths and allow players to move their pieces up. Snakes depicted on the gameboard symbolize challenges and require that players move their pieces down. Gameplay naturally mirrors the journey of personal growth and overcoming adversity.

Board games are beneficial in therapy for children as they mirror real-life developmental tasks and challenges. By observing children's choices, rule-breaking, and play styles, therapists gain insights into their emotional and psychological states (Bellinson, 2013). Engaging in these games allows children to express themselves, work through difficulties, and develop social skills, while therapists learn about and address their underlying issues.

Culturally relevant interventions are essential for meeting the unique needs of each child and engaging families from diverse backgrounds (Peterson et al., 2017). Studies examining the therapeutic benefits of traditional Indian games and cultural interventions suggest that Moksha Patam holds promise as a culturally relevant tool for promoting emotional regulation, resilience, and cultural identity among Indian children and families (Rahman et al., 2020), though the intervention may be applied to families from all cultural backgrounds.

Moksha Patam's narrative-rich gameplay presents an ideal platform for therapeutic exploration, as children engage in interactive play sessions, navigating the board and reflecting on their own life experiences and choices. This process promotes self-awareness, emotional expression, and problem-solving skills within a playful, safe, and supportive environment.

Setup

Prior to playing Moksha Patam with clients, acquire the game and familiarize yourself with the rules of gameplay. You may either access a preexisting digital version of the game, use one that is included in the supplemental materials that accompany this book (see Figure 46.1), or make your own.

To access a preexisting digital version of Moksha Patam, conduct an internet search for "Moksha Patam," "Snakes and Ladders," or "Chutes and Ladders." There is an array of digital variations of the game available on various websites (e.g., Google Play). When selecting which version of the game to use, consider the following:

- ***Advertisements and popups:*** Avoid using games that are on websites or applications that have advertisements and/or popups. These can be distracting for clients or potentially inappropriate depending on the content.
- ***Cultural relevance:*** Moksha Patam is the most culturally relevant version of the game, though it may be more difficult to access if you are physically located in a part of the world that does not commonly use this version of the game.
- ***Client fit:*** If you choose an alternative version of the game (e.g., Snakes and Ladders, Chutes and Ladders), consider the relevance of that version to the clients with whom you intend to play the game. For example, some versions of the game may be easier for younger clients to play than others. Alternatively, some clients may have a fear of snakes and may connect more easily with a version of the game that depicts slides rather than snakes (e.g., Chutes and Ladders).
- ***Number of players:*** Consider the number of players that the game allows to ensure that all members of the client system may engage in gameplay. If you are working with a family system with more members than is typically allowed, you may have clients create teams, use the variation of the game that is included in the supplemental materials that accompany this book, or create your own digitized version of the game.

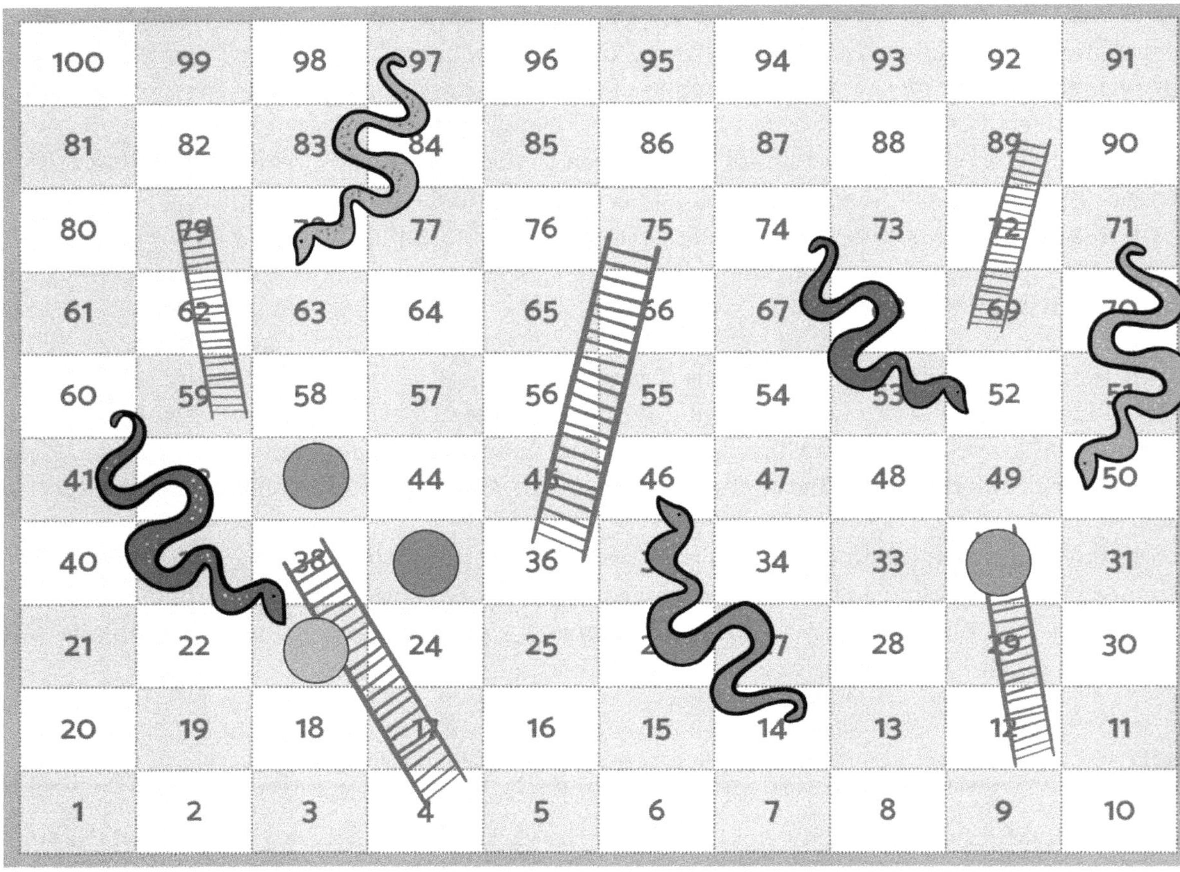

Figure 46.1 Moksha Patam game board. Credit: Simran K. Uppal, Dr. Christine Walsh Borst, and Rebecca A. Cobb.

If you prefer to make your own digitized version of the game, you may do this by following the subsequent steps:

1. ***Acquire an image of the gameboard.*** You may take a photo of a gameboard that you already have or search for preexisting images available on the internet.
2. ***Transfer the image to a PowerPoint slide.*** Expand the image so it fits most of the slide. You may need to change the slide's size or orientation to best fit the gameboard's image.
3. ***Add game pieces.*** You can use simple shapes such as circles and make them different colors. Alternatively, you may choose different shapes or images. You may even allow clients to make their own game pieces by selecting their favorite color, shape, or image to use as their game piece. Some clients may enjoy having their own photo used as a game piece so they can see themselves travel along the board on their journey! If you already have photographs of clients from another activity in this book (e.g., Chapter 26), you may ask clients if they would like to choose one of the photographs from that activity, take a new one, or use an entirely different object for their game piece. A benefit of making your own digitized version of the game is that you can include as many game pieces as you need to be able to include all members in the client system during gameplay. Prepare an extra game piece that you can use if clients want you to play the game with them.
4. ***Identify a website with a six-sided virtual die.*** Search for "six-sided virtual dice roller" or "online six-sided dice roller" and choose your preferred website for virtual dice.

Instructions

The following specifies instructions for this activity.

1. ***Introduce the activity.*** Tell client(s) that you have a game that they might be interested in playing. You might share your screen and show them the game itself, saying: "I have a game here. I'm wondering if you'd like to play it. This is Moksha Patam. Have you played it before?"

   Avoid assuming clients are familiar with the game. If they're unfamiliar with it, you might explain that "It's a bit like Snakes and Ladders or Chutes and Ladders."

   Expand on this by saying, "This is a special journey game that can help us explore different parts of life. You might like it because it's not just about rolling dice and moving tokens. It's like going on an adventure where we'll encounter challenges and victories, just like in real life. Want to give it a try?"

2. ***Provide access to the game.*** If you are using a preexisting digital version of the game, send clients a link to the game through the chat function of your teletherapy platform. If you create your own digital version of the game or use the one included in the supplemental materials that accompany this book (see Figure 46.1), you may move the game pieces for clients and simply send them a link to a website with digital dice. Alternatively, you may send clients a link to a website with digital dice and email the file containing the game that you created. This would allow clients to move game tokens on their own, which may be more engaging for clients. This option, however, may be more time-consuming.

3. ***Explain the rules.*** Explain that to play this game, each player takes turns, beginning at the bottom of the board, on square 1. Players take turns rolling a die to determine how many squares they will move forward. Players move their tokens forward the number of squares indicated by the dice roll. Some squares on the board feature illustrations of snakes or ladders. If a player lands on a square at the bottom of a ladder, they can climb up to the top of the ladder, advancing closer to the final square of the game. Conversely, if a player lands on a square with the head of a snake, they slide down the snake to the square at the snake's tail, setting them back on their journey.

   Depending on the age of the client(s), you might also explain that the values embedded in Moksha Patam align closely with the themes of virtue, karma, and spiritual growth found in Indian philosophy and culture. Ladders represent virtues and positive actions that lead to progress and enlightenment, while snakes symbolize vices and negative consequences that hinder one's spiritual journey.

4. ***Determine order of game play.*** Consider starting with the youngest family member and taking turns in order by age.

5. ***Begin game play.*** Ask the first player to roll the die. The number rolled determines how many squares their token moves forward on the board. Let's say the first player rolls a five. They then move their token five squares forward on the board, following the numbered path. Most digital versions of this game automatically move tokens after the die has been rolled. Once the first player completes their turn, it is the next person's turn to roll the die and move their token.

6. ***End the game.*** The game ends when someone successfully reaches the final square on the board, typically numbered 100. This final square represents liberation or enlightenment (i.e., moksha) and signifies the culmination of the spiritual journey depicted in the game.

   To win the game, a player must roll the exact number needed to land on the final square. For example, if a player is on square 97 and rolls a four, they cannot move forward because they need a roll of exactly three to reach square 100. In this case, the player must wait until they roll a three on their next turn to win the game.

Once a player reaches the final square and wins the game, they are considered to have achieved moksha, symbolizing the attainment of spiritual liberation and the end of the journey. The game typically concludes with congratulations and celebration for the winning player, marking the completion of their quest in Moksha Patam.

End gameplay 10 or 15 minutes before the session is over to allow time for processing.

Processing

Moksha Patam is a game of chance, so clients don't have control over how well they play. This, however, can be likened to many life events that are outside of one's control. Discussion of navigating the ups and downs of life and coping strategies utilized when setbacks occur can support clients in developing strategies for overcoming adversity. The gameboard can also be discussed as it relates to the client's life journey and conceptualized as a scale indicating progress toward identified goals. Solution-focused questions may be used to assess the client's journey. Throughout the game and upon its conclusion, ask processing questions about the client experience. Following is a list of questions that can be asked.

Navigating Ups and Downs

- What was it like for you to climb up the ladder?
- What was it like for you to slide down the snake?
- What was it like for you to see your [mom/dad/sister/brother/etc.] climb up the ladder?
- What was it like for you to see your [mom/dad/sister/brother/etc.] slide down the snake?
- Is there anything in your life that feels like a ladder?
- Is there anything in your life that feels like a snake?

Overcoming Adversity

- What strategies helped you navigate the challenges of the game?
- How might these strategies apply to managing difficult situations in real life?
- In what ways did playing the game help you practice the coping skills that we've discussed?
- Imagine your goals for therapy. Based on your experience with the game today, how might you apply these coping strategies in working toward your goals?
- Were there any times that someone in your family helped you to feel better when you had a setback in the game? What did they do that helped? How might you work together to do something similar when setbacks happen in real life?

Progressing Toward Therapeutic Goals

- If this gameboard represented your own life, what would you say the final square might represent?
- If this gameboard represented your own life, where would you say you are in the journey toward reaching your goals of therapy?

- Perhaps you don't need to reach the top of the gameboard. What square might feel like a good goal for your own journey?
- What do you think would need to happen to move from square [number where client indicates they would be] to square [number one or two higher than the number of the square that they identified]?
- What would it look like for you to move from square [number where client indicates they would be] to square [number one or two higher than the number of the square that they identified]?
- Is there anything that your [mom/dad/sister/brother/etc.] could do to help you in reaching that goal?

Processing the Karmic Journey

- The final square on the gameboard represents enlightenment. What do you think this [looks/feels] like? Have you ever experienced bits of that? If so, what was that like?
- If this gameboard represented your own life, where would you say you are in the karmic journey toward [enlightenment/spiritual liberation]?
- What snakes or other vices do you face that prevent you from reaching [enlightenment/spiritual liberation]?
- What helps you to progress toward [enlightenment/spiritual liberation]?
- How do you envision your life changing once you reach [enlightenment/spiritual liberation]?

Vignette

Samiya (11) presented in teletherapy due to escalating anxiety surrounding school attendance. Born into a first-generation Indian-Canadian family, Samiya navigated the intricate balance between her cultural heritage and the pressures of assimilation in her multicultural community. Samiya's father, Ajai (40), and her mother, Anaya (38), were keenly attuned to her emotional well-being and had growing concern for her distress both at home and in her academic environment. Recognizing the profound impact of Samiya's anxiety on her daily life, Ajai and Anaya sought professional support, leading to their referral for therapy.

In the teletherapy session with the family, the therapist began by explaining the therapeutic significance of incorporating Moksha Patam into their session. With the virtual game board displayed on the screen, each member of the family eagerly engaged in the interactive experience. The therapist took a moment to introduce the activity, highlighting how Moksha Patam offered a unique journey where they could explore challenges and victories akin to real-life experiences. The therapist explained the rules of the game, emphasizing that each player would take turns rolling the die and moving their tokens forward on the board, aiming to reach the final square that symbolized spiritual liberation.

As the family played the game, the therapist introduced solution-focused techniques aimed at building on the family's existing strengths and resources. Whenever someone's token landed on a snake, the therapist prompted them to explore coping mechanisms that help them in facing setbacks. When their tokens landed on ladders, the therapist guided them in reflecting on their strength and resilience.

At one point during the game, Samiya's token landed on a snake, causing her to slide back several squares. Samiya's face fell, visibly disappointed and anxious about the setback. Observing her reaction,

Ajai leaned in and offered words of encouragement, reminding Samiya of her past successes and her ability to overcome difficulties. He gently reassured her that it was just a part of the game, and just like in life, setbacks were temporary.

When Samiya experienced success by landing on a ladder, the therapist prompted her to think about similar instances in her life where she felt accomplished. The therapist asked questions like, "What was different about those times when you felt successful?" and "How can you use what you learned from those experiences to help you with your current challenges?" These questions helped Samiya recognize her own abilities and develop a clearer vision of her goals.

Drawing upon the family's cultural heritage, the therapist incorporated elements of Indian mythology and symbolism found in Moksha Patam to enrich their therapeutic exploration. Snakes, traditionally depicted as symbols of challenges that lead to transformation and renewal in Indian folklore, became metaphors for Samiya's journey toward overcoming her fears and embracing resilience. With the therapist's guidance, Samiya began to view her anxiety as a temporary obstacle on her path to growth and self-discovery.

After the game concluded, the therapist initiated a processing discussion with the family. She asked Samiya how she felt when she landed on the snake and what it was like to receive support from her father. Samiya shared that although she felt upset initially, her father's encouragement helped her feel more confident and less alone.

By the end of the session, the family experienced newfound insights regarding preexisting coping strategies that they could use to help Samiya manage her anxiety, which included reliance on and reassurance from her parents.

Suggestions for Follow-Up

Many children and adolescents who play Moksha Patam in therapy request to play the game in future sessions. Some make it a practice of playing every session. When this happens, you might review discussions had regarding gameplay from prior sessions and make relevant connections between current and past gameplay and conversations. For example, you might ask:

- How is your journey different than the last time we played?
- Are there any new challenges or triumphs you've experienced since we last played? How do they compare to previous sessions?
- What themes or patterns do you notice in your progress through the game? How do they relate to your own experiences outside of the game?
- Are there any moments from our previous discussions during gameplay that stand out to you now? How do they resonate with you today?

Contraindications

The intervention outlined in this chapter may not be fitting for all clients. Make adaptations to fit the needs, likes, preferences, and cultural backgrounds of each client. It may be helpful to offer different variations of the game as options for play. There is an extensive array of versions of this game available, ranging from vintage Sleds and Toboggans (c. 1895) to more recent versions such as Hasbro's *Dora the Explorer* edition. Dora is a fictional 7-year-old bilingual Latina heroine from a popular Nickelodeon cartoon, which may make this version of the game particularly relevant for working with Latina/o children.

References

Bellinson, J. (2013). Games children play. *Child and Adolescent Psychiatric Clinics of North America, 22*(2), 283–293. https://doi.org/10.1016/j.chc.2012.12.003

Mukherjee, S. (2018 Sept. 15). *Gyan chaupar to snakes and ladders: How a game about a karmic journey became a plaything for kids.* https://scroll.in/article/972864/gyan-chaupar-to-snakes-and-ladders-how-a-game-about-a-karmic-journey-became-a-plaything-for-kids

Peterson, L. S., Villarreal, V., & Castro, M. J. (2017). Models and frameworks for culturally responsive adaptations of interventions. *Contemporary School Psychology, 21*(3), 181–190. https://doi.org/10.1007/s40688-016-0115-9

Rahman, M., Raja, K., Rashid, M., & Kumar, K. (2020). Listing of Indian folk games for potential therapeutic benefits in children with neurodevelopmental disability. *Games for Health Journal, 9*(6), 453–460. https://doi.org/10.1089/g4h.2019.0191

Part 12

Green Screens

CHAPTER 47

GREEN SCREENS

TOOLS FOR THERAPEUTIC ENGAGEMENT

Sophia Ansari and Amy R. Nelson

Materials for Therapists: A 6-ft. × 6-ft. (or larger) solid green or blue background (e.g., large piece of felt, paper, tablecloth, solid-colored sheet, curtain, painted wall) and a Health Insurance Portability and Accountability Act-consistent version of Zoom. Other teletherapy platforms may offer green screen features but may be limited in capabilities compared to Zoom at the time of this publication. An additional piece of colored material that matches the color of the green screen can optionally be used to cover your chair.

Materials for Clients: None.

Objective

Green screens have emerged as a valuable tool in teletherapy, offering innovative and interactive ways to engage clients in therapeutic activities. Whether it is creating fantastical landscapes or interactive games, green screens provide endless possibilities for sparking creativity and playfulness. By leveraging green screens in teletherapy, therapists can transcend the limitations of physical space and create immersive, engaging environments that support clients on their journey toward healing and self-discovery. This chapter provides instructions on how to set up and use a green screen for teletherapy intervention.

Rationale for Use

In the world of film and television, green screens function by positioning the subject against a large, uniformly green backdrop. This green hue is subsequently digitally removed, or "keyed out," in post-production. A new image is then projected onto the space where the green backdrop once appeared, with the subject visible in front of it. This process allows for a seamless blend of the subject and the chosen background. This technique is used to create scenes that would be difficult or impossible to film in real locations. By using green screens, filmmakers can digitally transport actors to any imaginable environment, from outer space to fantasy realms, without leaving the studio.

DOI: 10.4324/9781003330912-59

In teletherapy, green screens offer similar benefits. Many teletherapy platforms offer pre-designed virtual backgrounds, but these can often be glitchy or inconsistent, especially when users move or adjust lighting. A green screen, by contrast, provides a stable, blank canvas onto which any desired background can be seamlessly applied. This results in fewer visual disruptions and an enhanced sense of immersion. It enables therapists to create personalized virtual environments that are clear and uninterrupted by the common blurring or "cut-off" issues seen in standard virtual backgrounds. With a green screen, therapists can project calming nature scenes, interactive activities (including images of worksheets or game boards), symbolic imagery, or videos to facilitate therapeutic interventions without worrying about visual disruptions.

By using a green screen with various images and a few supplies, therapists can create magical experiences such as feeding unicorns, visiting other worlds, and casting levitation spells. These playful moments lend the way to rapport building, attunement, and connection through the screen in special ways that can't occur in an in-person therapy room.

Green screens are uniquely suited to teletherapy, providing therapists with a tool to create immersive and personalized environments that transcend the limitations of traditional in-person therapy. This versatility allows therapists to engage clients in creative activities, visualization exercises, and exposure therapy in a controlled and safe virtual space.

Setup

1. ***Acquire a green screen.*** Use a 6-ft. x 6-ft. (or larger) solid green or blue piece of material that can be used as a background. Example materials may include a large piece of felt, paper, tablecloth, solid-colored sheet, curtain, or painted wall. Recommended colors for a green screen are Chroma Key Green or Chroma Key Blue because they are the opposite of natural hair and skin color, but any green or blue shade will work if the color is not found in your clothing or skin tone. To avoid appearing as a floating head on the green screen or having parts of your face or body appear transparent, refrain from wearing clothing, jewelry, and makeup that is the same color as your green screen. Even the slightest hint of green can appear transparent against the green screen. Likewise, any green or blue colored objects that match the green screen will also show up as transparent.

2. ***Set up the material.*** Place the material behind where you plan to sit or stand during teletherapy sessions. Fabric screens can be attached to a wall with temporary hooks. The material must lay flat and be wrinkle free as wrinkles can cause shadows.

3. ***Check your video.*** Ensure the green screen material fills the entire background behind you. Look at a video of yourself and your therapy space from the device that you use for teletherapy to ensure that only the green or blue color can be seen in your camera's field of vision. Higher-quality cameras result in a clearer, more stable virtual background by capturing details with greater precision, reducing the risk of visual glitches or blurring around the edges.

4. ***Cover your chair.*** If you will be sitting in a chair during teletherapy sessions and if the chair is in your camera's view, cover it in green screen material to blend it into the background. The material covering the chair should be the same color as the background.

5. ***Ensure proper lighting.*** Achieving maximum clarity with your green screen hinges on minimizing natural lighting. Natural light can result in pixelation and a less clear appearance, often causing a halo effect. To mitigate this, close curtains and blinds to block out natural light and use artificial lighting for optimal results. Insufficient lighting may cause rough or pixelated edges to appear.

6. ***Choose a virtual background.*** When selecting a virtual background for teletherapy, consider client preferences and treatment goals. A background that aligns with the client's interests, preferences, or therapeutic needs can contribute to a more engaging and comfortable therapy experience. Additionally, the selected background should be appropriate for the activities involved in the session. You may use a fixed image as your background, or you might consider the use of interactive backgrounds or videos.

    - ***Interactive backgrounds:*** You may upload images of worksheets, board games, or visuals relevant to the session. A felt green screen along with felt cut-out images enables you to directly place items onto the board or scene, providing a fun and dynamic interaction with the background! This creative setup can make activities more engaging, especially for clients who benefit from hands-on interaction.
    - ***Video backgrounds:*** Many teletherapy platforms support videos as backgrounds, allowing you to enhance the session with gentle movement or soothing imagery. Videos can provide a sensory experience that static images cannot, such as slow-moving clouds, forest streams, or aquarium fish swimming calmly. These moving visuals can help regulate emotions, reduce anxiety, or set the tone for mindfulness exercises. For example, if the therapy session involves relaxation techniques or mindfulness exercises, a looping video of waves gently lapping at the shore can offer an immersive, calming visual backdrop.

    Some platforms come with a selection of built-in video backgrounds that you can use directly. However, if you want to use your own video, here are some things to consider:

    - ***File format and compatibility:*** Ensure the video is in a supported format (e.g., MP4, MOV) and meets the size requirements of the platform.
    - ***Looping videos:*** A seamless, looping video can maintain continuity without noticeable interruptions during the session. This is especially useful for longer therapy activities.
    - ***Internet bandwidth:*** Videos may require more bandwidth than static images. Ensure both you and clients have a stable internet connection to prevent lag or disruptions.
    - ***Audio management:*** Some video backgrounds include sound (e.g., waves, rain). Depending on the session goals, you may either mute the video or use it as ambient sound to complement therapeutic activities.

    Ultimately, whether you choose an image or video, it should support the therapeutic goals of the session and enhance the client's overall experience.

7. ***Add the virtual background image or video.*** Follow your teletherapy platform's specific instructions on how to apply a virtual background. Upon applying your background image, the green screen behind you will be replaced by the image or video that you selected.

    When it comes to deciding when to add a virtual background in your teletherapy sessions, the timing largely depends on personal preference and the specific needs of the therapy session. Consider the following as it relates to adding virtual backgrounds before session, adding them mid-session, or changing backgrounds mid-session.

    - ***Adding before session:*** You may set up your virtual background before the session starts. This allows you to appear with the chosen background from the beginning, creating a consistent and professional appearance. It can also help set the tone for the session and create a visually appealing environment.

- ***Adding mid-session:*** Alternatively, you may add a virtual background during the session if the need arises, given the topic of conversation or needs of a particular activity.
- ***Changing mid-session:*** You may also change virtual backgrounds mid-session for various reasons. This could include transitioning to a different topic or activity that warrants a different background, or simply to keep the session engaging and dynamic.

Use best judgment to decide when to add or change virtual backgrounds. Consider the flow of the therapy session, needs for assessment and intervention, and the client's preferences. Some clients may appreciate a consistent background throughout the session, while others may enjoy the variety and creativity of changing backgrounds. Assess your client's experience and adapt accordingly to ensure a positive and effective teletherapy experience.

8. ***Add green screen magic!*** Though you may use a simple image or video with your green screen for successful intervention, there are many other ways in which green screens can be applied for creative interventions to further engage clients in teletherapy sessions. See Chapter 48 for more information on appearing and disappearing objects with the use of green screen pockets, Chapter 49 for a floating objects illusion, and Chapter 50 for an invisibility cloak intervention.

Contraindications

While green screens can enhance teletherapy sessions in many ways, there are some contraindications to consider, including therapist competency, the possibility of distraction, and other ethical considerations.

Therapists must be proficient in using green screens and integrating them effectively into teletherapy sessions. Lack of familiarity or expertise with green screen technology may hinder the therapist's ability to facilitate meaningful therapeutic interactions. You may watch additional tutorials to learn more. Play Spark (2020a, 2020b, 2020c) offers YouTube video tutorials on how to set up and utilize green screens for teletherapy sessions. Tutorials are specific to the Zoom platform, but the concepts can be applied to other platforms that allow similar green screen functionality. Practice the aforementioned steps and troubleshoot any challenges before using this telehealth feature with clients.

For some clients, the use of green screens may be distracting or overwhelming, particularly if they have difficulty focusing or processing visual stimuli. Also consider ethical considerations related to privacy when using green screens in teletherapy. Therapists may inadvertently reveal personal information or surroundings that they did not intend to share if the green screen is not set up properly or if there are technical glitches. Use best judgment in determining whether it is appropriate to apply this intervention in teletherapy with children, adolescents, and their families.

References

PlaySpark. (2020a, May 24). Getting started with green screen: Distance learning [Video]. YouTube. https://www.youtube.com/watch?v=Q0w-2Vp8edU

PlaySpark. (2020b, September 30). Using worksheets on green screen - teletherapy on Zoom [Video]. YouTube. https://www.youtube.com/watch?v=4F_ItBtD74o

PlaySpark. (2020c, December 9). Winter wonderland board game on zoom with green screen! (PLUS Additional Free Board Games!) [Video]. YouTube. https://www.youtube.com/watch?v=YcAxzdu4ZLA

CHAPTER 48

APPEARING AND DISAPPEARING OBJECTS

Sophia Ansari and Amy R. Nelson

Materials for Therapists: In addition to materials required for setting up a green screen, you will need a piece of fabric in the same color as your green screen and safety pins, Velcro, double-sided tape, or adhesive strips.

Materials for Clients: None.

Objective

Simple accessories such as pockets that are the same color as your green screen can help you to create fun effects to further engage clients in teletherapy sessions. The following describes how to create an appearing/disappearing object effect using a green screen for teletherapy intervention.

Rationale for Use

This technique may be used to make nearly any small object appear and disappear on screen, allowing you to lead clients on a magical journey. This chapter presents an example using a scene set in a castle with a dragon, a treasure chest, and appearing gems that reveal client strengths. You may adapt the images, objects, and storytelling to suit each client's needs and goals of therapy.

Setup

1. ***Set up a green screen.*** See Chapter 47 for instructions on setting up a green screen.
2. ***Select a background.*** Choose a background that is fitting given your client's personal interests, presenting problem, and the needs of any particular intervention that you wish to implement. For this example, the scene is set by using an enchanting background image that includes a sleeping dragon and a treasure chest (see Figure 48.1).
3. ***Make a "pocket."*** To create a pocket that can be used on a green screen for a fun effect, such as reaching into a treasure chest, start by cutting a piece of fabric in the same color as your green screen. You may also sew a pocket with a backing if preferred, which creates a more durable option. Use safety pins, double-sided tape, or adhesive strips to attach the pocket securely. If you are using a green screen made of felt material, you may attach Velcro to the back of the pocket and affix it

DOI: 10.4324/9781003330912-60

Figure 48.1 Example green screen background. Credit: Amy R. Nelson.

to the green screen; this allows for easy removal and repositioning. Make sure the pocket is deep enough to accommodate the items you plan to retrieve.

4. ***Place the pocket.*** Place the pocket on the green screen (see Figure 48.2). Ensure that it is aligned with the digital location from which you intend to have objects appear/disappear. For example, a pocket may be placed over the treasure chest to reveal treasure or over the dragon's mouth to create the illusion of feeding the dragon. It is helpful to have your camera on with the background that you intend to use while you place the pocket to help in determining its appropriate location.
5. ***Choose or create the object.*** You can use any object that you think will support the therapeutic intervention, as long as it fits in the pocket that you created. You may use a preexisting object or create a new one for the purpose of the intervention. For example, you may create a "gem" inscribed with a specific personal strength, such as kindness, creativity, bravery, or perseverance. You can do this by using design tools like Canva or other graphic design software, and printing and cutting out the image. Alternatively, you may draw the gem by hand and write the strength directly on the image.
6. ***Place the object.*** Place the object inside of the pocket that you created, ensuring that it is deep enough in the pocket so it cannot be seen. For example, the "gem" may be placed in a pocket that is strategically placed within the treasure chest.

Figure 48.2 Green screen setup with pocket feature. Credit: Amy R. Nelson.

Instructions

When you are in session, conjure the illusion by pulling the object out of the pocket. For example, you may pull treasure (i.e., the "gem") out of the chest (see Figure 48.3) and say something like,

> As we explore this special space together, imagine that you've just discovered a hidden treasure chest filled with gems that represent your personal strengths. I'll reach in and see what we find. Each gem I pull out holds a unique quality—like kindness, creativity, bravery, or perseverance—that makes you who you are. As I pull out each gem, describe how you use this strength in your everyday life.

This engaging narrative not only enhances the immersive experience but also encourages clients to reflect on their strengths in a fun and interactive way.

For additional "magic," see Chapter 49 for instructions on how to make the gems "float" through the air as you remove them from the pocket.

Figure 48.3. Reaching into the treasure box. Credit: Amy R. Nelson.

Processing

Facilitate a discussion about the object that appeared. Depending on the object and topic of conversation, you may discuss the following:

- What is it like for you when __________ [appears/disappears]?
- How do you think __________ appears?
- What do you do to help __________ appear when you need it most? What do [friends/family] do to help with this?
- How do you think __________ disappears?
- What do you do to help make __________ disappear when you need it gone? What do [friends/family] do to help with this?

For example, with the appearing gems, discuss the chosen strength. Explore how the client uses that strength in various aspects of their life, including at home, school, and in their relationships. You can also encourage clients to consider how their friends, family, heroes, or favorite pop culture characters exemplify that strength. Discussing these examples can help clients connect their personal experiences to broader narratives and inspire them to see the value of their strengths in different contexts.

Contraindications

When using the appearing/disappearing green screen effect in therapy, consider the client's developmental stage and ability to process the illusion. For clients who have not yet developed object permanence, the effect may be confusing or distressing, as they might perceive the objects as literally appearing and disappearing. Assess the client's ability to differentiate between reality and fantasy to avoid potential distress or misinterpretation.

For clients who are beyond this developmental stage, the intervention can be used more freely, but transparency is still essential. If clients express curiosity or concern about the experience, be prepared to explain how the effect works. This helps maintain trust and ensures that the intervention aligns with their understanding and comfort level. Always ensure that the use of this technique supports therapeutic goals and fosters a sense of safety and engagement in the session.

CHAPTER 49

FLOATING OBJECTS ILLUSION

Sophia Ansari and Amy R. Nelson

Materials for Therapists: In addition to materials required for setting up a green screen, you will need extra material that is the same color as your green screen, a ruler or similarly sized/shaped object, Velcro, double-sided tape, or adhesive strips, and an image that you would like to "float" through the air.

Materials for Clients: None.

Objective

Simple accessories can help you to create even more fun effects to engage clients in teletherapy sessions using a green screen. The following describes how to create a floating objects illusion using a green screen for teletherapy intervention.

Rationale for Use

This technique may be used to make nearly any small object float across the screen. This chapter builds on the example provided in Chapter 48 in which a scene is set in a castle with a dragon and a treasure chest. The addition of the floating objects illusion enhances the therapeutic experience of the previous intervention, making it more engaging and immersive for clients. By incorporating dynamic visual elements, you can capture the imagination of clients and encourage them to explore new perspectives, ultimately fostering a deeper connection to the therapeutic process. Adapt the images, objects, and storytelling to suit each client's needs and goals of therapy.

Setup

1. ***Set up a green screen.*** See Chapter 47 for instructions on setting up a green screen.
2. ***Select a background.*** Choose a background that is fitting given your client's personal interests, presenting problem, and the needs of any particular intervention that you wish to implement. For this example, the scene is set by using an enchanting background image that includes a sleeping dragon and a treasure chest.
3. ***Make a stick.*** Cover a ruler or similarly sized/shaped object in paper, fabric, or paint that matches the color of your green screen background (see Figure 49.1).

DOI: 10.4324/9781003330912-61

Figure 49.1 Green stick interactive prop. Credit: Amy R. Nelson.

4. ***Choose or create the object.*** You can use any object that you think will support the therapeutic intervention. You may use a preexisting object or create a new one for the purpose of the intervention. To attach the object to the stick, ensure it is made from a lightweight material, such as paper, that can easily adhere to the stick.

   Using the example from Chapter 48 on appearing and disappearing objects, you may create a "gem" inscribed with a specific personal strength, such as kindness, creativity, bravery, or perseverance. You can do this by using design tools like Canva or other graphic design software, and printing and cutting out the image. Alternatively, you may draw the gem by hand and write the strength directly on the image.

5. ***Place the image onto the stick.*** Attach a printed image to the end of the stick (see Figure 49.2). You may use Velcro for easy removal and swapping of images, or secure it with glue, double-sided tape, or adhesive putty, depending on your needs and how often you plan to change the image.

Instructions

When you are in session, conjure the illusion by moving the stick across the green screen with the selected object attached to it. When you move the stick across the green screen, it should appear as if the object is floating through the air. This effect can be discreetly executed out of the camera's view by

Figure 49.2 Levitating an object using a green stick. Credit: Amy R. Nelson.

either attaching the image to the stick before the session or, for those skilled in sleight of hand, in real time without the client noticing. Using Velcro on the stick ensures a smooth transition.

You can further engage clients who enjoy fantasy by inviting them to select a wand-like object in their own physical location, such as a pencil or chopstick, and wave it while reciting a playful "levitation spell." They can create their own spell or borrow one from a favorite movie or show. This spell activates the "magic" on screen, performed by the therapist, allowing the client to feel more involved, in control, and magical!

For example, when using a magic pocket from Chapter 48, after you retrieve a gem from the treasure chest, ask the client to recite a levitation spell while you lift the gem with the wand and create the illusion of the gem floating in mid-air (see Figure 49.3).

Contraindications

Consider the developmental age of each client as the concept of "magic" might be confusing or unsettling. Assess each client's ability to differentiate between reality and fantasy to avoid potential distress or misinterpretation.

Some cultural contexts might interpret levitation or other illusions as inappropriate, supernatural, or unsettling. Inquire about and respect each client's cultural background, faith traditions, and personal preferences before introducing such interventions.

Figure 49.3 Levitating object effect. Credit: Amy R. Nelson.

Additionally, using illusions might blur the boundaries of therapeutic transparency, especially if clients aren't fully informed about how the effect is created. Providing a clear explanation of the intervention's purpose helps maintain trust and uphold ethical standards.

Finally, consider whether the intervention supports the client's progress and enhances the therapeutic process. Ensure the levitation effect is aligned with the objectives of therapy, rather than solely for entertainment or novelty.

CHAPTER 50

SECRETS OF THE GREEN SCREEN

THE POWER OF INVISIBILITY

Sophia Ansari and Amy R. Nelson

Materials for Therapists: In addition to materials required for setting up a green screen, you will need a piece of material that matches the color of the green screen.

Materials for Clients: None. A copy of the image uploaded as a virtual background and a solid green or blue item to serve as the "invisibility cloak" (e.g., green or blue file folder, piece of construction paper, tablecloth, solid color sheet or curtain) are optional.

Objective

Asking children to think about which superpowers they would have and what they would do with those powers supports exploration of identity and strengths (Rubin, 2006). It encourages children to reflect on their own qualities, desires, and aspirations, and to think about what abilities they value and how they envision themselves in different roles or situations. Children often gravitate toward abilities or traits they admire or wish they had. This can highlight their existing strengths and talents, as well as areas they may want to develop further. Imagining themselves with superpowers overcoming challenges and obstacles may also help them feel more equipped to face real-life difficulties. Exploring superpowers enables children to visualize themselves as capable and powerful beings, fostering the development of a more positive self-image and heightened confidence in their abilities. Children who feel invisible or overlooked may be drawn to the power of invisibility, indicating a desire to be seen and heard. Conversely, children who frequently face punishment or experience abuse may also yearn for the ability to disappear, seeking a form of escape or protection from their challenging environments. This chapter provides instructions on how to use an "invisibility cloak" with a green screen to playfully facilitate these discussions in a non-threatening and imaginative way.

Rationale for Use

The invisibility cloak intervention, particularly within the framework of narrative therapy, offers a creative and powerful way to explore personal narratives, perceptions, and coping skills with children and adolescents. Narrative therapy emphasizes the idea that individuals construct their identities

DOI: 10.4324/9781003330912-62

and understandings of the world through the stories they tell about themselves and their experiences (Cattanach, 2006; White & Epston, 1990). By externalizing problems and viewing them as separate from the individual, narrative therapy empowers clients to rewrite their stories in more empowering ways.

The invisibility cloak can serve as a metaphorical tool to externalize and explore various aspects of a client's life or identity. For example, by imagining themselves wearing an invisibility cloak, clients can discuss and reflect on moments when they might feel unseen, unheard, or overlooked in their lives. This process allows them to externalize these feelings, viewing them as separate from their core identity, which can be a crucial step in reframing their narrative. It can also serve as a powerful tool for clients to explore feelings of safety and boundaries in various ways. Invisibility can provide a shield of privacy, allowing individuals to retreat from social interactions or unwanted attention. This sense of invisibility can create a safe space for them to recharge and reflect. By discussing the power of invisibility, children, adolescents, and families can explore how they would use this power to protect themselves or navigate difficult situations, empowering them to assert boundaries and advocate for their needs. The following provides instructions on how to use an "invisibility cloak" with a green screen for teletherapy assessment and intervention.

Setup

1. ***Set up a green screen.*** See Chapter 47 for instructions.
2. ***Acquire an additional piece of material that matches the color of your green screen.*** Examples of materials that can be used include a file folder, piece of construction paper, tablecloth, sheet, or curtain. Leave this material at arm's reach from where you conduct teletherapy, but in a place that's not visible to clients during the session.
3. ***Choose a virtual background image.*** Any virtual image or video can be selected for this intervention. Consider choosing a background that is relevant to the session's theme or the client's preferences, whether it's a serene natural landscape, a cozy indoor setting, or even abstract patterns that spark creativity and reflection. If the client is excited to discuss superheroes, you might search for images of 'superhero lairs' or use ChatGPT's image generator to create customized images that match each client's unique preferences (e.g., a superhero lair that's mostly pink and purple and styled as a fun cartoon).
4. ***Practice.*** Before implementing the intervention with clients, try it out on your own or with a colleague using the following instructions.

Instructions

1. ***Discuss the superpower of invisibility.*** Engage clients in meaningful conversations about the significance of invisibility in their own lives and experiences. These discussions may include examples from the client's favorite superhero or pop culture characters. For example, many superheroes such as Doctor Strange, Martian Manhunter, Miles Morales, Scarlet Witch, The Invisible Woman, and Harry Potter (through his invisibility cloak) can harness the power of invisibility.
2. ***Add a virtual background image.*** See Chapter 47 for instructions.
3. ***Activate the "invisibility cloak."*** Cover yourself with the material chosen as the invisibility cloak, or hold it in front of you, saying something like, "Watch closely. I'm disappearing!" or "Here

Figure 50.1 Using green fabric prior to creating the invisibility effect. Credit: Amy R. Nelson.

comes the magic!" (see Figure 50.1). The background image will now project onto the cloak, creating the illusion that you're invisible on the screen (see Figure 50.2).

4. ***Gradually reappear.*** Peek out from under the cloak to become partially visible, perhaps saying something like, "Am I back yet?" or "I wonder if you can see me now?" Finally, fully remove the cloak to make yourself completely visible again. You could even use this transition to discuss how it feels to disappear and then return.

Processing

Use the following processing questions to explore what it means to be seen versus invisible.

- If you could turn invisible, when would you want to hide and when would you want to stay visible?
- What fun things would you do if you were invisible?
- If you were invisible, how might you act differently?
- How would you feel if you could disappear and no one could see you?
- Are there things about yourself that you might want to keep secret or hidden?

Figure 50.2 Projecting a background image onto green fabric to create the invisibility effect. Credit: Amy R. Nelson.

- Can you think of times when hiding might help you feel safe or more comfortable?
- If you could stop being invisible whenever you wanted, when would you do it and why?
- What things do you want to let others see about you?
- How does it feel when someone notices you or pays attention to you?
- What does it mean to you when someone sees you and understands you?
- What are some things about you that make it easy for others to notice you?
- What would it be like if your friend or family member could turn invisible?
- How do you think your friends or family would feel if you had the power of invisibility?
- What are some good things and some not-so-good things about being invisible?
- Do you think you could do everything you need to do in life if you were always invisible? Why or why not?
- What other superpowers would you have and why?

For more superhero-specific processing questions, ask the following.

- Superheroes like Miles Morales and Doctor Strange can disappear and be invisible. How do you think being invisible helps them? Can you tell me about a time when you wished you could be invisible?

- Sometimes superheroes can turn invisible when they want to feel safe or hide from danger. Can you think of a time when you wanted to hide or be invisible? What made you feel that way, and what did you do?
- If you could turn invisible like a superhero, how would it make you feel? What would you do if you were invisible? Do you think being invisible could help you feel brave or strong in tough situations?
- If you had the invisibility cloak like Harry Potter, how would it change your life? What would you do with that power? How do you think it would make you feel?

Vignette

Maryam was a 13-year-old South Asian American female. She was referred to teletherapy due to depression and failing grades after moving to a new school. Maryam reported that she was having a difficult time adjusting to her new school and making friends. During the initial teletherapy session, the therapist asked Maryam about special interests, meaningful activities, and hobbies she enjoyed. She enthusiastically spoke of her love of reading books, especially books from the science fiction and fantasy genres.

With Maryam's interests in mind and considering her struggles with low self-esteem and the concerns she raised about feeling like she didn't belong, her therapist asked her to explore the power of invisibility.

Therapist: "Imagine having the power to control when you want to be seen and when you want to be invisible. Let's explore what that might mean for you. When do you feel the most seen by others?"

Maryam: "I guess when I'm with my family or close friends and they listen to me and understand me."

Therapist: "That's wonderful to hear. Now, when do you feel invisible?"

Maryam: "When I'm at school and no one pays attention to me, or when I'm in a big group and I feel like I don't belong."

Therapist: "It sounds like feeling seen is really important to you. Let's explore how we can help you feel more visible and confident. Imagine putting on an invisibility cloak whenever you feel the need to hide. What would you do if you were invisible?"

Maryam: "I think I would explore places without anyone noticing me, like going on adventures or helping people without them knowing."

Therapist: "That sounds like a lot of fun! Now, let's imagine taking off that cloak and stepping into the spotlight. What are some strengths and qualities about yourself that you would want others to see?"

Maryam: "Well, I'm really good at drawing, and I'm a good listener. I think people would like those things about me if they noticed."

Therapist: "Those are wonderful strengths, Maryam. And remember, even when you feel invisible, your strengths are always there, waiting to be seen. Together, we can work on helping you feel more confident and visible in all aspects of your life."

With the green screen backdrop and a pre-prepared virtual image already in place, the therapist utilized the magic of the green screen to demonstrate the disappearing effect. By holding up the "invisibility cloak" (i.e., piece of fabric the same color as the green screen), parts of the therapist appeared to vanish.

This dynamic demonstration brought the concept of the magical item to life! Maryam's reaction was one of delight, clearly engaged and captivated by the interactive display.

The therapist taught Maryam how to create an invisibility effect using just a green folder, without needing a full green screen setup. Maryam selected a virtual background in her video settings (see Figure 50.3), and as she moved the folder slightly, the virtual background projected onto it, blending seamlessly with her surroundings. This created the illusion that parts of her were disappearing behind the 'magical' folder, even though her actual background wasn't green (see Figure 50.4). While the effect was slightly glitchy without a green screen, it worked well enough to give Maryam a sense of magic and accessibility to the experience.

The therapist then engaged in a role-playing exercise using the following processing questions: *"What would it be like to be in a relationship if you had powers of invisibility?" "What would it be like to be in a relationship with a person who had powers of invisibility?"* During this exercise the therapist and Maryam took turns being the invisible person and speaking to the invisible person.

After the role-playing exercise, the therapist engaged Maryam in a discussion processing what it felt like to be both the invisible person and to speak to the invisible person. The discussion revolved around the themes of connection, attunement, and the need to feel validated, seen, and heard. Over the course of this session, Maryam explored her strengths and how to literally and metaphorically take down her invisibility cloak – the cloak that hid parts of herself that she felt she could not share. The parts that she ultimately recognized were the parts that made *her magical.*

The invisibility cloak intervention helped Maryam make significant progress toward her therapy goals, particularly in bolstering her confidence and embracing her strengths. This narrative therapy approach helped Maryam externalize her challenges, viewing them as separate from her core identity.

Figure 50.3 Using a green folder in preparation of creating the invisibility effect. Credit: Sophia Ansari.

Figure 50.4 Demonstrating the invisibility effect by projecting the background image onto a green folder. Credit: Sophia Ansari.

By imagining herself wielding the power of invisibility, Maryam gained a sense of control over her circumstances, allowing her to actively shape her own story and destiny. This intervention paved the way for future sessions where the therapist helped Maryam explore boundaries and self-compassion. She gained the confidence to assert herself and advocate for her needs, while also learning to accept and embrace all aspects of herself, both seen and unseen.

Suggestions for Follow-Up

Clients' interests in superheroes and superpowers can also be incorporated in strengths-based therapy (Ansari & Scott, 2019) by focusing on "what's strong" instead of on "what's wrong." The ability to become invisible can be seen as a metaphor for adaptability and resilience. Just as invisibility allows individuals to navigate challenging situations by evading detection, clients can explore how their innate strengths enable them to adapt and overcome obstacles in their lives.

Clients are often curious as to how therapists make the invisibility cloak work. Subsequent to the application of the initial intervention, you can teach clients how to create their own "invisibility cloak." This can help foster a sense of mastery and accomplishment.

Contraindications

Integrating superheroes and pop culture into therapy should be client driven. Interventions should also be developmentally appropriate for each client. For example, a young child who has not developed object permanence may become startled at the disappearing effect created through the green screen. It would not be appropriate for use with clients who are unable to decipher reality from fiction.

References

Ansari, S., & Scott, C. M. (2019). Flourishing after the origin story: Using positive psychology to explore well-being in superheroes and supervillains. In L. C. Rubin (Ed.), *Using superheroes and villains in counseling and play therapy* (pp. 9–28). Routledge.

Cattanach, A. (2006). Narrative play therapy. In C. E. Schaefer, C. & H. G. Kaduson (Eds.), *Contemporary play therapy: Theory, research, and practice* (1st ed., pp. 82–99). Guilford Press.

Rubin, L. C. (Ed.). (2006). *Using superheroes in counseling and play therapy*. Springer.

White, M., & Epston, D. (1990). *Narrative means to therapeutic ends*. WW Norton & Company.

INDEX

For Product Safety Concerns and Information please contact our EU
representative GPSR@taylorandfrancis.com
Taylor & Francis Verlag GmbH, Kaufingerstraße 24, 80331 München, Germany

www.ingramcontent.com/pod-product-compliance
Ingram Content Group UK Ltd.
Pitfield, Milton Keynes, MK11 3LW, UK
UKHW050235200926
475702UK00020B/3044
9781032362403